Gambero Rosso

2018

D1291312

TOP ITALIAN
FOOD & BEVERAGE
Experience

OVER 1200 COMPANIES

TOP ITALIAN FOOD & BEVERAGE Experience

entries
Stefania Annese
Serena Ciurcina
Indra Galbo
Clara Ippolito
Michela Marano
Mara Nocilla
Stefano Polacchi
William Pregentelli

translations
Angela Arnone
David Davidson
Jordan Joseph Alan De Maio
Sonia Hill
Ailsa Wood

Gambero Rosso®
Gambero Rosso S.p.A.
via Ottavio Gasparri, 13/17
00152 Roma
tel. 06 551121
fax 06 55112260
www.gamberorosso.it
redazione.guide@gamberorosso.it

editorial director
Laura Mantovano

graphics
Chiara Buosi

production
Angelica Sorbara

commercial director
Francesco Dammicco

sales and distribution
Eugenia Durando

advertising office
Paola Persi
ufficio.pubblicita@gamberorosso.it

newsagent
distribution for Italy
SO.DI.P Angelo Patuzzi Spa
via Bettoia, 18
20092 Cinisello Balsamo (MI)
tel. 02 660301
fax 02 66030320

bookstore distribution
Messaggerie Libri Spa
via Verdi, 8
20090 Assago (MI)
tel. 02 457741
fax 02 45701032

ISBN 978-88-6641-137-6

The guide editing was completed
on 31 July 2017

Printed for
Gambero Rosso S.p.A.
September 2017
by Fp Design srl
via Atto Tigri, 11
00197 Roma ITALY

Table of contents

3

Top Italian Food Guide
Over 1200 of Italy's best foods
ready for export

Gambero Rosso's Top Italian Food Experience, now on its third edition, is the only guide in Italy classified by product category to bring together over 1200 exceptional businesses, all ready and willing to export a range of quality items. The guide thus affirms its role as an indispensable tool for foodies, industry players and buyers all over the world.

In these three decades, Gambero Rosso has become the benchmark for professionals and connoisseurs worldwide, certifying the best "Made-in-Italy" foods and fine wines. Gambero Rosso, in striving to credibly promote the country's food and wine industry, is the only entity to have successfully organized international events for Italy's winemakers and food producers. Moreover, Gambero Rosso has established the largest, most widespread private Academy geared towards food industry professionals; it's also given a significant push to the sector, especially in terms of exports towards fast-growing markets. Gambero Rosso's events offer opportunities for Italian businesses to meet traders, journalists and interested gourmet food experts, and its courses are among the most reputable in Italy, as well as the world, when it comes to education for food and wine industry professionals.

Top Italian Food Experience is a tool for promoting "Made-in-Italy" products. In addition to large, well-known corporate entities, it lists over 980 SMEs, who offer everything from vinegar to charcuterie, cheeses, EVOO, patisserie, preserves, pasta, rice, honey, chocolate, flour, pulses and grains, coffee, and lots more. And these are small and medium-size businesses, not micro enterprises, thus well-developed and well-structured, with production volumes capable of allowing them to expand into foreign markets. They are rare pearls, ambassadors of Italy's finest, most appreciated gourmet lines, which are sought after around the world. A second section is dedicated to leading brands, over 250 of them, featuring Italy's largest and most beloved businesses, renowned at international level. These icons of "Made-in-Italy" vaunt the brands and logos that distinguish Italian cuisine. Last, but not least, 100% organic companies are identified in green.

The Top Italian Food Experience guide is available in English, both in print and in digital version. This is not a mere directory of large and small companies, as each business has its own profile, making it an excellent way for the industry to promote its products to the general public. This includes fans and foodies, but also (and especially) foreign buyers and influencers.

Villorba (TV)
Figulì

via Trieste, 80/5
☎ (+39) 0422444154
✆ figuli.it
✉ info@figuli.it
shop: yes
e-commerce: no

The company was started in 1954, with the goal of producing light sheets of Visnadello, a tasty treat of crusty bread made with EVOO, unrefined Cervia sea salt and wheat flour. Besides the classics we also have oregano, rosemary, sesame, sweet paprika and chilli. Then there are ramì, crispy sticks of yeast-free bread, classic or with rosemary; tele, a kind of cracker in classic and rosemary flavours. All products are still made by hand.

Riccione (RN)
Fresco Piada

via dell'Industria, 8
☎ (+39) 0541691477
✆ www.frescopiada.com
✉ info@frescopiada.com
shop: yes
e-commerce: no

A master producer of the very thin Riccione piadina, this company makes typical Romagna bread (piada and cascione) with ingredients deriving almost exclusively from the surrounding area, as tradition demands. The range includes classic piada made with suet and brewer's yeast, as well as those made with starter dough or extra virgin olive oil. No preservatives are added to the dough and the individual products are pre-cooked manually to preserve as much as possible of their softness and authenticity.

Matera
Fratelli Laurieri

via G. Agnelli zona Industriale La Martella
☎ (+39) 0835302809
✆ www.laurieri.it
✉ info@laurieri.com
shop: no
e-commerce: no

Founded in 1976 as a small workshop in the heart of town, since 2007 the company has extended and now covers thousands of square metres installed with modern equipment. The entire cycle is subject to strict controls that are documented and recorded, thus offering guarantees to the consumer. The production range includes biscuits (like limoncelli or nocciolato), savoury snacks called scrocchi (a kind of small cracker in various flavours), and crespini (a kind of grissino), then there are taralli, both traditional and flavoured.

Borgomanero (NO)

MastroCesare
Antico Forno Piemontese

v.lo Sorga, 3
☎ (+39) 0322 860739
🕸 www.mastrocesare.it
✉ info@mastrocesare.it
shop: no
e-commerce: no

MastroCesare was founded almost a century ago by Cesare Valsesia. Today the shop is managed with passion and professional skill by his grandson Marco, who adopted the same principles of tradition and guaranteeing flavor. Grissini breadsticks, prepared with select ingredients and the utmost care, steal the show. There are classic and organic varieties, but variations abound: with olives, sesame, rosemary, onion, nebbiolo grapes and nuts... There's even chocolate, a real treat! The biscotti, breads and cakes are all also delicious.

Rocchetta Tanaro (AT)

Il Panatè Mario Fongo

via Case Sparse Piana, 17
☎ (+39) 0141644764
🕸 www.mariofongo.com
✉ info@mariofongo.com
shop: no
e-commerce: no

Mario
"Il Panatè" Fongo

For the last 70 years this family firm has been expanding and evolving to meet the changing needs of customers, but never forgetting tradition and attention to quality. The ingredients are simple: flour, water, oil, salt. But above all long natural leavening that makes lightweight, fragrant products that are easy to digest. The grissini are delicious, both classic and flavoured, as the rubatà (rolled grissini), and lingua di suocera breadsticks. Also available are pasta, piadina, sauces and on the sweet side, chocolate grissini and amaretti.

Beer

Pederobba (TV)
32 Via dei Birrai

loc. Onigo I via Cal Lusent, 41
☎ (+39) 0423681983
🖳 www.32viadeibirrai.it
✉ info@32viadeibirrai.com
shop: no
e-commerce: yes

32
Via dei birrai

One of Italy's best and most famous breweries, 32 Via dei Birrai, was the brainchild of three partners, who were passionate about creating a new product in the beer-making landscape, both in style and concept. Quality, originality and research underpin the eight versions available, from a double-malt lager called Audace to the hop-rich pale Oppale, spicy Curmi and Tre+Due Qormi, and the double-malts Nebra, A Tra, Admiral, and Nectar, the latter with honey. There is also a beer vinegar, Ace To 32, made by very slow oxidation.

Loreto Aprutino (PE)
Birra Almond '22

c.da Remartello, 47h
☎ (+39) 0858208154
🖳 www.birraalmond.com
✉ info@birraalmond.com
shop: yes
e-commerce: no

Here, way back in 1922, there was an almond processing plant for production of comfits. Today, in homage to the history of the building, this microbrewery has called itself Almond '22. Since 2003 the company has grown significantly, becoming one of the best-known breweries in Italy. The beer undergoes second fermentation in the bottle, like Champagne, and processing is manual, with no filtering or pasteurizing. Lots of types on offer, from porters to IPAs, ales, blanches, and many aromas, with prime hops, spices, peated malt.

Arcidosso (GR)
Birra Amiata

loc. Zancona I via Podere Poderino, 1
☎ (+39) 0564966865 I 0564966570
🖳 www.birra-amiata.it
✉ info@birra-amiata.it
shop: yes
e-commerce: yes

Here, on the slopes of Mount Amiata, in some stunning countryside for nature and landscape, this craft brewery opened for business in 2006. It seeks out the best ingredients worldwide always, but some are local, to underscore and reinforce its ties with the territory. Some examples? Water, chestnuts, honey, and saffron. The range includes 14 labels, of which one is a Christmas beer, all processed in different styles, with some aged in barrique.

Beer

Maracalagonis (CA)

Barley

via C. Colombo
☎ (+39) 070789496
❀ www.barley.it
✉ info@barley.it
shop: yes
e-commerce: yes

Nicola Perra and Isidoro Mascia opened their brewery in 2006, with an ambitious goal: quality production while experimenting with new ideas. The first labels were Friska, Sella del Diavolo, and Toccadibò, available on the market throughout the year. Then came BB10, the first Italian craft beer to meet the wine through the use of cannonau saba, followed by BBevò, produced with the addition of native nasco grape saba, and BB9, a golden strong ale with the addition of Malvasia di Bosa saba. Also worthy of note, Zagara, with its addition of organic orange honey, and Tuvi Tuvi, Meda, Duenna Macca.

Olgiate Comasco (CO)

Bi-Du

via Torino, 50
☎ (+39) 031945418
❀ www.bi-du.it
✉ info@bi-du.it
shop: yes
e-commerce: no

Beppe Vento opened his brewery in 2002 and his standards are now acknowledged in and out of Italy. Here we find the Artigianale, which is one of the finest Italian interpretations of an English bitter, and the Rodersch, which is inspired by the German kölsch. Also worthy of note, the H10OP5, an almost unreadable formula that describes the use of no less than ten different hops in five different stages of the process, the Leyline flavoured with bearberry honey, and the original Saltinmalto, with coriander and Cervia mild salt.

Assisi (PG)

Birra dell'Eremo

loc. Capodacqua I via Monte Peglia, 5
☎ (+39) 0758064602
❀ www.birradelleremo.it
✉ info@birradelleremo.it
shop: yes
e-commerce: yes

The brewery was founded in 2012, in a hamlet on the slopes of Mount Subasio, by the passionately determined Gertrude Salvatori Franchi and her husband Enrico Ciani. They were quick off the mark with their six very drinkable products (Terra, Nobile, Fiera, Saggia, Magnifica, Fuoco) all of high quality, some of which have taken home prestigious awards. There is focus not only on ingredients, but also on sustainability, using recyclable packaging, from the glass used for the bottles to disposable kegs that are then reused in farming.

Fiumicino (RM)

Birradamare

via Falzarego, 8
☎ (+39) 066582021
❀ www.birradamare.it
✉ info@birradamare.it
shop: yes
e-commerce: yes

The company, founded in 2004 by great craft beer enthusiasts Elio Miceli and Massimo Salvatori, has developed three brands. First there is Birradamare, then 'nabiretta and Birra Roma, targeting mainly the restaurant market. There are about a dozen beers in the production range: lagers, amber, and dark, not to mention some special versions. The brewery's secret is its careful selection of ingredients, sourced mainly in the surrounding farmlands, and it has developed a whole range of fun, beer-themed gadgets, from glasses to t-shirts.

Conversano (BA)

Birranova

fraz. Triggianello I via Lepanto, 11
☎ (+39) 08040850000
❀ www.birranova.it
✉ info@birranova.it
shop: no
e-commerce: no

Birranova, operational since 2007, is undoubtedly among the more notable food producers in southern Italy. Its products are known for their high quality and unique personality. Donato di Palma, the owner and master brewer, highlights his region's attributes by drawing on recipes that are native to the territory. The brands are divided into three: 'Classic' (classic brews), 'Limited Edition' (experimental brews that use special ingredients) and the 'Why Not' (for strong beers with additional hopping).

Pietrasanta (LU)

Birrificio del Forte

loc. Portone - Parco degli Artigiani
via della Breccia Violetta, 5a
☎ (+39) 0584793384 I 3311303073
❀ www.birrificiodelforte.it
✉ info@birrificiodelforte.it
shop: yes
e-commerce: no

In just five years in business, this brewery has found a prime place in the coterie of Italian beer makers. The Forte in its name is in homage to Forte dei Marmi, a charming Versilia tourist resort of international appeal. In developing the beers the aim was to make them drinkable without discarding temperament and character, and ensuring rigorous selection of ingredients. Applying this philosophy, the result was six types found all year round, plus a series of seasonal specials.

Limido Comasco (CO)
Birrificio Italiano

via Marconi, 27
☎ (+39) 0315481162
🌐 www.birrificio.it
✉ info@birrificio.it
shop: no
e-commerce: no

One of the first in the region and now with almost two decades of experience behind it, this craft microbrewery stands out for dependability and quality standards. It produces about 16 different types of beer, some of which have won international awards, and range from fresh, drinkable versions to the more challenging for alcohol, nose and body. The company continues to experiment and evolve, as well as searching out the best ingredients, whether hops and malts, or spices, honey and flowers.

Isola Vicentina (VI)
Birrone

via Fossanigo, 6
☎ (+39) 0444975702
🌐 www.birrone.it
✉ info@birrone.it
shop: yes
e-commerce: no

Owner Simone Dal Cortivo was voted Italian brewer of 2014, bringing great satisfaction for a craft business like this, founded only very recently. There are other reasons for Simone to be proud, however, because since the beginning his beers have garnered many awards. There are ten different types, from the most straightforward to the cleverly spiced versions, made in various styles but all natural, without preservatives, pasteurization or filtration. There are also special brews, made and sold just for one season.

Codogno (LO)
Brewfist

via Molinari, 5
☎ (+39) 0377379814
🌐 www.brewfist.com
✉ info@brewfist.com
shop: no
e-commerce: no

Since day one, in 2010, this brewery has received the attention it deserved, its products able to win over even the most demanding enthusiasts. The helm is in the hands of a young, tightknit group that arrived at this project after various experiences in the field. All 20 labels are really enjoyable easy drinkers, from the excellent Spaceman IPA, to the Czech Norris Pils, or the original Spaghetti Western coffee stout, made in partnership with an Oklahoma brewery. Themed gadgets also available.

Trecate (NO)
Croce di Malto

c.so Roma, 51a
☎ (+39) 03211856101
❀ www.crocedimalto.it
✉ info@crocedimalto.it
shop: no
e-commerce: no

Federico Casari and Alessio Selvaggio are the two skilled, enthusiastic owners of this Novara brewery. A modern plant, using quality hops and malt, prime ingredients like yeasts, spices, chestnuts, local rice, and scrupulous control of every manufacturing phase are the hallmark of production, offering very high standards, recognized and rewarded at national and international level. The dozen versions of beer include Platinum, a Christmas beer, also available in large sizes.

Busseto (PR)
Birrificio del Ducato

s.da Argine, 43
☎ (+39) 052490137
❀ www.birrificiodelducato.it
✉ info@birrificiodelducato.it
shop: yes
e-commerce: yes

Founded in 2007 by Giovanni Campari and Manuel Piccoli in the birthplace of Giuseppe Verdi, this brewery shot to the top of Italian quality ratings. They do a lot of "field research" for the very best ingredients like malt, hops, and yeast, and their unwavering passion and studies have taken production to levels of excellence. They have about 30 beers available, in different styles, including a Christmas brew in a special format, some aged in oak barriques for a few months.

Erba (CO)
Doppio Malto

via Milano, 9
☎ (+39) 0313334187
❀ www.doppiomalto.it
✉ fabbrica@doppiomalto.it
shop: yes
e-commerce: yes

Alessandro Campanini is the soul, as well as the founding partner of this craft brewery, which started business in 2003. All processing stages are monitored closely as is the upstream selection of raw materials, primarily water, which differs depending on the beer being prepared. He has a dozen types available, including a Christmas brew and a very special ginger version. Some have been awarded prestigious awards internationally and there are also gadgets on sale.

Comun Nuovo (BG)
Elav

via Autieri d'Italia, 268
☎ (+39) 035334206
❂ www.elavbrewery.com
✉ info@elavbrewery.com
shop: yes
e-commerce: yes

This "independent brewery", as they call themselves, was so successful that at the end of last year they opened a new facility and recently purchased land in Val d'Astino for growing hops, raspberries, blackberries, pumpkins, and medicinal herbs for their beer production. It all began in 2010, intending to produce beer for personal consumption in two of their own properties. The beers are natural, high-fermentation, unfiltered and unpasteurized. Of course the ingredients are first-rate, from the water to the rest. Today they offer 23 different types.

Torgiano (PG)
Fabbrica della Birra Perugia

fraz. Pontenuovo I via Tiberina, 20
☎ (+39) 0759888096
❂ www.birraperugia.it
✉ info@birraperugia.it
shop: yes
e-commerce: no

A modern, emerging brewery, in a delightful structure a stone's throw from the capital, along the E45 expressway. The shingle is actually a piece of history, its origins dating back to 1875, but in the 1920s the business fell into decline and closed. So this passionate young team deserve a round of applause for reviving the brand and restoring the quality that had marked production in its heyday. There are six different types of beer from the classics to some creative brews, last but least Suburbia, a tribute to the district.

Forni di Sopra (UD)
Birrificio Foglie d'Erba

via Nazionale, 12
☎ (+39) 043388066 I 3473555197
❂ birrificiofogliederba.it
✉ info@birrificiofogliederba.it
shop: yes
e-commerce: yes

Gino Perissutti, Italy's 2011 brewer of the year, is the owner of this craft brewery in a charming village located in the Alpine region of Carnia. The first beer was brewed in 2008 and since then Gino has never stopped, sustained by a great passion and a desire to imprint his beers with local character, using special ingredients such as dwarf pine resin and pine needles. He mas four labels available, each in a different style, some seasonal.

Tuscania (VT)
Free Lions Brewery

s.da prov.le Martana, km 0,700
☎ (+39) 0761434471
🕸 www.freelionsbeer.it
✉ info@freelionsbeer.it
shop: yes
e-commerce: no

Founded in 2011 by Andrea Fralleoni, a former IT specialist, hence the play on words on the shingle. Andrea is now flanked by Adriano Protopapa and Michele Penta, and in 2014 Massimo Serra joined as a partner. In just a few years the brewery has developed steadily, to a production range of nine labels (including stouts, bitters, golden ales, etc.), plus the seasonal brews like Fidelis at Christmas, Magical Mystery Gold for summer, the spicy Lexy, and the three variants of the Kamikaze line.

Villa d'Adda (BG)
Hammer

via Chioso, 3a
☎ (+39) 035793207
🕸 www.hammer-beer.it
✉ info@hammer-beer.it
shop: no
e-commerce: no

Hammer was launched in 2015, thanks to an investment made by the Brigati family. The size of the place alone gives you an idea of their commitment to excellence. One man has stepped up to manage a brewery that counts itself as among the largest in the country and proven he is equal to the task. Marco Valeriani, a food-techie and lifelong beer lover has experience to match his passion, demonstrating from the outset his ability to work magic with hops. His work is particularly inspired by Anglo-Saxon brewing traditions.

Burago di Molgora (MB)
Hibu

via A. M. Ampere, 6
☎ (+39) 0399711365
🕸 www.birrificiohibu.it
✉ info@birrificiohibu.it
shop: no
e-commerce: no

Hibu got its start in 2007 when Raimondo, Lorenz and Gian began brewing professionally. Today the brewery, headquartered in Brianza, can also call itself home-grown inasmuch as the grains (and shortly also the hops) used are all from land owned by the brewers themselves (in Lombardy and Basilicata). There is a broad selection that draws on different brewing traditions, from Belgium to Anglo-Saxon and German styles. Last summer, they opened their own pub in Copenhagen, 'Il Locale'.

Milano
Birrificio Lambrate

via Adelchi, 5
☎ (+39) 0270606746
🌐 www.birrificiolambrate.com
✉ comunicazione@birrificiolambrate.com
shop: no
e-commerce: no

After two decades in business, Lambrate continues to be a benchmark for every self-respecting craft beer buff or aficionado. Firstly for its renowned role as a pioneer in having added true culture to the world of malt and hops, and long before anyone else. Then for its unquestionable quality and the sheer variety of its products, with a dozen options plus seasonal and special brews. Only ingredients of the finest quality are used.

Marentino (TO)
LoverBeer

s.da Pellinciona, 7
☎ (+39) 3473636680
🌐 www.loverbeer.com
✉ info@loverbeer.it
shop: yes
e-commerce: no

Valter Loverier started out as an amateur brewer who managed to turn his passion into a real business. His love for the world of beer making means he selects all ingredients carefully, many for the local area, including the Slow Food Presidium damassin plum. He monitors all stages of processing, respects timing, has an unstoppable desire to experiment, all leading to production of undoubted quality. Valter makes seven types of beer, each with its own characteristics, each more interesting than the next.

Serrapetrona (MC)
MC 77

loc. Caccamo I via E. Mattei, 4
☎ (+39) 0733904132
🌐 www.mc-77.com
✉ info@mc-77.com
shop: yes
e-commerce: no

The name on the shingle of this craft brewery includes the initials of the owners, young Matteo and Cecilia, also the abbreviation of the province of the Marche region where it is located, and the number of highway 77 that leads there. They always have three beers: Queen Bee, a blond ale with honey; San Lorenzo, a blanche spiced with orange and coriander; Bastogne, an American pale ale. They produce special brews only at certain times of the year, like the award-winning Fleur Sophronia, scented with hibiscus flowers. Meticulous skill and good raw materials make the difference.

Montegioco (AL)
Birrificio Montegioco

fraz. Fabbrica, 1
☎ (+39) 0131029012 I 3355748181
❀ www.birrificiomontegioco.com
✉ birraio@birrificiomontegioco.com
shop: yes **e-commerce:** no

Here in Val Grue, in the Tortona area, Riccardo Franzese decided to start his craft microbrewery, naming it after the village where it is located. The main feature of the beers produced, which stand out from others, in addition to their slow ageing, is the fact that local ingredients are used, like volpedo peaches, bella garbagna cherries, or even timorasso grapes. There are about 20 labels, each with its own characteristics, and in the most varied of styles, from classic to seasonal.

Notaresco (TE)
Opperbacco

via Ponte Cavalcavia, 38
☎ (+39) 3200734714
❀ www.opperbacco.it
✉ info@opperbacco.it
shop: no
e-commerce: no

OPPERBACCO

Luigi Recchiuti and his wife Arianna started this brewery, thinking they would produce beers that they would like to drink themselves. His motto is "soul and passion", and that makes the difference. Attention to ingredients is the main thing, starting with the purest spring water, from Mount Gran Sasso. Then he carefully selects spices, hops and other ingredients found locally. He makes about ten beers, from the very drinkable 4punto7 to the more challenging Overdose.

Livorno
Piccolo Birrificio Clandestino Aura

via A. Nicolodi, 40
☎ (+39) 0586854439
❀ www.piccolobirrificioclandestino.it
✉ info@piccolobirrificioclandestino.it
shop: yes
e-commerce: yes

PICCOLO
BIRRIFICIO
CLANDESTINO

In 2010 a group of friends with a shared passion for beer decided to start up this craft microbrewery. Following its success, the premises were moved from the original base in Via Solferino, which is just the pub now, to a production shed on the southern outskirts of the city. The brewery offers 14 types of beer, available in various sizes, each with a name that pays homage to Livorno traditions, all made from carefully chosen ingredients, some local, like spelt.

Podenzano (PC)
Retorto

via A. Grandi, 10
☎ (+39) 05231998845
✆ www.retorto.it
✉ info@retorto.it
shop: yes
e-commerce: no

In just three years, the craft facility founded by brewer Marcello Ceresa with his siblings Monica and Davide, has risen brilliantly in the Italian ranks. Awards began to arrive right from the beginning, with the first four labels. Now there are nine types, including Black Bullaby, a Belgian String Ale scented with cocoa and vanilla, barrique-aged Malanima, and the incredible Bloody Mario from high fermentation with coriander, grapefruit and orange zest, and whole cherries.

Ponte di Piave (TV)
San Gabriel

fraz. Levada I via della Vittoria, 2
☎ (+39) 0422202188
✆ www.sangabriel.it
✉ info@sangabriel.it
shop: yes
e-commerce: no

Founded in 1997 by beer sommelier Gabriele Tonon, this is a prestigious company based in a stately home near a Benedictine Abbey which once produced beverages with therapeutic properties, including beer. There is an almost manic attention to ingredients, pure spring water to hops from the surrounding countryside, and barley grown on the estate. Local products like radicchio, chestnuts, pumpkins, and other fruit and vegetables, are used to make seasonal brews.

Fidenza (PR)
Toccalmatto

via San Michele Campagna, 22c
☎ (+39) 0524533289
✆ www.birratoccalmatto.com
✉ info@birratoccalmatto.it
shop: yes
e-commerce: yes

Bruno Carilli, a fan of Belgian and British beers above all, opened his microbrewery in 2008. In no time at all the operation has won the heart of many a beer enthusiast and recently the facility has been expanded significantly. Now there is a real barrel cellar and 33 cl bottles have been introduced. Bruno makes over 20 brews, each characterized by its own personality, extensive use of hops, aromas, and experiments on yeast and fermentation. The beers range from the easy style to those matured in oak barrels for a few months or years.

Chiaravalle (AN)
Salumeria dell'Abbazia

via A. Volta, 14
☎ (+39) 07194508 l 3357547702
✉ abbazia@salumerialucaioli.191.it
shop: yes
e-commerce: no

Pacifico Lucaioli, the "great master of charcuterie" from the birthplace of Maria Montessori, produces a range of local specialities, most of which are free from colourings, preservatives, additives and milk powder. The only ingredients in the salami and sausages are pork, salt and pepper. The secret of his charcuterie, inspired by the Marche tradition of Corallina and Fabriano salami, loin, jowl, pancetta etc., lies in the selection of strictly Italian raw ingredients, skilful, unhurried processing and slow ageing.

Mirto (ME)
Sebastiano Agostino Ninone La Paisanella

via San Rocco, 15
☎ (+39) 0941919403 l 3341892003
🌐 www.lapaisanella.com
✉ agostino@lapaisanella.com
shop: yes
e-commerce: no

Sebastiano Agostino Ninone's company, in the Parco dei Nebrodi, is a family business dedicated to the breeding of native wild black pig and production of superlative pressed meats and fron a complete production chain that excludes only cultivation of the cereals used for feeding the pigs, which live in the open air in oak woods and eat acorns, roots, mushrooms, and wild herbs. The flagship products are cured ham and capocollo.

Castelsantangelo sul Nera (MC)
Norcineria Alto Nera

via Roma, 14
☎ (+39) 073798309
🌐 www.norcinerialtonera.it
✉ norcineria.altonera@tiscali.it
shop: yes
e-commerce: no

A well-organized and mature, semi-artisan company producing quality salami from local and Italian-raised pork, fed on vegetable protein. The soft traditional salami (a non-certified ciauscolo alongside the IGP version) is made from Cinta Senese pork, raised locally and processed without preservatives. It is ages in temperature-controlled chambers, natural caves and cellars, and sold regionally mainly by large-scale distribution, and in stores and restaurants around Italy.

Soragna (PR)
Antica Ardenga

fraz. Diolo I loc. Chiavica, 61
☎ (+39) 0524598289 I 3394856800
🕸 www.anticardenga.it
✉ info@anticaardenga.it
shop: yes
e-commerce: no

This old Parma company is part of the Culatello di Zibello Consortium, and guarantees high quality in breeding and butchering, processing premises, naturally ventilated maturation cellars and limited production quantities. The pigs are fed on the farm's own GMO-free products and butchered when they weigh about 260 kg. The meat is manually salted and tied. The various charcuterie products include the Slow Food Presidium Culatello di Zibello, a good spalla cruda and ready-to-cook products.

Polesine Zibello (PR)
Antica Corte Pallavicina

s.da del Palazzo Due Torri, 3
☎ (+39) 052496136 I 0524936539
🕸 www.acpallavicina.com
✉ info@acpallavicina.com
shop: yes
e-commerce: no

This company, with its century-old tradition, is famous for Culatello di Zibello (also a Slow Food Presidium) and has always stuck by the precepts of typicality and quality, supported by a closed supply chain in the Terre Verdiane district. The traditional charcuterie (including strolghino di culatello and coppa) derives from native local pig varieties and the meat is processed in the traditional way. The farm includes a semi-wild herd of black and white pigs, a production area, age-old cellars, the family-run restaurant and an exclusive hotel.

Spilinga (VV)
L'Artigiano della 'nduja

via A. Moro, 15
☎ (+39) 096365470
🕸 www.artigianodellanduja.com
✉ info@artigianodellanduja.com
shop: no
e-commerce: no

L'arte del sapore piccante

Luigi Caccamo made his dream come true in 2002 when he started up a company whose only product, 'nduja, is among the best-loved in his area. To produce it, the meat of Italian-bred pigs is processed at Spilinga into 1,000 quintals of 'nduja every year, without preservatives and additives. The company is still family-run despite its prominent position on the national market and abroad. Today the 'nduja is also available as a Crespone, in traditional, natural gut, weighing about half a kilo.

Terrassa Padovana (PD)
Bazza

via Fossetta, 3 zona artigianale
☎ (+39) 0499501066 l 331447570
❀ www.salumibazza.it
✉ info@salumibazza.it
shop: yes
e-commerce: no

In 1995 Giovanni Bazza began producing pressed meats without additives, preservatives or antioxidants: only pork, salt, pepper, garlic, spices, and natural flavouring, like the old days. Since he started his business, he has applied a precise philosophy and methodology: excellent meat from heavy pigs, temperature control, a pork butcher's skill and experience. In addition to fresh pressed meats (salami and soppressa are his flagships), he makes ossocollo, cured pork loin, and cotechino, zampone and bondiola.

Langhirano (PR)
Egidio Bedogni

via Fanti d'Italia, 75
☎ (+39) 0521853348 l 0521853349
❀ www.bedogniegidio.it
✉ bedogni@bedogniegidio.it
shop: no
e-commerce: no

A benchmark producer of gourmet prosciutto crudo since 1954, the company's secret is the care taken over the raw materials (selected heavy pig thighs from the Parma ham PDO circuit), artisan processing procedures, maturation in natural cellars for no less than 24 months. Begogni pays the same attention to the selection of charcuterie from reliable artisans in the sector, from excellent bull bresaola to Alto Adige speck, and strolghino, all sold under their own brand name.

Coreglia Antelminelli (LU)
Antica Norcineria Bellandi

loc. Ghivizzano l via Rinascimento, 6
☎ (+39) 058377008
❀ www.anticanorcineria.it
✉ clienti@anticanorcineria.it
shop: yes
e-commerce: no

Alta Qualità
in Garfagnana
dal 1945

The business gathered momentum in 1973 with the opening of a meat-processing facility. Today it produces charcuterie from Cinta Senese and pigs crossed with rustic breeds. Its name is linked to Biroldo della Garfagnana and Bazzone ham (Slow Food Presidia). The pigs are reared semi-wild by local farms, fed with vegetables and chestnuts. The pressed meats are prepared on site; the hams are made by Micheletti of Capannori and Tanara of Langhirano. Products are aged in the cellars of Ghivizzano castle.

Trento

Salumeria Belli

loc. Sopramonte I p.zza Oveno, 1
☎ (+39) 0461866130 I 0461866040
❂ www.salumeriabelli.it
✉ info@salumeriabelli.it
shop: yes
e-commerce: no

BELLI
Antica Salumeria Trentina
...da sei generazioni...

Belli, Trentino's oldest charcuterie producer, now in its sixth generation, has been a byword for speck and more since the 1800s. It vaunts a long history as a great artisan, and the proof is to be tasted in all its charcuterie: cooked ham, porchetta, frankfurters, carne salada, corned tongue, salted lard, smoked and seasoned, fresh salamis and local pork specialities like Trentino lucanica and mortandela. These have now been integrated with a small range of charcuterie made with wild Sila pork.

Campotosto (AQ)

Berardi

fraz. Poggio Cancelli I via San Giorgio, 1
☎ (+39) 0862909260
❂ www.salumiberardi.it
✉ ernesto.berardi@tiscali.it
shop: yes
e-commerce: no

Berardi
LAVORAZIONE MORTADELLE di
CAMPOTOSTO e INSACCATI TIPICI

For generations Berardi has been producing charcuterie in a corner of Abruzzo famous for Campotosto mortadella, and today processes pork in the traditional method, from late October to spring. The meat is dried by wood smoke and derives mainly from pigs raised in the local microclimate of Parco Nazionale del Gran Sasso e sui Monti della Laga. As well as Campotosto mortadella, they also produce schiacciato salami, ventricina, and meat and liver sausages.

Brunico/Bruneck (BZ)

Karl Bernardi

via Centrale, 36
☎ (+39) 0474555472 I 0474411176
❂ www.bernardi-karl.it
✉ info@bernardi-karl.it
shop: yes
e-commerce: yes

K. BERNARDI
BRUNECK · BRUNICO

This is a modern, traditional family company, in business for decades, and successfully combining century-old tradition with avant-garde technology. Italian meat of the highest standard is used: pork, beef, game and turkey, all hand-processed in the plant with dry salting and ageing in natural cellars. The meat is cold smoked with beech wood at controlled temperatures, alternating smoke and fresh air. The company produces Alto Adige charcuterie, venison salami, canned goulash and other delicacies.

Arnad (AO)
Maison Bertolin

loc. Champagnolaz, 10
☎ (+39) 0125966127 I 0125966144
❀ www.bertolin.com
✉ info@bertolin.com
shop: yes
e-commerce: no

Maison Bertolin, in Arnad, opened as a butcher in 1957, and has long been synonymous with local lard, also famous for its salami made with roe and red deer, chamois, beef and goat, the latter from two native breeds. Together with national pork, bred in compliance with Prosciutto di Parma specifications, a fine assortment of products is available. Cattle and goats spend the summer in a semi-wild state, and are stalled in winter. Their meat is used for typical motzetta and Lo Boc, a cooked goat salami.

Castiglione d'Orcia (SI)
Biamiata

Casale Giardinetto di Sopra
☎ (+39) 0564986110 I 3475057247
❀ www.aiacolonna.it
✉ info@aiacolonna.it
shop: no
e-commerce: no

The company owns one of the largest organic Cinta Senese pig farms in Italy. The animals live in a semi-wild state between Val d'Orcia and Monte Amiata, at the Podere Bioamiata at Castiglione d'Orcia, and the Aia della Colonna farm holiday centre at Roccalbegna, where the head office is now located. The pigs are fed on cereals and vegetable proteins, and the meat is processed in the Gam di Montefiascone plant which specializes in organic products. Delicacies include typical Bastardo and soppressata.

Sinagra (ME)
F.lli Borrello

c.da Forte, 7
☎ (+39) 0941594844
❀ www.trattoriaborrello.it
✉ f.lli_borrello@virgilio.it
shop: yes
e-commerce: no

Salumi
di suino nero dei Nebrodi

The Borrello family company is an organic, self-sufficient farm operating a closed supply chain, founded in the 1960s and today extending over 100 hectares of land on the Nebrodi foothills. The farm includes semi-wild cows, sheep, goats and black pigs, for the production of meat, cheese and charcuterie, which are sold in the farm's butcher's shop and can be tasted in the annexed family restaurant. The pigs yield excellent charcuterie, in particular prosciutto crudo, pancetta and salami.

Faicchio (BN)
La Bottega del Gourmet

via Provinciale, 185
☎ (+39) 0824947404
🕸 www.labottegadelgourmet.com
✉ info@labottegadelgourmet.com
shop: no
e-commerce: no

Here, the Pelatello or Nero Casertano pig reigns supreme. The black stock, fed on vegetable proteins, is raised semi-wild and selected between the provinces of Caserta and Benevento. A local pork butcher processes the meat to make sausages, salami and soppressata, using recipes and suggestions by Enzo Martorella for his Bottega del Gourmet. All the charcuterie is processed with artisan methods, additive- and preservative-free, and matured in temperature-controlled chambers or cellars at 1,300 metres asl.

Felino (PR)
Branchi

v.le Roma, 11
☎ (+39) 0521835601
🕸 www.branchi.it
✉ info@branchi.it
shop: yes
e-commerce: no

BRANCHI
PROSCIUTTI

The business was established in 1987 by Tito Branchi, but was developed in the 1950s and 1960s by Erminio Branchi and his son Franco. They were the first in the area to produce prosciutto cotto and prosciutto di Praga, which made its name on the market. Today these products are joined by culaccia and prosciutto made from the meat of black pigs. Thanks to homemade brines and slow wood-smoking, the prosciutto, smoked and corned meats, and other charcuterie products are real delicacies.

Zocca (MO)
Ca' Lumaco

via Mazzoli, 740
☎ (+39) 059987642
🕸 www.calumaco.it
✉ emanuele.ferri@calumaco.it
shop: yes
e-commerce: no

The business opened in 2001 with three generations of experience, and is dedicated to breeding Mora Romagnola pigs in the wild on the family farm, where they can feed on acorns, chestnuts, roots and tubers. Their diet is integrated with barley, fava beans and organic corn, all grown on the farm, forming a complete production cycle: the butchering and processing take place in the company's small facility, producing charcuterie without preservatives. The meats are aged in temperature-controlled chambers, ventilated with fresh air.

San Daniele del Friuli (UD)
Il Camarin

via San Luca, 24/26
☎ (+39) 0432942125
☻ www.ilcamarin.it
✉ ilcamarin.prosciutti@tin.it
shop: yes
e-commerce: no

This is a small artisan ham production business with limited quantities sold to gourmet stores and high-end restaurants. Healthy fresh air, prestigious ingredients (large, selected thigh joints from farms around Mantua and Brescia included in the PDO zone), careful processing, well-judged salting and lengthy maturation (between 14 and 24 months) are Il Camarin's strong points. The company produces DOT San Daniele and Dolcenero, a San Daniele matured for 36 months, a "super riserva" that is not for sale but can be tasted in the family restaurant.

Borgonovo Val Tidone (PC)
Capitelli

via Borgonovo, 1 (s.s. 412)
☎ (+39) 0523862845
☻ capitelli.cibosano.pro
✉ capitelli@cibosano.pro
shop: no
e-commerce: no

The company, founded in 1977 by Claudio Capitelli, is located along the main road linking the town to Castel San Giovanni. Over the last decade it has focused on the production of prime cooked ham, reviving old traditions and adopting innovative processing techniques. Its key product is San Giovanni, a cooked ham available in the classic, brazed and smoked, and honey-coated flavours. There is also a Europa mortadella and the recently launched Giovanna, a succulent cooked pancetta.

Lanzada (SO)
Casa della Carne

via San Giovanni, 155
☎ (+39) 0342453278
☻ www.casadellacarne.com
✉ malenca@casadellacarne.com
shop: yes
e-commerce: no

The company has over a century of experience in artisan meat processing, including different varieties of venison, typical of the Valmalenco production area, in Valtellina. The original and typical products have earned the company praise thanks to the efforts of owner Mario Cardinale Bosio, a Milanese lawyer turned cured meat producer a few years ago. The traditional-style products include bresaola, typical charcuterie of the Valtellina area and the exclusive Malenca. The business also has a lovely butcher's shop.

Tizzano Val Parma (PR)
Casa Graziano

loc. Capoponte **l** s.da Massese, 29
☎ (+39) 0521855023
❀ www.casagraziano.com
✉ info@casagraziano.com
shop: yes
e-commerce: no

Graziano Casa's ham business was established in the Seventies, in the strip of Italy that was to become today's Food Valley. The quality of his cured meats is explained by the blend of technology and artisanal care as well as a touch of nature, namely a microclimate particularly well-suited to curing, here on the edge of Valle del Cedra e del Parma Regional Park. Quality and authenticity are the typical features of the company's three specialities, Prosciutto di Parma PDO, Gran Culatta, and Ghinaldo.

Casabona (KR)
Salumificio di Casabona Santa Barbara

via della Sila
☎ (+39) 0962889072 **l** 3402507989
❀ www.salumificiocasabona.it
✉ salumificiocasabona@tiscali.it
shop: yes
e-commerce: no

The family-run Casabona charcuterie factory is situated in the upper Crotone countryside, in a the district of Santa Barbara, hence the product brand name. It produces typical regional charcuterie like soppressata, capocollo, dried sausages, etc., from its own free-range Cinta Senese and Nero di Calabria pigs, which feed on local barley, corn and wheat. Products are preservative- and additive-free, containing just pork, salt, pepper, peppers, chilli and wild fennel.

Roncà (VR)
La Casara - Roncolato Romano

via Nuova, 1
☎ (+39) 0457460052
❀ www.lacasara.it
✉ info@lacasara.it
shop: yes
e-commerce: no

In the 1920s Ermenegildo Roncolato and sons Romano and Angelo, started a rotating dairy. In 1964, Romano took over the Caseificio Sociale di Roncà and turned it into a small cheese-making business. At the same time a heavy pig farm was started, the stock fed with cheese manufacturing by-products. Today, in addition to cheese made from local cow and goat milk (flagships are PDO Monte Veronese and the Ubriachi line), the company also makes traditional Veneto charcuterie including soppressa, speck and hand-processed hams aged in a natural cellar.

Morigerati (SA)

Salumi Cellito

fraz. Sicilì I loc. Cillitto
☎ (+39) 0974982136 I 3395335733
❀ www.casalecellito.it
✉ salumicellito@gmail.com
shop: yes
e-commerce: no

Cellito is a family-run farm in Valle dei Mulini, a WWF nature reserve in the Cilento – Vallo di Diano National Park. Established about 12 years ago with the aim of reviving and promoting heirloom charcuterie recipes, it used pork from its own free-range stock, producing traditional artisanal cured meats, free from preservatives. The range includes dried, sweet and spicy sausages, soppressata, capocollo, pancetta, prosciutello and salamino.

Scandolara Ravara (CR)

Aziende Agricole Cerati

loc. Castelponzone I via Fornace, 10
☎ (+39) 0375350193
❀ www.aziendeagricolecerati.it
✉ info.salumificio@agricolecerati.it
shop: yes
e-commerce: no

Cerati is an excellent example of the entrepreneurial and agricultural labour typical of the Po Valley. Starting life as a dairy farm, it now handles all aspects of agriculture. Most production focuses on charcuterie, with all the processing and aging taking place within the farm. Over recent years Cerati has started producing charcuterie free from sugar, gluten and dairy products, with a tiny quantity of preservatives. Its specialities include a broad selection of sausages, Cremonese garlic salami, and the flagship product Il 100.

Martina Franca (TA)

Salumi Cervellera
Capocollo di Martina Franca

via Mottola, 68
☎ (+39) 0804838812 I 3281441942
❀ www.capocollodimartinafranca.it
✉ info@ilcapocollomartinese.it
shop: yes
e-commerce: yes

Giuseppe and Gianluca Cervellera, father and son, produce typical charcuterie from Valle d'Itria, the triangle of Puglia between Bari, Brindisi and Taranto. In their workshop, annexed to the family butcher shop, they process pork preferably from free-range pigs reared in Puglia's lower Murgia district. Their flagship product is Martina Franca capocollo, a Slow Food Presidium soaked in mulled wine, smoked with typical Martina Franca fragno oak, and seasoned in a trullo for 90/180 days.

Venticano (AV)
Prosciuttificio Ciarcia

c.da Ilici zona Pip
☎ (+39) 0825965309
❀ www.vittoriociarcia.com
✉ info@vittoriociarcia.com
shop: yes
e-commerce: no

Ciarcia®
dal 1930

Irpinia hams have been produced here since 1930. Originally a small workshop, over the years the Venticano facility has grown into a modern company and is now a benchmark throughout Campania for processing cured hams and charcuterie made from pork leg, such as culatta, culatello and fiocco di prosciutto. The pork is from heavy pigs purchased within Italy. This is then salted by hand and aged in rooms with windows. Ciarcia also makes ham using Nero Casertano stock.

Airola (BN)
Salumificio Cillo

c.da Cortedona, 20
☎ (+39) 0823714422 | 335454723
❀ www.salumificiocillo.it
✉ cillosabatino@alice.it
shop: no
e-commerce: no

dal 1985
Cillo
passione per le carni

Cillo is not only famous for its excellent own-production charcuterie but also prestigious fresh meats, including Marchigiana and Chianina beef, Laticauda lamb and Aberdeen Angus. The feathers in this company's production cap are charcuterie, prosciutto, culatello, pork jowl, mortadella, all made from Sannio and Nero Casertano pork, and even frankfurters made from Chianina and Marchigiana beef. The meat is processed by hand and matured in temperature-controlled chambers and natural environments.

Viterbo
Coccia

via Lega dei Dodici Popoli, 7d
☎ (+39) 0761250879
❀ salumificiococcia.it
✉ info@cocciasesto.it
shop: yes
e-commerce: yes

Coccia Sesto
Prosciuttificio

Since the early 20th century, the Coccia family have been working as producers of pork-based foods, respecting tradition while taking advantage of modern techniques that don't detract from the artisanal quality of the products. The 'susianella' (a certified Slow Food) is among the most sought after products. This cured meat is a local speciality. But the guanciale, prosciutto, mortadella, tasty sausages and lardo are all noteworthy, as is their salami (especially the red onion variety).

San Daniele del Friuli (UD)

Prosciutti Coradazzi

via Kennedy, 128
☎ (+39) 0432957582
⊛ www.coradazzi.it
✉ info@coradazzi.it
shop: yes
e-commerce: yes

PROSCIUTTI
CORADAZZI

Coradazzi is a benchmark for PDO San Daniele prosciutto crudo. A ham that is as plain, unfussy and straightforward as its owners, brother Angelo working in production, and sister Teresa running the company. The strength of their cured hams, ranging from a minimum of 16 months up to 20 months of ageing, is the fresh mildness, with a classic taste, surprisingly youthful but with an aromatic complexity and the sophistication of a star player.

Mortara (PV)

Corte dell'Oca
Gioachino Palestro

via F. Sforza, 27
☎ (+39) 038498397
⊛ www.cortedelloca.com
✉ info@cortedelloca.com
shop: yes
e-commerce: no

Gioachino Palestro came to La Corte in 1988 with the goal of setting up a business to protect and promote traditional Lomellina charcuterie. Geese have always been the most widely bred animal hereabouts and are considered as a separate typology in this sector. PGI Mortara goose salami is the feather in La Corte's cap and can be bought to cook or already cooked. Other products include goose liver torcione, salami, breast and ham. Some of the pressed meats are kosher products.

Soragna (PR)

CroceDelizia

s.da Emilia, 1a
☎ (+39) 0524596061
⊛ www.crocedelizia.com
✉ info@crocedelizia.com
shop: yes
e-commerce: no

SALUMI DEI LUOGHI VERDIANI

Ernestino Carraglia learned pork butchering from his father Ugo. Today he supervises the entire charcuterie production process, using heavy pig meat from farms in Emilia and Lombardy, under the PDO Parma. His name is linked particularly to the Antichi Produttori brand of Zibello culatello. There is also an organic line of charcuterie (from pigs raised in a semi-wild state) without additives. The products are matured in natural cellars and there is also a factory shop.

Oggiono (LC)

Marco D'Oggiono Prosciutti

via Lazzaretto, 29
☎ (+39) 0341576285
☀ www.marcodoggiono.com
✉ info@marcodoggiono.com
shop: yes
e-commerce: yes

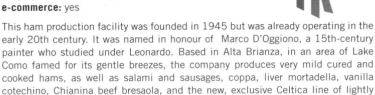

This ham production facility was founded in 1945 but was already operating in the early 20th century. It was named in honour of Marco D'Oggiono, a 15th-century painter who studied under Leonardo. Based in Alta Brianza, in an area of Lake Como famed for its gentle breezes, the company produces very mild cured and cooked hams, as well as salami and sausages, coppa, liver mortadella, vanilla cotechino, Chianina beef bresaola, and the new, exclusive Celtica line of lightly smoked charcuterie.

Cormòns (GO)

D'Osvaldo

via Dante, 40
☎ (+39) 048161644
☀ www.dosvaldo.it
✉ info@dosvaldo.it
shop: yes
e-commerce: no

Prosciutto di Cormòns

In 1940 smoking was a necessity: Luigi D'Osvaldo smoked his hams to preserve them and sell them in his butcher's shop. His grandchildren and son Lorenzo increased production while respecting tradition. A small quantity is smoked using milder cherry wood. The pork comes from small farmers in the Friuli area, and is mostly processed by hand and matured in well-ventilated rooms. The range includes not only Cormòns ham but also pancetta and speck.

Palmanova (UD)

Jolanda De Colò

via I Maggio, 21
☎ (+39) 0432920321
☀ www.jolandadecolo.it
✉ brunopessot@jolandadecolo.it
shop: yes
e-commerce: yes

Founded in 1976 to concentrate on traditional Friuli products and goose specialities, the company today is expanding its production facilities. The reins of the business are, however, always still in the hands of the Pessot-de Colò family, for whom quality remains a corporate priority. In addition to typical regional pressed meats, they make high-end products like foie gras and smoked salmon. Conventional pork is Italian mangalica, while goose comes from selected Hungarian farms.

Chiavenna (SO)

F.lli Del Curto

via F. Dolzino, 129
☎ (+39) 034332312
✉ delcurtosnc@gmail.com
shop: yes
e-commerce: no

Del Curto
Aldo e Enrico snc

A real Valchiavenna institution, at the very least because it is one of the few char-cuterie producers to make violino di capra, a goat ham and Slow Food Presidium. In addition to goat, pigs and cattle are also processed by Chiavenna facility. Cattle are raised on farms close, in full respect of nature and animal welfare. In addition to the violin, the Del Curto siblings also produce pressed meats in far northwest Lombardy, including and bastardèi salami made with pork and beef meat and fat.

Lesignano de' Bagni (PR)

Devodier

fraz. Mulazzano Ponte I via Ponticella, 4
☎ (+39) 0521 861070
✱ www.devodier.com
✉ info@devodier.com
shop: no
e-commerce: no

After over a century as pork butchers, in the mid-20th century the Devodiers under-stood the natural vocation of the area between Langhirano and Lesignano de'Bagni for maturing hams, and opened a specific business there. Since then they have produced various lines of PDO Prosciutto di Parma and exclusive reserve products, matured in old cellars rich in noble rot and enzymes: Mornello (20 months), "più di 24 lune" (over 24 months), Secretum (30 months), Eccellenze (36 months).

San Daniele del Friuli (UD)

Dok Dall'Ava

via Gemona, 29
☎ (+39) 0432940280
✱ www.dokdallava.com
✉ info@dallava.com
shop: yes
e-commerce: no

DOK DALL'AVA
prosciuttai-dal-1955

Dok Dall'Ava has been in the charcuterie business since 1955, building up a well-deserved reputation in processing PDO San Daniele, cru and reserve cured hams. Alongside the local product, which undergoes lengthy maturation and also light smoking, the company cures hams from game and pig breeds such as Nero Iberico, Nero dei Nebrodi, Mangalica, Nero Lucano. Fresh pasta and tortellini can also be tasted in the various delicatessens in the Triveneto region, as well as ready-sliced meats, and the Dall'Ava Bakery patisserie and baked goods.

Colorno (PR)
Salumificio Ducale

via al Macello, 10
☎ (+39) 0521815476
❖ www.salumificioducale.it
✉ info@salumificioducale.it
shop: yes
e-commerce: no

Ducale di Morini e Tortini charcuterie was founded in 1958 by a group of masèn (pork butchers) passionate about the typical Bassa Parmense charcuterie, like cooked shoulder from San Secondo, made using a medieval recipe. The ingredients are bought from local butchers dealing in heavy Italian pig breeds. The meat is mainly processed by hand and matured in naturally ventilated cellars. The leading products are PDO Zibello culatello, Felino salami and fiocchetto di prosciutto.

San Miniato (PI)
Sergio Falaschi

via A. Conti, 18
☎ (+39) 057143190
❖ www.sergiofalaschi.it
✉ info@sergiofalaschi.it
shop: yes
e-commerce: yes

In 1925 Guido Falaschi opened a butcher shop in San Miniato, with his two children working with him, but it was not until 1967, when Sergio arrived, that the business gathered momentum. He expanded the product range to include forgotten pressed meats and he revived the food chain concept. Now in the fourth generation, the business purchases grey and Cinta Senese pork from local farms where the stock is semi-wild. Artisanal processing for a range including all traditional Tuscan charcuterie.

Scerni (CH)
Fattorie del Tratturo

c.da Ragna, 59
☎ (+39) 0873914173 I 3393086378
❖ ventricina.com
✉ info@ventricina.com
shop: yes
e-commerce: no

The company is owned by Luigi Di Lello, founder of the Accademia della Ventricina and ambassador for this typical product of the Vasto area. Di Lello makes ventricina with prime pork thigh, loin and shoulder cuts, chopped with the knife point, flavoured with crushed dried bell peppers, pepper and wild fennel seeds; the product is dried by wood smoke and matured for at least three months. The liver salamella al vino cotto and capocollo di Montesorbo are also excellent. The meat is carefully selected with natural processing and maturing methods.

Altilia (CS)
Adriano Ferrari

c.da Monti
☎ (+39) 3345639303
🌐 www.nerocalabrese.it
✉ info@nerocalabrese.it
shop: yes
e-commerce: yes

Adriano Ferrari works to promote the black pig of Calabria, which he breeds in a semi-wild state on his farm in Altilia (Cosenza). He feeds the stock vegetal protein and slaughters at about two quintals in weight, producing a range of top-quality meats, flavoured with spices, black peppercorns, fennel seed, rosemary, and laurel in some. Capocollo, soppressata, and Atiliara sausage, lard, loin and typical Calabria 'nduja. All free of preservatives and additives.

Modena
Erio Ferrari

via Canaletto Nord, 565
☎ (+39) 059310015
🌐 www.salumiferrari.it
✉ info@salumiferrari.it
shop: no
e-commerce: no

The cured meat facility was established by Erio Ferrari in 1958, transforming a farm machinery depot into a meat processing plant with adjacent butcher. This was followed in 1995 by the new plant in Via Canaletto Nord. Here, cooked meats are produced from selected ingredients in the Emilia tradition, with a wide range that includes trotters and cotechino, the feather in the company's cap. The cured meats are produced in the Ferrari Cav. Bruno plant at Lesignano de' Bagni (PR).

Dubino (SO)
Ferraro

fraz. Nuova Olonio I via privata Molatore
☎ (+39) 0342687243 I 3936100010
🌐 www.bresaolaferraro.it
✉ info@bresaolaferraro.it
shop: no
e-commerce: no

Since 2005 Simone Ferraro has processed only fresh beef from France, Spain, Ireland and Italy, including the prestigious Piedmontese Fassona. There are no additives in his bresaola, just salt, pepper, spices, sugar and white wine. Another added value, as well as excellent ingredients, is the choice of cuts: top sirloin, tenderloin, round and bottom sirloin. The recipe is a family tradition, the processing (cutting, salting and manipulation) is carried out totally by hand. The slinzega made from bresaola trimmings is also worth tasting.

Montecilfone (CB)

Casa Florio

via Giordano, 6a
☎ (+39) 0875979727
❂ www.casaflorio.it
✉ info@casaflorio.it
shop: yes
e-commerce: yes

Casa Florio is a multifaceted producer where both 'national' and local cured meats are made. Both product lines have one thing in common: quality (both in terms of the pork used and techniques for working it). They don't raise their own pigs, but the meat used is strictly from suppliers belonging to the IPQ (Parma Quality Institute). Products are worked by hand and don't contain additives: only Cervia salt, and natural spices/aromatics. The ventricina and sausages are a must and can be enjoyed at an on-site eatery.

Sant'Egidio alla Vibrata (TE)

Fracassa Salumi

loc. Paolantonio I via Meucci, 41
☎ (+39) 0861842363
❂ www.fracassa.it
✉ info@fracassa.it
shop: yes
e-commerce: yes

FRACASSA
SALUMI

The Fracassa farm was originally established in the 1970s as a pig and sheep farm. When Roberto and Luigi joined the family business set up by their father Enrico, they began to produce charcuterie from heavy pork, including pigs reared on their own farm. The Fracassa family produces different types of salami, flavoured with Montepulciano d'Abruzzo, truffles and spices, bresaola and pork carpaccio, coppiette salami, liver sausage and classic "di Enrico" Teramo ventricina, a spreadable sausage delicious on bread.

Castel Focognano (AR)

Fracassi dal 1927

loc. Rassina I p.zza G. Mazzini, 24
☎ (+39) 0575591480 I 335343186
❂ www.simonefracassi.com
✉ info@macelleriafracassi.it
shop: yes
e-commerce: no

This butcher in Rassina, province of Arezzo, has been promoting Casentino grey for some time. This native stock is bred in the wild and Simone Fracassi, skilled fourth generation of a craft handed down over the years, has made the extraordinary ham famous. He monitors the production chain of prized IGP Chianina meat and uses it to make malenca, tagliata, nero and bianco di Chianina, stew, tripe, and burgers. Also available farmyard poultry, and Casentino lamb and rabbit.

Montefiascone (VT)

G.A.M.

via Verentana, 3 km 3,150
☎ (+39) 0761825471 I 3384787933
◈ www.salumificiogam.it
✉ socgam@libero.it
shop: yes
e-commerce: no

G.A.M. was founded in 1986 by a group of Montefiascone environmentalists as a kind of buying group. It evolved into a charcuterie producer serving butchers and grocers. Considered one of the best processing businesses in Central Italy, where organic breeders and Suino Nero pig farmers send their meat to be made into delicious cold meats. Its products are inspired by the charcuterie tradition of central Italy, but there is also room for classics from the rest of Italy. The pork saddle is to die for.

Gioi (SA)

G.ioi

via Chiaie snc
☎ (+39) 0974991135 I 3387354724
◈ www.soppressatadigioi.com
✉ info@gioisrl.com
shop: yes
e-commerce: no

This small artisan company works in the heart of the Cilento National Park and Vallo di Diano, in the tiny village of Gioi. The business processes the most prestigious cuts of pork raised in the park in a semi-wild state, and fed on vegetable protein. The meat is processed using time-honoured recipes, all by hand apart from mincing, and without preservatives, using only meat, salt, natural herbs and spices. The company is known for production of the Slow Food Presidium, soppressata di Gioi.

Langhirano (PR)

F.lli Galloni

via Roma, 84
☎ (+39) 0521354211
◈ www.galloniprosciutto.it
✉ info@galloniprosciutto.it
shop: no
e-commerce: no

This is undoubtedly one of the best Prosciutto di Parma industries. The hams are carefully processed, starting with selected thighs of heavy pig breeds (the largest and fattiest cuts) from the PDO and from trusted breeders. Processing is mostly manual with a longer-than-average maturation period, at least 15–16 months to three years. The range includes Magnus, a Prosciutto di Parma matured in barriques, a limited edition obtained from thighs of large, mature pigs of about a year in age.

Villa d'Almè (BG)
Edoardo Gamba

via G. Mazzini, 105
☎ (+39) 035541126
🌐 salumificio.it
✉ info@salumificio.it
shop: no
e-commerce: no

The history of this charcuterie began in 1880, when Giovanni Battista Gamba opened a butcher's shop with an annexed inn. Over a hundred years of business later, the company continues to make charcuterie with an eye on quality as well as innovation: meat from animals raised outdoors, organic certification, new spice combinations, no additives and preservatives in the bio line. Leading products include: pork and beef slinziga, spicy sausage, seasoned and game salamis.

Pontassieve (FI)
Gerini

v.le Hanoi, 50
☎ (+39) 0558368559 l 0558315207
🌐 www.gerinispa.it
✉ info@gerinispa.com
shop: no
e-commerce: no

Gerini got its start back in the 1700s, though the butcher shop's status was only officially formalized in 1882. Today Gerini can be called a veritable industry, exporting its products and producing its classic Tuscan salamis, though without losing sight of quality. Prosciutto is a featured product, from their Tuscan PDO to their Norcia PGI, both made in their own facility in Umbria, while their Aspromonte prosciutto, made from pigs bred in the wild, is produced at their Tuscan site.

Langhirano (PR)
Prosciuttificio Ghirardi Onesto

via Cascinapiano, 24
☎ (+39) 0521857617
🌐 www.ghirardionesto.com
✉ info@ghirardionesto.com
shop: no
e-commerce: no

The business was founded in 1972 at Langhirano, a few years after the Consorzio del Prosciutto di Parma and this is still the focus of all its activities. The processing is carried out manually with a close eye on the meat on and off the bone, and on the maturation which takes place in large rooms with traditional windows that are closed or open depending on the wind, humidity and outside temperature. The factory has its own small, independent weather station to benefit fully from the weather conditions.

Langhirano (PR)
Ghirardi Prosciutti

via B. Ferrari, 3
☎ (+39) 0521861155
⊛ ghirardiprosciutti.it
✉ info@ghirardiprosciutti.it
shop: yes
e-commerce: no

Albino Ghirardi began the business of processing and maturing ham in Langhirano in 1948. Over time production increased and the company became established on the Italian and foreign markets. In 2007 Ghirardi Prosciutti Srl was founded with its distinctive trademark butterfly, standing out over the cream of production. The meat derives from mature heavy pigs bred in Lombardy, Veneto and Emilia, with long maturation of the thigh joints (18–24 months) for hams on or off the bone, and other traditional charcuterie.

Canossa (RE)
Gianferrari

via Val d'Enza Nord, 143
☎ (+39) 0522878185
⊛ www.gianferrari.it
✉ info@gianferrari.it
shop: yes
e-commerce: no

Fernando Gianferrari began processing artisan charcuterie in Canossa in 1951, an art handed down from father to son resulting in high quality products. The meat, from heavy pig breeds born and raised in Italy, is processed by traditional methods with no preservatives. These features, along with lengthy maturation and the unusual climate of Val d'Enza, make this an unmistakeably tasty and high quality range of products including ham, coppa, strolghino, culatello.

Carrara (MS)
Giannarelli

fraz. Colonnata I via Comunale, 2
☎ (+39) 0585758093
⊛ www.lardogiannarelli.it
✉ info@lardogiannarelli.it
shop: yes
e-commerce: no

The business originated in Bedizzone, near Colonnata, as a butcher, but today is renowned as pork butcher, especially for the local lard produced. Processing is completely manual, non-GMO and gluten- and preservative-free. The classic charcuterie is made from the meat of Pianura Padana heavy white pigs, and the other line from Cinta Senese pigs bred on Oliviero Toscani's OT farm at Casale Marittimo. The pigs are semi-wild and fed a vegetable diet. The maturing takes place in natural caves and cellars.

Carpaneto Piacentino (PC)
Giordano

fraz. Case Draghi I s.da prov.le per Castell'Arquato, 28
☎ (+39) 0523859083
❀ www.salumigiordano.com
✉ info@salumigiordano.com
shop: yes
e-commerce: no

The Piacentino area's special humid climate, not prone to excessive temperature changes, is the secret of a long charcuterie tradition. Angela and Giuseppe Michelazzi, the owners of the Giordano charcuterie factory, produce all three Piacentina PDO products: salami, coppa and pancetta. They select pork from heavy pigs reared in Emilia Romagna and Lombardy, then process the meat and age the charcuterie a cool, damp underground cellar. Giordano also makes cotechino, strolghino and culatello.

Genola (CN)
La Granda

via Garetta, 8a
☎ (+39) 0172726178
❀ www.lagranda.it
✉ info@lagranda.it
shop: yes
e-commerce: no

La Granda
SALUMI

Granda Trasformazione, founded in 2004, is the natural evolution of the La Granda association, created by Sergio Capaldo, consisting of over 60 Piedmontese cow breeders. The meat is used for ready-to-eat specialities (roasts, sauces, tripe, beef tuna in jars etc.). Recently La Granda entered the charcuterie sector when it purchased the Dho di Centallo factory producing pork and beef salamis, cooked salami (a speciality of lower Piedmont), lard with herbs, galantina and other delicacies.

Carrara (MS)
Larderia Fausto Guadagni

loc. Colonnata I s.da Comunale, 4
☎ (+39) 0585768069 I 3356530268
❀ www.larderiafaustoguadagni.com
✉ larderiacolonnata@tiscali.it
shop: yes
e-commerce: no

The product range consists exclusively of lard: from PGI Colonnata in blocks, sliced and minced, to the delicious variations offered by Fausto Guadagni who runs the pork butcher's founded by his parents in 1949. The selected lards include: Gran Selezione Toscana, from Casentino grey pigs; LardoPic, from Calabrian black pigs raised wild in Aspromonte, and flavoured with chilli pepper; Selezione Mediterranea, from Calabrian black pigs, and flavoured with bergamot, wild fennel and Mediterranean herbs.

Spilimbergo (PN)
Lovison

via U. Foscolo, 18
☎ (+39) 04272068
🖑 www.salumilovison.it
✉ info@lovisonspa.com
shop: yes
e-commerce: no

We owe the invention of musetto, a type of cotechino with 110 years of history, to Lovison. In over a century the business has grown but without compromising the quality or the passion. In the Spilimbergo cured meat factory great care is taken over the ingredients (pigs raised and butchered in Friuli, fed on non-GMO fodder) and the processing, with heat dissection, and filling and tying by hand. Other charcuterie products by Lovison include soppressa, salami and an excellent matured lard.

Ferrere (AT)
Agrisalumeria Luiset

via Torino, 107
☎ (+39) 0141934326
🖑 www.agrisalumeria.it
✉ info@agrisalumeria.it
shop: yes
e-commerce: no

The Casetta family have created an eco-friendly closed-chain model, with pigs reared on the family farm, a processing facility, resources with minimal environmental impact, and a limited edition line of organic charcuterie. Cured and cooked charcuterie of traditional inspiration includes coppa, guanciale, brawn, trotters, and cotechino, and exclusive creations: double cured pork fat; Luiset pancetta with aromatic herbs; roast loin; and guster, a Piedmontese-style artisanal frankfurter.

Agliana (PT)
Macelleria Marini

loc. Ferruccia I via C. Levi snc
☎ (+39) 0574718119
🖑 www.macelleriamarini.it
✉ info@macelleriamarini.it
shop: yes
e-commerce: yes

Since 1906, four generations of the Marini family have drawn on their knowledge of meat, especially pork, to produce high-quality salamis and prosciuttos, all aged to perfection in their own cellars. Prosciutto is their speciality, but there's plenty more worth trying, including their guanciale, coppe, salami, lardo, sbriciolona (a local speciality), sausage and mortadella di Prato PGI (a certified Slow Food). They also sell various cuts of meat and other speciality food items.

Martina Franca (TA)

Martina Franca Salumi

via Vecchia Ceglie, 5 Zona L
☎ (+39) 0804490533 I 3281634715
✆ www.salumimartinafranca.it
✉ info@salumimartinafranca.it
shop: yes
e-commerce: no

Unique climate conditions and a long tradition of pig farming are decisive factors for the pork butcher business in Martina Franca, in the heart of Murgia dei Trulli and Valle d'Itria, where capocollo is the best-known product. This young company, created in 2010, is one of the best exponents of local charcuterie, lightly smoked with local Macedonian oak. The salamis from Aspromonte black pigs and the traditional local pagnotella pressed meat are recommended.

San Dorligo della Valle (TS)

Masè

via J. Ressel, 2
☎ (+39) 0402821011
✆ www.cottomase.com
✉ info@cottomase.com
shop: yes
e-commerce: yes

MASE'
Sapori d'autore dal 1870

In 2013 Masè was acquired by a group of Friuli businesspeople but this venerable brand of traditional Trieste charcuterie dates back to 1870, and has shops dotted around the towns of Saba and Svevo. The flagship is CottoTrieste, the typical ham cooked Trieste style. Alongside this pork speciality with its strong Mitteleuropa feel, and other classic local products, in recent years Masè has added unusual cooked hams, branded NeroTrieste, MieleTrieste, Spall8, and Panciotta.

San Casciano in Val di Pesa (FI)

Massanera

fraz. Chiesanuova I via Faltignano, 76
☎ (+39) 0558242222 I 0558242360
✆ massanera.com
✉ info@massanera.com
shop: yes
e-commerce: no

MASSANERA
... *un angolo di terra nel Chianti Classico* ...

Massanera is a fine Chianti Classico estate surrounding a villa, which began life as a hunting lodge for Florentine nobles, before becoming a farm in the 18th century. Here Carlo Cattaneo produces wines, grappa, EVOO, and excellent charcuterie, made from his own herd of Cinta Senese pigs. The additive- and preservative-free meat products, made by a butcher who is also a friend, are typical of Tuscany's charcuterie tradition: ham, salami, finocchiona, cured pork fat, flat and rolled pancetta, gota, capocollo and filetto.

Charcuterie

Predaia (TN)

Dal Massimo Goloso

loc. Coredo I p.zza dei Cigni, 6
☎ (+39) 0463536129 I 3381929010
❂ www.macelleriacorra.com
✉ macelleriacorra@tin.it
shop: yes
e-commerce: no

The story of Massimo Corrà goes back to a traditional general store established in the latter half of the 19th century. It produces classic regional charcuterie, sourcing pork from Trentino. Products include luganega sausage; Trentino speck including an additive- and preservative-free version; Val di Non mortandela; carne salada; game-based and smoked salamis; frankfurters and kaminwurst. It also vaunts a number of original creations, like luganega with walnuts, Pollospeck, Speckino with blueberry grappa, and speck spread.

Stra (VE)

Meggiolaro

via Brenton, 2
☎ (+39) 0498934562 I 3395766305
❂ www.meggiolarosrl.it
✉ info@meggiolarosrl.it
shop: no
e-commerce: no

Founded in 1966, Meggiolaro specializes in natural cooked charcuterie, using only meat, salt, pepper, and herbs. No preservatives or additives, thanks to innovative cooking methods that yield products with an authentic delicate flavour and some shelf life. The pre-cooked products (cotechino, zampone, bondiola) undergo tyndallization (double pasteurization at low temperatures). The sliced meats (starting with the flagship porchetta) are dry-cooked in the oven and seasoned when consumed.

Poggiridenti (SO)

Mottolini

via Lozzoni, 5
☎ (+39) 0342564070
❂ www.mottolini.it
✉ info@mottolini.it
shop: yes
e-commerce: no

Artisanal bresaola makers since 1986, the Mottolini family have always stood by traditional values, focusing on their partnership with the farming and processing industries. They source their meat from Italy, Europe and South America depending on the product. The key products include Fassone bresaola and, above all, L'Originaria, produced by the traditional method from beef reared and butchered in the province of Sondrio, Alpine salt, Valtellina red wine and organic herbs.

Paterno Calabro (CS)

Nero di Calabria

c.da Taverna (Piano Lago)
☎ (+39) 3483278422
✆ www.nerodicalabria.com
✉ info@nerodicalabria.com
shop: no
e-commerce: yes

A few Calabrian small-scale breeders and artisan charcuterie producers created a consortium in 2011 to promote the local black pigs. Every member must comply with specifications for typicality, self-discipline and strict quality control. The Calabrian black pigs are supplied by just 20 member breeders and live in a semi-wild state eating non-GMO flour, acorns and chestnuts. Processes is manual, with no preservatives or additives. The hams, pork jowl, pancetta, and capocollo are cellar-aged.

Vigevano (PV)

Oca Sforzesca

via F. Cavallotti, 8
☎ (+39) 0381450521
✆ www.ocasforzesca.eu
✉ info@ocasforzesca.eu
shop: no
e-commerce: yes

The company offers an artisanal production of goose charcuterie, typical of the Lomellina valley. The 100% free-range Italian animals are fed on corn and soya to keep them lean. The meat is processed within 72 hours from butchering, cured with mild Cervia salt and placed inside natural hand-sewn goose-skin. Products include cooked goose, also available with halal certification; aged cooked salami; smoked bresaola, cured breast; cotechino; gelatines.

Chiuro (SO)

Paganoni

via O. Cenini, 19
☎ (+39) 0342484349
✆ www.paganoni.com
✉ info@paganoni.com
shop: yes
e-commerce: no

Founded in the 1980s as a company selling fresh foods in Valtellina, Caiolo later began a niche production of typical local charcuterie and then expanded to the Chiuro plant. Today this is a large-scale business which does not, however, overlook raw materials: beef, pork, horse, and game purchased on national and international markets according to the type of product (bresaola, cured ham, local charcuterie).

Casciana Terme Lari (PI)

Paolo Parisi - Le Macchie

via delle Macchie, 1
☎ (+39) 0587685327 I 3483804656
❀ www.paoloparisi.it
✉ info@paoloparisi.it
shop: yes
e-commerce: no

Paolo Parisi used to be a medical equipment sales rep but he re-invented himself as a producer and breeder. His Livorno chicken eggs are a must in leading restaurants, and his charcuterie is no less prestigious. He breeds semi-wild mixed-breed pigs from a variety of breeds (Cinta Senese, Nero Casertano), fed on cereals and forest food. The meat is processed by Levoni, a venerable company with extensive experience, the aged in temperature-controlled chambers and natural cellars.

Bologna

Pasquini & Brusiani

via delle Tofane, 38
☎ (+39) 0516143697
❀ www.pasquiniebrusiani.com
✉ pasquiniebrusiani@libero.it
shop: yes
e-commerce: no

In 1950, Ennio Pasquini, a passionate cyclist, met Raimondi, who ran a small sports club at the time, but also owned a small butcher's. Ennio joined the club and, shortly after, also the company. In 1958 the butcher's was purchased by Ennio and Roberto Brusiani, a master butcher with 40 years of experience. The company produces a single type of mortadella, from pure Italian heavy pork, but also pancetta, coppa di testa, and typical pink Bologna salami, shaped like mortadella but with the scent and flavour of roast.

San Giovanni del Dosso (MN)

Pedrazzoli

via San Giovanni, 16a
☎ (+39) 0386757332
❀ www.salumificiopedrazzoli.it
✉ info@salumificiopedrazzoli.it
shop: no
e-commerce: no

Founded in 1951 this was one of the first Italian charcuterie businesses to believe in the supply chain system and closed cycle, linking the family-owned pig farm, abattoir and processing plant. There are several product lines: standard, from heavy pigs; Bio Primavera, from pigs raised in the open and fed on corn, barley, wheat, bran, and soya; Luxury Q+, premium charcuterie from wild black pigs, aged in natural cellars. No glutens, milk by-products or glutamates.

Alseno (PC)
Carlo Peveri

fraz. Chiaravalle della Colomba I via Chiaravalle, 3193/1
☎ (+39) 0523940156
✆ www.salumificiopevericarlo.com
✉ info@salumificiopevericarlo.com
shop: yes
e-commerce: no

Peveri is famous for typical Piacenza cured meats, including the three top local PDOs: coppa, salami and pancetta. The feather in the company's cap is coppa, with three different types to suit all tastes: coppa delle Fonti, leaner, soft and subtle; the PDO version, rougher, fattier and more substantial; and the nostrana, a super-version aged for one year, for connoisseurs. The meat comes from farms in Emilia Romagna and Lombardy, is dry-salted, hand-tied and then cured in natural cellars.

Postal/Burgstall (BZ)
Pfitscher

via Roma, 20
☎ (+39) 0473292358
✆ www.pfitscher.info
✉ info@pfitscher.info
shop: yes
e-commerce: no

METZGEREI × SALUMIFICIO

The Merano-based Pfitscher was once a small business specializing in speck, but is now a large, avant-garde company. It has expanded its range of specialities, but retains its strong links with South Tyrol tradition. Production capacity is now able that to meet export demands, with speck still the flagship, available in a number of versions, with and without IGP status, along with frankfurters in around 20 flavours, Bologna sausage, kaminwurzen and game salami. Cutting-edge technology here, and gluten and dairy-free products.

San Pancrazio/Sankt Pankraz (BZ)
Heinrich Pöder

loc. Gegend, 64
☎ (+39) 0473787147 I 3357033136
✉ aussererbhof@rolmail.net
shop: yes
e-commerce: no

Heinrich Pöder produces a typical speck on his own farm, made in traditional artisanal fashion using meat from his own pigs, processed without additives or preservatives, gently smoked and using the neck, loin, belly, and shoulder, as was the case in the past, and not just the leg. This unique speck, which stands out from those commonly found on the market, has IGP status and is aged for 7/8 months.

Colorno (PR)
Podere Cadassa

via Vedole, 68
☎ (+39) 0521816169
❀ www.poderecadassa.it
✉ info@poderecadassa.it
shop: yes
e-commerce: no

Podere Cadassa is home to Zibello, a culatello that can be tasted at Al Vèdel, the trattoria owned by the family since the 1700s. Only a few thousand hams are made and only in winter, without additives, aged in natural cellars. The reserve products aged for over 24 months are a Presidium brand. Other Terre Verdiane charcuterie: strolghino, San Secondo cooked pork shoulder, salame gentile, salame sfilsetta. The heavy pig meat comes from trusted breeders in Lombardy and Emilia Romagna.

Norcia (PG)
Poggio San Giorgio

fraz. Agriano I via San Luca
☎ (+39) 07438817794 I 0743817259
❀ www.poggiosangiorgio.it
✉ info@poggiosangiorgio.it
shop: yes
e-commerce: no

Poggio San Giorgio, the meat curing facility owned by Daniele and Alessandro Perticoni, is situated on Norcia's Agriano plateau. They produce first-class prosciutto from selected pork thighs, with moderate use of garlic, pepper, wine and salt, mountain air and no preservatives. The IGP prosciutto di Norcia, Peduccio di Frate Ginepro, a certified Umbrian product, and the Pregiutto Riserva Oro, from massive 17–18kg thighs, are all excellent. We also recommend Araldo culatta, Gonfalone fiocco di prosciutto and Barbozzo gola di suino.

San Daniele del Friuli (UD)
Prolongo

v.le Trento e Trieste, 129
☎ (+39) 0432957161
❀ www.prolongo.it
✉ prosciutti@prolongo.it
shop: yes
e-commerce: yes

In 1957 this small company was founded to produce prime San Daniele prosciutto, and is one of the few that still processes entirely in a workmanlike and artisanal manner. The hams are cured for up to 18 months, following the cycle of the seasons in age-old fashion, opening windows when temperature and humidity conditions allow. The raw material consists of selected thighs from the local PDO cured ham circuit, checked one by one. The factory has its own outlet.

San Ginesio (MC)

Re Norcino - Vitali

fraz. Pian di Peca I c.da Gualduccio, 13
☎ (+39) 0733694407 I 3355328193
❀ www.renorcino.it
✉ info@renorcino.it
shop: yes
e-commerce: yes

The Vitali family are born farmers and pig breeders. In 1957 their grandfather, Giuseppe, decided to close the chain and process the pork from his own pigs reared on the hills around Fermo. The business grows steadily, quality improvement accelerated thanks to the latest generation, Giuseppe and Giampiero, who have introduced a focus on natural processing for all the products, from ciauscolo campagnolo and salame lardellato, free from additives and preservatives, to norcidella, a rustic mortadella.

Bassiano (LT)

Reggiani

via Casanatola, 10
☎ (+39) 0773355024
❀ www.prosciuttobassiano.it
✉ info@prosciuttobassiano.it
shop: yes
e-commerce: no

Skilled Modena butcher Astro Muratori founded this company in 1964, specializing in Bassiano ham. The climate in the mountains around Latina was ideal for slow, natural ageing. Today the business is run by his son-in-law and daughters, carrying on the family tradition with all its secrets. The pigs come from selected breeders providing quality ingredients for hams on or off the bone, pork jowl and coppiette.

Serramazzoni (MO)

Regnani

via E. Fermi, 28
☎ (+39) 0536952060
❀ www.deliciaemensae.it
✉ info@deliciaemensae.it
shop: yes
e-commerce: no

The story of the Regnani family began in 1960 with a shop in Serramazzoni, in the Apennines near Modena. In 1972 they began producing salami, sausages, cotechino and zampone in the back room. Over time the business grew and specialized in cured meats, especially pre-cooked cotechino, pork shin, cappello del prete, cooked ham, and coppa di testa. The meat from heavy pigs comes from farms in the region, fed on vegetable protein.

Charcuterie

Urbino

Rinascimento a Tavola

via N. Pellipario, 24
☎ (+39) 3478354604
🕸 www.rinascimentoatavola.it
✉ info@rinascimentoatavola.it
shop: no
e-commerce: no

In other words, traditional Italian sausages, salami and biscuits, with delightful, spicy, old-style flavours, some dating back to the 16th-century Italian courts, others from popular Marche culture of the late 19th-early 20th-centuries. These are reworked by Daniela Storoni following the heritage recipes of Bartolomeo Scappi and Cristoforo da Messisbugo, or even old family recipes. The unique salamis are made from selected meats with wine and spices, no additives or preservatives, and go by the names of Salcizza, Salcizzone and Salamino.

Castell'Arquato (PC)

La Rocca

via Caneto s.da Castellana
☎ (+39) 0523805139
🕸 www.salumificiolarocca.com
✉ info@salumificiolarocca.com
shop: yes
e-commerce: no

The company was founded in 1963 in Castell'Arquato, a medieval village in the Apennines near Piacenza, and since then has expanded: today the founder's heirs combine tradition and innovation in the best possible way. The products are classic Piacenza cured meats, starting with the area's three PDOs of salami, coppa and pancetta, as well as culatello and fresh sausages. The meat is from heavy pigs bred in Emilia Romagna and Lombardy. The coppa and other long-aged products are matured in underground cellars.

Acri (CS)

Romano

via G. da Fiore, 36
☎ (+39) 0984953005 ǀ 3391825312
🕸 www.nerodicalabria.it
✉ extrabiol@libero.it
shop: yes
e-commerce: no

This company, established in the early 20th century, is located in Sila National Park and makes charcuterie from Suino Nero di Calabria pork. Now run by the third generation of the Romano family, with production using organic methods, without additives or preservatives and meat from its own farm. The free-range pigs graze in the mountains and on a broad natural terrace overlooking the Ionian Sea, feeding on the food they find in the wild, as well as meal produced by the farm. The Romanos offer capocollo, pancetta, soppressata, and 'nduja.

Traversetolo (PR)
Rosa dell'Angelo - Sagem

via Parma, 6
☎ (+39) 0521 844100 I 0521343924
❧ www.rosaangelo.it
✉ info@rosaangelo.it
shop: yes
e-commerce: no

The history of this pork butcher began with a Parma shop, opened in 1950, and continues with Sagem, the business set up in 1986 by Mauro Ziveri, specializing in the production of excellent prosciutto crudo aged for 24 months from the thighs of black pigs raised in its own farm, Fattoria di Rivalta, on the Parma hills. As well as a the selection of gourmet Emilian cured meats. Also on offer, sliced charcuterie in MAP trays. Moreover, Fattoria di Rivalta is dedicated to plant and animal biodiversity. Prosciutto bar Rosa dell'Angelo at Traversetolo and Parma-Eurotorri.

Fontanellato (PR)
Rossi - Ca' di Parma

loc. Sanguinaro I via Emilia, 129
☎ (+39) 0521825107
❧ www.salumificiorossi.it
✉ info@cadiparma.it
shop: yes
e-commerce: yes

SALUMIFICIO
ROSSI

In the 19th century the Rossi family already produced charcuterie on a small scale. It continues the tradition using meat from Large White, Cinta Senese and Duroc pigs, some home-bred and some purchased in Italy. The pigs have a natural diet and are slaughtered at one year. Manual processing, ageing in temperature-controlled chambers and 19th-century cellars, no gluten, dairy products, allergens, flavourings or GMOs are the main features of these products. The Culaccia® (culatello with bacon rind) is a registered trademark and famous product along with the lower Parma cured meats.

Langhirano (PR)
Ruliano

fraz. Riano I s.da Pranello, 6
☎ (+39) 0521357125
❧ www.ruliano.it
✉ ruliano@ruliano.it
shop: no
e-commerce: no

RULIANO
PEREX SUCTUM

"Prosciutto is an open book, telling the story of its previous life, and it always tells the truth," jokes Daniele Montali, who runs this ham production company which opened in 1949. Behind PDO Parma Ruliano are excellent thighs of heavy pigs raised comme il faut, experience, a series of strategies resulting from a lifetime's work, and the environment: cellars rich in enzymes where the hams are aged for 24–36 months. Also recommended is the spalla cruda, an old Parma Ruliano charcuterie product renamed Rudis Armus.

Monteriggioni (SI)
Salcis

loc. Pian del Casone I s.da prov.le Colligiana, 33
☎ (+39) 0577306724 I 0577306760
🌐 www.salcis.it
✉ salcis@salcis.it
shop: yes
e-commerce: no

Salcis was established in 1941 to bring together the pork butchers producing Sienese and Tuscan cured meats. It specializes in processing pork although since the 1960s it has worked alongside a dairy. Salcis is a benchmark for quality cured meats, using raw materials only from farms in the provinces of Siena and Arezzo, which are processed in a traditional way, like all the products on sale: Fionocchiona IGP, Tuscan salamino, Cinta Senese and wild boar cured meats.

Bormio (SO)
Il Salumaio Boscacci

via Peccedi, 20
☎ (+39) 0342903382
🌐 www.ilsalumaiobormio.it
✉ ilsalumaio@bormio.it
shop: yes
e-commerce: no

Since 1936 the company has been synonymous with bresaola, the most typical Valtellina charcuterie product, made here with the best beef rump, as well as with venison. Alongside bresaola, Boscacci makes its younger sister slinziga, no less delicious and made from the trimmings of rump beef; also violino ham made from roe deer or goat meat, liver mortadella, mountain lard with herbs, pancetta, prosciuttino with pepper and a good range of salamis.

Cembra (TN)
Il Salumificio di Casa Largher

s.da Lago Santo, 1
☎ (+39) 0461683082
🌐 www.largher.it
✉ loris@largher.it
shop: yes
e-commerce: no

In Val di Cembra, a consistently well-managed family business has found a way to bring together the traditional and the modern. Along with speck (of course) local speciality meats, like the 'salada trentina', 'mortandela' and 'luganega' (sausage) take center stage. Their halal certified sausages deserve a special mention, as well as their lactose-free and gluten-free products. We suggest visiting the Caneva, the old cellar used for aging meat, and the Becaria, their shop where you can find historic antiques and relics.

Coriano (RN)
San Patrignano

via San Patrignano, 53
☎ (+39) 0541362362 | 0541362111
❀ www.sanpatrignano.org
✉ mgiovagnoli@sanpatrignano.org
shop: yes
e-commerce: no

BUONO DUE VOLTE

This charcuterie production facility is one of 55 working businesses in the well-known rehabilitation community on the Rimini hills and its name is linked to Vincenzo Muccioli. The meat is Suino Brinato, a registered trademark crossbreed of Mora Romagnola and Large White raised semi-wild in the company's own farms between Romagna and Montefeltro, fed on vegetable leftovers and corn, barley, soya and bran. On sale also in Italian shops and restaurants.

Lesignano de' Bagni (PR)
Sant'Ilario

fraz. Mulazzano | via Ponticella, 18
☎ (+39) 0521857144
✉ info@s-ilarioprosciutti.it
shop: no
e-commerce: no

This is an outsider Parma ham: unusually mild in flavour, subtly tender, fresh, feminine, but also generous and complex with lingering aromas that leave an indelible impression after tasting. Proudly making just this one product, Sant'Ilario was founded in 1968 by Piero Montali and has always pursued extreme, uncompromising quality. Thorough and meticulous selection and processing of heavy pig thighs are the foundations of this ham, at its best after more than 30 months of ageing.

Cisternino (BR)
Santoro

c.da Marinelli via Isonzo
☎ (+39) 0804431297
❀ www.salumificiosantoro.it
✉ info@salumificiosantoro.it
shop: yes
e-commerce: yes

SANTORO
Salumi d'Eccellenza

Giuseppe Santoro and Piero Caramia started about 40 years ago in local butcher shops before opening their charcuterie factory in 2000. The pigs come from supervised local farms and live in the semi-wild, feeding on undergrowth in the surrounding forests. Capocollo di Martina Franca (a Slow Food Presidium) and lard-covered filet are hand-prepared and flavoured with pepper and Verdeca vino cotto. They are aged in temperature-controlled chambers and aged at length in natural cellars before release on the Italian market and abroad.

Sambuca Pistoiese (PT)
Savigni

loc. Pavana via della Chiesa, 36
☎ (+39) 053460072 I 0573892521
❀ www.savigni.com
✉ savigni@savigni.com
shop: yes
e-commerce: no

A closed cycle of farm, pork butcher and butcher, a byword for fine cured meats: from finocchiona to crema di lardo. Trade secrets include great experience, quality and monitoring of ingredients, from the company's own semi-wild organic farm. There are three product lines of Savigni charcuterie, all artisan-produced and non-GMO, with low preservative content and organic certification: Cinta Senese, Sambucano (a cross between Cinta and Suino Rosa) and game. The products are sold locally from a bright red Ape van flying the Savigni banner.

Itri (LT)
Scherzerino

c.so Vittorio Emanuele II, 76
☎ (+39) 0771727140 I 0771729385
❀ www.scherzerino.it
✉ info@scherzerino.it
shop: yes
e-commerce: no

The La Rocca family company vaunts a long tradition in the field, starting in the 1940s with grandfather Scherzerino. Today grandson Rino coordinates all the activities and focuses on searching out and selecting raw materials. Starting with pork from small local farms that raise conventional white pigs and black Casertano breed in a semi-wild state exclusively for him. Scherzerino processes in its own facility and uses no additives and preservatives, ageing the products in a basement cellar.

Pratovecchio Stia (AR)
Le Selve di Vallolmo

fraz. Pratovecchio I loc. Vallolmo
☎ (+39) 0575550085
❀ www.leselvedivallolmo.it
✉ prodotti@leselvedivallolmo.it
shop: yes
e-commerce: yes

The farm is situated in the attractive Tuscan countryside in an old country hamlet that also offers accommodation. The real virtue of this farm is the total control of the production chain: the Grigio del Casentino pigs are raised in the Foreste Casentinesi National Park and processed in-house. The top cured product is the Slow Food Presidium Prosciutto del Casentino, but the farm also produces Tuscan salamis, finocchiona, fresh and cured sausages, sambudello and capocollo.

Viterbo
Tenuta Serpepe

s.da Dogana, 8
☎ (+39) 3408116009 I 0761799203
❁ www.tenutaserpepe.it
✉ info@tenutaserpepe.it
shop: yes
e-commerce: no

On his 200-hectare organic farm, situated a few kilometres from Lake Bolsena, Domenico Fiorentini grows pulses and raises Sardinian sheep for cheese, as well as about a hundred Cinta Senese pigs. The latter are semi-wild, fed on cereals and pulses from the farm and everything they forage in the woods. They are butchered at two years of age and the meat is processed for certified organic hams and charcuterie.

Langhirano (PR)
Slega

via C. Battisti, 14bis
☎ (+39) 0521852841
❁ www.slega.it
✉ info@slega.it
shop: no
e-commerce: no

For this company producing ham means finding a balance between people, environment and local area. It was created in 1962 in the heart of Langhirano, by passionate Medardo Borchini, and is now one of the soundest in the sector, strictly producing only PDO Prosciutto di Parma. The hams (on or off the bone) are manually processed, from salting to piercing, with great care and experience. The ingredients, as prescribed by the regulations, all derive from the DPO Parma area and the hams are aged for 18–24 months. The whole production cycle takes place in house.

Soragna (PR)
Squisito

fraz. Diolo I via Azzali, 67
☎ (+39) 0524598206 I 3471493291
❁ www.salumificiosquisito.it
✉ salumificiosquisito@libero.it
shop: yes
e-commerce: no

This is a small facility. The meat used is partly from the company's own pigs, raised semi-wild, and partly from heavy pigs from a local breeder. The artisanal processing follows the specifications of the Prosciutto di Parma consortium. The traditional products apart from the ham are PDO Zibello culatello, strolghino and Felino salame (also organic), the black pig line and the specialities (Strolg Burger made only from pork thigh, Fortana wine and Maldon salt) operate a short supply chain and are gluten-free.

Vigonovo (VE)
Squizzato

via Padova, 188
☎ (+39) 049502758
✆ www.squizzato.info
✉ squizzato1952@yahoo.it
shop: no
e-commerce: no

Business began with Luigi Squizzato, a cattle dealer, who opened a butcher shop and factory in 1952. Initially production focused on classic Veneto charcuterie, before expanding to encompass products from other regions with the arrival of his son Fidelio. The range of specialities includes sausages, whole charcuterie, smoked products and raw charcuterie. Key products include aged cured pork fat and cappello di prete, cotechino, pork trotters and bondiola.

San Daniele del Friuli (UD)
Testa&Molinaro

via Tagliamento, 41
☎ (+39) 0432957353
✆ www.testaemolinaro.it
✉ info@testaemolinaro.it
shop: no
e-commerce: no

Since 1941 the Testa and Molinaro families, pork butchers and ham producers, have safeguarded their precious heritage, taken up by the Fantinels who continue to honour Prosciutto di San Daniele. There are two production plants and two prosciutto crudo lines. The Selezione Alta charcuterie line is more traditional, from pork thighs from ten Italian regions, complying with the PDO specifications and aged no longer than 16/17 months. Trentalune is Testa&Molinaro's more prestigious selection, aged for 18–20 months and sold to a niche market.

Cecima (PV)
Thogan Porri

loc. Casa Cucchi, 1
☎ (+39) 038359335 I 3386673400
✆ www.salamedivarzidop.it
✉ thogan@salamedivarzidop.it
shop: yes
e-commerce: no

The company, founded in 1967 in the Casa Zanellino district, moved to its new plant in Cecima, Valle Staffora, in 2001. It produces artisanal charcuterie, carefully selecting the meat from heavy pigs reared in Lombardy, Piedmont and Emilia Romagna. Upholding authentic rural traditions, the factory is now run by Giuseppe and his son Gentile. Its key product is Varzi salami, available in a full range of sizes: from the 500g short sausage to the gigantic cucito, weighing in at 1.7kg.

Daiano (TN)
Tito - Il Maso dello speck

loc. Pozze di Sopra, 2
☎ (+39) 0462342244
🌐 www.titospeck.it
✉ info@titospeck.it
shop: yes
e-commerce: no

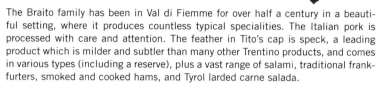

The Braito family has been in Val di Fiemme for over half a century in a beautiful setting, where it produces countless typical specialities. The Italian pork is processed with care and attention. The feather in Tito's cap is speck, a leading product which is milder and subtler than many other Trentino products, and comes in various types (including a reserve), plus a vast range of salami, traditional frankfurters, smoked and cooked hams, and Tyrol larded carne salada.

Faicchio (BN)
Tomaso Salumi

via Odi
☎ (+39) 0824863598
🌐 www.tomasosalumi.it
✉ info@tomasosalumi.it
shop: no
e-commerce: no

The family has been working in the charcuterie industry for two generations and is also a benchmark in promoting the Casertano black pig. The stock, from local farms, is bred in a semi-wild state and fed with cereal flours. The animals are slaughtered at 160 kg and the processing facility turns the meat into hams, sausages and lard, mainly working and tying by hand, respecting ancient local customs. The delicious Matese culatello is not processed in the traditional manner.

Jesi (AN)
Salumificio Tomassoni

via Don L. Sturzo, 4a
☎ (+39) 0731223464 I 073158761
🌐 www.salumitomassoni.com
✉ info@salumitomassoni.com
shop: yes
e-commerce: no

Sergio Tomassoni's firm produces classic Marche charcuterie. The pork from heavy pigs is selected from the circuit of classic great Italian ham and the trimming and tying processes are manual. The products are aged in temperature-controlled rooms after being dried by stove heat. Tomassoni products include charcuterie of traditional inspiration like ciauscolo, Fabriano salami and Lacrimello, a variant using Lacrima di Morro d'Alba wine.

Langhirano (PR)
Pio Tosini

via Fanti d'Italia, 23
☎ (+39) 0521861152 I 0521853945
✉ comunicazioni@piotosini.it
shop: no
e-commerce: no

One of the most famous Langhirano industries, producing fine quality of prosciutto di Parma on and off the bone since 1905. The thigh meat derives from a strict selection of the best heavy Italian pigs, in accordance with the specifications, and the hams are processed with slow, skilful care thanks to three generations of experience. The natural ageing process lasts 15/16 months to endow the hams with delicate aromas and mild flavour.

Sauris (UD)
Vecchia Sauris

fraz. Sauris di Sotto I loc. Gostach
☎ (+39) 0433866379
❀ www.vecchiasauris.it
✉ info@vecchiasauris.it
shop: yes
e-commerce: no

The company specializes in prosciutto di PGI Sauris. In accordance with production regulations, the pork thighs are purchased from national farms, salted, chilled, processed and lightly smoked with beech wood as is the local tradition. At Sauris smoking is an ancient art, linked to the people of Val Pusteria and the surrounding valleys. Vecchia Sauris also makes other charcuterie products, all using quality ingredients and high production standards.

Varzi (PV)
Vecchio Varzi

via Castelletto, 11
☎ (+39) 038352283
❀ www.vecchiovarzi.it
✉ info@vecchiovarzi.it
shop: yes
e-commerce: no

This company, set up in the 1970s by the Montagna family and owned today by the Nulli family, faithfully safeguards the venerable tradition of Varzi PDO salami, bringing together ancient skills and innovative technology, an ongoing pursuit of quality and growing production scale. The many excellent charcuterie products include lombata al Pinot, cotechino, lardo di spallone, pancetta al ginepro. The house specialities are Varzi salami, in various types: Varzino, Varzello, Cresponetto and Sottocrespone.

Carrara (MS)
Venanzio

via del Giardino, 12
☎ (+39) 0585758030 I 0585758046
❀ www.lardocolonnata-venanzio.it
✉ luigi@lardocolonnata-venanzio.it
shop: yes
e-commerce: no

Venanzio Vannucci is among those best equipped to promote Colonnata lard out-side the national frontiers (he is the owner of the "Conca dei Cain" marble block, the oldest in existence). The company was created in 2000 with the aim of pro-ducing and selling the famous product of heavy pigs from farms in Emilia and Lombardy. Entirely hand-processed, it is flavoured with garlic, pepper and spices, and aged in hollowed marble blocks in old rooms.

Torreano (UD)
Luigi Vida

via dei Laghi, 28
☎ (+39) 0432715232
❀ www.salumivida.it
✉ info@salumivida.it
shop: no
e-commerce: no

In half a century Vida, established in 1966, has transformed from an artisanal workshop to a modern food company, with avant-garde buildings and production techniques. Vida produces a full range of cooked and cured meats, from classic ham, speck, salami, pork fat, coppa, and bacon to cooked hams like Pandicotto; Brace ed Erbe without milk derivatives, additional polyphosphates, gluten or glu-tamate; and Alta Qualità from local pork. There is also a line of organic meats, called Biovida.

Negrar (VR)
Vigneto dei Salumi - Vinappeso

fraz. Arbizzano I via Casa Zamboni, 1
☎ (+39) 3296943331
❀ www.vinappeso.it
✉ info@vinappeso.it
shop: no
e-commerce: no

Vigneto Dei Salumi
I VALPOLICELLA I

It was seven years ago that Valpolicella-based cured meat producer Walter Ceradini tried to save a culatta that was too dry by wetting it with Recioto della Valpolicella. This was the birth of Vinappeso, the marriage of two noble products: the finest pork thigh and Valpolicella wines, Amarone and Recioto, on offer in three reserve versions with different flavour nuances. The barrique-aged line Vigneto dei Salumi also offers Speckwine, Salame Valpolicella and Cotevino (cotechino with wine).

Charcuterie

Appiano/Eppan (BZ)
Franz Windegger

loc. San Michele I via J.G. Plazer, 1
☎ (+39) 0471662153
❀ www.windegger.info
✉ mail@windegger.info
shop: yes
e-commerce: yes

Originally established as a butcher shop in 1901, Windegger has evolved over the years, opening a number of point-of-sale and expanding its range and production capacity. It makes typical regional charcuterie: small Tyrol salami called kiminwirzen; cooked ham in various flavours; a dozen types of frankfurter, sausages and luganega. Pride and joy is speck, the king of South Tyrol charcuterie, available in two different types: IGP and bauernspeck, the superior line made from pigs reared on local farms.

Sauris (UD)
Wolf Sauris

fraz. Sauris di Sotto, 88
☎ (+39) 043386054
❀ www.wolfsauris.it
✉ info@wolfsauris.it
shop: yes
e-commerce: yes

The business was handed down through the generations to Giuseppe Petris who, in 1962, created the prosciutto production company Wolf, now fully run by the Petris family. The meat is Italian pork from the Modena and Parma prosciutto crudo districts, processed by hand and by machine, without sources of gluten. The many products include culatello, ossocollo, salami, cotechino, pancetta, lardo alle erbe, pork jowl, fesa and shin, although the production flagships are ham and speck.

San Daniele del Friuli (UD)
Zanini Gio Batta

fraz. Villanova I via da l'Ancòne, 2
☎ (+39) 0432956017
✉ zaninigiobatta@libero.it
shop: yes
e-commerce: no

This prosciutto business earned a prominent place in the area's iconic product scenario, as one of the best exponents of San Daniele prosciutto, with strict monitoring and extreme care in production. The heavy pig thighs come from Italian PDO prosciutto areas and are selected for size, quantity of fat, and marbling of the muscle (indicating mature pork). Processing follows artisan methods, and the hams are aged in natural cellars.

Saludecio (RN)

Fausto Zavoli

via Pulzona, 3678
☎ (+39) 0541858041
❂ www.aziendaagricolazavoli.com
✉ az.agr.zavoli@gmail.com
shop: yes
e-commerce: no

For over 50 years the farm has raised semi-wild pink and Mora Romagnola pigs (a Slow Food Presidium) alongside their Romagnola cattle. The livestock is fed on grazing enriched with cereals grown and milled on the farm, as well as non-GMO soya and corn. The meat is processed in house, using artisan methods without preservatives. The vast range of charcuterie is based on Mora Romagnola pork (some products preserved in bees' wax) as well as the Rustichello Romagnolo line (cross bred with pink pigs).

Monzuno (BO)

Zivieri

p.zza XXIV Maggio, 9c
☎ (+39) 0516771533 l 335202403
❂ www.macelleriazivieri.it
✉ info@macelleriazivieri.it
shop: yes
e-commerce: no

MACELLERIA SALUMERIA
ZIVIERI MASSIMO

In 1987 the Zivieri family opened a butcher's shop in Monzuno, in the Reno valley. The turnaround came in 2005, when they started breeding free-range Cinta Senese and Mora Romagnola pigs on a 40-hectare farm in the Apennines outside Bologna, producing flavoursome charcuterie using natural techniques, and seasoned with Cervia salt and spices. There are a number of additive- and preservative-free products: cured ham, cured shoulder, cured pork fat, mountain salami and tasty mortadella, as well as an organic line and wild boar charcuterie.

Langhirano (PR)

Zuarina

via Cascinapiano, 2
☎ (+39) 0521861096
❂ www.zuarina.com
✉ qualita@zuarina.com
shop: no
e-commerce: no

The company is named after the founder's wife, Zuarina, who was born in 1873. The name has identified the hams of this brand, like Langhirano where the company is based, a quintessential area for quality prosciutto di Parma. These are important stamps for production and selection of the best heavy pig thighs, raised exclusively in Italy by selected breeders in the PDO prosciutto di Parma zones. There is an organic line for the local mild cured ham. Products are now exported to many countries worldwide.

Charcuterie

Oppeano (VR)

Cooperativa Agricola 8 Marzo Ca' Verde

loc. Oppeano I via delle Fosse, 10
☎ (+39) 04584153545
⚉ www.caverde.com
✉ caseificio@caverde.com
shop: yes
e-commerce: yes

The Ca' Verde dairy is the beating heart of an agricultural cooperative established in 1978, in an real agricultural and farming terrain, situated on the slopes of Mount Baldo and along the eastern shore of Lake Garda. The cheeses are made with cow and goat milk from the farm's own livestock, processed in a hygienic environment for fresh dairy products like yoghurt and ricotta, stretched-curd cheeses, ripe cow's milk cheeses, pecorino and the mouthwatering Monte Veronese PDO.

Vesime (AT)

Agrilanga

reg. Bricchetto, 60
☎ (+39) 3478867907
⚉ www.agrilanga.it
✉ robiola@agrilanga.it
shop: no
e-commerce: no

The farm stands on the green slopes of the Langa Astigiana area, where herds of goats can graze on over 50 hectares. The cheeses are organically produced with milk from the PDO Robiola di Roccaverano production area, in which Agrilanga is highly specialized. To be precise: Robiola di Roccaverano PDO in the old style, with raw full goat's milk, a Slow Food Presidium.

Mores (SS)

Coop. Allevatori di Mores

via Risorgimento, 4
☎ (+39) 079706002
⚉ www.coopmores.net
✉ coopmores@tiscali.it
shop: yes
e-commerce: no

A cooperative founded in 1951 by producers of typical Sardinian cheese. Over the years it has exported worldwide the quality and passion for the art of cheese-making from an area known for its shepherding tradition. The ewe's milk is used to produce above all an excellent Tenores PDO Pecorino Romano. Then there is Monte Acuto, aged 1–4 months; Ovilo; Isola Bianca; Moras; Moro del Logudoro. Not to mention Monteforte, a spread made from ewe's milk cheese and ricotta; fresh and aged Gentile sheep ricotta.

Bosia (CN)

Caseificio Alta Langa

s.da prov.le 31, 17
☎ (+39) 0173854174
🌐 www.caseificioaltalanga.it
✉ info@caseificioaltalanga.it
shop: no
e-commerce: no

The mission of this dairy has always been to produce entirely natural cheese using traditional recipes enhanced by the expertise of the makers, without preservatives, dyes and additives. Milk from cows, goats and sheep comes from certified farms, and is of premium quality. From this the company makes PDO Robiola di Roccaverano; Bianchina; Blu di Langa; goat cheese; robiola; Camembert; Carboncino with charcoal; and Rosso di Langa. Something for all tastes.

Dolianova (CA)

Argiolas Formaggi

s.da prov.le 14, 3
☎ (+39) 070740293
🌐 www.argiolasformaggi.com
✉ argiolas@argiolasformaggi.com
shop: yes
e-commerce: yes

The company has been in business for more than half a century, pursuing Sardinian cheese-making tradition with modern technologies, while protecting consumers who can take advantage of quality products made only from the milk of native sheep and goats. The choice is huge, from fresh produce like ricotta and stracchino, ripe or semi-ripe cheese, flanked by an organic line. Flagships include PDO Fiore Sardo from pure raw ewe's milk, and PDO Pecorino Romano and PDO Pecorino Sardo.

Taleggio (BG)

Arnoldi

fraz. Peghera I via Piazze, 156
☎ (+39) 034547550
🌐 www.arnoldivaltaleggio.it
✉ info@arnoldivaltaleggio.it
shop: no
e-commerce: no

For over 90 years the company has fielded passion, love of the area and much experience, working to process milk from the Val Taleggio and other pastures to make delicious cheeses, using astute, artisanal methods. The lion's share is, of course, PDO Taleggio in various versions, alongside Quartirolo, Bitto, Formai de Mut, Asiago, and Gorgonzola, all PDOs. Then there are butter, mascarpone, zola, fontina, crescenza, mozzarella, primo sale etc. Worthy of note are goat cheeses and an organic line.

Cheese

Taleggio (BG)
AS - Sergio Arrigoni

fraz. Olda di Taleggio I via Vittorio Veneto, 48
☎ (+39) 035543535
🌐 www.sergioarrigoni.it
✉ info@sergioarrigoni.it
shop: no
e-commerce: no

In 1859 the business run by the Arrigonis in Valtaleggio consisted of ageing and maturing cheeses. Over time it has become established as a benchmark for this market sector. Far-sighted Sergio Arrigoni has increased the range to include various fresh cow and goat cheeses, ripe cheese, blue cheese, and a line of Taleggio PDO, also using raw, still-warm milk, matured for at least 35 days.

Paestum (SA)
Barlotti

via Torre di Paestum, 1
☎ (+39) 0828811146
🌐 www.caseificiobarlotti.com
✉ info@barlotti.it
shop: yes
e-commerce: no

Founded at the beginning of the last century, this is one of Piana del Sele's oldest producers. The cheeses are made with milk from its own herd of buffalo, proudly on view next to the company's point of sale and eatery, or from members of the Consorzio Alba association of buffalo breeders, of which Barlotti is a member. Mozzarella in various sizes, provola and scamorza are the result of artisanal drawing and cutting. There is also plenty of milk, butter, ricotta, yogurt and buffalo meat.

Castel di Sasso (CE)
La Baronia

loc. Truli I s.s. 264
☎ (+39) 0823659014
🌐 www.labaronia.com
✉ labaronia@labaronia.com
shop: yes
e-commerce: yes

This cheese factory was founded in 1990 by the Cutillo family. Here they still make their cheeses according to tradition, by hand, while taking advantage of what the latest technology has to offer. Their buffalo mozzarella PDO is top-quality, made with 100% pure buffalo milk, controlled and guaranteed. It comes in various shapes and sizes (cherry-sized, larger balls, knots, twists etc.), in smoked varieties and certified halal (for Muslims). There's also butter, ricotta cheese, cream balls, burrata, smoked mozzarella and other stretched cheese varieties.

Castellazzo Novarese (NO)

Eredi Angelo Baruffaldi

via Roma, 32
☎ (+39) 032183717
❀ www.eredibaruffaldi.com
✉ info@eredibaruffaldi.com
shop: yes
e-commerce: no

The Baruffaldi family has been dairy farming for four generations, passionately going about its business with experience and skill. The premium milk makes an excellent PDO Gorgonzola, a product of this area and outstanding for its unique aromas and flavours. There are mild and ripe (which has won major awards) versions, or combined with mascarpone, or with mascarpone and walnuts. The production range also includes a delicious mascarpone, toma, PDO Taleggio, fontal and crescenza.

Sant'Anna d'Alfaedo (VR)

Corrado Benedetti

via Croce dello Schioppo, 1
☎ (+39) 0457545186 I 3284527217
❀ www.corradobenedetti.it
✉ info@corradobenedetti.it
shop: yes
e-commerce: no

A family-owned company devoted to the production of charcuterie, cheeses and preserves to serve with dairy products. In particular, Corrado Benedetti is famous for aging Verona and Lessinia cheeses. Alongside the house soppressa, Lessinia coppa, and Amarone salamino, the other musts are Monte Veronese cheese in various versions (with white passito, stravecchio, ubriaco), the "reserve cheeses" and the aged versions (in red or white marc, with cherries, pears, rosemary and sage, hay, walnut leaves etc.).

Medesano (PR)

Bertinelli

via Costa Garibalda, 25
☎ (+39) 0521 620776
❀ www.bertinelli.it
✉ info@bertinelli.it
shop: yes
e-commerce: no

BERTINELLI

AZIENDA AGRICOLA DAL 1895

This family company has long traditions behind it but over time it has developed and adapted to changing consumer demands, expanding and diversifying its offer. It vaunts 700 head of cattle, kept it the best conditions and fed with natural fodder, to produce 20 wheels of PDO Parmigiano Reggiano each day. The cheese is aged to three different stages: 15, 24 and 36 months. There are also Millesimato versions of 15, 24, 30 and 36 months. Last but not least, the Senza line with no lactose, sugar or gluten free.

Montechiarugolo (PR)
Bonati

loc. Piazza di Basilicanova I via Bosco, 3
☎ (+39) 0521 681707
❂ www.bonat.it
✉ info@bonat.it
shop: no
e-commerce: yes

The strict selection of raw material is the cornerstone of this company, which has produced Parmigiano Reggiano for 40 years. Giorgio Bonati, and son Gianluca, feed their Frisians with meadow hay, rich with herby fragrance. The entire processing cycle occurs in house with Parmigiano Reggiano reaching two years of age before being reassessed by the Consorzio di Tutela. Only the best wheels are accepted for the second extra branding. After this, only the best achieves three, four, five, six, seven or ten years of maturity.

Aprilia (LT)
Brunelli

via dei Giardini, 37
☎ (+39) 0692062025
✉ info@brunelli.it
shop: yes
e-commerce: no

dal 1938

Brunelli, established in 1938, is one of the key producers of Pecorino Romano and one of the few based in Lazio. It is far from small: a limited company distributing Italy and abroad, using not only milk from the Lazio countryside but also from Sardinia, as laid down in the PDO protocol. Its products are salted by hand and aged for longer than the minimum period provided for by the protocol. Brunelli distributes mainly to niche markets, in the best delicatessens and top restaurants.

Nepi (VT)
I Buonatavola Sini

via Cassia, km 41
☎ (+39) 0761571052
❂ www.ibuonatavolasini.com
✉ info@ibuonatavolasini.com
shop: no
e-commerce: no

From generation to generation two families, with years of experience behind them, have successfully upheld a craft dairy tradition using modern technological facilities. The results are appreciable, with a wide range of products, obtained from sheep's and cow's milk. Fresh products include various ricottas, including PDO Ricotta Romana. Then there are semi-ripe, aromatized (with chilli pepper) and ripe cheeses, including an outstanding PDO Pecorino Romano del Lazio.

Reggio Emilia

C.V.P.A.R.R. Consorzio Valorizzazione Prodotti Antica Razza Reggiana

loc. Coviolo I via F.lli Rosselli, 41/2
☎ (+39) 0522294655 I 0522286123
❀ www.consorziovaccherosse.it
✉ info@consorziovaccherosse.it
shop: yes
e-commerce: yes

In the 1980s, Reggio's prized Vacche Rosse breed of cattle ran a serious risk of extinction. A group of breeders devised this project to encourage a reprise in the number of animals. Since 1991, production regulations establish that the fodder shall include only grass, hay and certified feed, respecting the environment and with utmost attention to animal welfare and consumer health. Besides Parmigiano Reggiano of differing ages and sizes, the company also produces butter, yogurt and ricotta.

Cameri (NO)

Latteria Sociale di Cameri

via per Novara, 67
☎ (+39) 0321518224
❀ www.latteriadicameri.it
✉ latteriadicameri@libero.it
shop: yes
e-commerce: no

A cooperative set up over a century ago that now has hundreds of members and a modern dairy with a special ripening facility. Each day skilled master cheesemakers process approximately 270 quintals of milk with craft methods before proceeding to start ageing the cheeses on spruce planks in chambers at the right temperature and humidity. The main products are a mild, creamy and ripe Gorgonzolas, Taleggio, toma, Nivellina (Gorgonzola and mascarpone), and blue-veined Verdalpe goat cheese.

Aidone (EN)

Casalgismondo

s.da prov.le 103, km 13 c.da Casalgismondo
☎ (+39) 095892118 I 3355252799
❀ www.casalgismondo.it
✉ info@casalgismondo.it
shop: no
e-commerce: no

This farm can boast excellent organic production of cheese, made from Comiso ewe milk. In the 1990s the business was revamped and acquired a system of mechanized milking, but retained natural feed for livestock. The entire production cycle is nonetheless in house, starting from the cultivation of cereals intended for the sheep. The flagship product is the Piacentinu Ennese, but there are also tuma, pecorino primo sale, aged PDO Pecorino Siciliano. The farm also produces organic EVOO.

Roncà (VR)
La Casara Roncolato

via Nuova, 1
☎ (+39) 0457460052
❂ it.lacasara.com
✉ info@lacasara.it
shop: yes
e-commerce: no

The dairy opened for business in the 1920s in Brenton, where Ermenegildo Roncolato, with his sons Romano and Angelo, started up a rotating dairy. In 1964, Romano took over management of the Caseificio Sociale di Roncà and turned it into a small family-run cheese production business, christened La Casara, which went on to become a small-scale dairy. The production range includes cow and goat milk cheeses, especially Monte Veronese and traditional Veneto charcuterie.

Taleggio (BG)
CasArrigoni

fraz. Peghera, 575
☎ (+39) 034547421
❂ www.casarrigoni.it
✉ info@casarrigoni.it
shop: no
e-commerce: no

casArrigoni
storie di formaggi

The name identifies an admirable family with passion for its work in a field where it has operated for many years, producing and ripening cheeses in the local way, traditional to ValTaleggio. The flagship is the company's PDO Taleggio, available in tipico, tradizionale and basso versions. There are also Quartirolo, Salva Cremasco and Gorgonzola PDOs, and also worth noting La Belinda, Branzi, crescenza, robiola, primo sale, mascarpone, Gorgonzola, goat and organic cheeses.

Povegliano (TV)
La Casearia Carpenedo

fraz. Camalò I via Santandrà, 17
☎ (+39) 0422872178
❂ www.lacasearia.com
✉ info@lacasearia.com
shop: yes
e-commerce: no

Carpenedo is a family company that began selecting and ageing cheeses in 1976 when the first of the products ripened in wine and marc came about, named Ubriaco, meaning drunk. Today there are several hundred items in the catalogue, comprising different lines, from regional specialties from all over Italy, from Val d'Aosta Fontina to Sardinian Pecorino, to "cellar cheeses", with dozens of imaginative types, including cacioradicchio, caciobirraio, conciato al pepe with its pepper dressing. There are also classic products, like butter and casatella.

Verbania
La Casera di Eros Buratti

loc. Trobaso I via Vidic
☎ (+39) 0323517251
🌐 www.formaggidieros.it
✉ info@formaggidieros.it
shop: no
e-commerce: no

Eros Buratti IS La Casera! This true pro and passionate cheese affineur, hand picks from the best products locally and also further afield. A bespoke ripening path is developed for each product, respecting its origin but always adding that extra something. The product catalogue is in the hundreds, including PDO Murazzano, PDO Fiore Sardo, PDO Casciotta d'Urbino, various types of pecorino with marc, saffron, truffles, an IGP Moliterno; Farindola, a Slow Food Presidium; Romano, Siciliano and Toscano PDOs.

Ornavasso (VB)
Castagna

via A. di Dio, 185
☎ (+39) 0323837628
🌐 www.castagnasrl.com
✉ commerciale@castagnasrl.com
shop: no
e-commerce: no

Piccoli piaceri di montagna®

Giuseppe Castagna is the dynamic owner of a company bearing his name and for over 40 years he has sought out and selected in person the best dairy products. He works mostly with small producers who apply traditional and craft practices, and his catalogue vaunts hundreds of items in various lines: Taleggio, Quartirolo, Gorgonzola, Grana Padano, Parmigiano Reggiano, Fontina, Bra, Raschera, Toma, Castelmagno, Asiago, Monte Veronese, and Montasio, all PDOs. Then there are tomas, mountain (including a rare Bettelmatt) and Val Vigezzo cheeses.

Pomarico (MT)
Cavalli

c.da La Calcara
☎ (+39) 0835551473 I 3398286079
🌐 www.aziendagricolacavalli.it
✉ info@aziendaagricolacavalli.it
shop: yes
e-commerce: yes

Cavalli

The Cavalli family farm is set in 300 hectares of arable land, with olive groves and pastures that roll from the Pomarico hills as far as the River Basento. The owners are determined to integrate modern technologies and know-how with local traditions to create a model business, self-sufficient in terms of energy and able to produce quality cheeses. Their flagship is a PGI Canestrato di Moliterno, and there are also pecorino, goat cheeses, cacioricotta, caciotta, caciocavallo, ricotta, tomino in oil and other delights.

Vescovato (CR)
Ca' de' Stefani

via Padana Inferiore, 12
☎ (+39) 0372830270 I 3488060693
❂ www.latteriacadestefani.it
✉ info@latteriacadestefani.it
shop: yes
e-commerce: no

Latteria
Ca'De'Stefani

Founded in 1900, this was one of the first social cooperative dairies in the Po Valley, set up by farmers tired of milk prices imposed by the industry. Its facilities cover 60,000 square metres and it collects milk from Friesian cows for the entire in-house cheese production process. Annexed to the dairy is a pig farm producing fresh and cured meats, with a power supply provided by the whey waste. The two cheese products are both excellent: Gran Padano and Provolone (mild and ripe).

Serrenti (VS)
Central

loc. Villanova I s.s. 131, km 40, 250 zona industriale Villasanta
☎ (+39) 0709371363
❂ www.central.it
✉ central@central.it
shop: yes
e-commerce: no

Central Formaggi is a family company and a leader in Sardinia's dairy industry, producing about 50 different types of cheese under its own brand name. The key is its strategic position, which allows it to procure supplies from nearby farms, minimizing transportation and milk processing times. The fresh and ripe ricottas are noteworthy, as are the goat and sheep cheeses; fresh and ripe 100% goat cheeses; different ages of pecorino; spreads; PDO Pecorino Romano; and PDO Pecorino Maturo Sardo.

Introbio (LC)
Gildo Ciresa

via Vittorio Veneto, 11
☎ (+39) 0341 901401
❂ www.gildoformaggi.it
✉ info@gildoformaggi.it
shop: no
e-commerce: no

Here in Valsassina the land makes for excellent pasture, hence for farming. The farms and the natural forage are the starting point for cheese production. So, this business, run by the same family for three generations, aims to safeguard tradition, and the authenticity and quality of its products, some aged in ancient caves. There are four lines for a lengthy catalogue of products. In terms of typicity, try the Taleggio, Quartirolo and Gorgonzola, and the fresh goat, mountain and raw milk cheeses.

Fidenza (PR)
Caseificio Sociale Coduro

via Coduro, 9
☎ (+39) 0524523720 I 0521 774302
🕸 www.buonoperche.it
✉ noidicristian@live.it
shop: yes
e-commerce: no

The Caseificio Sociale Coduro makes Italy's most famous and celebrated product, Parmigiano Reggiano, using Friesian milk from member farms. A very short production chain and traditional processing methods are the basis for high quality. The cheese is matured for 24 or 36 months. Corduro is the benchmark dairy of Silvano Romani, founder of the eponymous brand, who has lent his name to the most excellent food products from the local area and the rest of Italy.

Grazzanise (CE)
La Contadina

via Andreozzi, 18
☎ (+39) 0823991850
🕸 www.caseificiocooplacontadina.com
✉ info@caseificiocooplacontadina.com
shop: no
e-commerce: no

Founded in 1950 as a farm devoted purely to raising buffalo and over time it has maximized its operating structure. Buffalo milk, collected daily across the territory from partner farms, is processed with cutting-edge plant and equipment. The Campania buffalo mozzarella is handmade or drawn by automated machinery to make various shapes and sizes: egg-shaped, braided, cherries, pearls, and a lactose-free version. The ricotta is also noteworthy.

Monesiglio (CN)
Società Agricola Cora

via alla Chiesa, 5
☎ (+39) 017492418
🕸 www.coraformaggi.it
✉ info.coraformaggi.bea@libero.it
shop: yes
e-commerce: no

The cheese dairy dates back to the 1990s here in the Alta Langa hills, an area particularly well-suited to breeding goats and producing cheese in a traditional style with the milk from the farm's own 300-strong herd. A short production chain and traceability are the most distinctive features. Top of the range are fresh and matured robiola cheeses, but products also include ripe cow's milk toma, blue cheeses and PDO cheeses.

Anela (SS)
Sa Costera

s.s. 132 reg. Torra Ischizzarolu
☎ (+39) 079791181
🌐 www.coopsacostera.it
✉ costera@tiscali.it
shop: yes
e-commerce: no

A dairy cooperative that now has 500 members and was founded in the 1960s. Controlled farms supply milk from livestock fed on forage rich in fragrant herbs, then modern machinery compliant with current legislation is used in the processing. The lengthy list of products includes sheep, goat, cow and mixed-milk cheeses, available in different ages. The flagship is the PDO Pecorino Romano but there is no lack of choice for ricotta, spreads, provolone, blue-veined cheeses, caciotta.

Vico Equense (NA)
De Gennaro

fraz. Pacognano I via R. Bosco, 956
☎ (+39) 0818028185
🌐 www.caseificiodegennaro.it
✉ info@caseificiodegennaro.it
shop: yes
e-commerce: yes

The dairy farm dates back to the first generation of dairymen who settled here in the 1700s. It is one of the best cheese production facilities in the area. Fernando, assisted by his wife and three children, and their families, uses only milk from cattle grazing on the Lattari mountains, and the zero-mile production is eco-friendly: fiordilatte, butter, smoked provolone, PDO Provolone del Monaco and caciocavallo cheese, all from raw milk and cut by hand. The fresh ricotta is amazing.

Castiglion Fiorentino (AR)
De' Magi - Alchimia dei Formaggi

via Tevere, 116
☎ (+39) 0575659995
🌐 www.demagi.it
✉ Info@demagi.it
shop: no
e-commerce: no

ALCHIMIA DE' FORMAGGI

Andrea Magi has been driven by his passion for cheese since childhood, and it turned into his raison d'être. He is tireless in his quest for the best cheeses to age himself or leave with his trusted cheesemakers. The results of his work are incredible, because Andrea loves to experiment, so each product has its own personality. For instance an amusing caciortaggi line of cow, ewe and goat cheeses aged with sage, radicchio, leek or other greens. Another is dedicated to the game of chess. And they are all excellent.

Varna/Vahrn (BZ)
DeGust

zona Bsackerau, 1
☎ (+39) 0472849873
❀ www.degust.com
✉ info@degust.com
shop: yes
e-commerce: no

The company, founded in 1995 with the aim of discovering and ageing special, small-scale dairy products, with a catalogue of mostly raw milk and mountain meadow cheeses. With 20 years of experience supporting the traditional ripening stage and the choice of raw materials, the company's products are very special and of impeccable quality. It would be impossible to mention them all, because owner Hansi Baumgartner is always trying and testing new ideas. He offers a targeted selection of niche specialities.

Bagnolo Piemonte (CN)
Carlo Del Clat - Montoso

via Bibiana, 54
☎ (+39) 0175391585
❀ www.carlodelclat.com
✉ info@carlodelclat.com
shop: yes
e-commerce: yes

This is the flagship of the Montoso dairy, founded in 1928. The cheeses bearing this label are produced in limited quantities and are special for their excellent raw materials, careful control of each phase of processing, and meticulous care at every step. The milk comes from surrounding farms and is processed by experts to make outright delights. The range includes dairy products like yoghurt, butter, mozzarella, stracchino, tomino primo sale, but also riper cheeses, like tasty tuma "dla pietra".

Agnone (IS)
Di Nucci

area artigianale Giovanni Paolo II, lotto 8
☎ (+39) 086577288
❀ www.caseificiodinucci.it
✉ info@caseificiodinucci.it
shop: yes
e-commerce: no

The company is also known outside the region for its dairy products, produced in pure Molise sheep-rearing tradition. Despite having a family-style business model, its working methods and professional standards bring to mind a modern, energetic company. Each product has well-defined flavours: scamorza, stracciata, manteca, salted and fresh ricotta, caciocavallo at various stages of ageing, and cheeses ripened in wicker baskets, unique for the use of Pezzata Rossa cow milk.

Cheese

Villafalletto (CN)
Le Fattorie Fiandino

via Termine, 25
☎ (+39) 0171930014
🌐 www.fiandino.it
✉ info@fiandino.it
shop: yes
e-commerce: no

Since 1948 the Fiandino dairy has been interpreting the art of cheese in Cuneo territory. Alongside traditional cheeses, the dairy offers more innovative types made with vegetable rennet. Milk, mainly from Italian Bruna Alpina and Piedmontese cow breeds, raw or pasteurized depending on the type of product to be made, comes in part from the farm's own stock, and in part is purchased in the Cuneo countryside. Production includes butter; Malga (an Antica Grangia toma); Grana Padano (aged 14–24 months); Selezione Fiandino, with a minimum of 20 months ageing.

Gaggio Montano (BO)
Fior di Latte

s.s. 324 loc. Torretta, 225
☎ (+39) 053431126 I 053430233
🌐 caseificiofiordilatte.it
✉ info@caseificiofiordilatte.it
shop: yes
e-commerce: yes

A social cooperative dairy, set up 70 years ago by a group of milk producers and today comprising 33 local partners, all from local farms. Some members are at altitudes of over 1,000 metres, ideal conditions for pastures and fodder. The admirable flagship product is the Parmigiano Reggiano, which has obtained several awards, available in 12, 24 and longer ageings. Also try the mozzarella, ricotta, yogurt, caciotta (fresh and aged) and other delicious dairy products.

Torremaggiore (FG)
Fattoria Fiorentino

loc. Castelfiorentino
☎ (+39) 3201197424
🌐 www.fattoriafiorentino.it
✉ info@fattoriafiorentino.it
shop: yes
e-commerce: no

Formaggi di Puglia

The farm, situated in the Foggia area, raises free-grazing Garganica goats and Podolica cattle, following natural timing and methods. Their diet is supplemented by pulses, oats, barley, and hay. All cheeses are made from raw milk in-house to the dairy, using ancient pastoral transhumance-related techniques. Goat cheese includes Ghibellino, cacio d'Armalù, Castelfiorentino, Guelfo aged in red wine, Argille, and Erborì. Cow-milk cheeses include Candidum, Rubeus, Florem, and Granum. Worth trying are the caciocavallo podolico and giuncata curds.

Roccalbegna (GR)
Il Fiorino

loc. Paiolaio
☎ (+39) 0564989059
❀ www.caseificioilfiorino.it
✉ info@caseificioilfiorino.it
shop: yes
e-commerce: yes

Founded in 1957 by Duilio Fiorini, the business collects ewe and cow milk from selected local breeders and processes it in its own cheese-making facility. The cheese is ripened naturally in controlled environments and in caves, where the particular microclimate and noble rot present endow it with aromas and character. The production range includes fresh cheeses (ricotta, fior di ricotta and raveggiolo), respected classics, and various types of pecorino, some aged in interesting ways (with chestnuts, saffron, Morellino wine etc.).

Vicchio (FI)
Il Forteto della Toscana

fraz. Rossoio, 6 I s.s. 551, km 19
☎ (+39) 0558448183
❀ www.forteto.it
✉ vendite@forteto.it
shop: yes
e-commerce: yes

This Alto Mugello cooperative was founded in 1977 and is now managed by Stefano Pezzati. Cheese-making is only one of its activities and it can count on a 3,500-square-metre dairy, processing up to 65,000 litres of milk a day, plus an in-house laboratory performing continuous quality control. Its flagship product is the PDO Pecorino Toscano, also in an aged version, but there are plenty of other cheeses, all appreciable: marzolino, caciotta, cacio di fossa, and pecorino in ash, wine, basil, truffle, chilli, pepper, aged in walnut leaves, and more.

Roncofreddo (FC)
Fossa dell'Abbondanza

p.zza Allende, 13
☎ (+39) 0541949200 I 05411930241
❀ www.fossadellabbondanza.com
✉ info@fossadellabbondanza.it
shop: yes
e-commerce: no

Renato Brancaleoni and daughter Anna are affineurs by family tradition. They choose cheeses produced locally and leave them to ripen in their own pit. The pride of their production is their excellent Pecorino di Fossa, but there is also the Vaccino of Fossa from cow milk, a raw-milk pecorino sottobosco, a semi-ripe, a wild blackberry blueberry, a saffron, another aged in hay, one with walnuts, Stravecchio, a Merlino, various types of Blu (Montefeltro, goat, Monte Rosa, Notte, Firenze), cow-milk Cerato, Birbetta (with beer) and Formaggio del Silenzio.

Sogliano al Rubicone (FC)
Fossa Pellegrini

via Le Greppe, 14
☎ (+39) 0541948542 I 0541948409
🌐 www.formaggiodifossa.it
✉ mpellegrini@rimini.com
shop: yes
e-commerce: no

A small family operation this, involved for many years in the processing and ageing of traditional Formaggio di Fossa in ancient caves. The cheese is matured underground for about three months until it acquires the characteristic flavour that transforms it into an unrivalled speciality. The Pellegrinis have the largest existing pit, at Sogliano, and select the best cow-milk, pecorino, mixed pecorino and goat-milk cheeses, ensuring they become quality products. The dairy is among the founding members of the consortium for the protection of Fossa.

Collecchio (PR)
Gennari

via Varra Superiore, 14a
☎ (+39) 0521805947
🌐 www.caseificiogennari.it
✉ info@caseificiogennari.it
shop: yes
e-commerce: no

Since 1953 this family operation has devoted itself to the entire Parmigiano Reggiano chain: from breeding Italian Bruna and Friesian cattle to processing and ageing the cheese. The experience of husband-and-wife Sergio and Maria was handed down to their four children, now involved in all aspects of the business. The youngest cheese is just 18 months old but the oldest is an astonishing 101 months and a unique multi-sensory experience. There are also Oronero cheeses, raw milk, semi-hard paste, aged just under nine months. Niche specialities are also available.

Bra (CN)
Giolito Formaggi

via Monte Grappa, 6
☎ (+39) 0172412920
🌐 www.giolitocheese.it
✉ info@giolitocheese.it
shop: yes
e-commerce: no

Fiorenzo Giolito is the most recent generation of a family of affineurs that has meticulously selected and aged cheese across the entire area for a century and more. He is now at the helm of the company, a microcosm of Italian dairy products (mainly from Piedmont), but also with some French and Spanish gems. There are the local PDOs of Bettelmatt, Castelmagno, Raschera d'alpeggio, and Bra; some Slow Food Presidia like Montebore; and then Gorgonzola, robiola creams and goat tomino, primintii pecorinos and Ragusa caciocavallo; and Sardinian Gavoi.

Motteggiana (MN)
Gonfo

fraz. Villa Saviola l s.da Argine Po, 88
☎ (+39) 0376527095
✉ zuccagraziano@virgilio.it
shop: yes
e-commerce: no

**Latteria Sociale
"GONFO"**

Originally a community dairy, it has evolved into a beautiful cooperative, with strong connections to the local area and an affinity for typical products. The flagship product is a quality Parmigiano Reggiano, made from the milk of cows raised on fodder grown on the farm. The key to success? A semi-artisan production approach combined with the outstanding technological skills of the new generation of entrepreneurs.

Arona (NO)
Luigi Guffanti 1876

via Milano, 140
☎ (+39) 0322242038 l 032247222
❂ www.guffantiformaggi.com
✉ info@guffantiformaggi.com
shop: yes
e-commerce: no

Formaggi per Tradizione

The Piedmont shore of Lake Maggiore is Italy's best calling card for cheeses. In the beginning there was PDO Gorgonzola and it is still the company's flagship product, available in various versions and reaping awards at many events, but with the passage of time countless other products have been added and today, in the region and beyond, there is something for everyone. Castelmagno, Caciocavallo Silano, Fontina, Asiago, Fiore Sardo, Casciotta di Urbino. Not to mention the great Tuscan and Lazio PDO Pecorinos, and much more.

Brusson (AO)
Fromagerie Haut Val d'Ayas

rue Trois Villages, 1
☎ (+39) 0125301117
❂ www.fromagerie.it
✉ info@fromagerie.it
shop: yes
e-commerce: yes

Founded in 2004, the cooperative brings together 65 manufacturers who contribute about two million litres of milk each year from native Valdostana cows. The operation treads the fine line between modern methods and age-old tradition. The result is production of artisan cheeses made with milk collected between the 1,200 metres of Brusson and the 3,000 of Mount Rosa. The flagship product is the PDO Fontina (organic also), aged for at least 90 days. There is also the PDO fromadzo, the tomas with rosemary, chilli, herbs, and juniper, in goat versions also; valdostana cheese.

Modena
Hombre

s.da Corletto Sud, 320
☎ (+39) 059510660
❀ www.hombre.it
✉ hombre@hombre.it
shop: yes
e-commerce: no

This 300-hectare farm is still known by the nickname attributed to Umberto Panini (who invented the famous Panini stickers) when he emigrated to Venezuela. It has certified organic, closed-loop production and makes Parmigiano Reggiano cheese with the milk from its own cows, raising about 500 Friesians, fed natural foods from the farm's own fields and mill. The cheese is available in whole wheels or in slabs of 200 grams upwards, aged from 12 to 36 months. Also worthy of note the butter and grated Parmigiano Reggiano.

Noci (BA)
Ignalat

via G. di Vittorio, 13
☎ (+39) 0804972478
❀ www.ignalat.it
✉ info@ignalat.it
shop: yes
e-commerce: no

The dairy, located in the Alta Murgia plains, has been producing traditional fresh and ripened Puglia cheeses for more than 50 years. The company has combined the skills inherited from master cheese-maker Vincenzo Ignazzi, who founded this small outfit in 1948, with rural culture and quality cow milk. It offers a full range of products, primarily dairy: mozzarella, butter, scamorza, stracciatella, burrata, ricotta bonbons. Then there is pecorino, ricotta forte, provolone, caciocavallo and, last but not least, giuncata curds.

Lesignano de' Bagni (PR)
Iris

loc. Rivalta I via Torchio, 3
☎ (+39) 0521863653 I 3487908677
❀ www.agricolairis.it
✉ info@agricolairis.it
shop: yes
e-commerce: no

Umberto Avanzini, wife Carolina and son Davide run this farm in the Apennine foohtills. They have 75 cows of their own, fed with forage and vegetables they grow themselves with organic methods. Every morning Umberto processes the milk himself to make cheese, and when we say cheese! About 1,400 wheels a year of excellent Parmgiano Reggiano Biologico, aged from 12–14 months to 24–26 and 30–32. In addition, butter, yogurt, ricotta, caciotta, spreads, panna cotta.

Cesiomaggiore (BL)

Lattebusche

fraz. Busche **I** via Nazionale, 59
☎ (+39) 04393191
❀ www.lattebusche.it
✉ info@lattebusche.it
shop: yes
e-commerce: yes

Located in the Feltrina Valley, this cooperative is a leading company in the dairy sector. Since it took its first steps in 1954 the mission has been to reconcile tradition with the technological progress. The range of products is extensive and includes milk, cream, butter, yogurt, ice cream (tubs, cones, sandwich, biscuits, bowls, sorbets, and desserts); fresh cheeses (mozzarella, mascarpone, stracchino, and many others); semi-ripe and ripe cheeses including Asiago, Piave, Grana Padano and Montasio.

Eboli (SA)

Casa Madaio

via Marino da Eboli, 9
☎ (+39) 0828364815
❀ www.casamadaio.it
✉ info@casamadaio.it
shop: no
e-commerce: yes

For four generations Casa Madaio has handed down the traditions and passion for making and ripening cheese, from father to son. The products fall into a number of categories: fresh items including cheese, yogurt and buffalo mozzarella; semi-ripe cheeses including a Manteca of string cheese and butter; Ficaccio wrapped in fig leaves and aged 40 days; ripe cheeses including Vetus caciocavallo podolico; Rosso with Senise pepper; Sbronzo using two types of milk, cow and buffalo; with Aglianico wine.

Crotone

Maiorano

loc. Pudano (bivio di Cutro) **I** s.da prov.le 43, km 0, n. 14
☎ (+39) 0962946135
❀ www.agricolamaiorano.it
✉ info@agricolamaiorano.it
shop: yes
e-commerce: no

The pecorino cheese made at Maiorano is at the top of its class. It's available on the market at various ages, from thirty days to 'gran riserva' (more than a year), with a flavor that goes from mild to decisive, with a slightly spicy aftertaste. We highly recommend their raw milk variety, which is aged in a cave and gives off a grassy aroma. The producer also offers an excellent ricotta, both fresh and smoked (orange wood or olive). Rounding out the selection is a cow ricotta and the local crotonese provola.

Cheese

Pavullo nel Frignano (MO)
Caseificio Malandrone 1477

fraz. Miceno I via per Polinago, 35
☎ (+39) 053621002 I 3287445447
❀ www.malandrone1477.com
✉ info@malandrone1477.com
shop: no
e-commerce: yes

With a herd of 300 Friesian cows fed with mountain forage rich in wild herbs, the dairy works daily to produce its excellent Parmigiano Reggiano Expert, ably assisted by the skilled gestures of an experienced master cheesemaker. It is unique for its lengthy and temperature-controlled ageing, to 24, 36 and 48 months, but some wheels are taken to 120, in a crescendo of perfectly balanced fragrance, aroma and texture.

Conco (VI)
Malga Verde - Fattoria Cortese

loc. Val Lastaro I via Malga Verde
☎ (+39) 0424700332 I 3395436022
❀ www.malgaverde.com
✉ info@malgaverde.com
shop: yes
e-commerce: no

In the early 1980s the Cortese brothers began their livestock farm and in 2003 took the plunge, starting process their excellent milk to make only prime cheeses. They combine traditional methods with compliance with legal regulations, especially in terms of hygiene. There are dairy products like ricotta, stracchino, butter, tosella, mozzarella, as well as caciotta, PDO Asiago of various ages (Mezzano, Vecchio and Stravecchio) and Malga Verde.

Gavoi (NU)
Sa Marchesa

loc. Tanca Sa Marchesa
☎ (+39) 3286027607 I 3289097404
❀ www.samarchesa.com
✉ samarchesa@alice.it
shop: yes
e-commerce: no

The life and soul of the company is Giuseppe Cugusi, who has been a shepherd practically all his life, and owner of 140 hectares of land, with Sarda sheep stock located up on the plateau. There are four cheeses, all raw milk and top quality, starting from PDO Fiore Sardo, made entirely by hand and aged at length. Then there is the Foz'e murta, flavoured with the myrtle juice, as well as thyme-flavoured Barone, and Sa Marchesa, a classic and very tasty pecorino table cheese.

Castelmagno (CN)
La Meiro

fraz. Chiappi I via dei Pinet, 1
☎ (+39) 3386261222 I 3356931946
❂ www.terredicastelmagno.com
✉ terredicastelmagno@hotmail.com
shop: yes
e-commerce: no

The farm has a modern manufacturing facility and a ripening centre in Chiappi, the municipality's highest district, in the stunning Santuario di Castelmagno basin. The owners have acquired precious pastures like Grange Nollo, Grange Rudu, Grange Bijoi and Grange Borgis. An important detail, because mountain milk is superior in quality and if properly processed the cheese reaches levels of absolute excellence. The business makes two versions of Castelmagno, the mountain and the alpine pasture, both PDO. Also on offer a genepy liqueur and Castelmagno honey.

Reggio Emilia
Montanari & Gruzza

loc. Gaida I via I. Newton, 38
☎ (+39) 0522944251
❂ www.montanari-gruzza.it
✉ info@montanari-gruzza.it
shop: no
e-commerce: yes

Since 1950 the quality cheeses made here use milk from herds of Rossa Reggiana and Bruna Alpina cattle. The results include about ten types of excellent butter (including one suitable for lactose intolerance); cream; a good PDO Parmigiano Reggiano of different ages; PDO Grana Padano without preservatives; and Cacionerone hard cheese, which takes its name from the intense black colour of the rind, and is ripened for at least 24 months. There is also an organic line.

Olzai (NU)
Montenieddu

via Brigata Sassari, 6
☎ (+39) 3476523390 I 3476523867
❂ www.montenieddu.com
✉ info@montenieddu.com
shop: yes
e-commerce: no

Montenieddu is a delightful, family-run producer that makes cheese using strictly artisanal methods and only with raw milk from their own sheep. Fiore Sardo PDO, made between December and June (according to tradition) and aged for a minimum of 105 days, is a mainstay. But there's so much more. Try their traditional pecorino, blue cheese, the 'granortzaesu', caciotta, ricotta (both fresh and aged) and creamy spreads, which can be used as toppings (there's also a spicy version).

Andria (BT)
Olanda

via Santa Maria dei Miracoli, 150
☎ (+39) 0883551810
❀ www.caseificioolanda.it
✉ caseificio.olanda@virgilio.it
shop: yes
e-commerce: no

A family-run dairy where experience melds with tradition, located close to Castel del Monte. The production is mostly fresh or semi-ripe cheese obtained from the milk of the Murgia Friesian breed, keeping faith with techniques of a bygone era and interpreting technological innovations with attention. The flagships are burrata and mozzarella, but the range includes nodini, bocconcini, treccia, scamorza, primo sale, caciocavallo, the latter also in a cave-aged version.

Scarperia e San Piero (FI)
Storica Fattoria Il Palagiaccio

via Senni, 40 int. 6
☎ (+39) 0558402103
❀ www.palagiaccio.com
✉ commercialepalagiaccio@gmail.com
shop: yes
e-commerce: yes

Palagiaccio's roots go back to before the turn of the first millennium, when a noble family, the Ubaldini, built a fortified stronghold on Mugello's fertile terrain. To this day, the historic farmstead serves as a benchmark for Florentine agriculture. They cultivate grains and meal. They also raise cattle and, most importantly, they produce milk, which is used for various cheeses (fresh, aged and blue cheese), their main product. Finally, they also produce honey and make pasta (fresh, dried and stuffed) using their own wheat.

Cavallirio (NO)
Palzola

via Europa, 21
☎ (+39) 016380940
❀ www.palzola.it
✉ info@palzola.it
shop: yes
e-commerce: no

Renato Paltrinieri runs a tight ship at his dairy. The secret of production quality lies in his careful checks on milk sources, the artisanal processing at each stage, and bespoke ageing from 70 to 150 days, depending on the type of cheese and in rooms where hygiene reigns supreme. The flagship is a Gorgonzola in mild or piquant versions, layered with mascarpone and another with chilli. Then there is Paltoma, a Piano Rosa toma from whole cow's milk.

Forenza (PZ)

Il Parco delle Bontà

c.da Piro Sorbo
☎ (+39) 0971773460
🌐 www.ilparcodellebonta.it
✉ caggiano@ilparcodellebonta.it
shop: yes
e-commerce: no

Farm, livestock and dairy, activities all monitored directly by the proprietors, the Summo and Caggiano families, from the forage for the stock to milking and production. The flagship product is Forenza pecorino, aged in tufa caves for a minimum of 6–8 months. There is also Forenza caciocavallo, matured from three months to two years; mozzarella, scamorza, burrino, butter, ricotta, and goat cheese. Also worth mentioning, a small but excellent charcuterie production line.

Asiago (VI)

Pennar

via Pennar, 313
☎ (+39) 0424462374
🌐 caseificiopennar.it
✉ caseificio.pennar@tiscali.it
shop: yes
e-commerce: no

The dairy, whose roots are lost in the mists of time, is located on the Asiago plateau and traditionally breeds native cattle that graze at 1,700 metres in altitude, using no silage fodder or fermented substances. Strictly raw milk is processed to achieve top dairy products, focused almost entirely on traditional PDO Asiago, both aged (medium, old and extra old, depending on ripending) and a younger version, ripened for no more than 60 days. The list continues with PDO Grana Padano, pennarone, tosela, caciotta, butter, ricotta, mascarpone and more.

San Pietro di Feletto (TV)

Latteria PER - Latteria Perenzin

loc. Bagnolo I via Cervano, 85
☎ (+39) 043821355
🌐 www.perenzin.com
✉ info@perenzin.com
shop: yes
e-commerce: no

For a century this expert family has produced and aged large cheeses using artisanal methods, advanced technologies and expertise that comes from passion and lifelong training. The processing starts with a careful selection of milk that will give the cheese grassy, hay fragrances, then proceeds to production, ripening and ageing. Goat and cow cheeses from organic farming, traditional recipes like PDO Montasio and experiments that give life to unique delights, like goat cheese aged in berries and rose petals.

Fagagna (UD)

Pezzetta

via Spilimbergo, 220
☎ (+39) 0432810827
✪ www.pezzetta.it
✉ info@pezzetta.it
shop: yes
e-commerce: no

SAPORI E RICETTE FRIULANE

The company has been in business for about 90 years, making and selecting cheeses and other delicacies. The cheeses it makes in house are sustained by strict quality control of milk and all processing stages, with maximum transparency for the consumer. The range includes Latteria, Montasio, fresh ricotta (also smoked), yogurt, caciotta, goat cheese rounds. The list of products are offers Formadi Frant, Frico, Formaggio Ubriaco and Blu Ramandolo.

Jesi (AN)

Piandelmedico

via Piandelmedico, 101
☎ (+39) 0731208397 I 3356393236
✪ www.caseificiopiandelmedico.it
✉ info@trionfihonorati.it
shop: yes
e-commerce: no

The Trionfi Honorati siblings created their dairy in 2004, relying on milk from their stock and the skills of master cheesemakers. They produce about 30 types of cheese, from dairy fresh to ripe, as well as mozzarella, treccia and bocconcino, then stracchino, robiola, taleggiello. The blue-veined mozzarella dadone and Castelmedico (a reinterpretation of Castelmagno) both used raw milk. Not to mention gessatina (a blue-veined cacioricotta cheese), bucarello (a kind of ripe robiola) and stracchinona (cow and buffalo cheese).

Filiano (PZ)

Piano della Spina

via Piano della Spina
☎ (+39) 0971808500
✪ www.pianodellaspina.it
✉ info@pianodellaspina.it
shop: yes
e-commerce: no

PianoDellaSpina

Latte, passione e tradizione.

The dairy was founded in 1987 in the hills of the Vulture area. over the years personal experience and traditional cheese-making skills have been integrated with technology, and today the company covers an area of 12,000 square metres, of which 4,500 are indoors. The milk supply comes only from local farms and is the secret of the quality of the cheese, but also of its quite unique flavour and aroma. The company produces PDO Silano caciocavallo, hard ricotta, Lucania provolone, butter, scamorza, mozzarella, goat cacioricotta and an excellent Filiano pecorino.

Volterra (PI)

Guido Pinzani dal 1969

loc. Montemiccioli I s.da prov.le 52 per Casole d'Elsa, km 3
☎ (+39) 058835043
❂ www.caseificiopinzani.com
✉ info@caseificiopinzani.com
shop: yes
e-commerce: no

The dairy was set up in 1969 by Guido Pinzani, who found himself attracted to the art of cheese-making after meeting a retired cheesemaker. Pinzani monitors each stage of production himself with loving care, and specializes in the production of raw-milk cheese. Other products vary from fresher Marzolino to the Da Serbo, a nice cheese aged over ten months; Rugoso, covered with natural mould; Pecorino Nero; peppered, saffron or truffle pecorinos. Finally, the ewe ricotta.

Sestu (CA)

Casearia Podda

ex s.s. 131, km 7,750
☎ (+39) 07022058 I 07022059
❂ www.ferrucciopodda.it
shop: no
e-commerce: no

Casearia Podda was established in 2012 when the Granarolo group, the largest Italian milk producer, purchased the Sardinian company Ferruccio Podda, with over 60 years of experience in the production of typical ripe cheeses, especially Sardinian and Roman pecorinos, with plenty of accolades under its belt. On behalf of the Bologna food company, Casearia Podda produces a pecorino romano of four saltings, which is pleasant, well-balanced and quite tangy considering it was made in Sardinia.

Castelmagno (CN)

La Poiana

p.zza Caduti, 1
☎ (+39) 0171986233
❂ cooperativalapoiana.it
✉ info@cooperativalapoiana.it
shop: no
e-commerce: yes

The cooperative, in the heart of Valle Grana, was founded in 1982, the same year that PDO Castelmagno cheese was awarded its label. While using the best modern technologies, processing follows traditional methods including the use of wood, ripening in whey, ageing in stone cellars and in the underground infernot. The flagship product is, of course, the alpine pasture Castelmagno, medium-aged, aged, and reserve cheeses. Then there is Bettelmatt, Berra, goat and ewe blue-veined cheese, Bra, PDO Fontina (also organic), PDO Murazzano, robiolas, testuns and much more.

Qualiano (NA)
Principe

c.ne Esterna, 37 (ex 24)
☎ (+39) 0818181794
❀ www.caseificioprincipe.com
✉ info@caseificioprincipe.it
shop: yes
e-commerce: no

At Principe, artisanal craft and modern technology come together beautifully. The cheesemaker, which was founded in 1965 by Domenico Buonanno, prides itself on the ingredients it uses (starting with milk, of course), all of which come from certified sources. From here the ingredients are worked into high-quality products like Buffalo Mozzarella PDO, available in different shapes and sizes. Smoked and vegan mozzarella cheeses are also available. Their shop sells wine and speciality food items as well.

Torrita Tiberina (RM)
Progetto Latte - Casearia Agri In

via Valle Carbone
☎ (+39) 0765322273
❀ www.agriin.it
✉ daniele.deroma@agriin.it
shop: no
e-commerce: no

This "taste farm" continues the old tradition of processing ewes' milk to enhance its generous sensory and nutritional features. Cheese is produced using only milk, rennet and salt, but what makes the difference is a respect for the natural pace here in the lush Tiber valley. Products include Pecorino Romano PDO, Pecorino di Fossa, and cheeses flavoured with walnuts, balsamic vinegar, or wood ashes.

Cologno al Serio (BG)
Quattro Portoni

via Crema, 69
☎ (+39) 035896507 I 3355943352
❀ www.quattroportoni.it
✉ info@quattroportoni.it
shop: yes
e-commerce: no

The Gritti family, who have owned farm in the heart of the Po Valley since 1968, began breeding Latina and Caserta buffalo in 2001. The livestock is raised in open barns, with controlled feeding, to ensure its wellbeing. The state-of-the-art Quattro Portoni in-house dairy farm processes the milk sold. There are over 20 types of cheeses aged here, including the award-winning Blu di Bufala, the maison's pride and joy. Also worthy are the ricotta, crescenza, scamorza, squacquerone, muratello, yogurt, mozzarella and caciocavallo.

Putignano (BA)
Querceta

s.da comunale Salita dell'Uomo, 1
☎ (+39) 0802145010 I 3283909682
❀ www.querceta.com
✉ info@querceta.com
shop: yes
e-commerce: no

The farm is located in a typical rural setting, surrounded by stone walls and age-old olive trees. The approach to business is based on preferring natural methods, from fertilization to stock breeding, milk processing to make certified organic dairy products. Among the cheeses, the burrata is a must, but also worthy are caciocavallo, cacioricotta, butter, mozzarella, fiordilatte, primo sale, scamorza, ricotta and a tasty stracciatella. Meat and olive oil are also available.

Malvicino (AL)
Le Ramate

loc. Ramate
☎ (+39) 0144340923 I 3485804749
❀ www.leramate.it
✉ info@leramate.it
shop: yes
e-commerce: no

Owned by the Cambiano family, this organic farming business occupies 17 hectares estate in the stunning Val di Erro landscape. Here Italian chamois goats are raised in the wild, and their milk is processed to make excellent cheese, following artisan methods. There are three products: the fresh Rubine Primo Amore; Rubine Primo Amore, a cheese blended from evening and morning milkings, matured for about 40 days; and Robiolone Max 1er, ripened at high altitude, unique for taste and fragrance.

Capaccio (SA)
Rivabianca

s.s. 18 Tirrena Inferiore, km 93
☎ (+39) 0828724030
❀ www.rivabianca.it
✉ info@rivabianca.it
shop: yes
e-commerce: yes

A farming cooperative specializing in buffalo, whose fresh milk is processed to make excellent products, applying the artisanal methods developed with years of experience (fermentation, spinning and cutting), but also working to all hygiene and healthcare standards. The catalogue is lengthy and includes ricotta; plain and smoked scamorza; cacioreale; smoked provola. Of course pride of place goes to buffalo mozzarella, braided in weights of 1.5 kg upwards, or in bocconcini of about 50 g each. Also classic mozzarella in a variety of formats.

Zocca (MO)
Caseificio Rosola

via Rosola, 1083
☎ (+39) 059987115
🌐 www.caseificiorosola.it
✉ info@caseificiorosola.it
shop: yes
e-commerce: no

A cooperative dairy breeding its own Bianca Modenese cows, whose milk makes Parmigiano Reggiano produced, aged and ripened in house at the company's premises on the Modena Apennine slopes. Rosola consists of seven operating units and is currently managed by the children and grandchildren of the partners that founded it, aiming to maintain local dairy traditions. In addition to traditional and mountain Parmigiano Reggiano, aged 22 to 30 months, the dairy also produces ricotta and meat from Modenese cattle.

Cervasca (CN)
La Sabaco d'Oc

loc. San Defendente I via Nazionale, 66
☎ (+39) 0171687449 I 3292082951
🌐 www.sabacodoc.it
✉ paolo@sabacodoc.it
shop: no
e-commerce: no

The Cuneo area is rich in fine cheese products made from precious ingredients and more often than not using artisan methods. This is the case for the business owned by Marco and Paolo Lopatriello. Sabaco offers three lines of dairy products and cheese made from as many types of milk: cow, ewe and goat. There is Famù yoghurt and other products, but the flagships are PDO cheeses, above all, the Robiola di Roccaverano Famè, made solely from Cuneo goat milk.

Ponzone (AL)
San Lorenzo - Arbiora

fraz. Caldasio, 119
☎ (+39) 3386251947 I 3406269168
🌐 www.sanlorenzoarbiora.it
✉ sanlorenzo.arbiora@gmail.com
shop: yes
e-commerce: no

Cheese-maker and ager Francesco Lauria and his son Fedele produce several lines of Roccaverano robiolas: Riserva della Filanda Arbiora, a classic brand acquired recently, aged for at least three weeks; the younger Robiola dall'Alpe and Formaggetta San Lorenzo, and the robiola del bec, traditionally made in September when the nanny goats are on heat. Lauria uses 100% goat's milk from their own farm, processed "au lait cru", then curdled.

Tezze sul Brenta (VI)
San Rocco

via Tre Case, 65
☎ (+39) 042489056
✪ www.caseificiosanrocco.it
✉ info@caseificiosanrocco.it
shop: yes
e-commerce: no

This social cooperative dairy opened in 1966. Today it is a leading company vaunting 400 quintals a day of milk processed to make quality products, monitored by cheese-making experts. The flagships are a fresh and a ripe PDO Asiago, but also worthy are the PDO Grana Padano, available in a Riserva version too, aged over 20 months. Then ricotta; rigatello (also with pepper and chilli); caciotta; tosella (including with paprika and chives); stracchino; and standard and aged Collina Veneta.

Montechiarugolo (PR)
Sangonelli & Delbono

loc. Basilicanova I via Case Nuove, 42
☎ (+39) 0521682235 I 3471714838
✪ www.sangonelli.it
✉ sangonelli@libero.it
shop: no
e-commerce: no

The farm run by Antonio Sangonelli and Gabriella Delbono has a strong cheese-making tradition behind it and is distinctive for its Italian Bruna livestock, now numbering 170 head. Their decision was inspired by the sturdy milk from these cows, which is perfect for producing cheese and drove the development of the Disolabruna consortium, of which Antonio and Gabriella are members and promoters. The company produces prime Parmigiano Reggiano, aged for at least 12 months, with some wheels reaching 30 months.

Vedeseta (BG)
Sant'Antonio Valtaleggio

fraz. Reggetto, 2
☎ (+39) 034547467
✪ www.santantoniovaltaleggio.com
✉ sca.santonio@virgilio.it
shop: yes
e-commerce: no

An agricultural cooperative found in Val Taleggio, established by an initiative of the Valle Brembana mountain community and Taleggio and Vedeseta municipal authorities. Chaired by Flaminio Locatelli, the cooperative today is a point of reference for local farmers and a a leading production facility for Italian Bruna cow cheeses made in the traditional way. Products also include butter, yogurt, Vedeseta stracchino, strachitunt, Taleggio, Alben, Magrera and formagella, all made in the same meticulous fashion with bespoke ripening times.

Serramazzoni (MO)
Santa Rita

via Pompeano, 2290
☎ (+39) 0536950193
✆ www.caseificiosantarita.com
✉ info@caseificiosantarita.com
shop: yes
e-commerce: no

The dairy is a farming cooperative set up over 50 years ago, collecting milk from Friesian and Bianca Modenese cattle, contributed by its members, all located in the area. The milk is processed raw and quickly to avoid altering the sensorial profile. The company follows a strict organic production process, starting from the cattle fodder grown on the land belonging to the member farms. Flying the company flag is a Parmigiano di Montagna available in different ages and of excellent quality.

Reggio Emilia
I Sapori delle Vacche Rosse

fraz. Villa Cella I s.s. 9 via G.B. Vico, 114
☎ (+39) 0522946569 I 335344279
✆ www.isaporidellarossa.com
✉ lucianocatellani@isaporidellarossa.com
shop: yes
e-commerce: no

The mastermind behind the business is Luciano Catellani, who started rearing livestock in the 1980s with the intention of saving and protecting the Vacca Rossa cow, an ancient Reggio breed. His production focuses mainly on an excellent Parmigiano Reggiano, aged 24, 30, 36, and 48 months, but there are also butter, yogurt, panna cotta, spreads, ice cream, mozzarella and caciotta, all made with milk from these cows. The deli department is a foodie paradise: lasagne, cappelletti, grissini, and sauces.

Olbia
Sardaformaggi

via Trento, 10
☎ (+39) 078921657 I 0558330046
✆ www.sardaformaggi.it
✉ info@sardaformaggi.it
shop: no
e-commerce: no

Sardaformaggi was set up in 1963 by three siblings and a cousin. The production is based on milk coming mainly from farmers in north-east Sardinia. Craft processing methods pump the milk directly into the cheese moulds and all steps are manual. The product list is lengthy, with fresh and aged ricotta; spun paste cheeses; various types of pecorino including semi-ripe and ripe; limited edition cheeses including one with thyme flowers. Last but not least, Pecorino Romano.

Morolo (FR)
Scarchilli

c.da Madonna del Piano, 12
☎ (+39) 0775806019
❀ www.grancacio.it
✉ info@scarchilli.it
shop: yes
e-commerce: no

Massimiliano Scarchilli wanted to breathe a hint of innovation into Gran Cacio di Morolo, a heritage Ciociaro spun-paste cow cheese. Roberto learned how to produce the cheese from his father but he wanted to revive and redevelop its image by selecting milk from local breeders and processing its raw. The cheese comes in wheels ranging from 1.2 kg to some of a spectacular 5–6 kg, called Riserva, aged in chambers for up to 18 months in wooden trays. In addition, there is the ciambella spun paste, which is slightly smoked, and a ciambella steccata.

Marene (CN)
Caseificio Sepertino

via Reale Nord, 2
☎ (+39) 0172742575
❀ www.caseificiosepertino.com
✉ info@caseificiosepertino.com
shop: no
e-commerce: no

The Sepertino family have been operating since 1930 and are now one of the most important businesses in the region. They offer a robust selection of high-quality cheeses, both fresh and aged, and from both goat and cow milk. Asiago stands out among their aged cheeses, along with the Bra, the Rashera and the Castelmagno PDO. Stracchino, primosale and robiola di Roccaverano PDO are among their featured fresh cheeses. Their butter also deserves to be mentioned (there's also a version with Himalayan salt). Organic cheeses from certified milk sources are also available.

Trecate (NO)
Sì Invernizzi

via Romentino, 98
☎ (+39) 0321783090
❀ www.invernizzisi.it
✉ info@invernizzisi.it
shop: no
e-commerce: no

caseificio

Sì INVERNIZZI

For three generations the Invernizzi family has produced and ripened Gorgonzola, this charming area's iconic cheese. The company is proud of its monitoring of each individual step of processing, for which it uses sophisticated state-of-the-art equipment. Gorgonzola aside, available in mild and piquant flavours, as well as the Dolce Panna and Bollo Nero types, there are also Effebi, a Gorgonzola and mascarpone cake, Taleggio, fontal and mascarpone.

Collecorvino (PE)

Taberna Imperiale

via Atri, 3
☎ (+39) 0858205008 I 3351311620
✆ www.tabernaimperiale.it
✉ info@tabernaimperiale.it
shop: no
e-commerce: no

Gianni Faieta is the man behind this company, founded over 30 years ago with the help of his brother Elio. Their intention was to select, ripen and mature quality cheeses. Today Gianni has a catalogue of a thousand dairy items, available in Italy and abroad, including some that are the result of unique experiments. There are several lines. One of PDO cheeses like Asiago, Bitto, Bra, Fiore Sardo, Castelmagno, Fontina, Gorgonzola, Grana Padano, and so on. Then fresh cheeses, blue-veined, hard and semi-hard.

Fornovo San Giovanni (BG)

Taddei

via San Vitale
☎ (+39) 036357120
✆ www.caseificiotaddei.it
✉ info@caseificiotaddei.it
shop: yes
e-commerce: no

For four generations traditional Bergamo cheeses have been made and aged here. The sheer quality of the various dairy products is due to the manual processing of milk brought only from selected local farms, combined with the expertise of the cheese-makers and affineurs. The flagship is the PDO Taleggio, one in blue wrapping, the other in red, the latter a prize-winning product. There are also a PDO Salva Cremasco, formaggella, Blutunt, caciotta, toma, Sbrisola, Pan di cacio, Regiur, Bergamina and Torta Orobica.

Borso del Grappa (TV)

Toniolo

via Molinetto, 47
☎ (+39) 0423910266
✆ www.toniolo.it
✉ toniolo@toniolo.it
shop: yes
e-commerce: no

Opening under the name of Toniolo Casearia in 1960, the company goes back another two generations with the Toniolo family of cheesemakers, originally from Vicenza and then moving to the Veneto foothills. Production revolves around the leading Veneto PDO cheeses of Asiago, Montasio, and Casatella Trevigiana, and about a dozen traditional dairy products. In addition, aged cheeses aromatized with herbs; camomile and mint; hay; ripened in red wine, and yet others; pure goat milk cheeses, ricotta, caciotta and butter.

Nurri (CA)
Unione Pastori Nurri

loc. Taccu I s.da prov.le 10 zona industriale, 57
☎ (+39) 0782849060 I 0782849309
❀ www.unionepastorinurri.com
✉ info@unionepastorinurri.com
shop: yes
e-commerce: no

A cooperative founded in 1962, today it has approximately 800 members. The mission was always to produce quality cheeses made from fresh sheep and goat milk from the rich pastures of Barbagia and the hills bordering the Flumendosa and Mulargia lakes. While it is true that the plant is cutting edge, the various processing phases are true to the heritage of ancient skills. The flagship cheese is a PDO Pecorino Romano, but also ricotta (sheep and mixed); pecorino with pepper; Miraluna sheep caciotta; Crabarida fresh goat cheese; spreads and more.

Urbino
Val d'Apsa

loc. Viapiana I via Ca' Bergamo, 1
☎ (+39) 072252088 I 072252187
❀ www.caseificiovaldapsa.it
✉ info@caseificiovaldapsa.it
shop: yes
e-commerce: no

The company, on the Urbino slope, preserves traditions rooted in the recipes handed down for centuries but also responds to growing market demands by installing state-of-the-art equipment and facilities. The dairy is outstanding also for its use of milk collected directly in the surrounding farms and proper processing of local products. The range is extensive, with Casciotta di Urbino and PDO Fossa di Sogliano, as well as primo sale, ricotta, pecorino, cow cheeses and others that are mixed, aged, flavoured.

Gerola Alta (SO)
Valli del Bitto

via Nazionale, 31
☎ (+39) 0342690081 I 3343325366
❀ www.formaggiobitto.com
✉ info@formaggiobitto.com
shop: yes
e-commerce: no

The main product is Bitto cheese whose unique properties are linked to its setting. It is a Slow Food Presidium and the only cheese to undergo over ten years of ageing. The merit goes to the Valli del Bitto producers' association, which includes 15 alp herders and has acquired the heritage pastures of in the Gerola and Albaredo valleys. Skills are handed down from generation to generation, together with the wholesome milk of Orobica goat and cow breeds, making each wheel of cheese a unique product each year.

Torrile (PR)

Valserena

loc. Gainago I s.da della Repubblica, 21
☎ (+39) 0521819114
◈ valserena.com
✉ info@valserena.com
shop: yes
e-commerce: yes

Here the processing of Parmigiano Reggiano has very ancient roots. From day one the dairy set itself the objective of safeguarding the craftsmanship and skill required to achieve a product coveted the world over and with many imitations. The milk is used raw and without chemical additives, taken from Italian Bruna cows fed on natural forage, rich in fragrant herbs. Products include Parmigiano Reggiano aged over 14, over 24 and over 30 months.

Brignano Gera d'Adda (BG)

La Via Lattea

s.da prov.le per Verdello, 33
☎ (+39) 0363817001
◈ www.la-vialattea.it
✉ caseificiolavialattea@live.it
shop: yes
e-commerce: no

In this small family-run company the chief is Valentina Canò, who studied and attends refresher courses in France. With the invaluable support of husband Roberto, she produces excellent cheeses from raw goat milk. The range includes fresh, ripe, aged, and blue-veined cheeses. Fresh goat cheeses include Morla (which has won several awards abroad) and Capricandido; the original Ol Sciur, a blue-veined cheese with rose petals and berries; and Bucun de la Regiura, matured in brandy and bran or in cornmeal.

Guardia Perticara (PZ)

Mario Viola

c.da Aria di Tutti i Venti
☎ (+39) 0835560500 I 3687512144
✉ azienda.viola@virgilio.it
shop: yes
e-commerce: no

Mario Pietro Viola, a businessman who studied veterinary medicine and agricultural sciences, conceived his company on a wave of a personal passion. Processing techniques are meticulous and bound to tradition, using quality milk from Viola's own livestock, underpinning a high-profile dairy. His specialities are goat and pecorino cheese, some flavoured, caciocavallo podolico and Moliterno canestrato. He is also the only breeder of the famous local black pig, which gives prized hams.

Tuglie (LE)

Alda

via A. Moro, 143a
☎ (+39) 0833598168
❀ www.alda.it
✉ info@alda.it
shop: no
e-commerce: no

ALDA

DOLCI TRADIZIONI

Three generations of pastry chefs are bringing together quality, tradition, top ingredients (especially local almonds, figs and extra-virgin olive oil), cutting edge technology and creativity. Almond paste production is at center stage, together with a rich and appetizing selection of chocolates and pralines. Don't forget about their chocolate-covered candied fruits, biscotti, local Salento sweets, cream spreads and liquors.

Pontedera (PI)

Amedei

loc. La Rotta I via San Gervaso, 29
☎ (+39) 0587484849
❀ www.amedei.it
✉ amedei@amedei.it
shop: no
e-commerce: yes

Amedei is a giant in artisanal chocolate-making and a revolutionary in the industry. The company controls the entire cocoa chain, from selection of beans directly in plantations to processing. Its range vaunts an appealing section of themed products, from dozens of napolitains that offer a tour of world cocoa; dark chocolate bars including excellent single-origin crus; pralines; drops; spreads; Tuscan square bars; hot chocolate mixes; tasteful gift caskets.

Cuneo

Arione

p.zza Galimberti, 14
☎ (+39) 0171692539
❀ www.arionecuneo.it
✉ info@arionecuneo.it
shop: yes
e-commerce: yes

Cuneesi al rhum are iconic confectionery made by this historic patisserie since 1923. Cuneesi vaunt many imitations but are really inimitable bonbons made with Andrea Arione's legendary recipe of a double meringue containing chocolate and rum cream, dipped in more chocolate for the classic version and with a Grand Marnier option. Then there are hazelnut, cremino, chestnut cream versions. Other artisanal delights include baci dorati, marrons glacés, gianduiotti, pralines, génepy and Piedmontese mountain spirits.

Chocolate

Cherasco (CN)
Barbero

c.so Luigi Einaudi, 32
☎ (+39) 0172488373
❂ www.pasticceriabarbero.com
✉ info@pasticceriabarbero.com
shop: yes
e-commerce: no

Confetteria Barbero is a legend dating back to 1881, acquired several years ago by Mr and Mrs Torta. The patisserie is a byword for the famous Baci di Cherasco, delicious morsels of fine dark chocolate mix blended with Piedmont hazelnuts toasted according to an ancient recipe and coarsely crushed. Then there are pralines, truffles, gianduiotti, dragées, chocolate bars, hot chocolate mixes, and chocolate-dipped Sicilian candied orange peel, coffee beans and even grissini.

Grottaglie (TA)
Bernardi

v.le Jonio, 18 Z.I.
☎ (+39) 0995623273
❂ www.bernardinet.it
✉ bernardi@bernardinet.it
shop: no
e-commerce: yes

Easy to reach from the Taranto-Brindisi freeway junction, this producer features a large showroom where it's possible to buy an infinite variety of delicacies, all made using artisanal, yet modern, methods. Care is taken that the best ingredients are used and that quality is maintained during all the different stages of production. During winter the focus is on chocolate, pralines, chocolate liquors, nougat and pannetone. In the hotter months attention shifts to fruit jelly drops, sugared almonds and dragée. In any case, it's chocolate, in all its forms, that reigns supreme here.

Novi Ligure (AL)
Bodrato

s.da del Turchino, 41
☎ (+39) 0143468902
❂ www.bodratocioccolato.it
✉ info@bodratocioccolato.it
shop: yes
e-commerce: yes

A shrine for Piedmontese chocolate. All thanks to prime raw materials like cocoa mass from Africa and South America, and Langhe hazelnuts, processed with the hand of an artisan. The speciality here is the boero, with Vignola cherries heady with grappa made in local vineyards, dredged in sugar and chocolate. Equally worthy are the classic chocolate bars, the cremino, gianduiotto, chocolate-coated citrus peel, dragées, pralines and spreads. At Easter look out for chocolate eggs with classic and bespoke decoration.

Modica (RG)
Antica Dolceria Bonajuto

c.so Umberto I, 159
☎ (+39) 0932941225
❀ www.bonajuto.it
✉ info@bonajuto.it
shop: yes
e-commerce: yes

ANTICA DOLCERIA BONAJUTO

Modica chocolate is very special, with a pleasant mouthfeel left by the grainy texture typical of cold processing and lack of conching, a technique derived from the Aztec recipe. Sugar is added to the cocoa paste at about 36 degrees and no cocoa butter is used. A heritage chocolate with a style of its own and the Antica Dolceria Bonajuto, founded in 1880, is a loyal chocolatier working true to tradition. The range comes in different cocoa concentrations and is flavoured with cinnamon and vanilla. For Christmas, try classic Sicilian nougats.

Jesi (AN)
Il Cioccolato di BruCo

via Don Battistoni, 11
☎ (+39) 0731215649
❀ www.cioccolatodibruco.com
✉ info@cioccolatodibruco.com
shop: yes
e-commerce: yes

BruCo, from the initials of Bruna Gibellini and Costantino Tiranti who invented aniseed chocolate in the 1900s. After lengthy trials the recipe inspired the founding of the Jesi company in 2001. The chocolate bars, pralines and chocolate creations are made from the best criollo, trinitario and forastero aromatio cocoa from South America, flavoured with star anise, cinnamon, chilli, and vanilla, presented in attractive packaging.

San Marco dei Cavoti (BN)
Casa Autore

via Beviera, 64
☎ (+39) 0824984749
❀ www.casaautore.com
✉ info@casaautore.com
shop: no
e-commerce: yes

CIOCCOLATO ARTIGIANALE

San Marco dei Cavoti

This small manufacturer specializes in the production of 'croccantino', a local sweet. Here it is made according to an old, traditional recipe that calls for a delicious coat of dark chocolate. Over the years other variations have emerged, for example using coffee or honey and figs. There's also a rich assortment of pralines, in various flavors, and cookies with a soft filling of dried fruit and honey. There's even a beer (made possible by a partnership with the brewer Karma), flavored with cocoa and dark chocolate: a real treat!

Giaveno (TO)

Guido Castagna

via Torino, 54
☎ (+39) 0119766618 I 3288659305
⊕ www.guidocastagna.it
✉ info@guidocastagna.it
shop: yes
e-commerce: yes

From beans to bar. In Guido Castagna's case the effect is surprising as he runs a very small chocolate crafting outfit but his production is on a par with bigger businesses. He selects raw materials directly from plantations and purchases from certified cooperatives, with production chain traceability taking in the field, cocoa bean processing, toasting, conching, right to the finished product. All the products are excellent: chocolate bar, the spice and aromatic herb cremino and, best of all, gianduia hazelnut specialities from the gianduiotto to spreads.

Vicoforte (CN)

Le Delizie di Silvio Bessone

loc. Santuario I via F. Gallo, 19
☎ (+39) 0174563312
⊕ www.silviobessone.it
✉ info@silviobessone.it
shop: yes
e-commerce: yes

Silvio Bessone, chef and patisseur, had a dream. He wanted to be able to choose his own cocoa. So after he created his house of chocolate with its modern workshop, restaurant, Cioccolocanda inn, and museum, he went to Sao Tomé to select in person the plantations and the best bean varieties, which he toasts himself. Silvio has an outright chocolate production chain and his Delizie range includes Rosa and Oro gianduiotti; pralines; herb-flavoured Fuego; single-origin chocolate bars: from Sao Tomé to Venezuela, from Cuba to Grenada, from Ceylon to Papua.

Calenzano (FI)

Fonderia del Cacao

via delle Bartoline, 41
☎ (+39) 0558878480
⊕ www.fonderiadelcacao.it
✉ info@fonderiadelcacao.it
shop: no
e-commerce: no

F%

F%NDERIA DEL CACAO

Fonderia is a project that uses advanced technology to promote fine cocoa powder among consumers. To guarantee control of the bean-to-bar production process, the team of passionate entrepreneurs behind the company select the Fino de Aroma cocoa in Ecuador, within a Fair Trade context. The products are mainly monovarietal dark chocolate with different percentages of cocoa, but all tastes are catered for, with white and milk chocolate bars and napolitains, as well as flavoured creminos, spreads and dragées. 99% of production is organic.

Forlì

Gardini

fraz. Vecchiazzano zona artigianale, 7 I via E. Benini, 38
☎ (+39) 0543480375
❀ www.gardinicioccolato.it
✉ info@gardinicioccolato.it
shop: yes
e-commerce: no

Brothers Fabio and Manuele Gardini are famous in Italy and abroad for some special chocolate creations inspired by the flavours of Romagna. An explosive mix of creativity and innovation, combined with passion and dedication, bringing to life the Cioccolato e Profumi del Territorio line: chocolate made with mild Cervia salt; pralines with Fossa cheese, Brisighella olive oil, Modena balsamic vinegar or Cesena relish. Then there are savoury gianduia chocolate bars, sour cherry cremino, Sangiovese Passito cream, Albana Passito bonbons.

Leinì (TO)

Giordano

via Volpiano, 77
☎ (+39) 0119988380
❀ www.giordanocioccolato.it
✉ info@giordanocioccolato.it
shop: no
e-commerce: no

For more than a century, the Giordano brand has meant quality. Here tradition is as dominant as ever, with gianduiotti chocolates made entirely by hand: from cutting to wrapping. At Giordano you'll also find an impressive selection of pralines, various white chocolate offerings, chocolate Easter eggs that can be custom decorated, nougat (at Christmas), cream spreads, bars and much more.

Castellazzo Bormida (AL)

Giraudi

loc. Micarella I via B. Giraudi, 498
☎ (+39) 0131278472
❀ www.giraudi.it
✉ info@giraudi.it
shop: yes
e-commerce: yes

Creativity, craftsmanship and passion applied to chocolate. Opened in 1907 as a mill and bakery, over time becoming a patisserie and, in 2005, Giraudi was converted to a chocolate boutique, with adjoining workshop and café. Not to be missed are its mandrugnin, a liqueur chocolate similar to a cuneese with seven different fillings, and the giacometta gianduia cream spread in four options. Be sure to try the amazing chocolates; excellent bars that include some single origins; gianduiotto; classic napolitain; cremino; nugatelli and dragées.

Torino
Guido Gobino

via Cagliari, 15b
☎ (+39) 0112476245
🕸 www.guidogobino.it
✉ info@guidogobino.it
shop: yes
e-commerce: no

Guido Gobino is a cult name for Italian chocolate. He makes many products with the black nectar but his name is linked above all to the tourinot, a miniaturized version of the gianduiotto, a gourmet morsel that swathes the palate like a caress. The dark and milk chocolate are excellent as are the chocolate eggs, spreads, pralines, and many themed creations. He uses premium raw materials, ranging from Piedmont PGI hazelnuts to chocolate made directly from the cocoa bean.

Maglie (LE)
Maglio

via V. Zara, 2 zona PIP
☎ (+39) 0836427444
🕸 www.cioccolatomaglio.it
✉ info@cioccolatomaglio.it
shop: no
e-commerce: yes

Cioccolato Italiano dal 1875

The long-established Salento company Maglio has 140 years of honourable service to its name and offers an extensive assortment of products made from chocolate including its Origine, mini sampling bars. But also cream-filled chocolates; bonbons; truffles; almond and hazelnut chocolates; cremino slabs for slicing; spreads; delicious candied fruit or dried figs stuffed with almonds, with chocolate coating, produced in house. All made with an artisan's skill, a careful selection of raw materials and premium cocoa mass.

Quarrata (PT)
La Molina

via Bologna, 21
☎ (+39) 0573774379
🕸 www.lamolina.it
✉ info@lamolina.it
shop: yes
e-commerce: yes

CIOCCOLATO
LA MOLINA

Behind La Molina is the passion for the arts, including the art of the 'delicious'. This has given life to a range of premium chocolates, which impress from the outset thanks to sophisticated packaging and original design. Pralines, bars, creamy spreads, chocolate eggs (in glass jars)... Their whole selection is made possible thanks to premium ingredients, creativity and an ethic that rejects artificial conservatives, colors and flavors.

Padova

Racca

via P.F. Calvi, 8
☎ (+39) 0498759855
◉ www.pasticceriaracca.com
✉ info@coutureraccachocolate.com
shop: yes
e-commerce: no

Monica Lazzarini, art director, and Gianni Zaghetto, maître chocolatier, create chocolate delights with passion, artistic flair and a spirit of innovation. They started life as patisseurs in 1990 and extended a classical repertoire of desserts and wedding cake a few years ago by adding chocolate with a strong creative twist. They offer about 50 kinds of pralines: cream-based French style; traditional Italian with nuts and liqueurs; inspired by contemporary art; and fusion range in which chocolate meets and patisserie. All made with excellent raw materials.

Modica (RG)

Sabadì

via Resistenza Partigiana, 124
☎ (+39) 0932906638
◉ www.sabadi.it
✉ info@sabadi.it
shop: yes
e-commerce: yes

Sabadì was founded by Simone Sabaini, an entrepreneur from Verona, in 2011. They make top-quality Modican chocolate using only organic ingredients that are worked slowly and in a low-temperature environment so as to stabilize the properties of the cocoa. Their selection includes a line of milk chocolates (the 'latte' varieties), more experimental varieties ('funzionali', with seeds, root extracts and spices), raw chocolate '('Crude'), the neapolitan 'Sicula Terra', sweet chocolate ('Zuccheri'), nougat and handmade candies. Their shop address is 105 Corso San Giorgio.

Monsummano Terme (PT)

Slitti

via Francesca Sud, 1268
☎ (+39) 0572640240
◉ www.slitti.com
✉ info@slitti.it
shop: yes
e-commerce: no

Andrea Slitti is a renowned artisan on the new Tuscan chocolate-making scenario. Everything is superlative quality, from the simple single-origin cocoa bars to tasty spreads, blocks, Ferri Vecchi chocolate tools, and Slitti's exclusive own invention LatteNero, a very chocolatey LatteNero milk chocolate. All of excellent quality that starts with the cocoa bean using cutting-edge machinery, consistent with the style and rigour of one of Italy's most reliable maîtres chocolatiers.

Chocolate

Milano
T'a Sentimento Italiano

via Tortona, 37
☎ (+39) 0297375919
❀ www.tamilano.com
✉ info@tamilano.com
shop: yes
e-commerce: yes

SENTIMENTO ITALIANO
CIOCCOLATO HAND MADE
TANCREDI E ALBERTO ALEMAGNA - MILANO

With T'a Sentimento Italiano handmade chocolate the Alemagna siblings provide an example of how passion for beauty can make something totally delicious. This iconic Italian family in the confectionery field produce a wide range of specialties in its Cerro Maggiore (Milan) plant: chocolate bars, chocolates, dragées, pralines, mini truffles, spreads and napolitains, which come in tasty, fragrant variants. Like the 100% Frutta on-the-go line of sweets, with the power of chocolate enfolding a centre in various fruity flavours.

Firenze
TortaPistocchi

via del Ponte di Mezzo, 20
☎ (+39) 0550516939
❀ www.tortapistocchi.it
✉ info@tortapistocchi.it
shop: yes
e-commerce: no

TORTAPISTOCCHI®
FIRENZE

Siblings Claudio and Claudia Pistocchi are famous for the cake named after them: an artisanal large, soft handcrafted chocolate bonbon made only with dark chocolate, dark cocoa powder and a little cream. No sugar, eggs, butter, flour or preservatives. To die for and invented by Claudio in 1990, with the classic version now flanked with chilli, sour cherry, Sicilian citrus, coffee, pear, strawberry, white chocolate and orange peel variants. There is also the exotic Torta Elisa cake and other sweet temptations.

Scandicci (FI)
Urzi

via V. Monti, 14a
☎ (+39) 055253739
❀ www.urzicioccolato.com
✉ urzi@interfree.it
shop: yes
e-commerce: no

Urzi
Lavorazione artigianale
Ciocc lato

For over ten years Francesco Montrone, owner of Bar Urzi, a gourmanderie at the gates of Florence, has been devoted to fine chocolate. As well as the best Venezuelan cocoa crus, his shop works with excellent ingredients: Piemonte PGI hazelnuts, Amalfi lemons, Slow Food Presidium Toritto almonds, Bronte pistachios, Cervia salt. The results? Sophisticated and delicious blends and textures: classic and flavoured bars, dragées, pastilles, spreads and soluble blends, as well as hot, mouthfilling hot chocolate.

Arezzo

Vestri

via Romana, 161a
☎ (+39) 0575907315
🌣 www.vestri.it
✉ info@vestri.it
shop: yes
e-commerce: no

The Vestri family have been operating since 1960, and now that they have their own cocoa plantation in Santo Dominingo, they can boast carrying out every stage of production with care. The variety of chocolates they offer seems limitless, from classic bars to pralines of every type, to experimental pairings with spices. During spring and summer you can also enjoy delicious artisanal ice cream made only with natural ingredients. At Easter you can find various types of chocolate eggs. They also have a shop in Florence.

Chocolate

Napoli
Anhelo Caffè

via G. Martucci, 27
☎ (+39) 3357226405
🖝 www.anhelo.it
✉ lucaferrari@anhelo.it
shop: yes
e-commerce: no

The Anhelo coffee blend quickly made its name with coffee connoisseurs both in Naples and farther afield. Made with the finest Arabica coffees from Central America and Brazil, and a percentage of Robusta from Indian and Ethiopian plantations, all roasted separately, it is sold in various sizes, including retail packs for home use. As well as its coffee, Anhelo is also known for an excellent selection of around 30 teas and tisanes, mostly organic and sold to small niche businesses. Cups, machines and other accessories also available.

Milano
L'Arte di Offrire il Thè

via M. Melloni, 35
☎ (+39) 027154421 022829753
🖝 www.artedelricevere.com
✉ artedelricevere@ar-tea.it
shop: yes
e-commerce: yes

This elegant shop and tea bar is owned by Francesca Natali, the author of a number of books on the subject. She has been in business for over ten years and her aim is to promote the culture of tea drinking. Francesca has also created some original packaging, unusual cocktails and unique blends. The shop sells around 250 types of tea, including organic and fair-trade, black, smoked, post-fermented, green, white, yellow, oolong, Darjeeling, contemplation, tisanes, rooibos and many more varieties. Accessories are also available.

Montegranaro (FM)
Caffè del Faro

c.da Guazzetti
☎ (+39) 0734889283
🖝 www.caffedelfaro.com
✉ caffe@caffedelfaro.com
shop: yes
e-commerce: no

Montegranaro is a major shoe production town, but over recent years it has also become home to another kind of business, set up by three young siblings who decided to select and produce quality coffee using highly automated procedures. The products range from Suprema 100% Arabica to decaffeinated, available for home use, in pods, and for businesses. Captivating modern packaging has been developed for each product, along with a variety of promotional items like cups, sugar, T-shirts and grinders.

Castel Goffredo (MN)
Ferri dal 1905

c.da Romanini, 111
☎ (+39) 0376779436
❀ www.ferridal1905.com
✉ info@ferridal1905.com
shop: no
e-commerce: no

Established over 100 years ago, this company has specialized in selecting and processing quality dried vegetables over the years. It produces a wide variety of teas, infusions, spices and fruit, as well as salt, sugar, pulses, but also accessories like mugs, kettles, strainers, and pepper mills. The products infused with prized Japanese Matcha tea, dried and stone milled are well worth a try, particularly its exclusive Matcha Cappuccino. All the raw ingredients are carefully selected and products are packaged by hand.

Pistoia
Espresso Giada

l.go Molinuzzo, 9
☎ (+39) 0573904596
❀ www.espressogiada.it
✉ info@espressogiada.it
shop: yes
e-commerce: no

This Pistoia-based firm roasts its coffee beans slowly so as to cook them evenly and preserve their sensorial properties. Its markets three different lines, ranging from single-origin blends sourced in Indonesia, El Salvador, Kenya, Ethiopia, Guatemala, Cuba, India, to its Eccellenza line, also single origin (including Jamaica Blue Mountain), and a variety of blends (including 100% Arabica and decaffeinated), as well as its barley coffee, also available with ginseng.

Verona
Giamaica Caffè

via V. Merighi , 5
☎ (+39) 045 569499
✉ info@ltgc.it
shop: no
e-commerce: no

Established in 1947, Torrefazione Giamaica has preserved its artisanal direct-flame roasting process over the generations. Using machinery from the 1950s, no longer available on the market, it processes 60 kilos of beans at a time and takes exactly quarter of an hour, otherwise the coffee alters and loses its special traits. The beans are then left to cool and rest for 48 hours, after which they need to be consumed relatively quickly. This coffee, available in around ten different varieties, is only available to a select clientele.

Coffee, tea, infusions

Ivrea (TO)

Caffè Giordano 1938

via Burolo, 22
☎ (+39) 0125617626
🌐 www.giordano1938.it
✉ giordano@giordano1938.it
shop: no
e-commerce: no

Over the course of several decades, Attilio Bottola's company has selected coffee from plantations in around 80 countries worldwide, producing premium coffees, including single-origin varieties, grand crus and blends, to suit a range of tastes. It focuses particularly on small-scale plantations to help safeguard biodiversity, and produces around a dozen single-origin coffees, from Brazil, Santo Domingo, India, Nepal and Guatemala, as well as five blends and a gourmet line.

Preganziol (TV)

Goppion

s.da Terraglio, 48
☎ (+39) 0422490921
🌐 www.goppioncaffe.it
✉ info@goppioncaffe.it
shop: no
e-commerce: yes

The story of Goppion goes all the way back to 1859, with roots that are artisanal to the core. It's a family story, and a lovely one at that. Today, with the fifth generation in charge, Goppion has been transformed into a full-blown industry, but it still hasn't lost its rigorous attention to quality, starting with identifying the best varieties of coffee in the most prominent territories (foremost Africa and South America) and the meticulous production of different types of coffee. In addition to supplying cafés and offices, they have coffee for home brewing and plenty of gift ideas... all of the highest quality.

Arzano (NA)

Kenon L'Oro di Napoli

s.da privata F. Graziano, 16
☎ (+39) 0817313965
🌐 www.kenon.it
✉ info@kenon.it
shop: no
e-commerce: no

At Kennon, coffee is chosen with an almost obsessive attention to detail, and only the top beans are taken into consideration. With more than 100 years of experience (it was founded in 1892), it's not surprising that this family-run business is pretty much unstoppable. They have coffee for every type of need, supplying cafés or for home brewing, with quality always a top priority. They also offer a line of coffee pods, great for use in the office or in restaurants.

Bologna
Caffè Lelli

via del Mobiliere, 1 zona Roveri
☎ (+39) 051531608
❀ www.caffelelli.com
✉ info@caffelelli.com
shop: no
e-commerce: yes

Leonardo Lelli, a true coffee connoisseur, set up his business to source the finest coffees. He only procures prize, hand-harvested and wet-processed coffees, each with a different aroma and each suited to different times of day, selling three different lines: seven 100% single-origin Assolo varieties selected worldwide; two fine Assolo Grand Cru varieties; and four Concerto varieties, special blends of different percentages of Arabica and Robusta coffee. Products can be purchased online at www.ilpiaceredelcaffe.it

Modica (RG)
Caffè Moak

v.le delle Industrie
☎ (+39) 0932904755
❀ www.caffemoak.com
✉ info@caffemoak.com
shop: no
e-commerce: yes

Started 50 years ago by Giovanni Spadola, Caffé Moak boasts a 10,000 square meter facility with state of the art systems. From harvest to processing the beans, every step is carried out with the utmost care so as to guarantee a standard of quality that is consistent and consistently high. Their efforts have earned them certifications as organic and kosher (and not only). They offer a variety of blends, all presented in sophisticated packing, for every occasion, from commercial grinds for cafés to home brews.

Faenza (RA)
Mokador

via Granarolo, 139
☎ (+39) 054628332
❀ www.mokador.it
✉ mokador@mokador.it
shop: no
e-commerce: yes

Mokador, founded in 1967, has undergone a number of changes over the last 50 years and is now one of Italy's most consistent players in the field of coffee production. Today, under the Castellari family, who purchased the Sacao and Caffé Gualtieri brands, the business continues to seek out ways to provide consumers with products that meet their expectations. Thanks to their innovative pods, their blends can be enjoyed in cafés, in the home and office. They have other products as well, like the intriguing coffee beer.

Borgo San Lorenzo (FI)
Mokarico

loc. La Torre I via del Bagnone, 24
☎ (+39) 0558495085
⊕ www.mokarico.com
✉ info@mokarico.com
shop: no
e-commerce: no

The history of the brand dates back to the 1930s when La casa del Caffè, founded in the early 20th century in Florence, was taken over by the Paladini family. Today the company head office can be found in the Mugello countryside, just outside Borgo San Lorenzo. The coffee beans are selected from the best growing areas: Brazil, Colombia, India, Indonesia. The roasting process is carefully monitored to guarantee the tempting aromas and unique features in the various blends of arabica, noir and mild coffees.

Monteprandone (AP)
Orlandi Passion

loc. Centobuchi I via del Terziario, Seconda Traversa, 6
☎ (+39) 0735655142 I 0735656024
⊕ www.orlandipassion.com
✉ info@orlandipassion.com
shop: yes
e-commerce: no

Orlandi Passion is a temple of many good things, split into three departments: coffee roasting, chocolate and biscuits, although the coffee is the core business. Mauro Cipolla, who has plenty of experience in the art of roasting coffee and exporting to the USA, produces various blends in a very modern plant. The blends for moka pot or pod coffeemakers are made with select arabica beans. The same care is taken over the creation of chocolate and biscuits inspired by old regional recipes. The spreads are excellent.

Roma
Paranà

via Portuense, 351b
☎ (+39) 0655389505
⊕ www.caffeparana.it
✉ info@caffeparana.it
shop: no
e-commerce: no

The coffee-roasting business started in the 1960s, when Ruggero Giannelli began selling raw coffee beans. Today the company is still run by the family but has moved forward and developed to garner well-earned success. It sells coffee blends and monovarietal coffees in Italy and abroad, selecting beans from the best production districts. Apart from the classics, Paranà offers decaffeinated arabica and an organic blend with Fairtrade certification.

Monte Cerignone (PU)
Pascucci

via Circonvallazione, 16a
☎ (+39) 0546978524
❀ www.pascucci.it
✉ info@pascucci.it
shop: no
e-commerce: yes

From the outset, this historic family-run business chose to make respect for the environment, a commitment to quality and a willingness to innovate the pillars of its philosophy. The effort has paid off, with results that are the envy of the field. Their coffee blends are the cornerstone of their product line, all made using carefully selected beans (especially organic) and with skillful, proven methods. There are also teas, herbal infusions and drinks, in addition to accessories that have been realized specifically so as to make coffee consumption more enjoyable.

Torino
Pausa Café

via A. Aglietta, 35
☎ (+39) 3355905537 I 01119714278
❀ www.pausacafe.org
✉ info@pausacafe.org
shop: no
e-commerce: no

The Pausa Café social cooperative was founded in 2004 with the objective of employing disadvantaged people and promoting fair and sustainable social and economic development. Its slow, artisanal roasting over wood enhances the properties of the coffee, purchased directly from the producers. Pure coffee comes from Huehuetenango (Guatemala) and Terre Alte; a blend of coffee from Sierra Cafetalera (Santo Domingo) and Huehuetenango, both Slow Food Presidia.

Altidona (FM)
Perfero

loc. Marina di Altidona I via Piave, 5 zona artigianale
☎ (+39) 3496889186 I 3282713391
❀ www.perferocaffe.it
✉ info@perferocaffe.it
shop: yes
e-commerce: no

Simone Meriggi and Daniele Pioppi's business venture began five years ago. They start by selecting only the finest raw ingredients, focusing on organic or fair-trade products. La Perfero produces coffee beans, ground coffee and organic pods). Customers can choose from a variety of blends, from Unica (100% Arabica) to Mild (75% Arabica and 25% Robusta), and speciality coffees (single-origin coffees from top-quality beans). The range is completed by the two Slow Food Presidia, Guatemala Huehuetenango and Ethiopia Harenna Wild Forest.

Coffee, tea, infusions

Bagno a Ripoli (FI)
Piansa

loc. Ponte a Ema I via A. Meucci, 1
☎ (+39) 055645774
🖫 www.caffepiansa.com
✉ torrefazione@caffepiansa.com
shop: yes
e-commerce: no

www.caffepiansa.com

Pietro Staderini opened his coffee-roasting business in 1976 because he was un-happy with coffee on offer and wanted to give his customers something better. He only works with premium varieties, from the world's best coffee-growing countries like El Salvador, Ethiopia, Costa Rica, Kenya, Cuba, Brazil, Honduras and Guate-mala. The beans are toasted using artisanal methods to product top-quality blends. The range includes organic coffee from Nicaragua and rare coffees from Puerto Rico and Hawaii. Pietro's son Alessandro works with him, following in his father's footsteps to maintain high production standards.

Livorno
Le Piantagioni del Caffè

via Provinciale Pisana, 583b
☎ (+39) 0586429094
🖫 www.lepiantagionidelcaffe.com
✉ office@lepiantagionidelcaffe.it
shop: yes
e-commerce: no

LE PIANTAGIONI
DEL CAFFÈ

This company has been selecting prized coffees for over ten years, supervising the entire production process from picking the different varieties to planting, har-vesting, drying, and roasting, the latter using traditional methods. It sells 12 dif-ferent types, including decaffeinated and the following single-plantation coffees: Harenna, Ethiopia, Slow Food Speciality, 100% Arabica; San Luis, El Salvador, 100% Arabica; Yrgalem, Ethiopia, 100% Arabica; Lagoa do Morro, Brazil, 100% Arabica; Alto Palomar, organic, 100% Arabica, Peru.

Signa (FI)
La Tosteria

via P. Gobetti, 9
☎ (+39) 055876669
🖫 www.latosteria.it
✉ info@latosteria.it
shop: no
e-commerce: no

laTOSTERIA

This firm has always focused on sourcing top quality products, as well as promoting culture and raising awareness, not just for its flagship product of coffee, but also teas, tisanes, infusions, herbs and spices. Its 16 coffee varieties are strictly select-ed from the best plantations, where the growing and harvesting methods are care-fully monitored. The beans are slow roasted before making the different blends.

Buti (PI)
Trinci

fraz. Cascine I via Olanda, 18
☎ (+39) 0587722026
❀ www.impressioni.it
✉ info@impressioni.it
shop: yes
e-commerce: no

Ercole Trinci established his Florence coffee-roasting business in 1939 but it was his son Andrea, still at the helm today with sister Chiara, who developed it and despite ups and downs, expanded into other fields, including wine and chocolate, developed it further and expanded. Its partnership with Slow Food grew thanks to its work with two prize blends, Impressioni, made from Slow Food Presidium coffees, and later with the production of small and large milk and dark chocolate bars, as well as some flavoured with San Rossore honey, chilli and vanilla.

Melle (CN)
Valverbe

via Prato, 9
☎ (+39) 0175978276
❀ www.valverbe.it
✉ valverbe@valverbe.it
shop: yes
e-commerce: no

This firm was founded 30 years ago in the heart of the unspoilt Valle Varaita, at 1500 metres above sea level. Here it grows, dries and processes organic medicinal plants. Freshly harvested herbs are washed, cleansed of bacteria, ground, mixed and then packaged in filters. Apart from the fruits of the forest and the wellbeing line, there are also digestive, draining and relaxing tisanes. Also available, herbs for cooking, infusions, teas (some aromatized) and much more.

Impruneta (FI)
La Via del Tè

loc. Cascine del Riccio I via Ponte a Iozzi, 8/1
☎ (+39) 0552094076
❀ www.laviadelte.it
✉ snak@laviadelte.it
shop: no
e-commerce: yes

Alfredo Carrai, a great tea enthusiast and a pioneering traveller to the East, set up this company over 50 years ago although todays' brand dates back to the early 1980s. His aim was to introduce the Italian public to all the properties of this noble beverage by importing directly top versions of different varieties. Most of the teas are grown in China, India, Kenya and Sri Lanka, followed by South America and Africa. The range includes green, black, oolong, white and pu-erh teas, alongside blends and aromatized varieties, so you will be spoilt for choice.

Scicli (RG)
Gli Aromi di Russino

loc. Cava d'Aliga I c.da Santa Rosalia
☎ (+39) 3478169770 I 3420616781
❁ www.gliaromi.it
✉ info@gliaromi.it
shop: yes
e-commerce: yes

Enrico Russino's firm is based in the Ragusa countryside, just inland from the coast. It markets typical herbs and spices from Sicily and further afield, both in pots and cut. Capers are its key product and are also sold as an ornamental plant. Enrico also produces oregano, thyme, sage, basil and a selection of exotic plants. Visitors are welcome if they call first to go over and breathe in the flavour and fragrance of all his wonderful leaves, mouth-watering sauces he makes with them, and other typically Sicilian ingredients.

Margherita di Savoia (BT)
Atisale

c.so Vittorio Emanuele, 90
☎ (+39) 0883871000
❁ www.atisale.com
✉ atisale@atisale.com
shop: no
e-commerce: no

solo sale italiano

The company has been managing salt flats in various Italian regions (Puglia, Sardinia, Tuscany) since 1994, primarily extracting two types of salt: sea and rock. Its table salt ranges from the ultrafine, from Volterra's underground deposits, to whole Sardinia salt, healthy iodized and diet salt, and salt mixed with spices, ideal for adding a touch of flavour to meats and roasts. There is also a "chef's" line of pure salt crystals.

Castiglione della Pescaia (GR)
Il Boschetto

loc. Porta a Colle
☎ (+39) 0564944311
❁ www.ilboschetto.net
✉ info@ilboschetto.net
shop: yes
e-commerce: yes

il Boschetto®
Maremma Toscana -Italy

Situated in the heart of Maremma, this model company boasts a number of different brands. It produces and markets top-quality extra virgin olive oil, also available in versions flavoured with aromatic herbs or spices, as well as salt, pepper, must, and vinegar developed to season various dishes, from simple salads to soups, meats, fish and more. The firm focuses heavily on the packaging and design of its various bottles and grinders, which have proved a hit in prestigious shop windows across Italy and abroad.

Navelli (AQ)
Casa Verde

loc. Civitaretenga I v.le Umberto I, 9
☎ (+39) 0862959163
🖉 www.casaverdesarra.it
✉ paoletti.dina@libero.it
shop: yes
e-commerce: yes

This agritourism can be found between Gran Sasso and Majella. It has been run for many years by Salvatore Silvio Sarra and his sister Giovannina. There could be no better destination for those wanting to discover the natural beauty and scenery of an area still off the beaten track. Accommodation in quiet, comfortable rooms, with genuine local cuisine, but above all the tasty PDO saffron pistils, the main local product and considered to be one of the best in the world.

Pontecagnano Faiano (SA)
Elody

via Mar Mediterraneo, 18
☎ (+39) 089848322
🖉 www.elody.it
✉ info@elody.it
shop: yes
e-commerce: yes

Since the early 1900s, this company has produced and marketed aromatic herbs, grown in lovely pots in greenhouses on its Piana del Sele farmlands. As well as standard parsley and basil, we also find sage, rosemary, thyme, marjoram, dill, and more. There is also an extensive selection of semi-dried herbs, losing none of their fragrance and flavours. Quality is guaranteed by the short supply chain, with strict controls in place to ensure seeds are non-GMO and untreated, and irrigation water is monitored.

Pianfei (CN)
Erbe di Montagna

via Blangetti, 29
☎ (+39) 0174585433 I 3392387240
🖉 www.erbedimontagna.it
✉ info@erbedimontagna.it
shop: yes
e-commerce: yes

This family-run company based in a historic farmhouse at the foot of the Maritime Alps painstakingly selects its raw ingredients and works methodically, focusing on the use of clean energy. It uses skill and imagination to produce, blend and process aromatic and medicinal herbs; spices like saffron, pepper; salt; sugar; teas and tisanes; honey; rice and, more recently, gluten-free flours and seaweed-based items.

Condiments: salt, spices, herbs

Sulmona (AQ)
Garzisi

v.le delle Metamorfosi, 9
☎ (+39) 3488535039
❀ www.garzisi.com
✉ info@garzisi.com
shop: yes
e-commerce: yes

A young company, run by an equally young entrepreneur, Giulio Garzisi, who built his business on the concept of one prime product: saffron. The crop is grown on two plots, one in Gagliano Aterno and one in Sulmona. Nothing has been left to chance, including packaging, with each pack containing a pot of pistils, a pair of pincers and a mortar to crush the spice before use. Giulio also produces delicious pear and saffron jam and saffron honey.

Gergei (CA)
Gourmet Sardegna

via Municipio, 16
☎ (+39) 070242020
❀ www.gourmetsardegna.it
✉ info.gourmetsardegna@gmail.com
shop: yes
e-commerce: no

Andrea and Jessica set up their company in 2010 to produce and market whole fleur de sel, hand-raked from the Conti Vecchi salt flats in Cagliari, in Parco Naturale di Santa Gilla, then processed with natural ingredients free from chemical additives. The classic version is flanked by various flavoured and smoked options, as well as versions with spices, pepper with a balanced hot note, and wine. There is also an organic line with Sardinian herbs, saffron, citrus and myrtle.

Marsala (TP)
Saline Ettore Infersa

c.da Ettore Infersa
☎ (+39) 0923733003
❀ www.salineettoreinfersa.com
✉ info@salineettoreinfersa.com
shop: yes
e-commerce: yes

Saline Ettore Infersa's enviable surroundings make it well worth a visit. The magical natural setting is the Stagnone lagoon, opposite the islet of Mozia, where three ancient salt-grinding windmills loom on the horizon. Its products are genuinely outstanding and include crystals, flakes, and wisps. Some of the aromatized salt is used to add marvellous flavour all kinds of food. The company also sells original jewellery made from salt, and other crafts. Visitors can stay in its charming B&B.

Villarbasse (TO)
Il Mercante di Spezie

via Rivoli, 84
☎ (+39) 0112428095
❀ www.ilmercantedispezie.com
✉ info@ilmercantedispezie.com
shop: no
e-commerce: yes

Il Mercante di Spezie®

This company is driven by its passion and focus on quality, which have led it to develop a thorough knowledge of the world of spices, researching its culture, and progressing constantly towards new horizons. Every step is subject to strict controls, starting with the spice plantations. There are 20 or more products, featuring ginger, vanilla, saffron, aniseed, cinnamon, cardamom, fennel, aromatic herbs and others. An incredible world of fragrance, sensations, and colour. Fit also sells fleur de sel.

Roccafluvione (AP)
Mario Mercuri

loc. Ponte Paoletti I via Teverito, 80
☎ (+39) 3393342897
❀ www.zafferanopuroinfili.it
✉ zafferanopuroinfili@gmail.com
shop: no
e-commerce: no

In 2004 Mario Mercuri started growing saffron with a very clear idea in mind: an intensive focus on crops and small-scale production to guarantee a premium product. The plants flower in October and are harvested during the same month, strictly at dawn and by hand, so as to gather the pistils without breaking them. The saffron is then dried on a rack over wood embers. In addition to saffron, he also produces honey, liqueur, pasta, biscuits and sauces, all flavoured with the precious spice.

Paceco (TP)
Oro di Sicilia

loc. Nubia I via Garibaldi, 46a
☎ (+39) 0923867374
❀ www.salineculcasi.it
✉ info@salineculcasi.it
shop: yes
e-commerce: yes

Riserva del Mare®

Only pure and natural sea salt processed using traditional artisanal techniques, which has not undergone any chemical treatment. Rich in iodine, potassium and magnesium, its health-giving properties are unaltered. The sodium percentage is low and salting power is high, so that only a small quantity is needed. Available in various formats and sizes: coarse, fine, crystals, fleur de sel, and as slabs, used for special cooking processes. The partners in the firm include the curators of the interesting salt museum.

Bibbona (LI)
Peperita

loc. Calcinaiola Podere I Doccioni
☎ (+39) 3936209346
❀ www.peperita.it
✉ info@peperita.it
shop: yes
e-commerce: yes

Rita Salvatori's farm grows around 40 varieties of organic and biodynamic chillies, used to make Peperita-branded specialities for consumers and chefs. Products include chilli powder in glass vials, varying in strength from 1 to 16, from delicate aji chillies and banana peppers to fiery Seven Pods and Trinidad Scorpions; pastes; chopped chillies; flavoured oils; Cayenne pepper flakes; cider vinegar; condiments and flavourings. It also produces fruit relish, jams and preserves, and red-hot sweet creams.

San Vito dei Normanni (BR)
Sale della Vita – Tecnitron

via San Domenico, 53
☎ (+39) 0831982136
❀ www.saledellavita.com
✉ info@saledellavita.com
shop: yes
e-commerce: yes

One of the first companies in Europe to import top-quality salt from all over the world and offers a range of excellent products intended for true connoisseurs. From Hawaii's iron-rich salt to one flavoured with cuttlefish ink, a subtle Australian salt, and Danish salt smoked over oak and holm wood, each for different uses and recipes but not just for haute cuisine. Its products also include salt blocks for grating and "humidifying" boxes to keep the salt in perfect condition.

Cervia (RA)
Sale di Cervia

via Salara, 6
☎ (+39) 0544971765
❀ www.salinadicervia.it
✉ info@salinadicervia.it
shop: yes
e-commerce: yes

Salt production has boosted the economy in this part of the province of Ravenna, set back from the sea, ever since Roman times. After years of neglect, Cervia municipal council stepped in to manage the salt flats, an area that has acquired international importance for its natural features and landscape. It has now become part of Parco Regionale Delta del Po Emilia Romagna. Salt is harvested in basin number 89, called Saline Camillone, from June to September, using a traditional manual method to prevent the formation of "bitter salt".

Almese (TO)

Sali dal mondo

via Rocciamelone, 15
☎ (+39) 01119887326
✆ www.salidalmondo.it
✉ info@salidalmondo.it
shop: yes
e-commerce: no

The result of meticulous research conducted in the best salt flats around, this firm's salt selection is of the very highest standard. Customers are spoilt for choice, and the range is a gourmet feast for the eyes and palate. The salt flakes and tiny crystals come from Cyprus, Bali, Iran, Hawaii, the Himalayas, Peru, and the Algarve. Beech-smoked whole salt with its unique aroma is also available. Cooking with salt like this adds that extra something special to any dish.

Sermoneta (LT)

Simposio Gastronomia Storica Sermonetana

via della Conduttura, 2
☎ (+39) 3392846905
✆ www.simposio.it
✉ simposio.sermoneta@gmail.com
shop: yes
e-commerce: yes

The company specializes in processing and preserving excellent products, mainly from the Lepini hills. So it is no coincidence that the delicatessen has become a draw for gourmets looking for delicious treats of all kinds, from jams to wine, honey and vegetables in EVOO. A series of traditional products are on offer, prepared according to Simposio recipes like sauce made from a native Sermoneta lemon called trombolotto, Terracina anchovies marinated in trombolotto, Ciceroniana olive pâté and mullet bottarga flavoured with Armagnac.

Trapani

Sosalt

Molo Ronciglio
☎ (+39) 0923540344
✆ www.sosalt.it
✉ info@sosalt.it
shop: yes
e-commerce: yes

Founded in the early 1920s, this company has always focused on cultivating and harvesting salt in the Trapani salt flats. Its product acquired PGI designation a few years ago. The salt flats extend over a stretch of coast that is over 20 kilometres long. The salt here is incredibly pure and packed with beneficial trace elements such as calcium, magnesium, potassium, fluoride and iodine. The range also includes flavoured and iodized types.

Milano
Tutte le spezie del mondo

via Vittoria Colonna, 11
☎ (+39) 0239448065 I 3471500813
❀ www.tuttelespeziedelmondo.it
✉ info@tuttelespeziedelmondo.it
shop: yes
e-commerce: yes

After years of research, study and travel around the world, in 2013 Francesca Giorgetti opened a shop in Milan and an e-commerce site, for selling spices, preferably organic, imported directly from the production area. Hundreds of spices and aromatic herbs, curry, mixed spice and flavoured salts, with over 20 types of pepper, 50 of chili pepper, 40 kinds of tea, infusions and rooibos, liqueur products, flowers and natural colourings. Beautiful gift packs.

Belmonte Calabro (CS)
Nicola Colavolpe

p.le N. Colavolpe
☎ (+39) 098247017
✪ colavolpe.com
✉ info@colavolpe.com
shop: yes
e-commerce: yes

More than a century of history behind this family company, rightly considered among the best in the industry for processing figs, which are certainly the main product. In recent years new lines have been developed, however, all of exceptional standard. The range includes cross-shaped crocette, bow-shaped nocchette, and fig garlands; figs stuffed with walnuts and citrus peel, top-quality chestnut, fig, apple and liquorice, elderberry, bitter orange and bergamot jam and marmalades. The company also sells wine, and vegetables in oil, but not under their own label.

Montalto Uffugo (CS)
La Cosentina

via Camigliatello zona industriale
☎ (+39) 0984934728
✪ www.lacosentina.com
✉ info@lacosentina.com
shop: no
e-commerce: yes

Typical, top-quality sun-dried Calabria figs, also in classic options, with almonds and dipped in chocolate. The company uses cannizze cane trays to dry the dottato figs provided by small local farms. Also available are sun-dried tomatoes, jars and sachets of aromatic herbs and spices, above all chilli and fragrant oregano, but there is no lack of pepper, rosemary, sage, bay leaf, basil, onion, meat seasonings, garlic, parsley, fennel and mint.

Gallese (VT)
Deanocciola

loc. La Valle
☎ (+39) 0761405760
✪ www.deanocciola.com
✉ info@deanocciola.com
shop: no
e-commerce: no

Here in northern Lazio the area is perfect for cultivation of Tonda Gentile Romana hazelnuts and, in 1998, the De Angelis family began to produce spreads using this nut and ingredients provided by organic farming. Over time, the company has specialized in the production of spreads in general, especially for consumers with gluten and lactose intolerance. Apart from hazelnut, there are also peanut, almond, pumpkin seed, sunflower seed, and even light and dark tahini, made from sesame seeds.

San Michele Salentino (BR)
Feudo di San Giacomo

via L. Galvani, 6
☎ (+39) 0831964969
✆ www.feudosangiacomo.it
✉ info@feudosangiacomo.it
shop: yes
e-commerce: yes

In the 1940s, the company now run by three generations of the Barletta family, began producing olive oil. In addition to the virgin and extra virgin olive oil and Primitivo wine, Feudo di San Giacomo has gained a well-deserved reputation for processing and preserving white dottato figs, a variety prevalent in southern Italy. From cultivation to harvesting and drying, every stage is monitored with attention. Both the sun-dried almond-stuffed figs and the more tempting version dipped in milk or dark chocolate are excellent.

Montalto Uffugo (CS)
Garritano 1908

c.da Pianette
☎ (+39) 0984939154
✆ www.garritano1908.com
✉ info@garritano1908.com
shop: yes
e-commerce: yes

Now in its fourth generation, this family company specializes in processing PDO dottato figs, a Slow Food Presidium, using artisanal methods that are virtually unchanged from day one to the present. The product list also includes sun-dried figs stuffed with almonds or walnuts, in braided trecce and treccioni, cross-shaped crocette, in round palloni. Not to mention figs in honey, in jam, chocolate-coated, in rum, in Cointreau; chocolate-coated candied peel; chocolates filled with chilli, liquorice, citrus fruits; liquorice, chilli, chocolate, citrus fruit liqueurs; and lots of other treats.

Noto (SR)
Consorzio Produttori
Mandorle di Noto

via XX Settembre, 119
☎ (+39) 0931836893
✉ consorziomandorla@gmail.com
shop: no
e-commerce: no

The consortium brings together several almond growers to ensure that these nuts, a Slow Food Presidium, are sold directly to them. There are three local varieties: Romana, Pizzuta d'Avola and Fascionello. The first gives the best fruit from the sensorial perspective, but is less appreciated by the market for its irregular, bulky shape. The harvest takes place between July and August, beating the branches with very long rods to shake the almonds down onto large tarpaulins laid on the ground, where they are bagged, hulled and left to dry in the farmyard. Then they are shelled, roasted and processed.

Avola (SR)

Munafò

via G. Riscica, 4
☎ (+39) 0931823263
🌐 www.munafosrl.it
✉ info@munafosrl.it
shop: yes
e-commerce: no

Munafò....
—— Import - export ——
Commercio e lavorazione Mandorle

The Munafò family opened the company in 1950 and for three generations has worked to grow, promote and protect the pizzuta almond, also producing and processing other dried fruits. The key to its success is close monitoring of the entire production chain, which guarantees constant quality. The range includes shelled and/or peeled almonds of different sizes, and in different packaging. There is also almond flour, widely used for making biscuits, desserts and cakes.

Santa Maria del Cedro (CS)

Officine dei Cedri

via dell'Arco Piccolo, 18
☎ (+39) 3488916803
🌐 www.officinedeicedri.it
✉ info@officinedeicedri.it
shop: yes
e-commerce: yes

Here, in true citron country, an interesting multimedia museum has been dedicated to this citrus fruit. The company produces a tasty range of quality products: citron and dottato fig jams; fig and boiled must extra jam relish; figs, including those stuffed with walnuts and orange peel, caramel must; in chestnut honey and rum; in boiled must; panicelli, citron leaves tied with broom twice and filled with raisins and citron peel; papillons, citron leaves filled with dried figs stuffed with walnuts and citron.

Lequio Berria (CN)

Papa dei Boschi

via Pianravero, 13
☎ (+39) 0173522019
🌐 www.papadeiboschi.com
✉ info@papadeiboschi.com
shop: yes
e-commerce: no

Papa dei Boschi

In a small Alta Langa district, the 40 hectares of land produce PGI Langa Tonda Gentile hazelnuts which this family-run company processes uses to manufacture some tempting treats. Each stage of processing is carefully monitored to guarantee constant quality. In addition to various size packs of shelled hazelnuts, there are crushed hazelnuts and hazelnut paste, used extensively in patisserie and ice cream manufacturing. The spread is delicious.

Dried fruit

Montella (AV)

Castagne Perrotta

c.da Baruso zona Pip
☎ (+39) 0827601588 I 3299474080
◈ www.castagneperrotta.it
✉ info@castagneperrotta.it
shop: yes
e-commerce: no

Perrotta was conceived to promote one of the main local products but also to give traditional flavours a modern twist. The company offers quality products like soft chestnut snacks; boiled chestnuts, also flavoured with bay leaves and wild fennel; chestnut and cocoa cream; chestnuts and porcini mushrooms for pasta sauces or to serve with meat). Then there is chestnut flour, dried chestnuts, chestnut cream, also with cocoa; chestnuts in syrup, in grappa and in rum.

Cassano allo Ionio (CS)

Rango

via Francesco Bruno, 33
☎ (+39) 098171524 I 3336633139
◈ www.rango.it
✉ info@rango.it
shop: yes
e-commerce: yes

Antonio Rango founded his company to safeguard an old tradition for preserving highly nutritious figs. Along with his family, Antonio monitors all stages of work carefully, and his imagination is always busy thinking up new products to offer his customers, without losing any of the quality, of course. In addition to classic dried figs in braided trecce, cross-shaped crocette, bow-shaped nocchette, and garlands, there are those in rum, with chocolate or liquorice. Then there are chocolate-coated candied peel, chocolate bars, bite-size nougats and holiday specialities.

Bronte (CT)

'A Ricchigia

via Card. De Luca, 115
☎ (+39) 0957723326 I 3491501264
◈ www.aricchigia.com
✉ contatti@aricchigia.com
shop: yes
e-commerce: yes

This company was established about 50 years ago and has always stood out for its strong connection with the local area, and quality products. In an excellent position for Bronte's iconic green pistachio, known and enjoyed worldwide. Harvested every two years and subjected to strict quality control, the nuts become creams, sauces, flours, pastes and grains for use culinary and bakery use. The company also produces almond cream and a delicious pistachio panettone.

Prignano Cilento (SA)
Santomiele

via Salita San Giuseppe
☎ (+39) 0974833275
❂ www.santomiele.it
✉ info@santomiele.it
shop: yes
e-commerce: no

Antonio Longo and Corrado Del Verme were able to transform the simple fig (PDO Bianco del Cilento dottato variety) into a precious sweet for gourmet palates, controlling the entire production chain, from the pruning of trees to drying the fruit. There are two variants: the classic natural unpeeled fig and the white fig, peeled before drying, the latter a tradition typical of Prignano Cilento, produced in limited numbers. There are also exquisite almond-filled figs, fig paste filets with chocolate and other goodies.

Cravanzana (CN)
Terra delle Nocciole

via Provinciale, 14
☎ (+39) 3497937452
❂ www.terradellenocciole.it
✉ info@terradellenocciole.it
shop: yes
e-commerce: no

True enough, this is the homeland of hazelnuts, and Cravanzana is one of the most representative areas, even organizing a special dedicated event: Nocciolando. Here three passionate young partners created a business model that processes and preserves the IGP Langa Tonda Gentile hazelnut using meticulous craft techniques, all overseen in person. What is the result? In addition to fruits in different packs, crushed hazelnuts widely used in confectionery, and some semi-finished products.

Rovigo
Valier

fraz. Borsea I via Canalbianco Sinistro, 10
☎ (+39) 0425474575
❂ www.valier.it
✉ info@valier.it
shop: yes
e-commerce: no

Agronomist Alberto Valier, from an ancient family of Venetian nobles that has owned the business since 1474, took over the estate 40 years ago and converted part of it into walnut groves. There are three main varieties of walnuts, which are sold today but above all processed into excellent products by the annexed facility. We find oil, flour, Nocino liqueur, cake, and biscuits; chocolate-coated walnuts; green candied walnuts; others in syrup and in oil; and green walnuts in syrup and jam. There are also jams, fruit jellies and pralines.

Dried fruit

119

Montella (AV)
Vestuto

c.da Baruso zona Pip
☎ (+39) 0827601460 I 3280509338
🕸 www.vestutocastagne.it
✉ info@vestutocastagne.it
shop: yes
e-commerce: no

The Montella chestnut, recently vaunting its own museum, is a PGI product that Lorenzo Vestuto's Irpinia company processes using entirely artisanal methods, from gauging to selection, peeling and candying. We then find delicious marrons glacés, in jars and individually wrapped in elegant gift boxes. But this is not the only delight Vestuto has to offer, because there are also creams in classic, cocoa and dark chocolate flavours; marroncini chocolates, and flour. The range closes with candied fruits and jams made with organic oranges, strawberries, and apricots.

Bronte (CT)
Vincente Delicacies

v.le J. Kennedy zona artigianale, lotto 12/13
☎ (+39) 0957722300
🕸 www.vincentedelicacies.com
✉ info@vincentedelicacies.com
shop: yes
e-commerce: no

The PDO Bronte green pistachio grows here on the slopes of Mount Etna, and is the key element in this top-quality range, where there is a keen eye turned to a very refined packaging, and with new trends closely controlled. The collection includes almond pastries: Matador crispy logs of pistachio and almond: Eros crispy logs of in various flavours; soft pistachio nougat; Glamour bite-size nougats; Maravilha chocolates; Arabesque coated pistachios and spreads. Also worthy of note are the pesto, tuna in oil and marmalades.

Alghero (SS)
Accademia Olearia

loc. Ungias Galantè Lotto E1
☎ (+39) 079980394 I 3482833257
❀ www.accademiaolearia.com
✉ amministrazione@accademiaolearia.com
shop: no
e-commerce: no

The Alghero-based Accademia Olearia is headed up by Giuseppe Fois, whose family has been involved in olive growing for four generations. His passion and expertise are easily seen in the quality and products typical of the local area. The most widely used cultivar is bosana, which flourishes in this area thanks to the Mediterranean climate. The firm owns around 200 hectares of olive groves, producing over 100,000 kg of olives, much of which is exported to the UK and Germany.

Rossano (CS)
Frantolio Acri

c.da Amarelli, via Epiro II trav.
☎ (+39) 0983500037 I 3334596003
❀ www.frantolioacri.it
✉ info@frantolioacri.it
shop: no
e-commerce: no

Frantolio Acri was founded in 1952 and today is run by Giovanni, now the third generation of the Acri family. The groves are located in real olive country, on the Sibari plain. Of the estate's 11 hectares, seven are now organically farmed, with olives harvested from the estate's own 3,000 trees as well as some selected and purchased from other local growers. Acri makes use of avant-garde machinery to make the EVOO it sells direct, but also produces vegetables and vegetable preserves, selling them online, as well as exporting to Europe and America.

Buccheri (SR)
Agrestis

via Sabauda, 86a
☎ (+39) 0931315353 I 3338827657
❀ www.agrestis.eu
✉ info@agrestis.eu
shop: no
e-commerce: no

This dynamic cooperative is chaired by Giuseppe Paparone and was founded in 2003 by a group of farmers determined to establish high-quality oil production. Situated at 600–700 metres above sea level, it extends over around 60 hectares and boasts some 12,000 olive trees, many centuries old, and with 30 certified organic trees, with the rest are undergoing conversion. The products are popular with the market, not only for their origins in this true olive district, but also thanks to the loving care in every phase of processing.

Andria (BT)

Agrolio

s.da prov.le 231, km 55,120
☎ (+39) 0883546074
❀ www.agrolio.com
✉ info@agrolio.com
shop: no
e-commerce: no

Agrolio operates in an area that is considered Apulia's best for producing high-quality olive oil. Their olive groves are managed according to traditional and organic agricultural methods, and their extra-virgin oil is made with Coratina, the producer's speciality cultivar, as well as other select olives purchased from local growers. All their olives are pressed on-site within 12 hours of harvest. Theirs is a family-run business and, in addition to oil, they make wines and produce Cerignola olives.

Bagno a Ripoli (FI)

Allevamento dell'Apparita

via Roma, 587
☎ (+39) 055632221 I 3337821406
❀ aziendagricolapparita.jimdo.com
✉ arcangeli50@libero.it
shop: no
e-commerce: no

The estate can be found in the hills south-east of Florence, high above the road to San Donato in Collina. Allevamento dell'Apparita was developed thanks to the passion for the countryside that Antonio Arcangeli shares with wife Rossella Belegni and their daughter Arianna, an agronomist. Today this small but remarkable farm raises jumping horses and produces EVOO from 2,000 trees in four hectares of its own olive groves, and from two it rents with a precious heritage of moraiolo.

Tuscania (VT)

Le Amantine

loc. Le Mandrie
☎ (+39) 3478160676 I 0621931086
❀ www.leamantine.com
✉ info@leamantine.com
shop: no
e-commerce: no

LE AMANTINE
TUSCANIA 1936

Marina Gioacchini's Le Amantine was outstanding this year for the quality of production, following a year of management problems finally resolved to everyone's satisfaction. There are eight hectares of olive groves, with 2,000 trees of frantoio, leccino and canino varieties. Much of its production is exported to France.

Salento (SA)
Fattoria Ambrosio

loc. Coste
☎ (+39) 335412467
❧ www.fattoriaambrosio.it
✉ massimo.ambrosio@libero.it
shop: no
e-commerce: no

Massimo Ambrosio comes from a long line of dedicated olive growers, and today he is leading an organization that has for years distinguished itself for excellence. Of the 100 hectares spread out across Cilento, 21 are olive groves, from which three types of high-quality oil are made. They still don't have their own press but in the meantime Davide Monzo, from Pietrabianca, is helping to produce their oil.

Alghero (SS)
Antica Compagnia Olearia Sarda

via Vittorio Emanuele II, 225
☎ (+39) 079951597 I 3356429404
❧ www.anticacompagniaolearia.it
✉ info@anticacompagniaolearia.it
shop: no
e-commerce: no

Antonio Gavino Fois opened his Antica Compagnia Olearia 1860, and it is now a leading estate in Alghero, northern Sardinia, with over 170 hectares of olive trees, some estate-owned and others rented. The most widely grown variety is bosana, which finds its ideal terroir here, but the company is experimenting with others, like semidana, another of the island's top varieties. Excellent value for money.

Montefalco (PG)
Antonelli San Marco

loc. San Marco, 60
☎ (+39) 0742379158
❧ www.antonellisanmarco.it
✉ info@antonellisanmarco.it
shop: no
e-commerce: no

The Antonelli family name has longstanding links with wine production, contributing to the history of Sagrantino di Montefalco in Italy and abroad. However, its 170-hectare estate also includes a dozen hectares devoted to olive growing, with around 3,000 trees of the main local cultivars. The estate is also home to Casale Satriano, an agritourism with seven apartments.

Extra virgin olive oil

Andria (BT)

Felice Ardito

c.da La Pineta
☎ (+39) 0883546934
❀ www.org-olio.it
✉ info@org-olio.it
shop: no
e-commerce: no

Felice Ardito built this inspiring operation in the area of Andria, bolstered by his family's four generations of experience as olive-growers. Today, he manages it, along with his wife, Nicla, following all stages of production carefully, from cultivation to harvesting and pressing, The producer, which got its start in 2000, is growing by the year. Recently, they've been investing in communication and packaging, but also in their grove of 9500 Coratina trees that, today, spans 29 hectares.

Gaiole in Chianti (SI)

Badia a Coltibuono

loc. Badia a Coltibuono
☎ (+39) 057774481 I 0577746110
❀ www.coltibuono.com
✉ marketing@coltibuono.com
shop: no
e-commerce: no

Badia a Coltibuono is an institution for Chianti Classico, producing subtle, knife-edged wines that defy time. But they also produce EVOO from their own olive trees, organically farmed as the estate's philosophy dictates. The woods surrounding the vineyards and olive groves are a habitat of significant biodiversity. The estate's head office is in an old Vallombroso monastery, dating back to 1049, in a beautiful location open to the public, and including a restaurant.

Trapani

Barbàra

fraz. Rilievo I via Marsala, 593
☎ (+39) 3338515007 I 0923864346
❀ www.agricolabarbara.it
✉ info@agricolabarbara.it
shop: no
e-commerce: no

The Barbàra family has run this beautiful estate for over 40 years: 90 hectares, 60 of which are organically farmed. Many of the 7,000 olive trees are over a century old and there is with a good distribution of traditional cultivars: nocellara del Belice, biancolilla and cerasuola. The estate is in a stunning location, between the slopes of Mount Erice and the Stagnone lagoon islets, an area known for its sea breezes and remarkable day-night temperature variation.

Perugia
Giovanni Batta

via San Girolamo, 127
☎ (+39) 0755724782 | 3358176332
❀ www.frantoiobatta.it
✉ giovanni.batta@tin.it
shop: no
e-commerce: no

The Batta family name has historic links with olive growing in Umbria, where it started production back in 1923, focused on quality from the outset, achieving extremely high standards over recent years thanks to its work in the field and the oil mill. The proof of the pudding came this year with two product lines that tipped the peak of excellence. The olive grove has 3,400 trees planted over 11 hectares of land.

Bolsena (VT)
Frantoio Battaglini

via Cassia, km 111,700
☎ (+39) 0761798847 | 3476012932
❀ www.frantoiobattaglini.it
✉ oliodibolsena@frantoiobattaglini.it
shop: no
e-commerce: no

An ancient estate of clayey soil extending over the volcanic hills of the Lake Bolsena basin, with about 12 of the 35 hectares planted with olive groves. This year's harvest continued throughout October and the olives were processed within 12 hours in the estate's own mill, then preserved without oxygen. Other consistently high quality products over the years are honey and special cosmetics if which the organic EVOO is a key ingredient.

Priverno (LT)
Francesco Saverio Biancheri

via San Martino, 80
☎ (+39) 3299433008 | 0773903260
❀ www.colledelpolverino.it
✉ fbiancheri@gmail.com
shop: no
e-commerce: no

The estate run by Francesco Saverio Biancheri is in a breath-taking location. The lovely property is found on the slopes of the Lepini mountains, in the unspoiled Bosco del Polverino. Of the 20 hectares, seven are planted with 1,150 century-old olive trees, farmed under certified organic methods. Harvest and storage of the olives before they are taken to the oil mill is extremely meticulous.

Extra virgin olive oil

Torri del Benaco (VR)

Paolo Bonomelli
Boutique Olive Farm

via per Albisano, 95
☎ (+39) 0456296711 I 3273274925
✆ www.paolobonomelli.com
✉ info@paolobonomelli.com
shop: no
e-commerce: no

Paolo Bonomelli
BOUTIQUE OLIVE FARM

Paolo Bonomelli's Ca' Rainene is one of the most interesting and innovative farms in the area north-east of Lake Garda. The olive groves spread out over the Torri del Benaco hills, creating a sort of open-air artwork that enriches the hillside landscape. The farm has 3,000 olive trees used to make four types of oil, and it operates a short supply chain, with every processing phase traceable and certified. Products are exported to Germany and Japan.

Fiesole (FI)

Buonamici

via Montebeni, 11
☎ (+39) 055654991 I 05565499216
✆ www.buonamici.it
✉ info@buonamici.it
shop: no
e-commerce: no

CESARE
BUONAMICI
FIESOLE - FIRENZE

Founded by the Buonamici family in 1991, this firm is still headed by Cesare, assisted by his sister Cesara when she has time. They have shown their commitment to the environment with a number of choices made over the years and in 1995 they decided to apply organic methods to their 26,000 olive trees. They have installed biomass heating system fuelled by olive stones to help with energy saving. Olives are pressed with the mill's own equipment specifically for organically grown olives. As well as being known for its oil, Buonamici also produces EVOO-based cosmetics.

Brisighella (RA)

C.A.B. - Terra di Brisighella

via Strada, 2
☎ (+39) 054681103
✆ www.brisighello.net
✉ info@brisighello.net
shop: no
e-commerce: no

The cooperative of three hundred members with 80,000 trees vaunts almost unparalleled experience nationwide in interpreting the terroir. There is no doubt that the cooperative invented the first Italian olive oil PDO, Brisighella, still a benchmark for fine oil production. It is worth a trip to the Valle del Lamone to see the age-old terraces typical of one of the country's northernmost production areas.

Rionero in Vulture (PZ)
Cantine del Notaio

c.da Serra del Granato
☎ (+39) 0972723689 I 3356842483
🌐 www.cantinedelnotaio.com
✉ info@cantinedelnotaio.it
shop: no
e-commerce: no

This estate is famous in Italy and worldwide for its wine production but also has an impeccable reputation for extra virgin olive oil. Founded in 1998, the Basilicata estate has about 500 trees of typical olive varieties, located on five hectares in the Vulture hills. The olives are pitted before processing, which applies the so-called "oil according to Veronelli" method.

Montefalco (PG)
Arnaldo Caprai

loc. Torre
☎ (+39) 0742378802 I 345 0496385
🌐 www.arnaldocaprai.it
✉ info@arnaldocaprai.it
shop: no
e-commerce: no

ARNALDO·CAPRAI
Viticoltore in Montefalco

Caprai is a very well-known name in the Italian wine sector and a leader in the local area, widely acclaimed as the father of modern Sagrantino. The winery, set up in Montefalco in the Seventies, has an entrepreneurial vision and is skilled in research and communication. Inevitably, EVOO became part of its mission and recent improvements in quality have taken it to a leading position in regional ranks.

Molfetta (BA)
Maria Caputo

fraz. Terza Cala I s.s. 16 per Giovinazzo, km 778,5
☎ (+39) 0803978000 I 3476215430
🌐 www.oliogranpregio.com
✉ info@oliogranpregio.com
shop: no
e-commerce: no

GRAN·PREGIO

Situated in the Molfetta area, to the north of Puglia's regional capital, its 16 hectares are home to 4,500 olive trees, used exclusively to produce organic oil from native coratina olives. After bottling, this precious liquid is also exported to the United States and Germany. The continuous processing cycle, starting as soon as possible after harvesting by hand, ensures production of a good EVOO that has not been subjected to unnecessary stress.

Extra virgin olive oil

Bagnoregio (VT)

Tenuta di Carma

loc. Podere, 6
☎ (+39) 3339865174 I 3337168017
🌐 www.concarma.com
✉ matheus@pnap.it
shop: no
e-commerce: no

IL TRIANGOLO DELL'OLIO
THE OLIVE OIL TRIANGLE
www.concarma.com

Giulio Figarolo di Groppello and Gianluca Pizzo run the Tenuta di Carma, an organic farm founded in 1985, extending east of Lake Bolsena. The 20 hectares of olive groves are planted on clayey land at an altitude of 400 metres, with 5,200 trees of the typical northern Lazio varieties. The olives are hand-picked between October and November, and processed in the estate's own state-of-the-art mill, with temperature-controlled pressing and nitrogen-sparged storage.

Trequanda (SI)

Carraia

loc. Petrolio I Podere Carraia, 47
☎ (+39) 3334579446 I 0577665208
✉ oliobardi@hotmail.com
shop: no
e-commerce: no

Here on the Trequanda hills the surroundings are stunning, a setting of woods and cypresses, whose clay soils are home to Franco Bardi's 14 hectares of olive trees, producing top quality fruit and excellent results year in, year out. The careful harvesting work and short processing cycle prior to pressing enhance the characteristics of Tuscany's most traditional cultivars, including frantoio, pendolino, moraiolo, correggiolo, leccino and olivastra seggianese.

Tavarnelle Val di Pesa (FI)

Casa del Bosco

s.da del Cerro, 5
☎ (+39) 3477559369 I 3391293281
🌐 www.ilcerro.com
✉ agricolaelimar@gmail.com
shop: no
e-commerce: no

IL CERRO

This farm was established by Pier Luigi Cavallucci, a man with a passion for extra virgin olive oil who purchased the land in the early 1970s. He also produces wine but the real focus is oil: just over three hectares of olive groves are home to frantoio, moraiolo, leccino, and pendolino varieties typical of the Chianti area. Some of the production is exported to France, Belgium and the United States.

Isolabona (IM)

Paolo Cassini

via Roma, 62
☎ (+39) 0184208159 I 3358161771
❀ www.oliocassini.it
✉ info@oliocassini.it
shop: no
e-commerce: no

The Cassini family has been growing olives since 1962, although 13th-century Benedictine monks first introduced olive trees to this area. Today there are around 1,500 taggiasca olive trees distributed over 7.5 hectares of plots extending up to 500 metres above sea level. This farm is one of the best on the Italian Riviera, thanks in part to the fact it has its own olive pressing facility. It exports to Germany, Austria, the United States and Japan.

Castellina in Chianti (SI)

Castello di Fonterutoli

loc. Fonterutoli I via Ottone III di Sassonia, 5
☎ (+39) 057773571 I 0577735750
❀ www.mazzei.it
✉ mazzei@mazzei.it
shop: no
e-commerce: no

CASTELLO DI
FONTERUTOLI

The castle estate has been owned by the Mazzei family since 1435 and has changed little in appearance since then. The 650 hectares include 117 dedicated vineyards, beautifully aspected at between 230 and 500 metres above sea level. Fonterutoli also produces an excellent extra virgin oil from the 4,000 olive trees which include classic Tuscan cultivars: frantoio, leccino, moraiolo and pendolino.

Bibbona (LI)

Il Cavallino

loc. Case Sparse I via Paratino, 43
☎ (+39) 0586677383 I 3357629329
❀ www.ilcavallino.it
✉ info@ilcavallino.it
shop: no
e-commerce: no

Il Cavallino
AZIENDA AGRICOLA

Romina Salvadori makes EVOO in the Bibbona area, on the splendid Tuscan coast south of Livorno. Her father Franco breathed new life into the family tradition in the post-war period, laying the foundations for what is now considered a fine estate in the varied Tuscan olive oil scenario. The large olive plantation counts 16,000 productive trees, whose olives are processed in the estate's own mill.

Castelvetrano (TP)

Centonze

s.s. 115 dir. Selinunte, km 0,500, 103 c.da Latomie
☎ (+39) 0924 904231 I 330664802
⊗ www.oliocentonze.com
✉ commerciale@oliocentonze.com
shop: no
e-commerce: no

Since 1953 the Centonze family has managed this lovely farm where ancient olive trees and lush citrus orchards grow side by side. Today the beautiful estate, not far from the Selinunte Archeological Park, has 38 hectares with 8,000 olive trees, some truly ancient. Any citrus trees that die are replaced with olive cultivars: biancolilla, cerasuola and nocellara del Belìce. On the estate it is worth visiting the "latomie", tuffstone quarries over 2,600 years old, and the "conigliere", drystone wall that are mostly intact.

Strongoli (KR)

Roberto Ceraudo

loc. Marina di Strongoli I c.da Dattilo
☎ (+39) 0962865613
⊗ www.dattilo.it
✉ info@dattilo.it
shop: no
e-commerce: no

CERAUDO

Roberto Ceraudo's 60-hectare estate includes 40 of olive groves, as well as vineyards and citrus orchards. The 7,000 olive trees are native local carolea and tonda di Strongoli cultivars. The olives are harvested as soon as they are ripe, and processed immediately at controlled temperatures, in a continuous cycle. Dattilo, which exports to Germany, the Netherlands, Denmark and the USA, has guest facilities including eight rooms and a restaurant offering good local high cuisine.

Castelnuovo di Farfa (RI)

Il Cervo Rampante

loc. Lo Stazzo I via delle Macerine
☎ (+39) 3338345364
⊗ www.ilcervorampante.it
✉ info@ilcervorampante.it
shop: no
e-commerce: no

IL CERVO  RAMPANTE

In 2007, the Gurgo siblings Camillo, Angela Maria and Maria Idria, of Castelmenardo, established this farm on the hills in the province of Rieti, in the heart of the Sabina PDO district. Their oil, made mainly from carboncella, frantoio, leccino, and pendolino olives, processed within 12 hours of harvesting in a local continuous-cycle olive press, has grown in quality over recent years. In addition to its Sabina PDO, monovarietal and aromatized oils, the firm also produces mouthwatering sweet and savoury spreads, preserves and EVOO-based cosmetics.

Sonnino (LT)
Alfredo Cetrone

via Consolare Frasso, 5800
☎ (+39) 0773 949008 I 3488918518
🌍 www.cetrone.it
✉ info@cetrone.it
shop: no
e-commerce: no

Founded in 1860 by another Alfredo Cetrone, ancestor of today's owner, this estate extends over the rocky Ausoni slopes, at 500 metres above sea level. The farm is a benchmark for the entire area and covers 100 hectares, with 20,000 itrana trees exposed to the beneficial sea breeze. It exports products to many different countries, including Germany, the Netherlands, Sweden, Switzerland, Northern Ireland, Japan, and the United States.

Chianciano Terme (SI)
Chiarentana

loc. Chiarentana I s.da della Fornace, 12
☎ (+39) 057869101 I 3357022077
🌍 www.chiarentanaolio.com
✉ info@chiarentanaolio.com
shop: no
e-commerce: no

CHIARENTANA

Founded as La Foce by Antonio and Irisi Dorigo more than 90 years ago, at a time when the Val d'Orcia had a very small population and was little known, the estate was split between the two daughters, and Donata went on to develop the Chiarentana section. As well as producing oil, which is made entirely on site thanks to an in-house olive press, the estate also boasts an agritourism with 35 guest rooms and part of the land is set aside for growing wheat.

Molfetta (BA)
Giuseppe Ciccolella

c.da Coppa d'Oro
☎ (+39) 3472265987 I 3470783451
🌍 www.olociccolella.it
✉ info@oliociccolella.it
shop: no
e-commerce: no

To the north of Bari, in magnificent olive-growing terrain, between Molfetta, Terlizzi and Giovinazzo, around 6,000 coratina trees grow alongside a small selection of cima di Bitonto olive trees. The olives are cultivated with traditional methods, harvested by hand at just the right level of ripeness, and then crushed in local presses that use continuous-cycle systems. Some of the production is destined for the German market.

Extra virgin olive oil

Chiaramonte Gulfi (RG)
Cinque Colli

c.da Mazzarronello
☎ (+39) 0932921643 I 3334490005
🕸 www.cinquecolli.it
✉ info@cinquecolli.it
shop: no
e-commerce: no

In 1998, dynamic Sebastiano Giaquinta decided to take over the family estate, purchased in 1976. At the time much of was devoted to growing grapes but he has converted it into a specialist olive farm, later purchasing a large plot of neighbouring land. Today it extends over around 45 hectares, with more than 5,000 olive trees of different ages, most of which are the prized local cultivar tonda iblea. The quality of production is guaranteed by very attentive and expert management, and by the fact that the drupes are pressed immediately at a nearby mill.

Sonnino (LT)
Filomena Coletta - Casino Re

loc. Rave Bianche I fraz. Capocroce I via Vallerotta, 31
☎ (+39) 0773947439 I 3277037668
🕸 www.casinore.it
✉ casino.re@libero.it
shop: no
e-commerce: no

Filomena Coletta manages the estate on the slopes of the Ausoni mountains, with ten hectares of olive groves on rocky terraces planted with 2,500 age-old itrana trees. Within a few hours of harvesting, olives are processed in the estate mill and the oil is stored in oxygen-free conditions. The estate also produces Gaeta table olives, and complies with the Alta Qualità certified traceability project.

Priverno (LT)
Colle Rotondo

loc. Ceriara I via Colle Rotondo
☎ (+39) 0678206751 3495037188
🕸 www.colle-rotondo.it
✉ info@colle-rotondo.it
shop: no
e-commerce: no

Salvatore Reali's family has owned the Colle Rotondo farm in Priverno, in the south of the province of Latina, since 1800. This is an organic farm on a hilly area of volcanic origin, at 400 metres above sea level, covering more than 13 hectares. The 4,000 olive trees are the itrana variety, which has been typical of the area since antiquity. Exports are mainly to France, Belgium and the Netherlands, and to Japan.

Cinigiano (GR)

ColleMassari

loc. Poggi del Sasso
☎ (+39) 0564990496
⊕ www.collemassari.it
✉ info@collemassari.it
shop: no
e-commerce: no

The farming project started by brother and sister team Claudio Tipa and Maria Iris Tipa Bertarelli began here. Now there are another three farms in prestigious, well-established districts. ColleMassari has made a fundamental contribution to bringing one of Tuscany's great unknown areas, Montecucco, to the attention of the rest of the world, drawing out of the shadow of nearby Montalcino. The estate of over 1,000 hectares is planted with 12,000 olive trees. Temperature variation due to breezes from Mount Amiata gives the EVOO freshness, complexity and elegant balsamic notes.

Blera (VT)

Colli Etruschi

via degli Ulivi, 2
☎ (+39) 0761470469 I 3282881851
⊕ www.collietruschi.it
✉ info@collietruschi.it
shop: no
e-commerce: no

The Colli Etruschi cooperative is in the PDO Tuscia zone on hills of volcanic origin, and opened in 1965. The estates of the 390 members are on clayey tufaceous substrata, for 800 hectares of olive groves and 40,000 plants of the caninese, frantoio and leccino varieties. All members adhere to strict organic farming rules and all the cultivation and harvesting phases are monitored carefully to ensure a high quality product. Colli Etruschi exports primarily to Europe and the US.

Carmignano (PO)

Colline San Biagio

fraz. Bacchereto I via San Biagio, 6b
☎ (+39) 0558717143 I 3292441152
⊕ www.collinesanbiagio.it
✉ info@collinesanbiagio.it
shop: no
e-commerce: no

This beautiful agritourism on the Tuscan hills is located in an elegantly renovated historic convent. It produces good IGT Toscano oil, processing moraiolo, frantoio and leccino olives from its own estate, and also makes its own wines (Carmignano DOCG Sancti Blasii, Sangiovese PGI Donna Mingarda, Merlot IGT Toscana) and Riserva Carmignano grappa, from its own vineyard harvests. Also worthy of note are the natural preserves made from its own seasonal fruits.

Extra virgin olive oil

Puegnago sul Garda (BS)
Comincioli

loc. Castello I via Roma, 10
☎ (+39) 0365651141
✹ www.comincioli.it
✉ info@comincioli.it
shop: no
e-commerce: no

The Comincioli family has lived in Valtenesi for over six centuries, in a spot where olive and grape growing have always reigned supreme. It is here that Giancarlo Comincioli produces his wonderful oil thanks to the modern olive mill that also pits all the olives produced by 2,500 olive trees on a ten-hectare estate. The farm also produces top-quality wine and grappa, exporting to Austria, Germany, Switzerland, Mexico, Japan, France and the United Arab Emirates.

Bassano in Teverina (VT)
Rete d'Imprese Concerto

via della Valle, 5
☎ (+39) 3382450712
✹ www.oliomammamia.it
✉ oliomammamia@gmail.com
shop: no
e-commerce: no

M/M
MAMMAMIA
OLIO EXTRAVERGINE DI OLIVA

These five high-profile olive farms producing in the heart of Tuscia started a joint venture involving businesses owned by Gisella and Elena Acenzi in Viterbo, Alessandra Boselli in Bassano in Teverina, Colli Etruschi in Blera, Laura De Parri in Canino and Frantoio Battaglini in Bolsena. The estates add up 900 hectares of olive groves, with 56,700 trees, mainly of the caninese variety. The goal is to produce an EVOO that offers the best possible expression of the terroir, through selection of each farm's top production.

Ugento (LE)
Luigi Congedi

via Marina
☎ (+39) 0833555263
✹ www.oliocongedi.com
✉ info@oliocongedi.com
shop: no
e-commerce: no

For almost a century, Oleificio Congedi has handed down its extra virgin olive oil tradition, from generation to generation. It bottles oil from olives grown on its 170 trees in the mild Salento climate, in a favourable geographic position between the Adriatic and Ionian Sea, and also uses olives from other carefully selected producers. The drupes are processed in its own olive mill, using marble millstones. The farm also markets a line of vegetable pâtés and marinated olives, exporting to South Africa, Sweden, the United States, Australia, Canada, Switzerland and Germany.

Monteciccardo (PU)

Il Conventino di Monteciccardo

loc. Conventino I via G. Turcato, 4
☎ (+39) 0721910574 I 3457112597
❂ www.il-conventino.it
✉ info@conventinomonteciccardo.bio
shop: no
e-commerce: no

Il Conventino farm is run by the Marcantoni family, a father and sons who have been working here since 2008 to produce quality extra virgin olive oil and wine. Although their groves are still young, they produce organic olives that are processed within 12 hours of harvesting. The olives are pressed in the farm's own modern mill during a liquid nitrogen-cooled crushing phase. The farm has 7,500 trees distributed over 20 hectares of olive groves and exports its products to the Netherlands, Belgium, Germany, the United States and Brazil.

San Secondo Parmense (PR)

Coppini Arte Olearia
L'Albero d'Argento

s.da al Grugno, 3
☎ (+39) 0521877611 I 0521877617
❂ www.coppini.it
✉ info@coppini.it
shop: no
e-commerce: no

Coppini Arte Olearia is a national and international leader in the production and distribution of extra-virgin olive oil. Their line includes organic oils, oils for chefs, the food industry and shops. Founded in 1946, and now on their third generation, Coppini's logistics and sales networks are coordinated in Parma, while harvesting and pressing take place in those areas best-suited to cultivation: Abruzzo, Apulia and Sicily (in collaboration with the the National Association of Italian Olive-Growers). They also offer a T.O.P. line (Traceability, Origins, and Product) for restaurants.

Cinto Euganeo (PD)

Frantoio di Cornoleda

via Cornoleda, 15
☎ (+39) 3807177284 I 0429647123
❂ www.frantoiodicornoleda.com
✉ info@frantoiodicornoleda.com
shop: no
e-commerce: no

The Zanaica family established this olive mill in 2008, on the road that leads to the town from which it takes its name, at the foot of Mount Gemola. In addition to the olive mill, the site boasts around 2,000 olive trees from the main local cultivars, spread over four hectares of land. It also produces olive pâté, honey, wine, liqueurs, preserves, and fresh fruit, currently exporting most of its produce to Germany.

Extra virgin olive oil

San Casciano in Val di Pesa (FI)

Fattoria Corzano e Paterno

loc. San Pancrazio I via San Vito di Sopra
☎ (+39) 0558248179 I 3356159469

❂ www.corzanoepaterno.com
✉ info@corzanoepaterno.it
shop: no
e-commerce: no

Founded in 1969, Corzano e Paterno was originally two different farms, merged thanks to the visionary thinking of architect Wendelin Gelpke. Today Wendelin's heirs are a large family and continue the work on the farm, enamoured of the land. The cheese, wine and EVOO are of extraordinarily high quality, with the oil side run by nephew Aljoscha Goldschmidt, who tends the 3,000 olive trees scattered across the 200-hectare estate.

Chiaramonte Gulfi (RG)

Frantoi Cutrera

c.da Piano dell'Acqua, 71
☎ (+39) 0932926187 I 3332049186
❂ www.frantoicutrera.it
✉ olio@frantoicutrera.it
shop: no
e-commerce: no

A 50-hectare estate with over 10,000 trees, many of which are over a century old. This quality benchmark for Sicilian and Italian olive growing has been headed by the Cutrera family for generations. Giovanni and Maria built a modern olive mill here in 1979, together with other facilities. In 2000, their children Giuseppina, Maria and Salvatore, and their respective spouses, took over the business, bringing in new enthusiasm and more up-to-date expertise. The meticulous monitoring of all stages in the production chain and the focus on the commercial side of the business mean their products are now appreciated worldwide.

Bitritto (BA)

Frantoio De Carlo

via XXIV Maggio, 54b
☎ (+39) 080630767 I 3356007705
❂ www.oliodecarlo.com
✉ info@oliodecarlo.com
shop: no
e-commerce: no

The historic De Carlo family is well-known in Puglia's olive-growing circles. Written records show that the family first became involved in the industry in the late 18th century, obtaining the necessary permissions for oil retail and wholesale in the first decades of the 19th century and pursuing the business from then on. For many years the farm has supplemented its products with preserves such as creams and sundried tomatoes, and oils aromatized by milling the olives with natural flavouring but never using essences. It also produces table olives. Its products are exported to the United States, Japan and Europe.

Canino (VT)
Laura De Parri - Cerrosughero

loc. Cerrosughero I s.s. 312, km 22,600
☎ (+39) 0761438594 I 3396792306
🌐 www.oliocerrosughero.it
✉ lauradeparri@libero.it
shop: no
e-commerce: no

Laura De Parri's estate, an important reference point for the area as a whole, extends over the hills between Lake Bolsena and the Maremma coast, near the border with Tuscany. This is the heart of the PDO Canino area, a clayey tufaceous terrain, and the 210 hectares are surrounded by meadows and woods, including 20 planted with 5,000 caninese, frantoio, pendolino, leccino and maurino olive trees. Its products are exported to Germany and the UK.

Ancona
Del Carmine

fraz. Torrette I via del Carmine, 51
☎ (+39) 071889403 I 3337016537
🌐 www.aziendadelcarmine.it
✉ info@aziendadelcarmine.it
shop: no
e-commerce: no

Del Carmine

The Del Carmine estate is in constant evolution. Antonio Roversi, his daughter, and their staff keep a close eye on innovation without neglecting healthy growing and milling practices. From the restaurant to the farm, everything is kept as natural as possible. The farm sells EVOO in various formats (including bag-in-box) and also produces natural cosmetics, paté, jams and pasta made from wheat grown on the farm.

Vetralla (VT)
Sergio Delle Monache

s.da prov.le Norchia, 20
☎ (+39) 07611768270 I 3498533236
🌐 www.oliotamia.com
✉ info@oliotamia.com
shop: no
e-commerce: no

TAMÍA
EXTRA VIRGIN OLIVE OIL
ORGANIC
ITALY

Sergio Delle Monache's farm dates back to 1928 and covers ten hectares on the volcanic hills in the heart of the Tuscia PDO. The seven hectares of organically farmed olive groves are planted on clayey soil at altitudes between 300 and 400 metres, with 1,700 trees of the typical Tuscia Viterbese varieties, chiefly caninese, frantoio, maurino and leccino. The olives are processed within a few hours in a local mill, and pressed in an oxygen-free environment.

Gaeta (LT)
Cosmo Di Russo

loc. Pontone
☎ (+39) 0771462201 I 3277440969
🌐 www.olivadigaeta.it
✉ dirussocosmo@yahoo.it
shop: no
e-commerce: no

Cosmo Di Russo's property is set on clayey terrain of volcanic origin, just inland from the Tyrrhenian coast, where it benefits from the microclimate generated by the local sea breezes. It covers a total of seven hectares, with 2,200 itrana olive trees. As well as olive oil, it also produces Gaeta olives in brine, oil and as pâtés, exporting its goods to the UK and Germany.

Gaiole in Chianti (SI)
Olio di Dievole

fraz. Pianella I s.da prov.le 408
☎ (+39) 05771793001 I 3484657945
🌐 www.dievole.it
✉ matteo.giusti@dievole.it
shop: no
e-commerce: no

One of the oldest businesses in the area, with records of Dievole dating back to the 11th century. Not too far from town, this firm has made a quantum leap over recent years and is now a holiday resort, as well as producing wine and oil. An olive mill was purchased recently to enhance oil production. The farm covers a total of around 400 hectares and has about 12,000 olive trees.

Formia (LT)
È.D.Enrico

loc. Castellonorato I via Campole, 5
☎ (+39) 0415950687 I 3388828088
🌐 www.edenrico.com
✉ info@edenrico.com
shop: no
e-commerce: no

It was only recently that Enrico De Marco took up the old family tradition of growing olives. His decision to cultivate and promote the Itrana olive, introduced into Lazio by the ancient Romans, should be commended. His land spans 12 hectares and includes about 4000 trees. In addition to much sought after extra virgin olive oil, they produce olives in brine, cremes and aromatized oils. È.D.Enrico export their products to the USA.

Venticano (AV)
Oleificio Fam

c.da Ilici, 5
☎ (+39) 0825965829 I 082774232
✤ www.oliofam.it
✉ info@oliofam.it
shop: no
e-commerce: no

NATURA DA AMARE®

Siblings Flora, Antonio and Maria Tranfaglia have developed the business established by their father Marcianoche, who founded this Irpinia oil mill in 1997. The Tranfaglias have lived in Tauresi for many generations and they have seven hectares of land here, including more than three planted with ravece olives. The family's crops are supplemented by a selection of olives from local growers based in this area, also renowned for unique wines such as Taurasi, Greco di Tufo and Fiano di Avellino.

Castelnuovo Berardenga (SI)
Fèlsina

via del Chianti, 101
☎ (+39) 0577355117
✤ www.felsina.it
✉ info@felsina.it
shop: no
e-commerce: no

FÈLSINA

Domenico Poggiali bought the farm in 1966 as a hunting reserve. His brother-in-law, Giuseppe Mazzacolin, helped him develop it into one of the loveliest wine estates in southern Chianti Classico. Today his son Giovanni has taken over, but the farming spirit and passion for EVOO have not changed. This was one of the first estates to join the "oil according to Veronelli" project, which included special quality production regulations.

Monreale (PA)
Feudo Disisa

fraz. Grisì I c.da Disisa s.da prov.le, km 6
☎ (+39) 0916127109 I 3355344258
✤ www.vinidisisa.it
✉ info@vinidisisa.it
shop: no
e-commerce: no

FEUDO DISISA

The Di Lorenzo family has owned this huge 400-hectare estate for over 200 years, located at 450–500 metres above sea level, in the countryside outside Monreale, between the provinces of Palermo and Trapani. It grows a number of different crops, particularly grapes, but its main focus has always been olives, with 60 hectares of groves, including ten that are certified organic, and for a total of 9,000 trees. The extensive experience gained over the centuries and its own innovative continuous-cycle olive press make it a leading name both in Sicily and farther afield.

Extra virgin olive oil

Corigliano Calabro (CS)

Frantoio Figoli

c.da Ogliastretti
☎ (+39) 098382081 I 3383493202
❂ www.frantoiofigoli.it
✉ info@frantoiofigoli.it
shop: no
e-commerce: no

The business founded in 1939 by Leonardo Figoli is now in the hands of the fourth generation, namely Tommaso. The farm covers 45 hectares of which 32 are planted with 13,000 organic olive trees of varieties including frantoio, coratina and carolea. The olives are pressed in the estate's mill within 12 hours of harvesting, and the oil is bottled under nitrogen after natural decanting. Online sales; exports to Japan, England, Germany.

Castagneto Carducci (LI)

Fonte di Foiano

loc. Fonte di Foiano, 148
☎ (+39) 0565766043 I 3473790291
❂ www.fontedifoiano.it
✉ informazioni@fontedifoiano.it
shop: no
e-commerce: no

A remarkably attentive oil production firm, handed down by the original owners Paolo and Marina to their children, who are now fully involved in running the operation, which also includes an agritourism, although the oil is the main focus here thanks to the olive groves with a total of 5,000 trees. There are numerous varietals like pendolino, maurino, leccio del corno and Santa Caterina, as well as some cultivars not so well known in Tuscany, like coratina and ascolana. The olives are processed in the farm's own mill.

Città Sant'Angelo (PE)

Forcella

via V. Cilli, 45
☎ (+39) 3338146619 I 08573030
❂ www.agricolaforcella.it
✉ info@agricolaforcella.it
shop: no
e-commerce: no

The Iannetti brothers, Giovanni and Paolo, put great enthusiasm into running this historic farm, founded in 1924. The olive groves extend over 18 hectares and are located in two different municipalities, Città Sant'Angelo and Loreto Aprutino, districts with different soil and climate traits, but each suited to growing olives. Their products are primarily exported to the United States, Canada and Germany.

Castel del Piano (GR)
Frantoio Franci

fraz. Montenero d'Orcia I via A. Grandi, 5
☎ (+39) 0564954000 I 3473342040
✿ www.frantoiofranci.it
✉ info@frantoiofranci.it
shop: no
e-commerce: no

This company has been producing top-quality extra virgin olive oil for more than 60 years thanks to brothers Franco and Fernando, who decided to devote themselves to production, transforming a hay barn into an olive mill. The real turnaround came 40 years later, in 1995, when Fernando's son Giorgio joined the team. He succeeded in stepping things up, selling farther afield, devising a brand and an image that until then had only been known to the local population. The company now has 3,000 trees dotted over 60 hectares of land.

Recanati (MC)
Gabrielloni

fraz. Montefiore
☎ (+39) 0733852498 I 347 2100834
✿ www.gabrielloni.it
✉ info@gabrielloni.it
shop: no
e-commerce: no

The Gabrielloni family-run olive mill was established in 1955 by grandfather Marino, and then handed down from father to son. Today the business is run with passion and great expertise by his granddaughters, Gabriella and Elisabetta. The firm has around 2,300 olive trees in an area of seven hectares on the Recanati hills. It exports its goods mainly to Germany and Japan.

Bisceglie (BT)
Frantoio Galantino

via Corato Vecchia, 2
☎ (+39) 0803921320
✿ www.galantino.it
✉ info@galantino.it
shop: no
e-commerce: no

This historic family-run firm processes drupes from its 10,000 olive trees and from carefully selected small producers in its olive mill. Its catalogue comprises two different lines, one traditional and one organic. It also produces oils aromatized with citrus, herbs, oregano, mint and basil, as well as a line of olives and preserves, and olive oil-based cosmetics, exporting its products to various countries.

Extra virgin olive oil

Trevi (PG)

Frantoio Gaudenzi

fraz. Pigge I loc. Camporeale, 6
☎ (+39) 0742781107
🕸 www.frantoiogaudenzi.it
✉ info@frantoiogaudenzi.it
shop: no
e-commerce: no

The Gaudenzi family's association with oil began many years ago, back in the mid-18th century, when Vittorio Gaudenzi established the business now run by Francesco and his family. Today it is celebrating 55 years with Stefano and Andrea Brunetti at the helm. Thanks to the efforts and passion of their parents, Francesco and Rossana, they started out with much more than mere experience in the field. They now have 8,500 olive trees spread over 24 hectares of land.

Peccioli (PI)

Tenuta di Ghizzano

loc. Ghizzano I via della Chiesa, 4
☎ (+39) 0587630096
🕸 www.tenutadighizzano.com
✉ info@tenutadighizzano.com
shop: no
e-commerce: no

Organic practice is a life philosophy here. The 350-hectare estate, certified organic since 2008, is at Ghizzano, a small village on the Pisa hills: 20 hectares planted with vineyards and the remainder with cereal crops, woods and poplar groves. The cellar and oil mill surround the tower built by the Veronesi Pesciolini family in 1370. The oil is made from the frantoio, razzo, moraiolo and leccino varieties.

Cariati (CS)

Fattorie Greco

c.da Guardapiedi
☎ (+39) 0983969441
🕸 www.igreco.it
✉ ufficio_marketing@igreco.it
shop: no
e-commerce: no

The Greco family have a huge olive plantation on 2,000 hectares, 150 of which are organically farmed, with 200,000 trees of the carolea, roggianella and dolce di Rossano varieties. The estate was founded in 1963, when Tommaso Greco built the first oil mill in Cariati. The lands overlook the Ionian coast in a thriving farming and tourism area. As well as EVOO, the Greco family produce white, red, rosé, and sparkling wines, which they export to Europe, the USA, Japan and Canada.

Sonnino (LT)
Gregorio De Gregoris

via Consolare Capocroce, 4066
☎ (+39) 3491467085
✆ www.olitrana.it
✉ olitrana@gmail.com
shop: no
e-commerce: no

Gregorio De Gregoris is heir to a long EVOO producing tradition. His four hectares of olive groves on the slopes of the Ausoni mountains are planted on rocky terrain, with a clay bed, at 400 metres in altitude: 4,000 trees, all of the native itrana variety. The olives are processed within a few hours in the estate's mill and the oil is stored at a controlled temperature without oxygen. The Gaeta table olives are also excellent.

Pontassieve (FI)
Fattoria di Grignano

FATTORIA DI
GRIGNANO

via di Grignano, 22
☎ (+39) 0558398490
✆ www.fattoriadigrignano.com
✉ info@fattoriadigrignano.com
shop: no
e-commerce: no

Fattoria di Grignano can be found in the heart of Rufina, where the Sieve and Arno rivers meet. The estate covers 600 hectares with 47 farms, each with its own special features. Alongside arable crops, orchards and woods the particular agricultural focus are the vast areas devoted to vineyards and olive groves. In 1972 the villa, along with the whole estate, was purchased by the Inghirami family, one of the most famous benchmark names in Italian fashion.

Tocco da Casauria (PE)
Guardiani Farchione

via XX Settembre, 30
☎ (+39) 085880509 I 3343947415
✆ www.guardianifarchione.com
✉ info@guardianifarchione.it
shop: no
e-commerce: no

The Guardiani-Farchione family olive groves are the glory of the rolling Tocco da Casauria hillsides, reaching altitudes of up to 360 metres. The family has always been considered a winegrower, but it is also renowned for its oil, especially thanks to over 4,000 toccolana trees, a variety that has grown here since time immemorial. The harvesting and processing phases take place quickly in a reliable modern mill.

Extra virgin olive oil

Chiaramonte Gulfi (RG)
Oleificio Gulino

c.da Cicimia
☎ (+39) 0932921249 I 3356628230
✪ www.oleificiogulino.com
✉ info@oleificiogulino.com
shop: no
e-commerce: no

This story of this farm, now owned by Eugenio and Luciano Presti, goes back to 1880 with the Gulino family, when a decision was made to devote it almost exclusively to olive growing, leading to the gradual establishment of the company olive mill. The property covers 15 hectares, ten of which are certified organic, and it has around 1,250 olive trees, almost all over a century old. After being hand-harvested, the drupes are placed in small crates and crushed a few hours later in the farm's own modern continuous-cycle olive mill.

Penne (PE)
Frantoio Hermes

c.da Planoianni, 13
☎ (+39) 0858279937 I 3397646347
✪ www.frantoiohermes.it
✉ info@frantoiohermes.it
shop: no
e-commerce: no

Despite coming from a completely different sector, Claudio Di Mercurio revived the family olive mill in 2009, completely refurbishing it and making his mark. Although he started the venture almost as a hobby, it soon became a priority and also involved his wife Olga, who has supported him throughout. This dynamic, constantly expanding firm, boasts 16 hectares of organic olive groves with 4,000 trees, around half of which are centuries old.

Sonnino (LT)
Lucia Iannotta

via Capocroce, 10
☎ (+39) 0773947005 I 3393445032
✪ www.olioiannotta.it
✉ info@olioiannotta.it
shop: no
e-commerce: no

Lucia Iannotta's farm has been operating in this area, at the foot of the Ausoni mountains, for four generations. The entire estate, with its 16 hectares of rocky calcareous terrain at 500 metres above sea level, is planted with around 4,000 itrana trees, distributed over two separate plots exposed to the mild sea breeze. Export destinations are Japan, Colombia and Austria.

Sonnino (LT)

Impero Biol - Maggiarra Impero

via Cap. V. Pellegrini, 10
☎ (+39) 0773 98019 I 393 9666154
❀ www.imperomaggiarra.it
✉ maggiarra-impero@libero.it
shop: no
e-commerce: no

The Maggiarra family has been growing and processing olives since 1947. Its property extends over hillside plots at 400–500 metres above sea level, on the northern slopes of the Ausoni mountains. The four hectares of olive groves are planted with 3,000 itrana trees, and are all certified organic, also producing table olives. It exports its products primarily to Europe.

Alberobello (BA)

Olio Intini

c.da Popoleto
☎ (+39) 0804325983 I 3479603450
❀ www.oliointini.it
✉ info@oliointini.it
shop: no
e-commerce: no

Pietro Intini is a reference point in Puglia for top-quality production, making six monovarietal extra virgin olive oils, iinterpreting the area in a style that epitomizes this part of Italy. A few years ago Intini made major investments in improving production and conservation processes, resulting in some mouthwatering extra virgin olive oils evocative of the Alberobello area, between the provinces of Bari and Brindisi. The firm is open for visits. Exports reach Japan, Sweden, France, Belgium and Germany.

Castelleone di Suasa (AN)

Valter L'Olivaio

via Case Nuove, 25
☎ (+39) 071966123 I 3391891967
❀ www.lolivaio.it
✉ info@lolivaio.it
shop: no
e-commerce: no

From millers to growers, all the experience of three generations comes together in this firm's products. The modern production methods are under constant review, improving the oils produced by the firm, which now runs 20 hectares of olive groves, mostly planted with native Marche varieties. The estate is in Castellone di Suasa, a quiet hillside location not far from the sea at Senigallia. The ideal conditions of the land, the immediate milling of the harvested olives and the continuous-cycle extraction all contribute to the quality of its products. A point-of-purchase is located in Pagliere del Tronto (AP).

Cerchiara di Calabria (CS)
Rosa Laino

c.da Piana
☎ (+39) 0981994204 I 3396704866
❀ www.eleusi.net
✉ info@eleusi.net
shop: no
e-commerce: no

A family-run firm that focuses on cultivating a small number of trees and producing top-quality extra virgin olive oil, also using olives purchased locally. Here, in Piana di Sibari, next to Pollino national park, the location is perfect for production that focuses on native varieties. Oil is exported to Germany and a number of English-speaking countries.

Vaccarizzo Albanese (CS)
Tenute Librandi Pasquale

via Marina, 23
☎ (+39) 098384068 I 098384321
❀ www.oliolibrandi.it
✉ info@oliolibrandi.it
shop: no
e-commerce: no

This oil-production firm was founded by Pasquale Librandi in 1967 and is now run by his four children. It produces significant quantities of good quality oil using olives from its 30,000 organic trees planted over an area of 153 hectares. The estate is on the northern slopes of the pre-Sila Greca, just outside the historic village of Graeco-Albanian origin and tradition. The farm also has five guestrooms offering overnight accommodation. Librandi oil is exported outside national borders to the rest of Europe, Russia, Japan and the United States.

Serre (SA)
Madonna dell'Olivo

via G. Garibaldi, 18
☎ (+39) 0828974950 I 3355273347
❀ www.madonnaolivo.it
✉ info@madonnaolivo.it
shop: no
e-commerce: no

Antonino Mennella is a real star who combines the talent (and sensitivity) of an artist with scientific method. Year after year the standard of his production continues to improve, taking the company to an almost incomparable level of reliability in Italy. His efforts have been rewarded by the leading role universally attributed to him in Campania. The firm has seven hectares with 2,050 ravece, rotondella, picholine, carpelles and pisciottana olive trees, with products exported to Germany and the United States.

Arco (TN)

Madonna delle Vittorie

via Linfano, 81
☎ (+39) 0464505432 I 3356245115
✆ www.madonnadellevittorie.it
✉ info@madonnadellevittorie.it
shop: no
e-commerce: no

A name that has been associated with top-quality wine and oil since 1970. The seven hectares are planted with 1,500 frantoio and casaliva olive trees, whose drupes are processed in the company mill. The farm also has two comfortable apartments available to rent during holiday periods.

San Mauro Forte (MT)

La Majatica

via A. De Gasperi, 121
☎ (+39) 0835674113 I 3396174083
✆ www.lamajatica.it
✉ info@lamajatica.it
shop: no
e-commerce: no

FRANTOIO OLEARIO VALLUZZI

This beautiful farm at more than 550 metres in altitude consistently produces top-quality oil. It is has just a small olive grove and an excellent continuous-cycle three-phase milling facility, which is also open for use by third parties. The owners' passion for oil has enabled them to preserve and promote an important native variety, majatica. Two guestrooms are available for those wishing to stay overnight.

Alghero (SS)

Domenico Manca - San Giuliano

via Carrabuffas CP 56
☎ (+39) 079977215 I 079980349
✆ www.sangiuliano.it
✉ info@sangiuliano.it
shop: no
e-commerce: no

Bolstered by more than 250 hectares of olive groves in the territory of Alghero, San Giuliano is one of the largest island food producers in the country. Their impressive production volumes haven't compromised quality, however. The producer was founded in the early 20th century by Pasquale Manca, the grandfather of its current chief, Domenico. San Giuliano produce a wide range of extra virgin olive oils, as well as vegetables bottled in oil, olives and a recently introduced line of cosmetics made with olive oil.

Extra virgin olive oil

Palma di Montechiaro (AG)

Mandranova

s.s. 115, km 217 strada di servizio
☎ (+39) 3939862169
❂ www.mandranova.com
✉ info@mandranova.com
shop: no
e-commerce: no

A modern 180-hectare estate found near the town that inspired Tomasi di Lampedusa's famous Gattopardo. In a beautiful hillside setting, with intense, almost dazzling light and colours, Giuseppe and Silvia Di Vincenzo manage the operation with admirable enthusiasm. This unique terroir has always been an agricultural haven, caressed by the loving breeze from the nearby sea. It specializes in growing olives and its most recent grove vaunts almost 10,000 trees, some of which are more than a century old. Its innovative olive mill permits optimum processing of the drupes. The refined resort has hotel and restaurant facilities.

Custonaci (TP)

Manfredi Barbera & Figli

c.da Forgia
☎ (+39) 091582900 ❙ 3298782041
❂ www.oliobarbera.it
✉ barbera@oliobarbera.it
shop: no
e-commerce: no

This important business has been operating on international markets since 1888. It is now headed by the tirelessly competent Manfredi Barbera, the fourth generation of a family that has left its mark on the history of Italian olive production. The firm coordinates a network of small and micro producers, all of whom benefit from specialist technical assistance and next-generation technology. Its well-established international marketing network, which has been in place since time immemorial, succeeds in promoting various products on the market, produced using the olives from 600,000 trees planted over 3,000 hectares.

Campello sul Clitunno (PG)

Marfuga

v.le Firenze
☎ (+39) 0743521338 ❙ 3494200063
❂ www.marfuga.it
✉ marfuga@marfuga.it
shop: no
e-commerce: no

Back in the early 20th century Domenico Gradassi began making a goof profit selling demijohns of his oil to northern Italy, but the real turnaround in terms of quality came in the 1960s under his son Ettore. Today Marfuga is one of the most important regional production firms, standing out for its consistent production quality, even during difficult harvests, like last year. Its 30-hectare olive grove contains around 13,000 trees. It also has an agritourism with five guestrooms.

Rosciano (PE)

Marramiero

c.da Sant'Andrea, 1
☎ (+39) 0858505766
❀ www.marramiero.it
✉ info@marramiero.it
shop: no
e-commerce: no

Marramiero is primarily an established, award-winning winery, acknowledged to be one of the best in Abruzzo. A family that loves what its land is able to produce, proudly exporting its products all over the world. A few years ago these values led to the idea of producing quality extra virgin olive oil to sell alongside its renowned wines. It exports primarily to the United States, Japan and Germany.

Morigerati (SA)

Nicolangelo Marsicani

fraz. Sicilì I c.da Croceviale
☎ (+39) 3382906364 I 0974982074
❀ www.marsicani.com
✉ frantoio@marsicani.com
shop: no
e-commerce: no

Nicolangelo Marsicani operates in Cilento, where he's become a reference point even for young oil producers. Despite some difficult years, he's been able to establish a reputation for quality oil thanks to his experience in the field. Marsicani cultivates about 6,000 plants over 50 hectares, all of which are certified PDO. In addition to oil he grows apples, figs, artichokes and wild asparagus. Products can be bought online at their website.

Matera

Vincenzo Marvulli

via Dante, 9
☎ (+39) 3386079006 I 0835332568
✉ giovanni.marvulli@yahoo.it
shop: no
e-commerce: no

azienda agricola
vincenzo marvulli

This is one of the best estates in the region, not only in terms of EVOO production but also of pulses, pearl barley, farro pasta, and Senatore Cappelli durum wheat pasta. Estate manager Giovanni Marvulli founded the farm thanks to the investments made by his father Vincenzo in 1960. Today, about 2,700 trees are scattered over 24 hectares of certified organic olive groves.

Extra virgin olive oil

Trevi (PG)

Mascio

loc. Falcione
☎ (+39) 0742780955 I 335356645
❀ www.agricolamascio.it
✉ agricolamascio@offnet.it
shop: no
e-commerce: no

Mascio

A firm locally renowned for its quality, and since 2006 for its consistent production and product focus thanks to the tenacity of Giuseppe Giancarlini. It has around 8,000 olive trees of main local varieties (frantoio, leccino, moraiolo), distributed over 22 hectares of perfectly exposed terrain.

Marsciano (PG)

Castello Monte Vibiano Vecchio

fraz. Mercatello I voc. Bocca di Rigo
☎ (+39) 0758783001
❀ www.montevibiano.it
✉ info@montevibiano.it
shop: no
e-commerce: no

CASTELLO
MONTE VIBIANO
———— VECCHIO ————

This charming estate can be found in some of Umbria's loveliest countryside, on the way from Perugia to Marsciano, in the Perugia hills. Here, the Fasola Bologna family cultivate vineyards and olive groves to produce wine and EVOO. And they do so with outstanding environmental awareness and particular attention to CO_2 emissions.

Morro d'Oro (TE)

Frantoio Montecchia

c.da Case di Pasquale, 29
☎ (+39) 085895141 I 3483959952-3
❀ www.frantoiomontecchia.it
✉ info@frantoiomontecchia.it
shop: no
e-commerce: no

FRANTOIO
MONTECCHIA
olio extra vergine di oliva

The Montecchia family has been growing olives for around thirty years. Headed by Gennaro, it is one of the most important firms in the province of Teramo. It has 26,000 trees, new and old, in Morro d'Oro, at around 250 metres above sea level. They are spread over 80 hectares belonging to the family. Such large numbers of trees are needed to meet the growing demand from local and foreign markets.

Villamaina (AV)

Oleificio Montuori

c.da Toppoli
☎ (+39) 0825442175 I 3384016634
✉ oleificiomontuori@libero.it
shop: no
e-commerce: no

Emilio Montuori runs an estate of around 100 hectares, with six given over to olives. The firm has 2,200 trees, whose drupes are processed in the family's own oil mill together with olives from reliable local organic producers. We are in the area between the Villamaiana and Torella dei Lombardi hills, a short distance from the sulphurous crater in Valle dell'Ansanto, cited by Virgil in his Aeneid, indicated as one of the "gates of Hell".

Serrungarina (PU)

Massimo Mosconi

via Tomba, 50a
☎ (+39) 3204414610 I 072123230
⊛ www.emozioneolio.com
✉ info@emozioneolio.com
shop: no
e-commerce: no

MASSIMO MOSCONI
AZIENDA AGRICOLA

Massimo Mosconi opened in 2012 and his farm is an excellent example of how things can get off to an immediate good start. Although Massimo is a doctor, his great passion for the countryside led him to embark on this venture with the support of his family and a number of highly skilled consultants. His three hectares of olive groves stand on the hills outside Pesaro, partly within the borders of the PDO Cartoceto district.

Soriano nel Cimino (VT)

Alessandro Musco

via della Montagna, 20
☎ (+39) 063227676 I 3442970429
⊛ www.alessandromusco.it
✉ info@alessandromusco.it
shop: no
e-commerce: no

With a strong family tradition of olive growing behind him, Alessandro Musco is now promoting a new business project that is widespread in northern European countries: acquiring technical knowledge to then select the producers and product, and market it. His selections, working with the Frantoio Paolocci in Vetralla, favour production deriving from the volcanic land on the Cimini hillsides, in the eastern province of Viterbo, at altitudes of 400–500 metres.

Arco (TN)

OlioCRU

via A. Moro, 1
☎ (+39) 0464715344 I 3287447414
❂ www.oliocru.it
✉ info@oliocru.it
shop: no
e-commerce: no

An ambitious and successful business project, started in 2011 by Mario Morandini and Stefano Bonamico, when they combined their individual farms. The result is ten hectares of olive groves with 2,000 trees. The main cultivars are casaliva and frantoio, and the process is managed with avant-garde technology and innovative quality concepts. The results have been more than impressive, making it necessary to purchase other olives alongside the 500 quintals produced by the estate.

Canino (VT)

Coop. Olivicola di Canino

via P. Nenni, 1
☎ (+39) 0761438095 I 3356436436
❂ www.olivicolacanino.it
✉ info@olivicolacanino.it
shop: no
e-commerce: no

Coop. Olivicola
di Canino a r.l.

Sapori di
Terra Etrusca

Luciano Stocchi is at the helm of this cooperative, founded in 1988. Today's 130 members grow olives in the Canino PDO and constitute a network of strong roots. The stony hillsides of volcanic origin are at 300 metres in altitude, between Lake Bolsena and the sea. Member-owned groves cover 300 hectares on the Tuscan border: 35,000 trees of local varieties whose olives are processed within 24 hours in the cooperative's own mill. The EVOO is filtered with natural cotton and preserved in nitrogen-sparged containers.

Priverno (LT)

Paola Orsini

loc. San Martino I via Villa Meri
☎ (+39) 0773913030 I 3392964172
❂ www.olioorsini.it
✉ info@olioorsini.it
shop: no
e-commerce: no

Paola Orsini's olive farm is certainly one of the best in the Colline Pontine area, covering 40 hectares, of which 30 are olive groves planted only with 4,000 age-old itrana trees. The quality of production is influenced by the exposure of the olive groves to the sea breeze, but also to the extensive experience of the owners and the organic methods they prefer. The olives are processed within a few hours of harvesting in the next-generation, continuous-cycle, certified organic olive mill. The farm exports its products to Japan, the United States and Great Britain.

Pianella (PE)
Marina Palusci

c.da Fonte Gallo, 2
☎ (+39) 3392285185
✆ www.olivetopependone.com
✉ info@olivetopependone.com
shop: no
e-commerce: no

Massimiliano D'Addario is the driving force behind this firm, based inland of Pescara, in Pianella, and which has been one of Abruzzo's leading oil production names four generations here. Indeed, Palusci is now synonymous with quality and respect for local values. Massimiliano, a young oleologist and professional taster, harvests healthy, intact fruits each year from his 4,000 olive trees, processing prized oils that are much in demand.

Montespertoli (FI)
Fattorie Parri

via Vallone, 4
☎ (+39) 0571674057
✆ www.fattorieparri.it
✉ info@fattorieparri.it
shop: no
e-commerce: no

The Parri family has run this farm for four generations. Their love of the local land was handed down to descendants, the current owners. Wine is the main product, but extra virgin olive oil also plays a particularly important role, with 40 hectares of olive groves containing almost 8,000 trees made up of the four main local varieties: moraiolo, leccino, pendolino and frantoio.

Castrocaro Terme e Terra del Sole (FC)
Tenuta Pennita

via Pianello, 34
☎ (+39) 0543767451 I 3482333510
✆ www.lapennita.it
✉ info@lapennita.it
shop: no
e-commerce: no

Gianluca Tumidei has invested great energy and resources in this business, making it a benchmark for the entire Emilia Romagna region over the course of just a few years. Gianluca's strict methods and skill are key to a selection that delivers some of the best expressions of the Brisighella area each year, for oils that are always extremely limpid and pure. The firm has expanded further and processes olives from 15,200 trees set in 45 hectares of olive groves. It exports mostly to Europe, the United States and Japan.

Extra virgin olive oil

Atri (TE)

Persiani

c.da San Martino, 43
☎ (+39) 0858700246 I 3383642724
❧ www.aziendapersiani.it
✉ agricolapersiani@libero.it
shop: no
e-commerce: no

The Atri hills, at 380 metres above sea level between Gran Sasso and the Adriatic sea, are home to Persiani olive groves, an 18-hectare farm (with a total of 4,500 trees) managed by Mattia Persiani and Helvia Tini, who delight us with their quality oils produced with great passion and love of the land. Their products are exported to France, Australia, the United States and Belgium.

Buccheri (SR)

Tenuta del Pettirosso

c.da Vernera, 3
☎ (+39) 3492480746
✉ flucer@tin.it
shop: no
e-commerce: no

Francesco Lucerna set up his operation in 2005, and the production of his "green gold" is progressing in leaps and bounds. There are 14 hectares of olive groves with a total of 1,650 typical local cultivars. He is a great believer in manual harvesting of drupes and in proper processing times. In addition to EVOO, he produces vegetables bottled in olive oil, sun-dried tomatoes and jams, also exported to France and Germany.

Apricena (FG)

Piano

loc. Palombino I s.da prov.le 28, km 2
☎ (+39) 0882643676 I 3493950096
❧ www.agricolapiano.com
✉ info@agricolapiano.com
shop: no
e-commerce: no

A family business and for several decades a producer of EVOO in the hilly countryside behind the Gargano promontory, in the province of Foggia. It focuses on small-scale production of the provenzale cultivar better known as peranzana, which thrives in the mild climate and has a perfect habitat in the local soil. The firm is currently converting to organic methods and exports to various European countries and North America.

Casal Velino (SA)
Pietrabianca di Davide Monzo

fraz. Marina I via Portararo, 32
☎ (+39) 0974907384 I 3472301542
❀ www.oliodelcilento.it
✉ info@monzo.it
shop: no
e-commerce: no

PIETRABIANCA
- FRANTOIO OLEARIO -

This family-run firm dates back to the early 20th century, when the Monzo family began to cultivate the olive trees that are now quite an age but still productive. Pietrabianca was founded in 1993 by Antonio Monzo, the father of Davide who runs these 35 hectares today, primarily planted with salella, pisciottana, rotondella, frantoio and leccino varieties. The farm is in a beautiful spot in the Cilento national park, in the heart of Basso Cilento, with its stunning landscapes and fascinating history.

Menfi (AG)
Planeta

c.da Dispensa
☎ (+39) 091327965
❀ www.planeta.it
✉ planeta@planeta.it
shop: no
e-commerce: no

An internationally renowned wine brand for over 20 years thanks to the consistency and quality of its products, which has made a fundamental contribution to the establishment of Sicilian wine production, and also a top-quality oil producer. The 98-hectare estate has 26,000 olive trees and is in Menfi, in Contrada Capparina, amidst stunningly beautiful scenery. Scrupulous attention to detail is combined with respect for tradition and the most recent technology.

Fasano (BR)
Profumi di Castro
Adriatica Vivai

fraz. Speziale I via Lecce di Speziale
☎ (+39) 3394101859 I 0804810989
❀ www.profumidicastro.it
✉ info@profumidicastro.it
shop: no
e-commerce: no

Profumi di Castro

This firm began producing oil in the 1990s following its decision to purchase various plots of land in the scenic district between Fasano, Ostuni, Villa Castelli, and Montemesola, in the Brindisi area. Since 2011, a next-generation extraction plant has enabled the firm to take control of the entire production chain, from the field to bottling. Products are exported to Germany, Great Britain and Denmark.

Extra virgin olive oil

Greve in Chianti (FI)
Pruneti

loc. San Polo in Chianti I via dell'Oliveto, 24
☎ (+39) 0558555091 I 3317133833
✆ www.pruneti.it
✉ frantoio@pruneti.it
shop: no
e-commerce: no

The Pruneti family has been
in the area since at least the mid-19th century and has been producing oil for at
least 100 years, as well as growing irises, and have now added saffron as a crop,
but oil is still the key product for Gionni and Paolo, the fourth generation of the
Pruneti family. There are numerous cultivars to be found in the 80 hectares of olive
groves, starting with the most common local varieties such as moraiolo, leccino
and frantoio, also used to make monovarietal oils. The presence of the company
olive mill ensures consistently high quality.

Alatri (FR)
Americo Quattrociocchi

via Mole Santa Maria, 11
☎ (+39) 0775435392 I 3393289548
✆ www.olioquattrociocchi.it
✉ info@olioquattrociocchi.it
shop: no
e-commerce: no

Since 1888 the Quattrociocchi family, now steered by Americo, has been one
of the leading names in quality oil production in the Frosinone area. This organic farm is in a rocky area, with plots extending over 112 hectares, planted
with around 30,000 itrana, moraiolo, frantoio and leccino olive trees. The olives
are processed within four hours of harvesting, in the farm's own next-generation
continuous-cycle oil press, and stored in nitrogen-saturated stainless steel tanks.

Bagno a Ripoli (FI)
Fattoria Ramerino

loc. La Fonte I fraz. Osteria Nuova I via Roma, 404
☎ (+39) 055631520 I 335434399
✆ www.fattoriaramerino.it
✉ info@fattoriaramerino.it
shop: no
e-commerce: no

Fattoria Ramerino

In 2000, owner Filippo Alampi decided to take over management of the farm,
rescuing it from neglect and resuming large-scale oil production, thanks to the
olives saved from the big freeze of 1985. He began to farm the land applying
organic methods and achieved organic certification in 2004. The 25-hectare farm
is planted with 5,500 trees, and as well as the moraiolo, frantoio and leccino cultivars typical of the area, Filippo has added the americano variety.

Riva del Garda (TN)
Frantoio Di Riva

via San Nazzaro, 4
☎ (+39) 0464552133 I 3358795369
✪ www.agririva.it
✉ info@agririva.it
shop: no
e-commerce: no

The Riva del Garda cooperative founded in 1926 is now one of the most important agricultural structures on Lake Garda. Its new headquarters have a winery and olive mill as well as two shops that it runs directly. The cooperative aimed to develop the short-chain concept here, combining concepts of quality and sustainability. While there are only 80 actual members, 1,200 growers are involved for oil production and use of the olive mill. Agririva accounts for 65% of all Garda Trentino oil production.

Ponte (BN)
Tenuta Romano

via Candele, 13
☎ (+39) 0824874332 I 3395742717
✪ www.frantoioromano.it
✉ info@frantoioromano.it
shop: no
e-commerce: no

This venerable Sannio estate is known especially for EVOO production. Here, in an area also famous for Aglianico wine production, the fourth generation of the family now runs the oil mill, with its modern continuous-cycle system installed in 2004. As well as EVOO, the estate also produces wine and offers six comfortable guestrooms for rents. The olive plantation of 1,600 trees lies on six hectares.

Finale Ligure (SV)
Domenico Ruffino

loc. Colle di Varigotti I s.da del Borriolo, 9
☎ (+39) 3484521161 I 3387001640
✉ domenicoruffino@hotmail.com
shop: no
e-commerce: no

Domenico Ruffino is one of northern Italy's top olive growers and has built his reputation over the years by working on his estate with a rare passion, while never overlooking the work done in the olive mill. This has produced tangible results year in, year out, in his monovarietal oils made from colombaia olives, a cultivar introduced to this area by Benedictine monks in the 12th century. He exports his products to a number of European countries and to Japan.

Extra virgin olive oil

Comiso (RG)

Frantoio Raffaele Sallemi

via Piave, 1
☎ (+39) 0932963424 I 3334370111
❀ frantoiosallemi.it
✉ sallemi@tin.it
shop: no
e-commerce: no

An olive-growing tradition that dates back to the second half of the 19th century and the installation of the first olive mill. Raffaele Sallemi's business continues today, known for quality that is repeated year after year and that few succeed in imitating. He works with great experience and passion from this lovely estate in the Ragusa area, where 3,000 olive trees are dotted over 24 hectares of land.

Zungoli (AV)

Frantoio San Comaio

c.da Carpineto
☎ (+39) 0825845013 I 3338977118
❀ www.sancomaio.it
✉ info@sancomaio.it
shop: no
e-commerce: no

Pasquale, Roberto, Raffaella and Francesca Caruso are the siblings who manage this "modern family business", as they call it, convinced that modernity must be upheld by the most deep-rooted traditions. This catchphrase sums up a wonderful experiment that in recent years has spoiled us with the extraordinary oils obtained from the 2,000 trees they own, including ravece, ogliarola, marinese, peranzana and leccino varieties. Products are exported throughout Europe.

San Giorgio Morgeto (RC)

Olearia San Giorgio

c.da Ricevuto, 18
☎ (+39) 0966935321 I 0966940569
❀ www.olearia.it
✉ info@olearia.it
shop: no
e-commerce: no

Domenico Fazari founded the business over 70 years ago and it is still a family concern, run by his children and grandchildren. The estate of over 140 hectares, with about 25,000 olive trees, is located in San Giorgio Morgeto and Cittanova, in Aspromonte national park. There are 11 hectares of olive groves under certified organic management, and a mill that also applies a certified supply chain traceability system for each batch, with a reference code on the label to guarantee origin and authenticity. Exports go to Europe and further afield.

Aprilia (LT)
Casale San Giorgio

via Casalazzara, 1
☎ (+39) 3460214349 I 069256388
❀ www.casalesangiorgio.it
✉ casalesangiorgio@alice.it
shop: no
e-commerce: no

A daring and unusual decision led Casale San Giorgio to start super-intensive cultivation of Spanish and Italian olive varieties. After a radical restructuring of the family business, in 2010 the super-intensive method was organized for Spanish varieties like arbequina, koroneiki, arbosana and sikitita, as well as a number of experimental Italian cultivars, under observation by the University of Florence. The olive groves, with 18,000 trees, cover ten hectares and are found on the coast south of Rome.

Pineto (TE)
Tenuta Sant'Ilario - Colancecco

fraz. Borgo Santa Maria I via Costa del Mulino, 1
☎ (+39) 0859492089 I 3356555187
❀ www.tenutasantilario.com
✉ info@tenutasantilario.com
shop: no
e-commerce: no

Since 2009, Laila Colancecco has dedicated her life to her olive groves in Borgo Santa Maria, in Pineto. The 31 hectares are planted with over 5,500 trees that yield healthy, lush fruit every year thanks to their favourable geographical location. This year the estate's new-generation mill produced 200 quintals of excellent EVOO. The olives are harvested manually and pressed within six hours.

Santa Venerina (CT)
Emanuele Scammacca del Murgo

via Zafferana, 13
☎ (+39) 095950520 I 3351376443
❀ www.murgo.it
✉ info@murgo.it
shop: no
e-commerce: no

One of Catania's top operations was the brainchild of Barone Emanuele Scammacca del Murgo, who set it up. The history of this farm has always been linked to wine production even though the EVOO gives equally satisfying results. Today, the olive grove vaunts about 5,000 nocellara etnea trees, covering 18 hectares of land. In addition to oil and wine, the business also produces jams, pâtés and honey, and welcomes guests to its farmhouse accommodation of 15 comfortable rooms.

Extra virgin olive oil

Binetto (BA)
Schiralli

s.da prov.le Bitetto-Binetto
☎ (+39) 0807831755 I 3497152705
❀ www.crudo.it
✉ info@crudo.it
shop: no
e-commerce: no

In a nutshell, the Schiralli siblings have a young company and are determined not just to improve it but to strive for excellence. They have their own small olive mill so they cut out the need for go-betweens and are in direct control of processing their stellar Crudo, the flagship of their production. Bitetto is famous for a special table olive, the termite di Bitetto, which the Schirallis package in water and salt, or use to make a pâté. The company also produces traditional tomato sauce, as well as baked products like taralli using its own EVOO, tozzetti with Cervia salt and almond treccine.

Vasto (CH)
La Selvotta

via Buonanotte, 10
☎ (+39) 0873801658 I 3358154427
❀ www.laselvotta.it
✉ info@laselvotta.it
shop: no
e-commerce: no

The Sputore siblings, whose farm is in Vasto, have become known for the quality of their production. The family owns 12.5 hectares of olive groves scattered around the best areas of the Vasto hills, near the sea, enjoying plenty of sun, rich soils and a breezy climate. All this makes the area an agricultural and landscape gem. The company also offers farmhouse accommodation. Products are exported to Europe, the United States and Japan.

Spinetoli (AP)
Oleificio Silvestri Rosina

loc. Pagliare del Tronto I via Schiavoni, 3
☎ (+39) 0736890027 I 3478653743
❀ www.oliosilvestri.it
✉ info@oliosilvestri.it
shop: no
e-commerce: no

For generations the Albertini family has managed this olive mill and has succeeded in combining passion, experience and renewal. Now the business is supported by two operating systems, one traditional, using antique granite wheels, and the other a continuous centrifugal extraction plant. We are in the Piceno hills where the tender ascolana olive has been grown for centuries. Alongside its oil, the company offers cosmetic products, delicious chocolate spreads made with EVOO, black olive preserves and condiments.

Lenola (LT)
La Tenuta dei Ricordi

via Roma, 46
☎ (+39) 0771598555 I 3474907894
🖑 www.latenutadeiricordi.net
✉ latenutadeiricordi@gmail.com
shop: no
e-commerce: no

Ilenia Labbadia started her farm in 1999, and it is now a local point of reference for its focus on production quality. Ilenia has signed up for the traceability project for 100% Italian olive oil. The property, six hectares of volcanic rock, is situated on the northern slopes of the Monti Aurunci regional park, at an altitude of 450 metres. Terraced olive groves, with 1,500 itrana trees, cover four hectares. For the time being exports are mainly to Germany.

Trapani
Titone

fraz. Locogrande I via Piro, 68
☎ (+39) 0923842102 I 3357629634
🖑 www.titone.it
✉ info@titone.it
shop: no
e-commerce: no

A prestigious olive operation, between Trapani and Marsala, with 5,000 trees on 19 hectares, founded in 1936 by Nicolò Titone, an expert in the industry. He set himself the goal of producing the best oils while respecting the environment, and this awareness and expertise has been handed down to the rest of the family, which includes several pharmacy graduates. In 1985 the operation converted to organic farming, quite rare at the time. The estate is now in the hands of Antonella Titone, whom we admire for her dedication and deep commitment. The company has its own continuous-cycle mill for instant grinding of drupes.

Battipaglia (SA)
Torretta

fraz. Torretta I via Serroni Alto, 29
☎ (+39) 0828672615 I 3358038809
🖑 www.oliotorretta.com
✉ info@oliotorretta.it
shop: no
e-commerce: no

Once again, this year we see confirmation of the quality of Maria Provenza's work as marketing and production manager of the Torretta a Battipaglia cooperative in the Salerno hills. The cooperative has been in business since the 1960s but was modernized in 1998. The mill boasts innovative technology and qualified technical staff, co-ordinated by the owner in the EVOO production process. The estate owns ten olive groves with 6,000 trees, many of which are heirloom.

Extra virgin olive oil

161

Casoli (CH)
Trappeto di Caprafico

c.da Caprafico, 35
☎ (+39) 0871897457 I 3473320228
🕸 www.trappetodicaprafico.com
✉ info@trappetodicaprafico.com
shop: no
e-commerce: no

TRAPPÈTO
DI
CAPRAFICO

The Masciantonio family roots in the oil business are lost in the mists of time, with one generation following the next since 1874. Today the company is in the able hands of Tommaso Masciantonio, a young and passionate producer. There are 16 hectares of olive groves, entirely under organic management since 2004, on the rolling hills between Casoli and Guardiagrele, with a total of 4,000 plants. Exports are concentrated in Europe, United States and Japan.

Giovinazzo (BA)
Le Tre Colonne

s.da prov.le 107 Giovinazzo-Terlizzi km 0,200 c.da Caldarola
☎ (+39) 0803941570 I 3475220457
🕸 www.letrecolonne.com
✉ info@letrecolonne.com
shop: no
e-commerce: no

Salvatore Stallone's company is on a mission to excellence, seen in his constant commitment to enhancing quality. Le Tre Colonne, the three pillars, is named for tradition, taste and authenticity, the three rules underpinning its production of extra virgin olive oil. A fairly young company that began in 1986, making a quantum leap in 2008 when it was awarded its PDO label. Le Tre Colonne uses special equipment to minimize oxidative stress so drupes can give their best. Export destination include Britain, Germany and Canada.

Trevi (PG)
Trevi Il Frantoio

loc. Torre Matigge I via Bastia, 1
☎ (+39) 0742391631 I 3201710087
🕸 www.olioflaminio.it
✉ info@olioflaminio.it
shop: no
e-commerce: no

fLa MINIO
IT tastes good!

The Trevi cooperative opened for business in 1968 thanks to a few farmers who joined forces. It is named after the municipality, renowned for olive cultivation and the production of excellent EVOO. The overall surface area is currently around 300 hectares split between about 60 members. A sea of olives, which provides ample opportunities for choice and selection.

Vetralla (VT)
Frantoio Tuscus

v.le Eugenio IV, 107
☎ (+39) 0761 477889
❀ www.frantoiotuscus.com
✉ info@frantoiotuscus.com
shop: no
e-commerce: no

Giampaolo Sodano and Fabrizia Cusani have created a real bellwether in the region with Frantoio Tuscus, the oil producer from Tuscia known for its high-quality extra virgin olive oil. Their success in maintaining such high standards is thanks in part to a collaboration between the Olivaia farm and the modern facilities of Tuscus (which can be visited during the growing season), both of which are privately owned. Their website also features an easy-to-use online shop. They export to France and Japan.

Orosei (NU)
Olivicoltori Valle del Cedrino

loc. Conculas I s.s. 125, km 225
☎ (+39) 0784 997103 I 3460357650
❀ www.costadegliolivi.it
✉ costadegliolivi@tiscali.it
shop: no
e-commerce: no

COSTA DEGLI OLIVI

The Cooperativa Agricola Olivicoltori Valle del Cedrino was founded in 1999 by nine members on a mission to produce quality EVOO. The cooperative thus managed to save an ancient olive grove estate, an integral part of a unique habitat. The cooperative is named after the valley where it is located, an area starting on rough, wild mountainsides and meandering towards the sea. In this setting, the River Cedrino plays a key role in the local microclimate. The cooperative has about 50 hectares of olive groves of which 90% are given over to the bosana cultivar.

Verona
Cantina Valpantena

fraz. Quinto di Valpantena I via Colonia Orfani di Guerra, 5b
☎ (+39) 045550032
❀ www.cantinavalpantena.it
✉ samantha@cantinavalpantena.it
shop: no
e-commerce: no

This leading wine cooperative, active in the area since 1958, counts about 300 members. Since about half of them also own olive groves, the company equipped itself with an oil mill in the years following its establishment, and now produces EVOO exclusively from the native grignano and favoral varieties. Here, on the outskirts of Verona, towards the Lessini hills, the countryside resists the urban sprawl in an area aptly known as the Valley of the Gods by the poets and historians of ancient Rome.

Grottaglie (TA)
Tenuta Venterra

c.da Mannara
☎ (+39) 0999915296 I 3929992246
✆ www.tenutaventerra.it
✉ info@tenutaventerra.it
shop: no
e-commerce: no

Tenuta Venterra is a farm that has made sustainability its business philosophy. The new mill, 3.5 metres below the level of the surrounding countryside, uses solar energy to produce electricity, while ground olive pits are used as fuel and olive cake as fertilizer. About 67,000 trees are farmed with organic methods in the countryside between Grottaglie and Ceglie Messapica, in the province of Taranto. Much of the production is exported to the rest of Europe.

Sassocorvaro (PU)
Oleificio Venturi Agape

fraz. Mercatale I via Nuova, 46
☎ (+39) 3391553556 I 3488370706
✆ www.olioagape.it
✉ info@olioagape.it
shop: no
e-commerce: no

The Venturi oil mill, in a charming medieval village in the shadow of Mount Carpegna, has a long history in the cultivation of olive trees. Located in the Marche, right below San Marino, the company today is run by Nirvana Guerra, who took over from her father and pursues quality in the same way. The business does not have its own olive groves so selection is very stringent and relies on a good base guaranteed by batches from top local growers. Export destinations include the Netherlands, Germany and France.

Buccheri (SR)
Vernèra

via Umberto, 21/23
☎ (+39) 3383622868 I 3381450213
✆ www.vernera.it
✉ vernera1984@gmail.com
shop: no
e-commerce: no

In the heart of the Hyblaean mountains, this stunning natural setting, dense with thick woods and vast pine groves, stands at 500–700 metres above sea level. The estate owned by Gaetano, Mariagrazia and Tania Spanò, fourth generation of a family that has combined professional careers with farming, vaunts 70 hectares and 9,500 olive trees, almost all of a venerable age. Products are exported mainly to Germany.

Greve in Chianti (FI)
Vignamaggio

via Petriolo, 5
☎ (+39) 055854661 I 3483035155
❀ www.vignamaggio.com
✉ prodotti@vignamaggio.com
shop: no
e-commerce: no

VIGNAMAGGIO

The 200 hectares in the heart of Chianti Classico are owned today by Paul Patrice Tavarella. This very attractive estate is documented as far back as the 15th century. It is thought that the Vignamaggio landscape provided the background for Leonardo Da Vinci's Mona Lisa. Alongside the 60 hectares of vineyards there are 30 hectares of groves with 5,000 olive trees of traditional Chianti cultivars: frantoio, leccino, moraiolo and pendolino, open-centre pruned and organically farmed since 2014.

Foligno (PG)
Viola

fraz. Sant'Eraclio I via Borgo San Giovanni, 11b
☎ (+39) 074267515 I 3355742329
❀ www.viola.it
✉ info@viola.it
shop: no
e-commerce: no

VIOLA

Marco Viola is a key player in Umbrian and Italian quality olive growing. He never loses touch with the olive grove while still managing to do an amazing job in the mill. In doing so he has managed to build a business that is an inspiration today for anybody who aiming for a quality product. Marco's estate has about 27,000 trees occupying over 80 hectares of land, many of them certified organic, and he also produces pulses, grains and flours.

Incisa in Val d'Arno (FI)
Il Violone

loc. Entrata, 1
☎ (+39) 0558336873 I 3286652746
✉ staff@campusviola.com
shop: no
e-commerce: no

TENUTA
L'ENTRATA

In 2003, the della Valle family, owners of ACF Florence, bought the historic producer Tenuta dell'Entrata, named for its geographic position as a kind of entranceway between Incisa and Chianti. On the estate you can find a villa built in 1578 by the Bagnesi family, who are among Florence's oldest aristocratic families. At about 200 meters above sea level, they oversee a total of 130 hectares, comprising 12 vineyards and and an olive grove of 3000 of the most venerable trees of the region. Il Violone exports to Asia, especially South Korea and Japan.

Extra virgin olive oil

Chiaramonte Gulfi (RG)

Viragì

c.da Mazzarronello
☎ (+39) 3939299344 I 3809025045
🌐 www.viragi.it
✉ info@viragi.it
shop: no
e-commerce: no

Traditional olive growing, revived in 2007, developed with renewed enthusiasm and fresh skills from a tightknit family in a district that has always been famous for its belief in quality production. The estate stands at over 450 metres in altitude and has a total area of 30 hectares, with over 3,000 trees, almost all tonda iblea, with a percentage of nocellara del Belìce, mostly very old, some very ancient. About five hectares of this estate are managed using certified organic farming methods. The acknowledged quality of the oils produced is down to the meticulous care at all stages of the supply chain.

Trevi (PG)

Sorelle Zappelli Cardarelli

loc. Bovara Fondaccio, 6
☎ (+39) 074278669 I 335498309
🌐 www.agriturismoimandorli.com
✉ info@agriturismoimandorli.com
shop: no
e-commerce: no

Maria, Alessandra and Sara Zappelli Cardarelli play a key role in this beautiful farm, found in an area that enjoys one of the longest traditions of Umbrian olive oil. The olive grove vaunts 5,500 trees with organic certification, distributed across 14 hectares, but vegetables, jams, spelt, fruit and vegetables are also produced here, not to mention the charming farmhouse accommodation facility.

Canino (VT)

Ione Zobbi

loc. Gioacchina I via del Tufo
☎ (+39) 0761437601 I 3283765629
🌐 www.iandp.it
✉ paolo.borzatta@iandp.it
shop: no
e-commerce: no

Ione Zobbi and Paolo Borzatta, with the precious help of professor Maurizio Servili, have set themselves apart for their innovative cultivation techniques, harvesting and pressing, which is performed separately for each cultivar. The 19 hectares of olive groves, which host about 1300 plants, reach an altitude of about 300 meters above sea level. Olives are processed shortly after harvest in a press that is at the vanguard of what's available today. In addition to maintaining an easy-to-use online shop, they export to the USA, Holland, UK and France.

Chiaramonte Gulfi (RG)

Villa Zottopera

via D. Cimarosa, 75
☎ (+39) 3357851044 I 0932621442
🌐 www.villazottopera.it
✉ zottopera@gmail.com
shop: no
e-commerce: no

A stunning agritourism facility dating back to the late 1700s, surrounded by olive groves, and comprising five welcoming houses. Apart from the magical setting, however, there is also some impressive excellent extra virgin olive oil. This is one of the area's top operations, outstanding for its reliable quality, as well as 2,500 splendid tonda iblea variety trees in its olive grove.

Extra virgin olive oil

San Venanzo (TR)

Guido Alberti

loc. Poggio Aquilone I via Centro, 12
☎ (+39) 0758743365 I 3389902573
✪ www.prodottibioalberti.it
✉ info@prodottibioalberti.it
shop: yes
e-commerce: no

The farm estate covers 560 hectares that roll between the provinces of Perugia and Terni. A certified organic outfit, managed with passion and love for the land by agronomist Guido Alberti and his wife Paola. The product range is rich and varied, but the lion's share goes to pulses and cereals: chickpeas, lentils, grass peas, beans, cowpeas, mixed soups with cereals, barley and spelt, and even a chickpea pâté. There is no shortage of flour (chickpea, spelt, Senatore Cappelli durum wheat), olive oil, pasta and even organic Chianina meat.

Antignano (AT)

Antignano Prodotto Tipico

fraz. Perosini
☎ (+39) 3333029056
✪ www.antignanoprodottotipico.it
✉ info@antignanoprodottotipico.net
shop: no
e-commerce: no

This firm produces otto file corn, known locally as the "king's corn" because it was consumed by King Vittorio Emanuele II. It is grown in small, carefully monitored plots of land and is stone ground after harvesting to produce a premium flour with a unique flavour, perfect for making polenta and much more. The firm also produces various types of pasta, melba toast and other delicacies.

Norcia (PG)

Bettini - Agrisviluppo Todiano

v.le della Stazione, 7
☎ (+39) 0743938022
✪ www.bettinibio.com
✉ info@bettinibio.com
shop: yes
e-commerce: yes

A family-run operation, which opened in 1992, producing and selling only organic typical mountain crops. Each process is monitored meticulously, from sowing to harvesting to processing, and is a virtuous example of the closed chain. Hence the noteworthy quality of the chick peas, grass peas, spelt (pearl, puffed and cracked, pasta, flour, puffed cakes), field pea, Bettini lentil, Castelluccio lentil, Monti Sibillini lentil, barley, mixes for various soups.

Mortegliano (UD)
La Blave di Mortean

via Flumignano, 23
☎ (+39) 0432760547
✆ www.lablavedimortean.com
✉ info@lablavedimortean.com
shop: no
e-commerce: no

In the heart of an area mostly dedicated to the cultivation of corn, this cooperative has for years dedicated itself to safeguarding this crop, from sowing to selecting the ears to the harvest itself. The next step is processing the kernels so as to produce a top-quality flour that is white and yellow and neither too fine nor too thick. Wheat, barley and rice flour are also made here. La Blave di Mortean also produce delicious and healthy snacks.

Onano (VT)
Marco Camilli

loc. Bicchiere I via Cavour, 80
☎ (+39) 076378018 I 3284187301
✆ www.marcocamilli.it
✉ info@marcocamilli.it
shop: yes
e-commerce: no

In 1996, Marco Camilli gave up a career as a pharmacist to start up this organic farm. He specializes in production of cereals and pulses, especially native species with different morphological and sensorial traits. So there are various types of chickpeas (cerere, flora, otello), grass peas, beans (ciavattone, cocco, giallo, solfarino, verdolino, purgatorio), spelt (cracked and pearl), barley meal, pearl barley, delicious Onano lentils that cook fast without being soaked in advance.

Monteleone di Spoleto (PG)
Cicchetti

loc. Ruscio
☎ (+39) 0743755841 I 0743755869
✆ www.farrocicchetti.it
✉ Info@farrocicchetti.it
shop: yes
e-commerce: no

The business was founded in 1995 by Giulio Cicchetti and sister-in-law Roberta Gervasoni, and in the past ten years has evolved radically, especially the product range. Quality is the watchword for every item: PDO and organic spelt above all, sold cracked, semi-pearl, shucked, puffed. Then there are puffed spelt cakes, plain and chocolate-coated, crackers, honey-coated grains, flour, meal, various pasta shapes. Also available are soup mixes, lentils, chickpeas and grass peas, beans, pearl barley, field peas.

Gragnano Trebbiense (PC)
Molino DallaGiovanna

loc. Gragnanino I via Madonna del Pilastro, 2
☎ (+39) 0523787155 I 0523787338
✆ www.dallagiovanna.it
✉ info@dallagiovanna.it
shop: yes
e-commerce: yes

Since 1832, the Dalla Giovanna family has produced flours with the sole objective of offering quality to its customers. First it carefully selects raw ingredients, the cereals and grains, then it monitors all subsequent stages, from storage temperature in the silos to the slow grinding and ensuing blending process. The Dalla Giovannas produce a number of all-purpose flours, together with more specific types including organic and wholemeal. They also market a line of gluten-free products and a range for people with dairy intolerances.

Gazzo (PD)
Francesco De Tacchi

loc. Grantortino I via Garibaldi, 54
☎ (+39) 0495995067
✆ www.detacchi.it
✉ ufficio.commerciale@detacchi.it
shop: yes
e-commerce: yes

DeTacchi
RISARE dal 1570

Francesco De Tacchi's farm is a centuries-old operation that has always devoted outstanding care and attention to its crops, from seeds to harvest and processing of products. The jewel in the crown is the excellent rice, part of which is Carnaroli and Vialone Nano, aged for a surprising 22 months. Then there is flour (including instant and stoneground) and artisanal corn pasta, monovarietal biancoperla and maranello corn beers, and biscuits (Venetian buffetti and tondi de luna) also made from corn.

Casalnuovo Monterotaro (FG)
Molini De Vita

via G. Donizetti, 16
☎ (+39) 0881558556 I 3409641335
✆ www.molinidevita.it
✉ info@molinidevita.it
shop: no
e-commerce: no

MOLINO
DeVita

The De Vita family has always grown wheat in an ideal area for this crop, almost on the border with Molise, but it was not until 1997 that it developed a modern plant, with minimal environmental impact, for grinding flour in near the farm. Now it has total control over the entire cycle and guarantees the excellent quality of the end product. They have organic, traditional, and health lines, as well as Kamut, spelt and Senatore Cappelli wheat flours, with various wholemeal and multigrain varieties.

Viterbo
Fornovecchino

s.da prov.le Ombrone, km 4,800
☎ (+39) 0761823654 I 3393601998
✉ claudio.pagliaccia@libero.it
shop: yes
e-commerce: no

Fornovecchino is a farm, mill, processing and pasta maker facility. Claudio Pagliaccia and his wife Romina grow organic heirloom pulses and cereals: Purgatorio beans, solco dritto chick peas, Onano lentils, emmer and einkorn, Senatore Cappelli and Khorasan durum wheat, Frassineto, Gentilrosso, Verna and Maiorca soft wheat, rye, oats, millet, barley, Marano corn, grass peas, dall'occhio and verdolino beans. Natural grindstones are used and the pasta is bronze-drawn.

Monte San Giovanni Campano (FR)
Il Frantoio

loc. Colli I via Araietta, 6
☎ (+39) 0775866003
⊕ www.ilfrantoionline.it
✉ biofrant@tin.it
shop: yes
e-commerce: no

In addition to good organic EVOO, the farm produces its own prime quality items, and acquires from cooperatives and other businesses that apply natural working methods. The product list includes over 400 entries, including pulses, grain and puffed cereals, muesli, stone-milled flour, pasta made from different types of cereals (durum wheat, spelt, soya, Kamut, rice, corn, rye, buckwheat), bread and bakery products, couscous, vegetable stock cubes, dried fruits, canned tomato sauce, sea salt, wine, beer and fruit juices.

Castelbello Ciardes/Kastelbell Tschars (BZ)
Fuchs

via della Palude, 11
☎ (+39) 0473624756
⊕ www.fuchs-cereals.com
✉ info@fuchs-cereals.com
shop: no
e-commerce: no

The farm has been producing excellent lines of cereals since 1922, thanks to careful quality control of ingredients and various work processes. The range includes the classic cornflake in numerous variations (plain, chocolate, spelt, honey pops); muesli mixes with honey or pieces of fruit; and a range of prized grains and flours like wholemeal and buckwheat; oat, spelt, barley, millet, barley and hulled millet. Without overlooking pumpkin, sunflower, flax, and hulled sesame seeds, plus the organic line.

Panicale (PG)
Molino Gatti

via Olmini, 45
☎ (+39) 075837336 I 3347721777
✆ molinogatti.it
✉ info@molinogatti.it
shop: yes
e-commerce: yes

For over half a century, this family-run business has produced excellent flours for food use. It uses organic fertilizers and grows its crops in as sustainable a fashion as possible. The wheat harvest is monitored closely, as are the various processing stages, which do not use any chemical additives. It produces dozens of different types, suited to various types of foods and available in different sizes, including "0", "00", wholemeal, strong etc. It also produces an organic line and instant dried yeast.

Parma
Molino Grassi

loc. Fraore I via Emilia Ovest, 347
☎ (+39) 0521662511
✆ www.molinograssi.it
✉ silviograssi@molinograssi.it
shop: no
e-commerce: yes

Creiamo qualità

With 80 years of experience behind it, this business has built up a tried and tested chain over the years. It produces top-quality products and always keeps one eye on changing customer requirements. Its seven flour lines have been developed specifically for bread-making, pizza, pasta, pastry-making and so on, both for catering industry professionals and for use at home. It has an interesting organic segment, with einkorn, emmer and spelt, Kamut, durum wheat, Manitoba and wholemeal flours.

Medicina (BO)
Marchesi

via Licurgo Fava, 150
☎ (+39) 051857551
✆ www.marchesi-srl.it
✉ info@marchesi-srl.it
shop: no
e-commerce: no

A business founded in the 1950s and a cereal specialist producing mainly couscous, not only from traditional durum wheat meal and semolina, but also from quinoa and chickpea, lentil and chickpea, whole durum wheat and green lentil, wholemeal, whole corn, or with larger grains, semolina, and polenta. There is also an organic line of durum wheat, spelt, corn, rice, wholemeal Kamut, whole barley, whole rice, whole buckwheat and corn, four whole grains (durum wheat, spelt, corn, Kamut).

Cossano Belbo (CN)

Mulino Marino

via Caduti per la Patria, 41
☎ (+39) 014188129
❂ www.mulinomarino.it
✉ info@mulinomarino.it
shop: yes
e-commerce: no

The Marino brothers are the third generation of a family that has been in the milling industry since the 1950s, using natural stone and roller mills. They have achieved great success over recent years thanks to a focus on biodiversity, processing pure-ground traditional organic cereals. Its millstones include one for processing otto file corn, one for soft and durum wheat, and one for grinding cereals suitable for gluten intolerance. They also sell pulses and cereals in grain form.

Castelvetrano (TP)

Molini del Ponte

via G. Parini, 29
☎ (+39) 0924904162 I 3357457677
❂ www.molinidelponte.it
✉ info@molinidelponte.it
shop: yes
e-commerce: yes

For four generations, the Drago family has produced fine flours made from traditional native Sicilian wheat. Every stage of the process is handled internally and subjected to strict controls. The wholemeal flours are all stoneground and free from colourings, preservatives and additives. The varieties available include tumminia, used to make the renowned Castelvetrano black bread, a Slow Food Presidium. There are five different brands: Molini del Ponte primarily for couscous; F.lli Drago; Le Farine del Palmento; Tumminia for pasta; and Fa.Bio, the organic line.

Rieti

Molino del Cantaro

via di Villa Mari, 3
☎ (+39) 0746484478 I 3292333646
❂ www.molinodelcantaro.com
✉ molinodelcantaro@tiscali.it
shop: yes
e-commerce: no

Domenico Mari works about 60 hectares of land situated inside the Laghi Lungo e Ripassottile nature reserve, applying scrupulous organic farming principles to his cereal and pulse crops. The grains are then used to make flour in an old stone mill dating back to the 1600s, still powered by the waters of the Rio Cantaro. Domenico sells rye, oat, corn and wheat flours in various packagings and weights, and also offers chickpeas, lentils, grass peas, oats, corn for popcorn and sunflower seeds.

San Lorenzo in Campo (PU)

Monterosso

via Costantinopoli, 9
☎ (+39) 0721776511
✆ www.mrosso.it
✉ info@mrosso.it
shop: yes
e-commerce: yes

This business cultivates farro delle Marche, an emmer wheat and one of the oldest types of spelt. On the 500-hectare estate every stage, from sowing to harvesting and processing is subject to strict controls. Its stoneground flours preserve optimum nutritional properties thanks to the grinding temperature. It also produces different types of long and short pasta, as well as cracked and pearl emmer, perfect for soups and broths.

Firenzuola (FI)

Poggio del Farro

loc. Mazzetta I via Pietramala, 670a
☎ (+39) 055818186
✆ www.poggiodelfarro.com
✉ info@poggiodelfarro.com
shop: no
e-commerce: no

The efforts of more than a hundred farm workers produce organic spelt here in a territory that is particularly well-suited to its cultivation, with a maximum respect for the environment and the aid of renewable energy sources. Flour comes first, but there's a whole lot more, starting with various types of pasta (whole wheat, egg, gnocchi), crackers and bread substitutes, snacks, biscotti, sweets, baked goods, pearled spelt (perfect for salads and soups) and even beer.

Urbino

Prometeo

fraz. Canavaccio I via Metauro, 10
☎ (+39) 072253520
✆ www.prometeourbino.it
✉ info@prometeourbino.it
shop: yes
e-commerce: no

Founded in 1991, in the small-business district, the company specializes in processing spelt, especially certain genealogically engineered emmer varieties designed to make the most of this heritage cereal's innate properties. As well as biscuits, wholemeal couscous, mouth-watering sweet and savoury snacks, pasta in a variety of shapes, including wholemeal, and puffed, cracked and pearl emmer, it also produces white and wholemeal flour suitable for use in many different recipes.

Pontelongo (PD)
Molino Rossetto

via Indipendenza, 156
☎ (+39) 0499775010
❀ www.molinorossetto.com
✉ info@molinorossetto.com
shop: yes
e-commerce: yes

Established in 1760, this business has evolved over the years and is now a leading name in the flour and cereal sector. As well as focusing on quality and technology, it also keeps pace with changing customer demands. The range is incredibly varied and includes products for various uses including bread, pastries and pizzas, as well as durum wheat, wholemeal, and semi-processed flour. The range includes stoneground, gluten-free, corn, and special flours from Kamut, oats, spelt, grano arso, puffed cereals and grains, yeasts.

Buttapietra (VR)
Antico Molino Rosso

via Bovolino, 1
☎ (+39) 0456660506
❀ www.molinorosso.com
✉ gaetano@molinorosso.com
shop: yes
e-commerce: yes

ANTICO MOLINO ROSSO®

This reliable, attentive business stands out for its expertise, innovation and on-going research. Its cereals are stored in silos with a modern ventilation system before being stoneground at low temperatures to preserve intact their wholesomeness. Antico Molino Rosso produces a varied range of organic flours, including gluten-frees, and a rich selection of organic cereals like spelt, Kamut, rye, barley, buckwheat, millet, and quinoa; dried fruit; pasta of various kinds; and sourdough starters.

Sondrio
Sala Cereali - Il Saraceno

v.le dello Stadio, 24
☎ (+39) 0342214068 I 0342571828
❀ www.salacereali.it
✉ salacereali@tin.it
shop: yes
e-commerce: no

IL SARACENO
SALA CEREALI
il Gusto della Ricerca

For over a century, generations of the Sala family have been active in the processing of grains, above all Valtellina native varieties. Careful selection of type of crop and monitoring of processes ensures quality products, including buckwheat flour for polenta taragna; cornmeal; wheat flour; wholemeal rye and spelt flours; rice flour; chickpea flour; almond flour; coconut flour; and chestnut flour. Then there are bread and breadsticks, rice, soup and breakfast cereals, pulses, dried mushrooms, honeys, jams and much more.

Flours, pulses, cereals

Martinengo (BG)
Salera

loc. Cascina Vallere I via Vallere, 65
☎ (+39) 0363987295 I 3356237378
❀ www.salera.it
✉ info@salera.it
shop: no
e-commerce: no

Love of the land and work ethic are the underpinning of a business that has made genuine products its flagship. Grains take the lion's share: spelt, oats, barley, millet, rye, heritage wheat, and buckwheat. Stone-milled flours come next: wheat, spelt, barley, rice, buckwheat, millet, five-grain, Manitoba, oats, wheat, einkorn, heritage wheat, flint corn. There are also yellow, red and white cornmeals (coarse and medium ground; whole) for polenta taragna; spelt and rye polenta flours; and a "vecchia polenta bergamasca". Gnocchi and baked goods also on offer.

Norcia (PG)
Sapori di Norcia - Cooperativa Lenticchia di Castelluccio

via del Lavoro
☎ (+39) 0743828174 I 0743817073
❀ www.lenticchiacastelluccio.it
✉ info@saporidinorcia.com
shop: yes
e-commerce: no

Castelluccio lentils, grown on the eponymous plain, in the Monti Sibillini National Park at 1500 metres in altitude, were awarded PGI in 1997. The cooperative was founded with the aim of protecting the consumer by offering a quality product, cultivated without the use of chemicals. These tiny pulses are delicious, with high nutritional value and cook fast without soaking in advance. The cooperative also sells beans, chickpeas, peas, grass peas, pearl barley, spelt, cereal and pulse soup mixes, spelt waffles and puffed spelt.

La Morra (CN)
Mulino Sobrino

via Roma, 108
☎ (+39) 017350118 I 0173 509860
❀ www.ilmulinosobrino.it
✉ info@ilmulinosobrino.it
shop: no
e-commerce: no

For generations, the Sobrino family have produced high-quality organic flour from their historic mill. Flours are produced using a variety of grains, from corn to oat, malt, rye, whole wheat, rice, spelt, Kamut and semolina, all without added enzymes or chemicals. They also make chestnut flour. There are so many varieties that choosing the best isn't an easy task. Their future projects include rediscovering flours from long-lost ancient grains and making them available to the public.

Foligno (PG)
La Valletta

via dei Villini, 35c
☎ (+39) 0742632106
✆ www.lenticchie.it
✉ amministrazione@lenticchie.it
shop: no
e-commerce: no

COLFIORITO

Founded in the 1980s by Antonio and Adriana Cappelletti, this family concern today has about 150 hectares of land mostly in the Colfiorito area. Production consists mainly of pulses (including hulled), with lentils at the top of the list, then grass peas, chickpeas, beans, and field peas. Followed by barley, spelt, soup mixes (some are very handy pre-cooked). Last but not least, spelt crackers, dried porcini mushrooms and pure saffron threads.

Flours, pulses, cereals

Tornareccio (CH)
Adi Apicoltura

via A. De Gasperi, 72
☎ (+39) 0872868160
❀ www.adiapicultura.it
✉ info@adiapicoltura.it
shop: yes
e-commerce: no

The Jacovanelli family has 150 years of experience in beekeeping to its name. A green, certified kosher business, it produces several lines of honey: organic, its top line, includes about ten varieties of Italian wildflower, acacia, cherry, rosemary, sunflower, sainfoin, honeysuckle, linden, chestnut, and eucalyptus honeys, including a unique winter savory (a subspecies of thyme), processed only when it rains. The products are entirely Italian and natural, integrated with a line of apiary by-products.

Termini Imerese (PA)
Carlo Amodeo

c.da Madonna Diana
☎ (+39) 0918114615 I 337967373
❀ www.amodeocarlo.com
✉ apicolturaamodeo@libero.it
shop: yes
e-commerce: no

Carlo Amodeo's interest in the taste of honey and the bee world inspired this business, working with renewable energy to manage 1,500 beehives and three workshops. Here the project regarding the Sicilian black bee was born, reintroduced nearly 20 years ago to the island's habitat and then elected a Slow Food Presidium. The honey is unique, along with the citrus, loquat, honeysuckle, and bramble, not to mention the very unusual thistle, carob, milkvetch (a rare type from high mountains), giant fennel (produced on the island of Filicudi in June), prickly pear and almond.

San Sperate (CA)
Coop. Apistica Mediterranea

s.da prov.le 4, km 12
☎ (+39) 0709601926
❀ www.apimed.com
✉ direzione.terrantiga@gmail.com
shop: yes
e-commerce: yes

Terrantiga
O.P. Apicoltori Sardi

The cooperative grew out of beekeeping experiences that the Caboni family developed in 1995, inspired by grandfather Salvatore's skills. He was the first to use frame hives and a drip-system honey melter, with other innovations to enhance processing, quality of honey and, above all, bee welfare. In 2001, organic certification arrived. The many types of honey include asphodel, strawberry tree, and eucalyptus, but the most noteworthy are those from Mediterranean maquis; thistle; and orange. Many other products include honey and mead sapa.

Caluso (TO)
Mario Bianco

via Morteo, 20
☎ (+39) 0119833441 I 3488708882
❀ www.mieleitalia.com
✉ contatti@mieleitalia.com
shop: yes
e-commerce: yes

i Mieli di Mario Bianco

Andrea and Lorenzo are the fourth generation of the Bianco family, beekeepers since the late 1800s, producing honey from stable hives in the best Italian habitats. There is linden in Val d'Ossola; wildflower and rhododendron in Parco del Gran Paradiso; sunflower in Tuscany; clementine in Calabria; eucalyptus, thyme and citrus in Sicily; strawberry tree in Sardinia. As well as rosemary, acacia, chestnut and dandelion. Their Mielò liqueur is made from Erbaluce di Caluso grappa and citrus honey, and there are exclusive delicacies like orange honey pralines.

Guardiagrele (CH)
Apicoltura Bianco

loc. Villa San Vincenzo I via Sciusciardo, 10
☎ (+39) 0871893422
❀ www.apicolturabianco.it
✉ apicolturabianco@libero.it
shop: yes
e-commerce: no

BIANCO

A family company from Guardiagrele, producing quality honey in many varieties. In addition to traditional honeycomb, mountain and wildflower, chestnut, eucalyptus, orange, sunflower, honeysuckle, sainfoin and alfalfa honey, there are countless original products like aromatized acacia honeys, hazelnut and honey spread, and recipes with honey and nuts, cocoa or saffron. There is also preservative-free jam with honey, called Scrùcchjata, and a bitter digestif made from honey and a local herb.

Bibbiena (AR)
Apicoltura Casentinese

via dell'Artigiano, 10/12
☎ (+39) 0575536494
❀ www.apicolturacasentinese.com
✉ info@apicolturacasentinese.com
shop: yes
e-commerce: no

APICOLTURA
CASENTINESE

A beekeeping park of thousands of certified organic hives makes this one of Italy's leading companies in the industry. It was founded in 1982 and then moved its hives from Calabria's valleys to central Italy, particularly Casentino and Maremma national parks. The range of honey products is varied, ranging from regional orange, citrus, clementine, eucalyptus and chestnut, to bio acacia, wildflower and honeydew. Apicoltura Casentinese has been certified for the quality of its honeys by the international body, CSQA.

Malalbergo (BO)
Cazzola

fraz. Altedo I via Canaletto, 15
☎ (+39) 0510473468
◈ www.apicolturacazzola.it
✉ info@apicolturacazzola.it
shop: yes
e-commerce: no

This bee farm's motto is "don't change what Nature has already perfected". It is committed to nomadic beekeeping so as to make honey with different botanical origins. The results are whole virgin honey; an extensive line that includes woodland and fir honeydew; traditional acacia, citrus, chestnut, and cherry honey; special borage, heather, alfalfa, apple, lavender, rosemary, dandelion, and linden honey. Noteworthy acacia honey mixed with apricots, dried fruit, almonds, hazelnuts, walnuts, and truffle.

Pratola Peligna (AQ)
Apicoltura Colle Salera

via Per Prezza, 58
☎ (+39) 0864271082 I 3333600083
◈ www.apicolturacollesalera.com
✉ info@apicolturacollesalera.com
shop: yes
e-commerce: no

Walter Pace has been passionate about bees for many years. His small, family firm devotes itself to the fine ancient agricultural skill of apiculture, in a particularly favourable setting: the green Valle Peligna, where the bees enjoy an unpolluted environment. As well as wildflower, sainfoin, citrus blossom, honeydew, acacia, chestnut, eucalyptus, and sunflower honeys, the organic products also include royal jelly, propolis, pollen and beeswax.

Monterenzio (BO)
Coop. Conapi - Mielizia

via Idice, 299
☎ (+39) 0516540411
◈ www.mielizia.it
✉ info@conapi.it
shop: yes
e-commerce: no

Attrazione Naturale

The CONAPI Italian national beekeepers' association was set up in 1978 by a group of young producers. Over time CONAPI has extended its products and the number of beekeepers throughout Italy. Approximately 2,500 tons of top wildflower and single-flower honey are sold in retail outlets and the HORECA circuit under the brand name Mielizia. Despite its large scale, CONAPI makes quality honeys, both organic and conventional. Some are typically Italian, some come in sachets, in squeezers and in the state-of-the-art fully compostable paper packs.

Salmour (CN)

Diale

via Trinità, 22
☎ (+39) 0172649329 I 3920066696
🕸 www.apicolturadiale.it
✉ andrea@apicolturadiale.it
shop: yes
e-commerce: yes

The company opened in 1970 thanks to the passion of Giuseppe Diale, who was determined to find the most precious Piedmontese flowers to make authentic honeys with sophisticated sensorial traits and of the best quality. His passion for beekeeping was inherited by son Andrea who still practises this noble art, creating quality honeys from acacia, rhododendron, basswood, chestnut and dandelion flowers, as well as woodland and fir honeydew, and a fragrant Valle Stura high-mountain honey.

Elva (CN)

Apicoltura biologica Floriano Turco

Baita San Giovanni
☎ (+39) 3382030388
✉ florianoapibio@yahoo.it
shop: yes
e-commerce: no

Floriano Turco makes "extreme honeys", in the Cuneo Alps near the French border, at about 2,000 metres altitude. They are organic and are part of the High-Mountain Honey Slow Food Presidium. Floriano practises closed-cycle beekeeping: he raises the queen bees and nuclei of the bee community, builds the hives, produces and bottles the honey. He makes four high-mountain honeys: rhododendron, wild thyme, wildflower and fir honeydew, as well as an exclusive crystallized acacia honey.

Rivoli (TO)

La Margherita

c.so Francia, 152
☎ (+39) 3384971274 I 3388094502
🕸 www.apicolturalamargherita.com
✉ info@apicolturalamargherita.it
shop: yes
e-commerce: no

Canavese, Val di Susa, Val Sangone and the Gran Paradiso National Park, are the location of owner Margherita Fogliati's apiaries. The bees graze far from the roads, sheltered from sources of pollution, to guarantee an authentic and healthy product. As well as the classic acacia, dandelion, wildflower, basswood, chestnut and woodland honeydew honeys, products include rare honeys from Alpine flora and rhododendrons, protected by a Slow Food Presidium.

Alife (CE)
Messidoro

via Vergini
☎ (+39) 0823783395
✉ messidoro@alice.it
shop: no
e-commerce: no

A beekeeping cooperative with members all over the Italian peninsula, especially in the south, and producing acacia, linden, orange, eucalyptus, borage, honeysuckle, clover, alfalfa, sunflower, and cherry honey; and Metcalfa honeydew named after an insect native to North and Central America. Contributing apiarists are nomadic. The honey is extracted cold using a spinner, then the product is left in ageing vats for about 40 days. At this point it is part is bottled and part is kept in drums to be sold as required.

Pescina (AQ)
Raggi di Sole

loc. Ponte San Valentino
☎ (+39) 086386231 I 3397566155
◈ www.mieleraggidisole.it
✉ info@mieleraggidisole.it
shop: yes
e-commerce: yes

Franco Troiani's apiaries can be found in the luxuriant, unblemished eastern Marsica. The insects feed at altitudes of 800–1,100 metres above sea level and these conditions combine to produce an extraordinary high-mountain honey. As well as the traditional acacia and wildflower varieties, the best honeys include horehound, ironwort and savory. The company also offers pollen, propolis and a line of cosmetics.

Ton (TN)
Mieli Thun - Andrea Paternoster

loc. Vigo I s.da Conte Zdenko Thun, 8
☎ (+39) 0461657929
◈ www.mielithun.it
✉ info@mielithun.it
shop: yes
e-commerce: yes

Andrea Paternoster, the third generation of a beekeeper family (with more than a thousand hives scattered throughout Italy), is a passionate defender and promoter of top-quality honey. Since the early 1990s he has been signing off on a rich range of wildflower products in addition to honey compotes, nectars sometimes combined with hazelnuts, walnuts and apples. The flagship Quintessenza is a sort of cru, made with virgin supers, created to achieve maximum purity. Rosemary honey and fir honeydew inspired the idea of honey vinegar.

Colle di Val d'Elsa (SI)

Distilleria Alboni

loc. Mensanello I zona industriale Pian dell'Olmino, 86
☎ (+39) 0577904424
🌐 www.distillati.it
✉ info@distillati.it
shop: no
e-commerce: no

ALBONI

TOSCANA
distilleria artigianale
a bagnomaria

In the heart of the Sienese hills, in Chianti, marc and fruit are distilled using the traditional bain-marie process. Alboni is a small artisan estate where the fruit is carefully selected for different types of spirits. As well as the classic monovarietal grappas, the stills are also used for honey brandy and beer spirits from artisan beers produced specifically for the purpose.

Merano/Meran (BZ)

Kellerei Algund Genossenschaft

Portici, 218
☎ (+39) 0473237147
🌐 www.algunderkellerei.it
✉ info@algunderkellerei.it
shop: no
e-commerce: no

**Algunder
Kellerei**

The fame of Lagundo wine and food is rooted in history but equally solidly bound to a great distillery: Lagundo cooperative winery. It was established on 24 February 1909 by 37 members, in the Marchetti retail building in the centre of Merano. Today, the distillery produces the famous Algunder Treber, and since the 1990s vaunts the Grappa label which upholds production standards for this prized Italian spirit The result is a beverage with a refined aroma and unmistakable character, made solely from grapes of the finest Italian vintages.

Canelli (AT)

Grapperia Artigianale Ali

via Indipendenza, 110
☎ (+39) 0141823440
🌐 www.artegrappa.it
✉ info@artegrappa.it
shop: no
e-commerce: no

Giuseppe Aliberti founded his Grapperia Artigianale Alì (hence the name Alì) in Canelli in the 1950s. It is now run by the third generation of the Poglio family, who work with complete respect for craft traditions. The passion that drives the Poglios means they make liqueurs or bespoke grappas, prepared with traditional recipes or following indications given by customers, who are also free to choose their own label for the product according to their taste or needs.

Aquileia (UD)

Distilleria Aquileia

via Julia Augusta, 87a
☎ (+39) 043191091
❂ www.distilleriaaquileia.com
✉ info@distilleriaaquileia.com
shop: no
e-commerce: no

In 1965 Flavio Comar decided to set up his Distilleria Aquileia. With huge determination he decided to start his own system with a pot still, built in 1938, and a continuous still built in 1965. Today his son Alessandro continues his father's work with great passion, following the distillation process step by step. The flagship product is certainly La Centenara Gran Riserva Flavio Comar, distilled from traminer, riesling, sauvignon and malvasia marcs, aged in new barriques.

Barbaresco (CN)

Distilleria del Barbaresco

s.da Ovello, 49
☎ (+39) 0173635217
✉ distil.barbaresco@tiscali.it
shop: no
e-commerce: no

Distilleria del Barbaresco is a cooperative founded in 1980 to promote the image of Barbaresco. Today it is known for its commitment to seeking enhanced quality in the production of grappa. To this end, the cooperative has installed cutting-edge distillation systems to create a grappa that preserves the characteristic fragrance, scent and aroma of marc. In addition, in 2002 installation began of a double-boiler distillation plant for processing not just grapes but fruit, wine and lees.

Costigliole d'Asti (AT)

Distilleria Beccaris

fraz. Broglietto I via Alba, 5
☎ (+39) 0141968127
❂ www.distilleriabeccaris.it
✉ info@distilleriabeccaris.it
shop: no
e-commerce: no

Cavaliere Elio Beccaris began his business adventure in the world of distilled spirits in 1951. Piedmont's heritage of prestigious wines is the underpinning for the Beccaris family's production of grappas, spirits and liqueurs. They experiment with various solutions to achieve excellent products, including continuous and discontinuous distillation, oak and cherrywood barrels, long maturation and solera method, as well as making grapeseed oil and delicious bottled fruit.

Mombaruzzo (AT)
Distillerie Berta

via Guasti, 34
☎ (+39) 0141739528
🌣 www.distillerieberta.it
✉ info@distillerieberta.it
shop: no
e-commerce: no

Francesco Berta founded this venerable distillery, located in Casalotto di Mombaruzzo, at the turn of the 20th century. He was bold and tenacious, and was not discouraged by the hard farming life, working the vineyards and seeking customers to purchase his products. Since then, four generations have taken their turn at the helm and contributed to the distillery's current success. The spirits are unique, in eye-catching packaging, and the wide range satisfies even the most demanding palates.

Mezzocorona (TN)
Distilleria G. Bertagnolli

via del Teroldego, 11
☎ (+39) 0461603800
🌣 www.bertagnolli.it
✉ info@bertagnolli.it
shop: yes
e-commerce: yes

A company with 144 years of history in making Trentino grappa and still run by the Bertagnolli family. The marc is distilled after first racking, using a discontinuous double-boiler alembic that enhances the aromatic profile of teroldego, nosiola, chardonnay, marzemino and gewürztraminer grape to produce grappa that is always clean and well-balanced.

Mestrino (PD)
Umberto Bonollo

via G. Galilei, 6
☎ (+39) 049900023
🌣 www.bonollo.it
✉ info@bonollo.it
shop: no
e-commerce: yes

The art of making grappa has been a prerogative of the Bonollo family since 1908, the year the founder of the family, Giuseppe Bonollo, experimented with an innovative steam still able to produce grappa with a better sensorial profile than that found in traditional types. In 1951 his son Umberto Bonollo decided to continue his father's company with his children, establishing the legal offices in the Padua area and starting up a production process that includes a special Riserva Grappa of Vintage Sei Stelle.

Liqueurs, syrups, distillates

Cuneo

Bordiga

via Valle Maira, 98
☎ (+39) 0171611191
❀ www.bordigaliquori.it
✉ info@bordigaliquori.it
shop: no
e-commerce: yes

The Bordiga family has always used the multitude of herbs, flowers, roots, and plants found on the mountains and in the valleys of Cuneo to give life to a range of products steeped in alpine scents, aromas and fragrances. Génépi, for example, is a key ingredient in one of Bordiga's most famous liqueurs, grows completely naturally on the mountain slopes of the Maira and Varaita valleys. Today the fourth generation of the Bordiga family is able to offer spirits that combine the ancient flavour and the goodness of craft production.

Ospedaletto (TN)

Borgo Vecchio Distillati

via Barricata, 12a
☎ (+39) 0461770000
❀ www.borgo-vecchio.it
✉ info@borgo-vecchio.it
shop: no
e-commerce: yes

Borgo Vecchio is one of the few distilleries entitled to use the Tridente label, issued by the most authoritative institute for origin and quality of Trento grappa. Over the years this distillery has developed unique, very drinkable meditation products that have garnered important awards. In 2006, its Grappa Gran Riserva 98 and Grappa Barrique were awarded prizes by ISW (International Spirituosen Wettbewerb) and its proven quality continues to be a constant across its wide range of products.

Castagneto Carducci (LI)

Premiata Fabbrica di Liquori Emilio Borsi

via Garibaldi, 7
☎ (+39) 0565766017
❀ www.borsiliquori.it
✉ info@borsiliquori.it
shop: yes
e-commerce: no

In April 1886 Francesco Borsi started his production of liqueurs in Castagneto Carducci, where he began to make his famous Elixir China Calisaja, which won awards at the Rome Expo of 1895 and 1899. This liqueur used Ecuador cinchona, used to extract quinine, the antimalarial drug used in the Maremma district at least until the early 1900s. When Francesco died, his son Emilio took over and continued traditional production. Today the company is managed by Anna Maria Costa, and produces Gran Liquore del Pastore, prepared with pure milk, sugar, vanilla and lemons.

Figline Vegliaturo (CS)
Bosco Liquori

loc. zona industriale Piano Lago I c.da Felicetta
☎ (+39) 0984969582
❀ www.boscoliquori.it
✉ info@boscoliquori.it
shop: no
e-commerce: no

In 1864, Raffaello Bosco created the first recipe for amaro silano, made from precious Calabrian herbs. Prior to this ingenious idea, the liqueur was only made in the rural homes, after careful selection of the herbs and for private consumption. Since then, Bosco liqueurs have made their mark and the products are purchased all over Italy, including by wealthy consumers. Today four new partners continue the production and mindful of the Bosco reputation for quality, consolidate and promote the brand in Italy and abroad.

Godega di Sant'Urbano (TV)
Bottega

fraz. Bibano I Villa Rosina v.lo A. Bottega, 2
☎ (+39) 04384067
❀ www.bottegaspa.com
✉ info@bottegaspa.com
shop: no
e-commerce: no

The Bottega distillery is inextricably linked to the name of Rosina Zambon Bottega and her husband who in acquired the business in Sartor, near Treviso, in 1967. A few years later Rosina was widowed but she never lost heart, and bravely continued to work hard in the business she had begun. The Alexander brand was launched in 1987, for the connoisseur consumer seeking a sophisticated, fragrant grappa. Today Rosina's children have taken over and safeguard the concept of excellence.

Montegalda (VI)
F.lli Brunello

via G. Roi, 51
☎ (+39) 0444737253
❀ www.brunello.it
✉ info@brunello.it
shop: no
e-commerce: no

At 170 years of age, this is the oldest artisan distillery in Italy, working over four generations to select the best marc. In the 1980s the latest offspring took over and is still in the saddle today: Giovanni, Paolo and Stefano brought new ideas that would meet the demands of a modern consumer looking for a softer but equally refined grappa. Here the Brunello family refined distillation techniques and extended the range, adding monovarietals to traditional spirits.

Liqueurs, syrups, distillates

Gorizia
Candolini

via Fatebenefratelli, 4
☎ (+39) 048133100
🌣 www.branca.it
✉ ufficiostampa@branca.it
shop: no
e-commerce: yes

CANDOLINI

Soft, limpid, authentic. Grappa Candolini vaunts a distinctive refined, fresh aroma. A flavour that swept away the Italian market and in 2008 took the brand's various lines to pole position. In 1987 t was taken over by the Branca group, a company famous for its Fernet-Branca bitter, an iconic name in Italy. The specialities worthy of note are the Sensea monovarietals from chardonnay, moscato, glera and pinot: a line for the most demanding, refined palates.

Rosà (VI)
Capovilla Distillati

via Giardini, 12
☎ (+39) 0424581222
🌣 www.capovilladistillati.it
✉ info@capovilladistillati.it
shop: no
e-commerce: no

CAPOVILLA
DISTILLATI

Artisans of the calibre of Gianni Capovilla can be counted on the fingers of one hand in the distillery world. His passion for spirits dates back to 1974, but became tangible with the production of pure products made from impeccable raw materials and double-boiler distillation. Production time is eight times longer than those aiming more for quantity than for quality, and the range is extensive, from fruit distillates to those made from beer, brandy and rum, all manufactured with great care. And there is plenty of choice.

Zeddiani (OR)
Silvio Carta

s.da prov.le 12, km 7,800
☎ (+39) 0783410314
🌣 www.silviocarta.it
✉ info@silviocarta.it
shop: no
e-commerce: no

Silvio Carta

Silvio Carta's winery was founded in the 1950s and soon became the icon of Vernaccia di Oristano well beyond regional boundaries. Today the founder works alongside his son Elio, and together they also produce fine spirits and traditional liqueurs. Their long journey led to the installation of an innovative plant with modern technology and an exclusive packaging style. The estate also produces artisan beers and essential oils from typical Sardinian medicinal herbs.

Donnas (AO)
Caves de Donnas

via Roma, 97
☎ (+39) 0125807096
🌐 www.donnasvini.it
✉ info@donnasvini.it
shop: no
e-commerce: no

Donnas is a small village in the lower Val d'Aosta, known mainly for its wine, which has been a DOC since 1971. Hence the Caves de Donnas cooperative was established, equipped with the most modern winemaking systems and oak barrels for ageing. In addition to the many wines produced, worthy of note is the feisty Caves de Donnas grappa, a true mountain spirit, made almost entirely from nebbiolo marc, with lingering notes of violets and a strong, persuasive flavour.

Fivizzano (MS)
China Clementi

via Ferriera, 4
☎ (+39) 058592056
🌐 www.chinaclementi.it
✉ info@chinaclementi.it
shop: no
e-commerce: no

In 1884, Doctor Giuseppe Clementi's pharmacy in Fivizzano produced a prodigious elixir made from two fine varieties of tropical cinchona, armomatic and medicinal herbs. Known as China Clementi, this renowned and precious product is still made with the traditional recipe. Of a characteristic orange colour, China Clementi is barrel-aged for two years to achieve a soft, intensely scented, virtuoso liqueur with a persistent finish.

Chambave (AO)
La Crotta di Vegneron

p.zza Roncas, 3
☎ (+39) 016646670
🌐 www.lacrotta.it
✉ info@lacrotta.it
shop: no
e-commerce: yes

La Crotta di Vegneron is a cooperative set up in in 1980 by about 25 members, expanding to 80 in 1985. This leading company collects the grapes of two famous production areas that give their names to the Nus and Chambave designations of origin, the underpinning to a vast production of wines and spirits. Particularly interesting is the wide range of chambave, bus, fumin, and müller thurgau grappa, with their subtle yet strikingly leisurely fragrance.

Liqueurs, syrups, distillates

Vigliano d'Asti (AT)

Distilleria Dellavalle

via Tiglione, 1
☎ (+39) 0141953926
✆ www.grappedellavalle.it
✉ distilleria@grappedellavalle.it
shop: no
e-commerce: no

Roberto Dellavalle put his oenological studies and passion for wine to work and created a distillery that has just celebrated 30 years of activity. As well as grappas from the Piedmontese winegrowing legacy, the range offers products made from the marc of great Italian wines like Amarone and Greco di Tufo, or spirits aged in barrels previously used for ageing Marsala, Passito di Pantelleria, Demerara rum or whisky. The grappas in the range are velvety, appealing and complex.

Barberino Val d'Elsa (FI)

Deta Distilleria

s.da di Poneta, 2/16
☎ (+39) 0558073173
✆ www.detadistilleria.it
✉ info@detadistilleria.it
shop: no
e-commerce: no

In 1926, the noble Torrigiani di Santa Cristina family founded a small distillery near the River Elsa. In 1978, Deta was set up to modernize the old distillery once called Lo Stillo. Over the years the facilities have developed and are now a leading distribution centre for grappa in Tuscany. Today modern technology with cutting-edge stills is used to make the grappa, employing highly specialized personnel. In addition to grappa, Deta also produces brandy, limoncino and grape aquavit.

Susa (TO)

Distilleria Erboristica Alpina

loc. Tra Due Rivi, 15/4
☎ (+39) 012231909
✆ www.grappadelnonno.it
✉ maurizio.zara@grappadelnonno.it
shop: no
e-commerce: no

This distillery was founded in 1997, in the heart of Val di Susa, with the mission of safeguarding the old, traditional recipes. Indeed, here herbs from the surrounding forests are distilled into an excellent génépy and, of course, the award-winning herb Amaro. The Chocolate Gianduiotto liquor is definitely worth trying, as is the Turin Chocolat, both are delicious. The liquorice, mint and rhubarb liqueurs are just as enticing. Finally, their selection is rounded out with grappas (of various flavors, including honey), syrups, gin and vodka.

Cividale del Friuli (UD)

Domenis 1898

via Darnazzacco, 30
☎ (+39) 0432731023
❂ www.domenis1898.com
✉ info@domenis1898.com
shop: no
e-commerce: no

DOMENIS1898
crystal clear **tradition**

Since its founding in 1898, four generations of the Domenis family have managed the distillery with unflinching dedication and attention. Tradition, quality and innovation are at the foundation of their production philosophy, which also includes a selection of organic spirits. Ingredients are supplied by local growers and then slowly and expertly worked by masters. Grappas, liquors and brandies, all of the highest quality, can also be bought in elegant gift packaging.

Roccabianca (PR)

Faled Distillerie

via Tolarolo, 6
☎ (+39) 0521374004
❂ www.spiritoverdiano.it
✉ roberta@faled.it
shop: no
e-commerce: no

The Faled distilleries have been in operation since 1945, distilling and ageing grappa, brandy, liqueurs, infusions of walnuts and other fruit, upholding a tradition that does not disdain the use of modern technologies. Both the grappa and the infusions are prepared by selecting prime raw materials and all production processes with extreme care. Worthy of note are the prize Grappa Lambrusco, Grappa Malvasia, Grappa delle Nebbie, Grappa Gutturnio and Grappa Fortana, all very drinkable and with heady fragrances.

Spilimbergo (PN)

Fantinel

fraz. Tauriano I via Tesis, 8
☎ (+39) 0427591511
❂ www.fantinel.com
✉ fantinel@fantinel.com
shop: no
e-commerce: no

Fantinel

The three generations that have worked in the business have made Fantinel the biggest operation of its genre on the Friuli wine scene. Its range of quality wines are known worldwide as an expression of their terroir and true drinkability. The family estate vaunts 300 hectares of priceless vineyards whose grapes also produce a fine pomace used for a grappa that is intense, elegant and lively. The Fantinel line includes Grappa Ramandolo and Grappa Refosco Barrique.

Cornaiano/Girlan (BZ)
Fischerhof

loc. Colterenzio, 12
☎ (+39) 0471660627
◈ www.fischerhof-mauracher.it
✉ info@fischerhof-mauracher.it
shop: no
e-commerce: no

The history of the Fischerhof distillery began half a century ago in Girlan, a village with a large number of wineries. Here the Maso distillery produces grappa from the marc provided by these wineries, as well as fruit brandies and liqueurs. The Williams pear distillate has a crisp, intense flavour, with a strong, lingering palate; the monovarietal moscato rosa gives a grappa with a subtle, velvety, pleasing fragrance; and a coffee-orange liqueur offers the delicate scent of oranges, sweet and fruity with coffee emerging in the finale. All products made with carefully selected prime raw materials.

Gussago (BS)
Distillerie Franciacorta

via Mandolossa, 80
☎ (+39) 030 2529311
◈ www.distilleriefranciacorta.it
✉ info@dfran.it
shop: no
e-commerce: no

The Gussago company is a prestigious operation opened in 1901 by wine producer Luigi Gozio. In 1930, his sons Paolo and Giuseppe were responsible for a turning point in the family firm when they installed a modern steam distillation facility to obtain purer, more subtle products. In 1977 the company became Distillerie Franciacorta Spa, a true industry with high-tech equipment to deal with new scales of production and distribution. The Franciacorta brand includes Grappa Selezione Cuore and René Briand brandy, two prestigious labels in the world of spirits.

Valdina (ME)
Distilleria Giovi

via Valdina, 30
☎ (+39) 0909942256
◈ www.distilleriagiovi.it
✉ giovisrl@tiscali.it
shop: no
e-commerce: no

The Giovi distillery is a relatively young concern, born in 1987 but quickly achieving very high levels of quality and winning numerous awards in the world of spirits. Giovanni La Fauci is the master distiller and the founder of this company located in Valdina, in the province of Messina. Giovanni procures the raw materials from top Sicilian wineries and fruit comes from crops dotted across the slopes of Mount Etna, while the marcs come from the best vineyard country. All spirits are typical of the raw material, preserving the fragrance and voice of their origins.

Silvano d'Orba (AL)
Distilleria Gualco

via XX Settembre, 5
☎ (+39) 0143841113
◉ www.distilleriagualco.it
✉ info@distilleriagualco.it
shop: no
e-commerce: no

The Gualco distillery is a magical place for anyone who wants to explore the ancient craft of making spirits as undertaken by Paolo Gualco, a former cooper. The company has been operating in the sector for 150 years, with its own venerable double-boiler stills and offers guided tours in the age-old marc storerooms and late-1700s ageing cellars. The company also has an authentic grappa boutique selling numerous products from young to aged spirits, aromatized grappa, liqueurs and imported beers.

Volpago del Montello (TV)
Loredan Gasparini

via Martignago, 24
☎ (+39) 0423870024
◉ www.loredangasparini.it
✉ info@loredangasparini.it
shop: no
e-commerce: no

In the late 1940s, Count Piero Loredan realized the winemaking potential of the Venegazzù area and invested here, planting vineyards in the hilly Alta Marca Trevigiana district of the province of Treviso. The territories between Asolo and Montello offer balanced, dynamic wines that express their terroir in no uncertain terms. The marc from these prestigious grapes are used to make Grappa Capo di Stato, from the iconic red wine produced by the winery, and its Riserva aged 60 months in oak barrels.

San Michele all'Adige (TN)
Fondazione Mach

via E. Mach, 1
☎ (+39) 0461615252
◉ www.iasma.it
✉ cantina@iasma.it
shop: no
e-commerce: no

FONDAZIONE EDMUND MACH

A few lines will not suffice to describe the history of this excellent facility and of Edmund Mach, the first principal of San Michele all'Adige school of agricultural studies. In 1871 Innsbruck Regional Diet acquired the monastery that is now home to the school and its estate, converting it into a school with a station for agricultural trials. Today, apart from teaching, the Foundation boasts 120 hectares of vines and apple orchards, a winery and a distillery. True to tradition the institute produces grappa with a discontinuous double-boiler still and creates a dozen monovarietals as well as the famous Castel San Michele grappa blend of two different grape varieties.

Casale Monferrato (AL)

Magnoberta

via Asti, 6
☎ (+39) 0142452022
🕲 www.magnoberta.com
✉ info@magnoberta.com
shop: no
e-commerce: no

The Magnoberta distillery is based in Casale Monferrato and is coming up for its centenary as it has been produces spirits, distillates and grappa since 1918. Right from the start the company began to win awards at major trade fairs. There is currently a wide range of grappa, and the noteworthy monovarietal flagship Pura line using native Piedmont marc from like dolcetto, brachetto, grignolino and barbera.

Altavilla Monferrato (AL)

Mazzetti d'Altavilla

v.le Unità d'Italia, 2
☎ (+39) 0142926147
🕲 www.mazzetti.it
✉ info@mazzetti.it
shop: no
e-commerce: yes

The distillery was founded before the Unification of Italy, in 1846, when Filippo Mazzetti began to distill in the heart of Monferrato. Now in its sixth generation of distillers, the Mazzetti family today may vaunt a unique history and experience in this sector, as is clear from the range of products: classic and aged grappas, collections, selections, aquavit and spirits that have garnered the company a place as a top award-winning distillery in Italy and in the world.

Ascoli Piceno

Meletti

zona industriale Campolungo
☎ (+39) 0736403493
🕲 www.meletti.it
✉ info@meletti.it
shop: yes
e-commerce: no

Silvio Meletti began to distil his Anisetta in 1870, perfecting a recipe inherited from his mother. The aniseed picked in this part of the Piceno area is renowned for its strong aromatic profile. Along with other natural flavourings, herbs and flowers used for the distillate, it confers unique notes, thanks to a very gentle distillation process. In addition to the classic Anisetta, Meletti also produces a dry version, and Mistrà, a Marche liqueur of pure anise.

Valdobbiadene (TV)

Distilleria Miotto

fraz. San Vito I via del Fossadel, 1
☎ (+39) 0423976428
✉ diviva.srl@virgilio.it
shop: no
e-commerce: no

DI.VI.VA.

Miotto, like Prosecco, is at home in Valdobbiadene. The company has been making wine and distilling grapes in Veneto since 1889. A story of four generations, of lengthy experience, still producing excellent distillates from glera marc, for young, fresh grappas that preserve all the aromas and subtlety of the grape.

Rodengo Saiano (BS)

Mirabella

via Cantarana, 2
☎ (+39) 030611197
⊕ www.mirabellafranciacorta.it
✉ info@mirabellafranciacorta.it
shop: no
e-commerce: yes

Mirabella
Franciacorta
1979

The company was founded in 1979, on a whim of Teresio Schiavi and Giacomo Cavalli, with a group of friends, owners of small vineyards in Franciacorta. They created a single brand under which each could contribute their property. The location is lovely and the winery is on the cutting edge, producing not only Franciacorta but also a grappa line using the marc from chardonnay, pinot bianco and pinot nero, the sparkling wine cultivars.

Alba (CN)

Distilleria Montanaro

fraz. Gallo I via Garibaldi, 6
☎ (+39) 0173262014
⊕ www.grappamontanaro.com
✉ grappamontanaro@grappamontanaro.com
shop: no
e-commerce: no

The history of the distillery began in 1885 with Francesco Trussoni, who decided to create one of the first grappas made from nebbiolo, the variety used exclusively in prestigious Barolo wines. In 1922 the estate passed into the hands of Mario Montanaro and his wife Angela Trussoni. Today the family still makes a wide range of products, based on the native local grape varieties, nebbiolo, dolcetto, arneis, barbera, moscato, in grappas that speak of the Piedmont area's aromas and flavours.

Palaia (PI)
Liquori Morelli

fraz. Forcoli I via A. Meucci, 29
☎ (+39) 0587628707
❀ www.liquorimorelli.it
✉ info@liquorimorelli.it
shop: no
e-commerce: no

The Morelli family's passion for spirits dates back to 1911 when Leonello, the owner of a small bar, had fun mixing essences and extracts to create liqueurs and infusions. Today this estate is well-known not only in Tuscany but also in France, Germany, Switzerland, Austria, Norway, Belgium and South Africa, all of which import the family's products. Piero's children, the fourth generation are now at the helm, and they use the most modern and sophisticated equipment to produce liqueurs, young or mature grappas, lemon or orange infusions, and creams from carefully selected ingredients.

Mareno di Piave (TV)
Negroni Antica Distilleria

via Ungheresca Sud, 64
☎ (+39) 0438492250 I 0423870024
❀ www.negronianticadistilleria.com
✉ info@negronianticadistilleria.com
shop: no
e-commerce: yes

Cavalier Guglielmo Negroni founded the company in the Marca Trevigiana area of Treviso. It was soon famous for cocktail and grappa production, and today it is owned by the Palla family. The range of grappa includes monovarietals, others from prosecco, chardonnay and cabernet marc; traditional liqueurs and punch. The cocktails are the solid underpinning of the company's production.

Aymavilles (AO)
Caves des Onze Communes

loc. Urbains, 14
☎ (+39) 0165902912
❀ www.caveonzecommunes.it
✉ info@caveonzecommunes.it
shop: no
e-commerce: no

La Cave des Onze Communes, which opened in 1990, is a cellar that collects and processes grapes from vineyards in 11 municipalities of central Val d'Aosta, located to the right and left of the River Dora Baltea. In addition to wines, the winery is also known for its production of distillates from native grapes, including the noteworthy fragrant chardonnay and petite arvine, harmonious gamay and fumin, and a scented petit rouge grappa.

Cengio (SV)
Laboratorio Origine Green Spirits

p.zza della Libertà, 21
☎ (+39) 019555669
✪ www.origine-laboratorio.it
✉ info@origine-laboratorio.it
shop: no
e-commerce: no

Laboratorio Origine, run by Luca Graffo and Alessandro Pancini, makes a wide range of products. The two friends, respectively a technician and a philosopher, created this distillery in a house they owned, installing avant-garde equipment. With the use of prime ingredients and pure aromatic herbs they prepare fine coffee and walnut liqueurs and vodka, in a wholesome, easily recognizable style.

Gussago (BS)
Distillerie Peroni Maddalena

via A. De Gasperi, 39
☎ (+39) 0302770640
✪ www.distillerieperoni.it
✉ info@distillerieperoni.it
shop: no
e-commerce: yes

DISTILLERIE
PERONI MADDALENA
ANTICA DISTILLERIA IN GUSSAGO

Gussago, a few kilometres from Brescia, is home to this distillery, and thanks to its strategic position it is able to represent many important wineries. Franciacorta chardonnay, Garda groppello, Lugana trebbiano, corvina, molinara, Amarone rondinella and many other grapes are used to make harmonious grappas, rich in fragrance and aroma. Also worthy of note, a bio grappa line from organic marc.

Faver (TN)
Pilzer

via Portegnago, 5
☎ (+39) 0461683326
✪ www.pilzer.it
✉ info@pilzer.it
shop: no
e-commerce: no

PILZER
DISTILLATORI IN TRENTINO DAL 1957

The philosophy that guides this distillery, nestled in the heart of Val di Cembra, is based on desire for innovation, appreciation for the past, and aspiration to improve further. Alongside grappas, it also distils several fruit varieties for aquavit from Williams pears, apricots, apples and others from grapes and wine, all products infused with freshness and fragrance.

Liqueurs, syrups, distillates

Lasino (TN)
Pravis

loc. Le Biolche, 1
☎ (+39) 0461564305
❀ www.pravis.it
✉ info@pravis.it
shop: no
e-commerce: no

A winery with 40 years of dedicated work in vineyards scattered across the lake shores and mountain slopes, with sustainability to the fore, supported by the intense passion of the artisan. In addition to true-to-type wines, Pravis offers a small range of grappa, obtained only with the marc of its grapes, grown on the Valle dei Laghi hills. These are distilled as soon as alcoholic fermentation is complete, preserving aromas and freshness, and concluding a virtuous cycle beginning with the soil and the vine.

Glorenza/Glurns (BZ)
Puni

via Muhlbach, 2
☎ (+39) 0473835500
❀ www.puni.com
✉ info@puni.com
shop: no
e-commerce: no

PUNI DISTILLERY

Located in the heart of Val Venosta, Puni is the first and only (at least for the moment) Italian distillery to produce whisky. It was the entrepreneur Albrecht Ebensperger who took on the challenge in 2010. This high-quality whisky is made using homegrown grains and the clear, fresh waters of the Puni creek. Three types of whisky are available (all of which come in brilliantly designed bottles): limited edition Puni Nero (aged in pinot nero casks), Alba (aged in Marsala casks) and the Nova (aged in American and European oak).

Zeddiani (OR)
Pure Sardinia

s.da prov.le 12, km 7,800 zona industriale
☎ (+39) 3939835425
❀ www.puresardinia.eu
✉ puresardinia@tiscali.it
shop: no
e-commerce: no

Vodka, vermouth, myrtle liqueur and Solo Wild Gin are all products that display the recognizable aromas and flavours of Sardinia. The spirits are made by infusion for 30 days in grain alcohol and subsequent distillation using the discontinuous method. The artisan production method yields expressive products with mouth-filling flavour and appealing aromas, like the Solo Wild Gin, obtained from wild juniper berries, growing wild along the coast and hand-picked. Gin that embodies the spirit of Sardinia.

Castelnuovo Don Bosco (AT)
Antica Distilleria Quaglia

v.le Europa, 3
☎ (+39) 0119876159
❀ www.distilleriaquaglia.it
✉ info@distilleriaquaglia.it
shop: no
e-commerce: no

Four generations of Quaglia family have managed this distillery since 1906 (though the business officially goes back to 1896). From grappa, distilled with care and aged in wood barrels, to liquors like rosolia, ratafià, genepy, gin, vodka and absinthe, their entire selection is notable for its high and consistent standard of quality. Their outstanding vermouth, with its herbs and spices (and available in different flavors), also deserves to be mentioned.

Chiaverano (TO)
Distilleria Revel Chion

via Casassa, 4
☎ (+39) 012554808
❀ www.distilleria-revelchion.it
✉ info@distilleria-revelchion.it
shop: no
e-commerce: no

The Canavese area is rich in breathtaking landscapes and fairy-tale castles. The Revel Chion family, distillers for seven generations, have been operative in this magical land for over a century. Attention to detail and an artisan production process are the distillery's distinctive traits, working with native Piedmontese varieties to make both from monovarietal and mixed marc grappas, to be consumed either young and fresh or matured and complex.

San Benedetto del Tronto (AP)
Anisetta Rosati

via Tagliamento, 23
☎ (+39) 335308086
❀ www.anisettarosati.com
✉ info@anisettarosati.com
shop: no
e-commerce: no

The recipe used by Anisetta Rosati (founded in the second half of the 19th century), was invented by the pharmaceutical-chemical laboratory of Umberto Rosati di Ascoli Piceno. The process starts with a slow, batch, bain-marie style distillation. The liqueur is flavored using select green anise seeds from Castignano, in the Piceno hills, and is rounded out with organically grown Mediterranean spices. The result is a liquor with a low sugar content that facilitates digestion and is extremely pleasing to drink.

Catania
Rossa Sicily

via P. Toselli, 35
☎ (+39) 0958265667
🌐 www.rossasicily.com
✉ info@rossasicily.com
shop: no
e-commerce: no

A young, dynamic company located on the slopes of Mount Etna and which has made the Sicilian red orange the main ingredient in its entire product range. While the flesh of this fruit is used for a tasty marmalade, the peel is used to flavour Modica chocolate and a bitter, produced by infusing herbs and sugar, a liqueur that embodies the warmth of the Mediterranean in every sip.

Asti
Distilleria Rovero

fraz. San Marzanotto, 216
☎ (+39) 0141592460
🌐 www.rovero.it
✉ info@rovero.it
shop: no
e-commerce: no

The Rovero family are the guardians of a tradition rooted in the 19th century. Today brothers Franco, Claudio, Michelino, and his son Enrico, continue the farming business producing grappas as well as organic wines. The family distil their own freshly drawn-off marc alongside marc from the most prestigious estates in Piedmont and the rest of Italy. The results are monovarietal grappas, some are fresh and lively, displaying all the varietal aromas of the grapes; others are complex and velvety, enriched by the warm tones of small oak barrels.

Santa Venerina (CT)
F.lli Russo

via D. Galimberti, 70
☎ (+39) 095953321
🌐 www.russo.it
✉ russo@russo.it
shop: no
e-commerce: yes

Distilleria Fratelli Russo, whose origins date back to 1870, is located on one of the Mount Etna foothills, not far from the Ionian coast, in the town of Santa Venerina. Grappa from native varieties, bitters, typical liqueurs, artisanal rosolio flavoured with local fruits and flowers: all part of a catalogue that upholds tradition and highlights the fragrances of Sicily as a guarantee of wholesome quality.

San Salvatore Monferrato (AL)
San Tommaso

reg. Guatrasone, 99
☎ (+39) 0131238249
❀ www.grappasantommaso.it
✉ info@san-tommaso.com
shop: no
e-commerce: no

Along with Langhe and Roero, Monferrato's wine-producing landscape is a UNES-CO World Heritage site, and this is the magnificent setting of the San Tommaso distillery. The range of grappas on offer will satisfy all palates: young, fresh, aromatic products as well as grappas matured for at least 12 months in barrels, and extra mature, reserve grappas aged in oak for no less than 18 months. Not to mention the grappas flavoured with natural ingredients like digestive herbs, fruits and roots.

Celle Enomondo (AT)
Distilleria Sancarlo

s.da Comunale Morandino, 5
☎ (+39) 0141205049
❀ www.distilleriasancarlo.com
✉ info@ditilleriasancarlo.com
shop: no
e-commerce: no

This is the smallest distillery in Italy, an artisan business working with care and attention. The passion for grappa handed down through the generations has led the Sancarlo family to take up the old Piedmontese bain-marie distillation method, for more focused aromas. The marc comes from small Langa, Roero and Monferrato producers, and is distilled while fresh, on arrival at the estate. Grappas are available in young versions or aged in small cherrywood barrels.

Firenze
Farmacia Santa Maria Novella

via della Scala, 16
☎ (+39) 0554368315
❀ www.smnovella.com
✉ press@smnovella.com
shop: yes
e-commerce: no

Casa Fondata nell'Anno 1612
Firenze

Unique in its genre, Officina Profumo-Farmaceutica di Santa Maria Novella vaunts eight centuries of cosmetic science and care that changed the history of beauty products. In 1221 the Dominican friars began to build their Florence convent, with adjoining vegetable garden where medicinal herbs were grown and used to prepare medicines, balms and ointments for the small infirmary. Today the ancient production of perfumes, soaps, cosmetics and liqueurs continues. The ample range offers from alchermes to elixir of roses, and even the famous Santa Maria and Medici liqueur, excellent with dessert and with excellent digestive properties.

Liqueurs, syrups, distillates

Alba (CN)

Santa Teresa - Marolo

c.so Canale, 105/1
☎ (+39) 017333144
❀ www.marolo.com
✉ grappe@marolo.com
shop: no
e-commerce: no

Besides being a land of great wines, the Langhe also offers excellent distillates. In the 1970s, Paolo Marolo was one of the first distillers to believe in the potential of the native grape of Piedmont. Today, joined in the enterprise by his son Lorenzo, his grappas show that he was right: nebbiolo, arneis, cortese and brachetto are the raw material for velvety, intriguing spirits that are the voice of the cultivar and the territory.

Castelnuovo del Garda (VR)

Scaramellini

fraz. Sandrà I via Garibaldi, 48
☎ (+39) 0457595006
❀ info@distilleriascaramellini.com
✉ info@distilleria-scaramellini.com
shop: no
e-commerce: no

The story of this distillery began in 1921 when Antonio Scaramellini founded his company in Sandrà. Today it continues to produce grappa with a discontinuous Charentais pot still, a truly traditional method. The amarone, bardolino and recioto marcs make grappas with a strong, well-defined character, velvety yet vital.

Costabissara (VI)

Schiavo

via G. Mazzini, 39
☎ (+39) 0444971025
❀ www.schiavograppa.com
✉ info@schiavograppa.com
shop: no
e-commerce: no

In 1887 Distilleria Schiavo opened for business in the town of Costabissara. Production has always relied on the freshness of the marc, distilled in a few hours by pressing in the cellar. In this way, treating the raw material with respect and ensuring a slow distillation process, the spirit is sure to have fresh fragrances and a clean palate.

Quart (AO)
Distillerie St. Roch

loc. Torrent de Maillod, 4
☎ (+39) 0165774111
❊ www.saintroch.it
✉ saintroch@saintroch.it
shop: no
e-commerce: yes

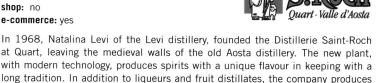

In 1968, Natalina Levi of the Levi distillery, founded the Distillerie Saint-Roch at Quart, leaving the medieval walls of the old Aosta distillery. The new plant, with modern technology, produces spirits with a unique flavour in keeping with a long tradition. In addition to liqueurs and fruit distillates, the company produces a Génépy, a wormwood liqueur, and the Sant'Orso monovarietal grappa line from chardonnay, moscato and petit rouge.

Saint Marcel (AO)
La Valdôtaine

zona industriale, 12
☎ (+39) 0165788919
❊ www.lavaldotaine.it
✉ info@lavaldotaine.it
shop: no
e-commerce: no

Founded in Verrés, in the lower Aosta Valley, La Valdotaine opened as a distillery in 1947 to produce grappa, and later genepy and bitter. In 1978 the business moved to Saint Marcel, where the company is located. Grappa, brandy-based liqueurs, fruit distillates, jams, marrons glacés, and hams are in the very varied catalogue. Look out for the Val d'Aosta grape grappas: Torrette, Picotendro, Gamay and Muscat de Chambave.

Tassullo (TN)
Distilleria Valentini 1872

via di San Vigilio, 43
☎ (+39) 0463450022
❊ www.myvalentini.com
✉ info@distillerievalentini.com
shop: no
e-commerce: yes

It all began with Von Damian Valentini, who started distilling marc to be aged in small barrels of five to fifty litres, in Val di Non. It was 1872 and spirits were consumed by the family, traded, or bartered to pay duty to the Austrian Empire. Now, 150 years on, Valentini's glory is untarnished thanks to very fine spirits and a perfectly balanced flavour. As well as monovarietal grappas, pear williams eau-de-vie, limoncello, and chocolate liqueurs, Valentini offers the original Luxury liqueur made from pure liquorice, to be drunk neat or on the rocks.

Liqueurs, syrups, distillates

Neive (CN)

Villa Rosati

via Gallo, 38
☎ (+39) 0173677757
🌐 www.villarosati.com
✉ info@villarosati.com
shop: no
e-commerce: no

Situated between the two villages of Neive and Mango, the Villa Rosati distillery was set up in an old renovated farmhouse which today houses the processing equipment. The whole production cycle is supervised here, from distilling to storage and bottling. The underground floor is home to the oak barrels used to age the spirits. The grappa processing system has a double function to ensure steam and bain-marie distillation. The spirits are young or aged, well-structured, with vibrant, pleasing aromas.

Castel Maggiore (BO)

Villa Zarri

via Ronco, 1
☎ (+39) 051700604
🌐 www.brandyvillazarri.com
✉ info@villazarri.com
shop: no
e-commerce: no

FONDATA 1729

Villa Zarri

Established in 1729, Villa Zarri is renowned in Italy for its excellent brandy, made through a process of slow, batch distillation with white wine (usually Tuscan Trebbiano or Romagolo) of low alcohol content, good acidity and without any trace of sulphur dioxides. In addition to their traditional brandy, they produce several prized brandies, aged from 10 to 25 years. Villa Zarri also make an excellent amaro, acquavite, nocino cherry and coffee brandy.

Appiano/Eppan (BZ)

Alfons Walcher

loc. Frangarto I via Pillhof, 99
☎ (+39) 0471631145
🌐 www.walcher.eu
✉ info@walcher.eu
shop: no
e-commerce: yes

WALCHER
SÜDTIROLER
GUTSBRENNEREI

Maso Turmbachhof soars over the small village of Turmbach, near Appiano. The estate, which grows fruit and grapes, has belonged to the Walcher family for nine generations. In 1966, Alfons Walcher began to distil spirits using the ancient double-boiler method, using chardonnay and pinot nero grapes. He soon acheived the great quality found today in the grappas, fruit aquavits, herb spirits and other luxurious specialities.

San Michele all'Adige (TN)
Zeni

via Stretta, 2
☎ (+39) 0461650456
❀ www.zeni.tn.it
✉ robezen@tin.it
shop: no
e-commerce: yes

The winery and the distillery were founded in 1975, when two brothers, Roberto and Andrea Zeni, developed their father's business. Today, the reins are in the hands of the next generation, the offspring of Roberto and Andrea, who run the cellars with an eye to innovation while upholding family tradition. Zeni spirits are made with grapes from its own vineyard, and teroldego, cabernet and chardonnay marc is immediately processed to give the distillates their unmistakable scents and aromas.

Castelrotto/Kastelruth (BZ)
Zu Plun

via San Valentino, 9
☎ (+39) 3356009556
❀ www.zuplun.it
✉ info@zuplun.it
shop: no
e-commerce: no

Florian Rabanser is the creator and master distiller of the estate, at 1,000 metres above sea level in the Dolomites. This is the birthplace of spirits made from plums, apricots, apples, pears, as well as eau-de-vie made from gentian violets, juniper and service berries, and seven types of grappa, two of which are aged in oak barrels. Since 2007 rum and gin are also available. These are not typical local products as they are only made from herbs and ingredients growing in the mountains. Lastly, the new entry: Alto Adige balsamic vinegar fermented in oak, chestnut and cherrywood barrels.

Liqueurs, syrups, distillates

Mushrooms, truffles

Montà (CN)
Alba Tartufi

via Cavour, 15
☎ (+39) 0173975670 I 3355218652
❀ www.albatartufi.com
✉ info@albatartufi.com
shop: yes
e-commerce: yes

Montà, in the heart of Roero, is where the Truffle Trail starts, but also home to Ugo Cauda, who has been selecting and selling fresh and preserved truffles since 1988. His products range from the prized white truffle to the sought-after black truffle, bianchetto or spring truffle, and products made from this noble tuber. There are white or black truffle creams; Pecorino with truffle; Grana Padano with truffle; ceps and truffle; artichoke, olive and truffle; truffle-infused olive oil; sliced truffles in brine.

Capracotta (IS)
Gli Alti Sapori - Le Miccole

via N. Falconi, 38
☎ (+39) 0865949141 I 3335703426
❀ www.altisapori.it
✉ info@altisapori.it
shop: yes
e-commerce: yes

Since he was a child, Antonio Beniamino has loved exploring the local area and woods. He knows them like the back of his hand, learning to source all the products he offers every season. Thanks to his extensive experience, the company is now able to market some truly exquisite products, including fresh white and black truffles, as well as other varieties; black or white truffle pasta, rice, butter, and creams with various ingredients, cold meats and cheeses with truffle, dried ceps, mushrooms with truffle, pulses, jams and more.

Roccafluvione (AP)
Angellozzi Tartuficoltura

via Ponte Pugliese, 13
☎ (+39) 0736365719
❀ www.angellozzi.it
✉ info@angellozzi.it
shop: yes
e-commerce: yes

ANGELLOZZI
TARTUFICOLTURA

The Angellozzis have long been renowned as truffle hunters. Truffles were once bartered here in exchange for other foods and truffle hunting has now become a very profitable business. White truffles and other varieties are sourced from the family's own truffle woods in different locations and at different altitudes. Most truffles are sold fresh, but some are frozen in packs of different weights. Truffles in brine, truffle carpaccio, minced truffles and creams are all available.

Valsamoggia (BO)

Appennino Funghi e Tartufi

loc. Savigno I via del Lavoro, 14b
☎ (+39) 051960984/5
❁ www.appenninofunghietartufi.it
✉ anaclaire.v@afood.it
shop: yes
e-commerce: no

Some years ago, brothers Luigi and Angelo Dattilo were inspired by their love of the land and its produce, particularly truffles, changed a hobby into a business. They now process and sell truffles and mushrooms, using cutting-edge machinery, selling fresh white and black, Burgundy and bianchetto truffles, among others. But also ceps, Caesar's and Saint George's mushrooms, chanterelles and others. They also preserve truffles in brine and use them for creams, pâtés, condiments, dressings and sauces, flours, pasta and honey, as well as an organic range.

Civitella in Val di Chiana (AR)

Boscovivo

loc. Badia al Pino I via dei Boschi, 34
☎ (+39) 0575410396
❁ www.boscovivo.it
✉ boscovivo@boscovivo.it
shop: yes
e-commerce: yes

Founded in 1982 by Alfredo Landucci and Franca Bianchini, the business initially focused on promoting and processing truffles. It then extended its range with numerous specialities, particularly Tuscan products. Delicious truffles are available fresh, preserved, or in creams and sauces. It also sells cheese, cold meats and truffle honey. Its range includes ceps (dried and in various products); condiments; game, meat and Chianina beef ragouts; ready stews and casseroles, including game; vegetables in oil; vinegars, jams and fruit in syrup.

Grosseto

Brezzi Oliviero & Figlio

via Ambra, 19
☎ (+39) 0564493087
❁ www.tartufotaste.it
✉ info@tartufotaste.it
shop: yes
e-commerce: no

Prized white and black, black summer scorzone, bianchetto spring truffles are the main ingredients in these preserves, which are extremely popular with gourmets the world over. White truffles are available bottled whole, in creams, butter and oil. Black truffles are available bottled whole, in creams, in Pecorino, in cheese fondue, in oil and in a spread for mouth-watering bruschetta, along with ceps cream, and in a sauce. Black summer scorzone and bianchetto spring truffles are sold bottled whole. The business also sells ceps cream.

Mushrooms, truffles

Campello sul Clitunno (PG)
Tartufi Alfonso Fortunati

via F. da Campello, 24
☎ (+39) 0743521124
❀ www.fortunati.com
✉ fortunati@fortunati.com
shop: yes
e-commerce: yes

This 40-year-old family business is one of the most reliable in the truffle sector, working meticulously to source the very best products, monitoring the various processing stages and targeting quality. Prized white and black truffles or black summer truffles are sold while in jars, in slices, in purées, and used for pâtés, sauces and creams. It also sells fresh, frozen and dried ceps, pasta, polenta and flour flavoured with truffles and mushrooms; honey, including with wine and dried fruit; pulses and cereals, oil and condiments, salami and cheeses with truffles.

Cagli (PU)
Italia Tartufi

via E. Fermi, 1
☎ (+39) 0721781388
❀ www.italiatartufi.it
✉ info@italiatartufi.com
shop: no
e-commerce: no

It was the passion and experience of two partners, both with a family background in truffles, that gave life to Italia Tartufi in 2011. Their goal is to spread truffle culture and knowledge, and also to improve the quality of what's being offered to consumers. This prized mushroom can be found almost year-round here, depending on the season, starting with the highly sought-after white variety all the way to the black, summer truffle. Delicious truffle sauces abound, along with dressings, pâtés, aromatized salt and honey, oils and vinegars. You can also find truffle salami, egg noodles, rice and polenta.

Urbania (PU)
Longhi

via Roma, 103
☎ (+39) 0722319459
❀ www.longhitartufi.com
✉ longhitartufi@libero.it
shop: yes
e-commerce: no

Domenico Longhi, restaurateur, started marketing truffles here in Alta Valle del Metauro in the 1960s, thanks to his bond of trust with local truffle hunters. The business is now run by the next generation, but has preserved its high quality standards. The truffles are used in the ready-to-cook products (four-cheese cream, soup, pumpkin cream); anchovies, salamis and cheese in oil; creams, pasta, rice, polenta, flour, sauces, butter, oil, vinegar and honey.

Acqualagna (PU)
Marini & Azzolini

v.le Risorgimento, 26
☎ (+39) 0721798629
❀ www.trufflespecialties.com
✉ info@trufflespecialties.com
shop: yes
e-commerce: no

For over 50 years, this business has been selecting the finest truffles thanks to its longstanding relationships with the area's most expert truffle hunters. It sells the best varieties of fresh seasonal truffles all year round. From late autumn to early winter, its star product is the wonderful white truffle but there are plenty of other products to try at other times of year, like mouth-watering truffles in brine and a whole range of flavoured specialities, such as creams, sauces, oil, butter and cheese.

Sirmione (BS)
Martelli Food

via Verona, 174
☎ (+39) 0309905197
❀ www.martellifood.it
✉ info@martellifood.it
shop: yes
e-commerce: yes

For many years the Martelli family has been busy selecting and marketing hundreds of fine food and wine products, including EVOO, cheese, and bottled preserves, all of outstanding quality. Their experience, intuition and expertise ensure that their range is always of the highest quality. Their key product is the selection of fresh and frozen truffles and mushrooms in various sizes, as well as butter, honey, creams, condiments, cheeses, salt, pasta, rice, polenta and salami: all flavoured with truffles.

Alba (CN)
Tartufi Morra

p.zza E. Pertinace, 3
☎ (+39) 0173364271 I 0173364272
❀ www.tartufimorra.com
✉ info@tartufimorra.com
shop: yes
e-commerce: no

TARTUFI
Morra
TARTUFALBA

Established in 1930 and run by various generations of the Morra family, this was the first Italian company to specialize in processing and marketing Alba white and other truffle varieties. Its range of fresh truffles includes white, black, black autumn and summer, and bianchetto. It also sells frozen truffles, bottled black and white truffles, purée and carpaccio of truffle, as well as truffle pâtés, creams and sauces, condiments (including butter, vinegar, oil, and salt), flour, honey and chocolates, and dried ceps.

Mushrooms, truffles

Campoli Appennino (FR)

Pagnani Tartufi

via Fontana, 4
☎ (+39) 07761806071
◈ www.pagnanitartufi.net
✉ info@pagnanitartufi.net
shop: yes
e-commerce: no

This family business was set up in 2002 and has always aimed high, offering truffles and other fine foods. Its range includes fresh prized black and white spring and summer truffles, as well as every possible type of preserve imaginable, made with prime ingredients like Ciociaro EVOO. Delicious creams and sauces with truffles and vegetables are sold alongside honey, pasta and cheese flavoured with truffle, truffle oil and liqueurs, whole or sliced truffles in brine.

Città di Castello (PG)

Penna Tartufi

via G. Sorel, 3b
☎ (+39) 0758510298 I 3476754018
◈ www.marcotartufi.com
✉ pmtartufi@hotmail.it
shop: yes
e-commerce: yes

For many years this business has specialized in marketing truffles, mushrooms and other gourmet delicacies. Its strong point is its direct, well-established relationship with the truffle hunters who work mainly in the Alto Tevere area. Its range includes fresh prized white and black truffles, as well as the various seasonal types; frozen products and in brine; creams; pâtés; sauces; condiments and more. It also sells ceps and other mushrooms fresh, in oil and dried, and makes niche food and wine products.

Trofarello (TO)

Piemont Fungo
Antiche Tradizioni

via Cuneo, 1
☎ (+39) 0114034831
◈ www.piemontfungo.com
✉ info@piemontfungo.com
shop: no
e-commerce: yes

Founded in 1999 by the Previdi brothers, Piemont Fungo Antiche Tradizioni sells all types of mushrooms, identifying the best products and selling them under their Antiche Tradizioni brand. The porcino mushroom, the king of the woods, takes center stage here. Only the most prized variety is sold, available in thin slices, whole, cut, baked, in dressing, dried and so on. Don't overlook the delicious chiodini and muschio mushrooms, not to mention their jarred vegetables (such as stuffed peperoncini), sauces and preserves.

Sulmona (AQ)
Pignatelli Tartufi

v.le della Repubblica, 14
☎ (+39) 086452559 I 337919714
❀ www.pignatellitartufi.it
✉ info@pignatellitartufi.it
shop: yes
e-commerce: no

One of Abruzzo's main companies devoted to marketing and processing truffles. The Pignatelli family has worked in the sector for many years, supplying quality products and a range of different lines for retail and the catering industry. Its range includes fresh precious white and black, scorzone and bianchetto truffles; preserved whole and sliced truffles; pâtés; various sauces; and truffle-flavoured butter.

Alba (CN)
Tartufi Ponzio

via Vittorio Emanuele, 7a
☎ (+39) 0173440456
❀ www.tartufiponzio.com
✉ info@tartufiponzio.com
shop: yes
e-commerce: yes

Ponzio, based near Piazza Duomo, has been a failsafe go-to for truffles since 1947. The experienced, highly professional Curti family sells a range of premium products. White, black and black summer truffles are used to flavour taglierini pasta, risotto, polenta, fondue, creams, sauces, butter, mouth-watering preserves anchovies, salamis, toma cheese in oil, EVOO, salt, balsamic cream, honey, grissini and cugnà jam. Its preserves include dried white and black truffles, and sliced truffles in oil or cream. Sweet truffles and other delicacies also abound.

Schiavi di Abruzzo (CH)
I Sapori della Terra

c.da Badia, 59
☎ (+39) 0873979379 I 3397545637
❀ www.saporidellaterra.net
✉ info@saporidellaterra.net
shop: yes
e-commerce: yes

I SAPORI
DELLA TERRA

Giancarlo Campati's business is based in a tiny historic village in the Alto Vastese mountain community, almost on the border with Molise. It has marketed truffles, mushrooms and select specialities since 2007. As well as fresh black and white truffles, and a selection of seasonal varieties, it also sells whole truffles in brine, and sliced and minced truffles. Its product range includes honey, sauces and creams, EVOO and butter condiments, polenta and rice, cheeses and salami, chocolates and dried figs.

Mushrooms, truffles

Vinchiaturo (CB)

Sapori di Bosco Molisani

c.da Monteverde, 17
☎ (+39) 0874348109 I 3283769248
❀ www.saporidibosco.it
✉ infosaporidibosco@alice.it
shop: yes
e-commerce: no

Molise is one of Italy's best truffle regions thanks to its extensive woodlands. This family company specializes in processing and selling truffles and truffle products, and was founded in 2002 because of its true passion for the tuber. Customers are spoilt for choice by whole truffles in brine or corn oil, minced or creamed truffles, sliced truffles in EVOO, truffles in various sauces, with honey, salt or oil, and also ceps creams and vegetable, and other products in oil.

Pisa

Savini Tartufi

loc. Montanelli I fraz. Forcoli I p.zza D'Ascanio
☎ (+39) 0587628037
❀ www.savinitartufi.it
✉ info@savinitartufi.it
shop: yes
e-commerce: no

Four generations of Savinis have marketed white and black, black winter, bianchetto, scorzone and Burgundy truffles, most sourced in the San Miniato area. It has three product lines: Tricolore, Elegance and the top-of-the-range Luxury, with an impressive selection of condiments (butters, oils, mayonnaise, mustards, salt), sauces, pâtés, creams, preserves (asparagus, anchovies, green peaches), pesto, rice, polenta, tagliolini pasta, potato flakes, honey, chocolates, as well as various types of bottled whole truffles and handy accessories.

Campoli Appennino (FR)

Sulpizio Tartufi

via Colle Polmone, 14
☎ (+39) 0776885031
❀ www.sulpiziotartufi.it
✉ info@sulpiziotartufi.it
shop: yes
e-commerce: yes

Many people are unaware that Lazio has its own truffle hunters and its best truffles are to be found in the hills and woods around Frosinone. Since 1987, various generations of the Sulpizio family have studied and processed the best truffles and mushrooms on the market to make top-quality products at competitive prices. As well as fresh white and black, bianchetto and summer black truffles, it also sells the tuber in jars, dried, in creams, sauces, condiments, cheese and salami, pasta, polenta and rice, and liqueurs, together with dried and preserved mushrooms.

Acqualagna (PU)

t&c Tartufi Tentazioni

via Pole, 26
☎ (+39) 0721799065
❀ www.tectartufi.it
✉ info@tectartufi.it
shop: no
e-commerce: yes

T&C was established in 1990 with the intention of selling truffles, the majestic mushroom that is a native to the lovely town of Acqualanga. They offer a variety of local mushrooms year-round thanks to modern conservation techniques. Their products are sought after by other shops, restaurants and processing plants. In addition to fresh varieties, dried and frozen mushrooms are available, as well as creams, toppings, sauces and much more.

Piobesi d'Alba (CN)

Tartuflanghe

loc. Catena Rossa, 7
☎ (+39) 0173361414
❀ www.tartuflanghe.com
✉ tartuflanghe@tartuflanghe.com
shop: yes
e-commerce: yes

After working in the catering industry for several years, Domenica Bortolusso and Beppe Montanaro decided to set up this business in 1980, in an area that boasts some of Italy's very best white truffles. The idea was to allow gourmets to enjoy truffle-based specialities even out of season, so they developed the first truffle pasta in the world. Since then they have come up with many other delicacies, including sauces, snacks, creams, anchovies with truffles, risottos, polenta, fresh pasta, salt and condiments, sauces, honey, fondue, fresh and dried truffles, and even pralines.

Montà (CN)

Dal Trifulè

p.zza Vittorio Veneto, 20
☎ (+39) 0173975455
❀ www.trifule.it
✉ trifule@trifule.it
shop: yes
e-commerce: yes

This company is built on the experience, passion and expertise of the Cerutti family, its founders. It is now run by Paolo, assisted by his wife Monica. The prime product range is based on a thorough knowledge of the local area and the raw ingredient. Satisfaction is guaranteed whichever product you choose: fresh truffles (white, black and other varieties); truffle-based products (condiments, salt, butter, sauces, creams, honey, pasta) and even cheeses, lard, salami and anchovies with truffles.

Mushrooms, truffles

Roccafluvione (AP)

Trivelli Tartufi

s.da prov.le Bivio Agelli, 86
☎ (+39) 0736365407
❂ www.trivellitartufi.it
✉ info@trivellitartufi.it
shop: yes
e-commerce: yes

In this family-run business, love of truffles has been handed down from father to son. It is thanks to this knowledge and experience that production (from its own truffle woods), selection and marketing processes meet the very highest standards. The truffles, especially the white and black types, are sold fresh or preserved, either just in brine or in the form of creams, pâtés, sliced, minced, as sauces with other ingredients or oil and butter condiments.

Gravina in Puglia (BA)

Andriani - Felicia

via N. Copernico Zona Pip
☎ (+39) 0803255801
❀ www.andrianispa.com
✉ info@andrianispa.com
shop: no
e-commerce: no

Andriani is one of the most important producers in the field of "innovation food", with an entire plant dedicated solely to gluten-free items. Their brand, Felicia, is comprised mostly of pasta made with gluten-free grains (whole rice, corn), pseudo-cereals (buckwheat, quinoa, amaranth) and legumes (lentils, peas, beans), 90% of which are organically grown. In 2016, they also launched a selection of flour mixes for sweet and savory baked goods.

Fara San Martino (CH)

Bioalimenta - Farabella

Zona Industriale
☎ (+39) 0872994053
❀ www.farabella.it
✉ info@bioalimentasrl.it
shop: no
e-commerce: no

Since 2000, Bioalimenta has made a name for itself producing gluten-free foods aimed at celiacs. Their selection, which goes under the brand Farabella, comprises gnocchi, pasta (both dried and fresh), bread, flours and baked goods. All their products are made with choice ingredients that are certified "Spiga barrata" (wheat-free) and GMO-free, with production carried out using modern equipment in their Bioalimenta plant in Fara San Martino. Their pasta, which is wire-drawn in bronze and dried at low temperatures, is available in a variety of shapes and sizes.

Calenzano (FI)

Probios

via degli Olmi, 13
☎ (+39) 055886931
❀ www.probios.it
✉ info@probios.it
shop: no
e-commerce: yes

Since it was established in 1978, the company has been committed to producing organic foods with selected ingredients of which 70% are Italian, grown according by ethical and sustainable methods, and GMO-free. A full range from drinks to pasta, pulses, baked cakes, spreads and condiments. Over the years, the Probios brand has been enriched with vegan, gluten-free and lactose-free products to meet the demands of an increasingly varied clientele.

Meduna di Livenza (TV)
Solo Mais

via E. Majorana, 16
☎ (+39) 3387321945
❀ www.solomais.com
✉ info@solomais.com
shop: yes
e-commerce: no

The name of this little family business is like a declaration of intent, as it is dedicated to processing a typical local product, corn, and careful selection of ingredients. The house specialities are polenta Soffi, cornflour breadsticks, salt, and extra virgin olive oil. But there are also the rosemary and chilli pepper Sfoglie, and breakfast biscuits made from wholegrain cornflour, free-range chicken's eggs, butter from Alto Adige farms and Madagascan vanilla.

Montemurlo (PO)
Vegan Delicious

via Montalese, 248
☎ (+39) 0574720918
❀ www.vegandelicious.it
✉ info@vegandelicious.it
shop: no
e-commerce: yes

Set up in an ex-butcher shop, Vegan Delicious is the brainchild of Fabio Mesana and his father, Piero. This family-run business shows that it's possible to bring together change and changing food needs with high-quality products and flavor. Take NoGluty, an organic vegetable sausage, aged perfectly and flavored with natural ingredients. Obviously it is gluten-free and is available in different flavors, including spicy. Another surprising product is the vegetable cheese, similar to mozzarella, called FioDiVegan. It too is organic and gluten-free.

Pasta

Gragnano (NA)
Afeltra

via Roma, 20
☎ (+39) 0818736080 I 0818795579
✉ www.pastificioafeltra.it
✉ ordini@afeltra.it
shop: yes
e-commerce: no

DAL 1848
PREMIATO PASTIFICIO
AFELTRA
GRAGNANO
(NAPOLI)

In 1848 a pasta-making facility opened in the heart of Gragnano, home to a dry pasta craft industry. Since then, Afeltra has safeguarded quality and tradition through its production processes using bronze dies, careful control of raw materials, and creative skills applied to handmade pasta such as fusilli, the most typical shape. The skills of a bygone age are lavished on all the lines, from the most conventional to the most special, prepared only the with highest quality of durum wheat and spring water from the Lattari Mountains.

Campofilone (FM)
La Campofilone

loc. Ficiarà, 27
☎ (+39) 0734931294
✉ www.lacampofilone.it
✉ lacampofilone@lacampofilone.it
shop: yes
e-commerce: yes

"la Campofilone"
pasta all'uovo dal 1912

Here we have a benchmark producer of the famous capello d'angelo pasta, made in the new Ficiarà plant along with a dozen other egg pasta types, from maltagliati to lasagne sheets. The flour comes from the Marche and is GMO-free, the organic eggs are from farmyard hens. The company also has the Tabula brand of good white pasta, made with selected durum grains with high gluten content, produced under licence by a renowned pasta factory. There are three lines: long, short and special, with different aromas.

Guardiagrele (CH)
Casino di Caprafico

loc. Piane di Caprafico
☎ (+39) 0871897492
✉ www.casinodicaprafico.com
✉ info@casinodicaprafico.com
shop: no
e-commerce: no

CASINO DI CAPRAFICO
AZIENDA AGRICOLA
GIACOMO SANTOLERI

Giacomo Santoleri is an engineer who decided to become an organic farmer on the slopes of Mount Maiella. The pasta has always been original, from the initial spelt spaghetti made in 1993. Tasty artisanal pasta, made as Nature commands, in refined tobacco colour packs, with a dash of colour from the Casino di Caprafico logo. In 2001 the durum wheat and barley Ma'kaira line of pasta in chitarra and linguine versions, bronze-drawn and dried at a maximum 45 °C. Since 2006 it is also available in spelt and barley versions.

Maglie (LE)

Benedetto Cavalieri dal 1918

via Garibaldi, 64
☎ (+39) 0836484144
❀ www.benedettocavalieri.it
✉ info@benedettocavalieri.it
shop: yes
e-commerce: no

The Cavalieri family has grown wheat since the second half of the 1800s and has produces dry pasta for nearly a century. The rigorous selection of raw materials, delicate processing with prolonged kneading, slow mixing and pressing, bronze drawing, and drying at low temperatures, means that tradition, taste and product quality are all safe. The bronze-drawn thick, long spaghettoni are to die for, a true culinary cult, as are all the other shapes, including the wholemeal version.

Fara San Martino (CH)

Cav. Giuseppe Cocco

zona artigianale, 15
☎ (+39) 0872984121
❀ www.pastacocco.com
✉ info@pastacocco.com
shop: no
e-commerce: no

The Verde River springs and the ancient machines still used in Fara San Martino have given Cocco pasta its unmistakable taste for almost a hundred years. The top products include egg nests and skeins, durum wheat caserecci, coarse or refined pasta sheets with saffron, richer than the former as it is made following a rural tradition that sometimes added to its unrefined flour the bran discarded by the landowners.

Fano (PU)

Columbro - Iris

loc. Bellocchi I via G. Toniolo, 3a
☎ (+39) 0721854476
❀ www.columbro.com
✉ columbro@columbro.com
shop: no
e-commerce: no

Selected grains from virtuous productions, Senatore Cappelli durum wheat, timilia, khorosan bio and spelt flours; organic eggs from farmyard hens raised on healthy feed. The list of ingredients used to make Columbro bronze-drawn pasta before being completed by slow drying. The company has over 20 certified organic shapes, from egg specialities (above all capellini and fettuccine, some flavoured) to long and short durum wheat and spelt varieties.

Flumeri (AV)
Molino e Pastificio De Matteis

Valle Ufita
☎ (+39) 08254212
⊗ www.granoarmando.it
✉ info@granoarmando.it
shop: no
e-commerce: no

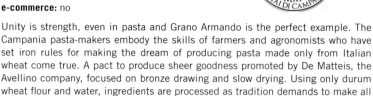

Unity is strength, even in pasta and Grano Armando is the perfect example. The Campania pasta-makers embody the skills of farmers and agronomists who have set iron rules for making the dream of producing pasta made only from Italian wheat come true. A pact to produce sheer goodness promoted by De Matteis, the Avellino company, focused on bronze drawing and slow drying. Using only durum wheat flour and water, ingredients are processed as tradition demands to make all the usual shapes and sizes.

Fermo
Di Mauro

fraz. San Mauro I via dell'Industria, 24
☎ (+39) 0734277338 I 3319323900
⊗ www.pastadimauro.com
✉ info@pastadimauro.com
shop: no
e-commerce: yes

Arte Pastaia Marchigiana
Pasta Art from the Marches

It starts by choosing the best semolina and the freshest eggs, and then drawing on the wisdom of masters who, according to tradition, work the dough slowly. From there they stretch it and then dry it at low temperatures, for no less than 24 hours. There are four different types of pastas: those with egg doughs, those with semolina, those with whole wheat flour, and those with spelt flour. There are both long and short varieties, as well as those infused with other flavors (garlic and parsley, truffle, squid ink...).

Enna
Pastificio Eag Miritello

Zona Industriale Valle del Dittaino
☎ (+39) 0935950662
⊗ www.valledelgrano.it
✉ info@pastificioeag.com
shop: yes
e-commerce: yes

Miritello have been cultivating durum wheat in Sicily since the late 1800s, and making pasta since the mid-20th century. Their name features a seal that expresses their approach to work: "The excellence of the ancient granaries". Their selection uses only local wheat that is then transformed into dough through a vacuum-sealed process. Their Valle del Grano pastas are wire-drawn in bronze so as to guarantee the product is sufficiently porous, and then dried at middle-low temperatures. They offer all the classic varieties (from spaghetti to rigatoni), in addition to traditional Sicilian anelli, gigli, gnochetti and small "acini di pepe".

Strada in Chianti (FI)
Fabbri

p.zza E. Landi, 17
☎ (+39) 055858013
❂ www.pastafabbri.it
✉ info@pastafabbri.it
shop: no
e-commerce: yes

At the end of the 1800s pasta workshops began to thrive and one such was Giovanni Fabbri's craft pasta production business. It vaunted outstanding attention and a passion for good things then and still does. Quality wheat, bronze dies, but also slow, careful crafting are the secrets of the company's various shapes and sizes of pasta. The catalogue is endless: short pasta, including the unusual dischi volanti; long reginelle and spaghettoni toscani; for broths; specials like stracci toscani; pasta in hanks; egg, durum wheat, semolina and wholemeal semolina pasta.

Gragnano (NA)
La Fabbrica della Pasta di Gragnano

v.le San Francesco, 30
☎ (+39) 0818011487
❂ www.lafabbricadellapastadigragnano.it
✉ marketing@lafabbricadellapasta.it
shop: yes
e-commerce: no

This is one of Gragnano's historic pasta makers, founded by Mario Moccia in 1976 and now run by the third generation. Past traditions and modern technology combine to create artisan pasta made from first extract semolina and spring water, bronze-drawn and dried at low temperatures of 40–50 °C. Over 100 traditional shapes are produced, as well as single portions like the exclusive "a Caccavella", over ten different types of fusilli, and more than 20 variations of excellent gluten-free pasta.

Gragnano (NA)
Faella

p.zza Marconi, 13/14
☎ (+39) 0818012985
❂ www.pastificiofaella.com
✉ info@pastificiofaella.com
shop: yes
e-commerce: no

Gragnano is the pasta capital and also home to this iconic family-run factory, one of the most interesting locations for bronze-extruded craft pasta. Over the years the doughty determination and the passion of Mario Faella perfected production based on a direct relationship and trust with the flour suppliers. Even today adding value to classic shapes and sizes, above all pennoni and paccheri, extra, short and long. Sometimes also packaged in plain paper.

Predazzo (TN)

Felicetti

via L. Felicetti, 9
☎ (+39) 0462501225
◉ www.felicetti.it
✉ info@felicetti.it
shop: no
e-commerce: yes

Known for its Monograno line and operating in Val di Fiemme since 1908, growing wheat and producing pasta with artisan methods. Today, Felicetti is more involved in organic products than ever with a selection that gourmets adore. Wholemeal Kamut (the ancestor of modern grains), matt, spelt or egg pasta, in any case the supreme quality is guaranteed by the quality of the flour and the spring water used. There are more than 11 varieties and over 200 shapes and sizes, specialities using Regiokorn spelt and Kamut.

Ancona

Filotea

via I Maggio, 56
☎ (+39) 071201070
◉ www.filoteasrl.com
✉ info@filoteapasta.com
shop: yes
e-commerce: yes

This small Marche facility is loyal to time-honoured manufacturing processes. For its pasta it uses the best eggs and the purest, finest flours, so various condiments (also part of its production) are enjoyed to their best. The pasta is easy to digest for its lightness, and all lines, from traditional (above all spaghetti chitarrone) to egg (vincisgrassi and other flavoured types) or durum wheat, are the result of tradition and long experience.

Gragnano (NA)

Pasta Gentile

via P. Nastro, 67
☎ (+39) 0818013417
◉ www.pastagentile.it
✉ info@pastagentile.com
shop: yes
e-commerce: yes

Manufacturers of macaroni since 1876 and makers of PGI Gragnano pasta using organic Senatore Cappelli durum wheat grown in the Matera countryside. There are more than 40 types of pasta, also in wholemeal organic flour, bronze-drawn and dried in the traditional Cirillo manner: cells fitted with fans that dry the pasta at up to 48 °C. The Zampino family also owns the San Nicola dei Miri brand of preserves; the Frantoio dei Grani Rossi oil brand; and the iconic San Leone patisserie brand.

Gragnano (NA)
Gerardo di Nola

via Roma, 25
☎ (+39) 0818733451 I 3889449766
✪ www.gerardodinola.it
✉ info@gerardodinola.it
shop: yes
e-commerce: no

Gerardo di Nola is linked to two typical Italian products: pasta and canned tomatoes. Pasta, among the best in Italy and famous throughout the world, is crafted from selected durum wheat, preferably Italian, then drawn by bronze into classic shapes and sizes. Excellent canned tomatoes include purées (from gourmet and Villa Literno tomatoes, grown by dryland farming) and tomatoes with their juice (dryland farmed tomatoes, tomato filets, peeled Nocerino Sarnese San Marzano tomatoes).

Torano Nuovo (TE)
Gioie di Fattoria

loc. Villa Fiore I c.da Petrella, 20
☎ (+39) 0861851873
✪ www.gioiedifattoria.net
✉ info@gioiedifattoria.net
shop: yes
e-commerce: no

This farm in Abruzzo grows spelt and wheat with organic methods in a perfect habitat. The philosophy pursued is the constant search for authenticity, simplicity and tradition, respecting the environment. All products are processed in house with classic methods: spelt, polenta, flour (including saragolla, an ancient typical local cereal), pasta of various shapes and sizes. Genuine jams and spelt biscuits.

Cercola (NA)
Leonessa

via Don G. Minzoni, 231
☎ (+39) 0815551107
✪ www.pastaleonessa.it
✉ info@pastaleonessa.it
shop: no
e-commerce: yes

Pasta Leonessa started in 1974 with the purpose of carrying on traditional pasta making methods. Their approach is characterized by a refusal to compromise: brass wire-drawing and slow drying are among the keys to a product whose 'only' ingredients are water and durum wheat semolina. Paccheri & co is their flagship pasta, but there's much more that's worth trying, from fresh pastas to stuffed varieties that include meat agnolotti and more original offerings, like monkfish. There's even a line of organic pasta products.

Monte San Pietrangeli (FM)
Pasta Mancini

c.da San Rustico
☎ (+39) 0734969311
❀ www.pastamancini.it
✉ info@pastamancini.it
shop: yes
e-commerce: no

San Carlo and Levante durum wheats are the two varieties selected and produced to become Mancini pasta. The farm is surrounded by a field of wheat, an island of goodness that looks Nature directly in the face, producing various shapes and sizes of pasta with traditional methods. The various types include spaghetti, trenette, spaghetti alla chitarra, penne, macaroni, fusilli, mezze maniche and tuffoli, all of great quality, available in designer packaging that also indicated the year the grain was harvested.

Gioia del Colle (BA)
Piccolo pastificio artigiano Marella

s.da prov.le per Putignano, km 0,300
☎ (+39) 0803434511
❀ www.pastamarella.it
✉ info@pastamarella.it
shop: no
e-commerce: no

Antonio Marella began his craft pasta adventure in the late 1980s, naming his company Il Pozzo del Re, famous for its oversized, flavoured special shapes. In recent years, with the opening of the new factory, production has expanded to embrace classic shapes and sizes, dozens of long and short types, both bronze-drawn and rolled, dried slowly in static frames at a temperature never exceeding 36–38 °C. The preference is for organic local or regional durum wheat, processed by small local mills.

Casciana Terme Lari (PI)
Martelli

via dei Pastifici, 3
☎ (+39) 0587684238
❀ www.famigliamartelli.it
✉ past@martelli.info
shop: yes
e-commerce: no

Martelli is a small but well-known family firm based in Lari, just outside Pisa. A passion for pasta is expressed in age-old production methods using durum wheat flour and drying for two days at the traditional low temperature of no more than 36 °C. The results are limited to just four types, with good porosity, a trait that allows the pasta to absorb condiment. Spaghetti, classic penne, Tuscan spaghettini and maccheroni, all packaged in distinctive yellow wrapping.

Pasta

223

Pratola Peligna (AQ)

Masciarelli

via Enopolio, 32
☎ (+39) 0864273137
❀ www.pastificiomasciarelli.it
✉ info@pastificiomasciarelli.it
shop: yes
e-commerce: no

dal 1867 Artigiani Pastai

This family craft pasta maker has been in business for almost a century and a half. The ancient crafting is now replaced by machinery able to reproduce tradition, keeping to its slow times and methods, and low drying temperatures, as well as using circular bronze dies. The 17 pasta shapes and sizes are made with durum wheat flour, high in gluten and protein, procured from Campobasso's Ferro mill, and packed in straw-coloured boxes featuring the Parco Nazionale della Majella seal.

Montopoli in Val d'Arno (PI)

Antico Pastificio Morelli 1860

fraz. San Romano I via San Francesco, 8
☎ (+39) 0571459032
❀ www.pastamorelli.it
✉ morelli@pastamorelli.it
shop: no
e-commerce: no

The ingredient that makes all the difference in this company's paste is wheat germ, never found in standard pasta. Dating back to 1860, after five generations Pastificio Morelli continues with the same specialities produced with age-old crafting, with no use of preservatives and colouring agents. The pasta is rich in flavour, like the wheat germ tacconi (also in the egg line) and traditional pici senesi and spelt tagliatelle pastas, not to mention a series of cereals and flavoured types.

Osimo (AN)

Pasta 60027 Carla Latini

via Simonetti, 3 c/o Pastificio e forno Dorico
☎ (+39) 3454241565
❀ www.pasta60027.it
✉ info@pasta60027.it
shop: no
e-commerce: yes

La Pasta di Carla Latini

After taking a few years off, Carla Latini, a major player in the field of pasta production, is back, thanks to a partnership with the Stoppani family. And now she's taken on a new challenge: Pasta 60027 (Carla knows 600 types of wheat and has produced 27 types of spaghetti through the years… but 60027 is also her zip code in Osimo). The pasta is made with top-quality Italian wheat and skilled, proven methods. 'Trucioli', the brainchild of the master chef Gualtiero Marchesi, stand out among the varieties being offered.

Monte San Giusto (MC)

La Pasta di Aldo

c.da Castelletta, 41
☎ (+39) 0733837120
❀ www.lapastadialdo.it
✉ aldo@lapastadialdo.it
shop: yes
e-commerce: no

An acronym for a pasta factory, the name made up of the first syllables of the names of Maria Alzapiedi and her husband, Luigi Donnari. Traditional shapes and sizes, tagliatelle, filini, chitarrine, now extended to include speciality products such as Farrine made with spelt flour, tagliatelle with truffles, and the Saracens made from buckwheat. Each pasta type has its own dedicated flour, strictly selected to ensure the sheets are spongy and even.

Ferrara

Pasta di Canossa

fraz. San Martino I via Buttifredo, 16
☎ (+39) 3456504610
❀ www.pastadicanossa.it
✉ info@pastadicanossa.it
shop: no
e-commerce: yes

In 2012 the Canossa family, with Alvise and his son Ottavio, decided to write a new chapter for the historic Tenuta Cuniola, at the gates of Ferrara. The 70-plus hectares of arable land produce durum wheat used for zero-kilometre pasta production, naturally good because it is a controlled network, bronze-drawn and slow-dried, as Italian tradition demands. The dough is used for spaghetti, gramigna, paccheri, fusilli and other shapes in the classic rough, porous appearance typical of quality pasta.

Gragnano (NA)

Pastai Gragnanesi

via Giovanni della Rocca, 20
☎ (+39) 0818012975
❀ www.pastaigragnanesi.it
✉ info@pastaigragnanesi.it
shop: yes
e-commerce: no

PASTAI GRAGNANESI
SOCIETÀ COOPERATIVA

One of the region's best-known pasta factories, whose secret for making a quality product is the perfect blend of durum wheat, as well as bronze drawing and long drying times (24–36 hours) at temperatures not in excess of 55 °C. Many operations are still manuals for a total production that never exceeds 40 quintals a day. Paccheri, lasagne, taccozzette, fusilli, ferrazzuoli, calamari, trecce and trofie del Vesuvio are the more traditional shapes and sizes, flanked variations on a theme, like paccheri rigati and paccheri ondulati.

Pontedera (PI)
Pastificio Caponi

loc. La Bianca I via della Virgola, 14
☎ (+39) 058752532
❀ www.pastacaponi.it
✉ info@pastificiocaponi.it
shop: no
e-commerce: no

TUSCANY
Lavorazione Artigianale Italiana
dal 1953

No industrial equipment is used in Alessandro Tagliagambe's pasta factory. The processing cycles are almost entirely manual with a daily production of about 200kg of pasta made from durum wheat and fresh eggs, for a niche clientele. Since 1953, the watchwords have been quality and respect for the ingredients. The pasta is dried slowly at room temperature to preserve the organoleptic features and nutritional qualities of the proteins and carbohydrates. The formats vary from classic to typically Tuscan.

Gragnano (NA)
Pastificio dei Campi

via dei Campi, 50
☎ (+39) 0818018430
❀ www.pastificiodeicampi.it
✉ info@pastificiodeicampi.it
shop: yes
e-commerce: yes

Pastificio dei Campi
GRAGNANO

Founded in 2007, the company was the brainchild of the younger partners of Pastificio Di Martino (dating back to 1912) who wanted to innovate. The mission of this facility is to produce high-end pasta, an expression of a tradition and a territory, but in step with the times. It produces 100% Italian pasta in various shapes and sizes, making only 30 quintals a day. Limited edition products, for a gourmet target, in Duet packs of 250 grams for two diners, and the Egoista single portion of 125 grams.

Calenzano (FI)
Michele Portoghese

loc. Settimello I via Baldanzese, 45
☎ (+39) 0558953869
❀ www.micheleportoghese.com
✉ info@micheleportoghese.com
shop: yes
e-commerce: no

pasta Michele PORTOGHESE
Artigiana
Tradizione
Italiana

In the 1970s Michele Portoghese opened a small pastry laboratory producing cantucci biscuits. Over the years it has retained its family-run scale but the company now specializes in pasta. Good quality and the desire to promote Italian ingredients and the value of a Mediterranean diet have been decisive factors in making this little pasta company famous beyond national borders. The focus is on classic shapes and the latest challenge is to produce the perfect pacchero: Pugliese wheat, slow drying and 17 minutes cooking time!

Palagano (MO)

Quinta Armonia
Pastificio Palaganese

loc. Monchio I via Panoramica, 197
☎ (+39) 059527683 I 3347902825
❀ www.quintaarmonia.it
✉ info@quintaarmonia.it
shop: no
e-commerce: no

The company works according to the principles of traditional Modenese, and more generally Emilian, cuisine. This means obeying the dictates of hand-made fresh pasta, using selected Italian wheat and free-range eggs to guarantee flavour and quality. The filled pasta products use typical local ingredients like PDO Prosciutto di Parma matured for 24 months, IGO mortadella, and PDO Parmigiano Reggiano matured for 30 months.

Cicciano (NA)

Nicola Russo

via Caserta, 79
☎ (+39) 0818248628
❀ www.pastificionicolarusso.it
✉ info@pastificionicolarusso.it
shop: no
e-commerce: yes

At the end of the 19th century the Russo family moved from Torre Annunziata to Cicciano and started the pasta-making business that it still operates to this very day. Passion and a commitment to traditional, artisanal methods are the keys to its success. Only choice semolina is used to make the dough, which is worked slowly before being drawn through brass, dried slowly and cooled at room temperature. Their selection is robust and diverse. Both short and long pasta varieties are available, as well as flavored pasta. Sauces and toppings are also available.

Pianella (PE)

Rustichella d'Abruzzo

p.zza Vestini, 20
☎ (+39) 085971308
❀ www.rustichella.it
✉ info@rustichella.it
shop: no
e-commerce: no

The business began in 1924 and since then the pasta has been crafted from the best durum wheat flour and pure mountain water. The Primograno line comes from 100 hectares of land planted with San Carlo, Varano and Mongibello cultivars, which are the source of spaghetti, spaghettoni, rustic penne and sagne pieces. Alongside the classic line, egg and special pasta, including handmade, regional, giants and rolled sheets.

Torre Annunziata (NA)
Setaro

via Mazzini, 47
☎ (+39) 0818611464 I 0818626913
❀ www.setaro.it
✉ info@setaro.it
shop: yes
e-commerce: no

Setaro began crafting pasta in 1939, respecting nature and tradition, using selected durum wheat flour and extra-pure spring water. Processing goes through vintage bronze dies and the pasta drying process is kept very slow (from 24 to 120 hours, depending on the type), at low temperatures. The product range is extensive: paccheri, millerighe, gigantoni, lumaconi for baked dishes, calamarata for fish sauces, taccole for chickpeas. And all packaged by hand.

Campofilone (FM)
Spinosi

via XXV Aprile, 21
☎ (+39) 0734932196
❀ www.spinosi.com
✉ info@spinosi.com
shop: yes
e-commerce: no

l'artigiano della pasta fatta in casa dal 1933

A heritage brand that goes back almost a century, with a story that began in 1933, when Nello Spinosi took his wife's homemade pasta to Rome as a gift for some acquaintances. The pasta goes by the name of Campofilone maccheroncini and became so popular that they soon drove a craft industry. Three generations of uninterrupted passion have carried the company into the present. There are a number of products: classic, special omega 3, special shapes, flavoured varieties. Confectionery specialities are also available now.

Thiesi (SS)
Tanda & Spada

s.s. 131bis
☎ (+39) 079886805
❀ www.tandaespada.it
✉ info@tandaespada.it
shop: no
e-commerce: no

Since 1990, Tanda & Spada have evolved notably, though they've done it without losing their commitment to quality and traditional, artisanal methods. Their selection includes pasta for large-scale distribution and an organic line of pasta, made with regular or whole wheat flour. In addition to local Sardinian specialities (gnocchetti, malloreddus and fregula), they offer some forty other varieties of pasta (short, long, flavored with sage, saffron, squid ink...).

Arcevia (AN)

La Terra e Il Cielo

fraz. Piticchio I b.go Emilio zona PIP, 229h
☎ (+39) 0731981906
❀ www.laterraeilcielo.it
✉ info@laterraeilcielo.it
shop: no
e-commerce: no

LA TERRA E IL CIELO

Founded in 1980, this cooperative was the first Italian example of a building to embrace principles of sustainability, bio-architecture and feng shui, guaranteeing the wellness of those who work there and purity of the products, all strictly bio. The range includes: dry pasta, including types made with rare cereals (La Terra e Il Cielo even has its own dehulling equipment for organic grains); oil, pulses, coffee (roasted in house), preserves, and some baked products.

Roseto degli Abruzzi (TE)

Verrigni

via Salara, 9
☎ (+39) 0859040269
❀ www.verrigni.com
✉ info@verrigni.com
shop: yes
e-commerce: yes

VERRIGNI
ANTICO PASTIFICIO ROSETANO DAL 1898

Over 30 years ago this was one of the first pasta factories to propose organic pasta, then wholemeal, and another made with alternative cereals like spelt and kamut. Then came pasta made from wheat produced by the Valentini winery, for a short, local chain, and the Oro line in five sizes, from the spaghettone to the fusillone, extruded with gold dies. Today the old Roseto pasta plant has expanded even further into the terroir and more edible excellence, selecting and distributing food specialities, including a gluten-free pasta.

Monte San Giusto (MC)

Zelo

via G. Rossa, 54
☎ (+39) 07331890907 I 3483720335
❀ www.zelopasta.it
✉ zelocommerciale@gmail.com
shop: no
e-commerce: yes

ZELO
Pasta Artigianale all'uovo

Brothers Matteo and Maurizio Zengarini, the former a master pasta maker and the latter working in public relations, have spent four years experimenting in pursuit of the perfect product: selection of ingredients, study of machinery and production methods. The result is excellent egg and durum wheat pasta. The format and flavours on offer include: classic tagliatelle, tagliolini and fettuccine, or flavoured with truffles, basil, farro, and on the horizon, citrus fruit. Striking packaging is in the colour of bread paper, with the long strings of pasta curled into nests.

Pasta

229

Sassello (SV)

Amaretti Giacobbe

loc. Pianferioso, 62
☎ (+39) 019724860
✆ www.amarettigiacobbe.it
✉ info@amarettigiacobbe.it
shop: no
e-commerce: no

Antonio Giacobbe's goal when he opened this company in 1955 was to make quality artisan products. Today it is run by his great-grandson who continues the family business with great passion. Production specializes in typical Sassellese amaretti, made according to tradition, with a few simple but authentic ingredients: sweet and bitter almonds, sugar and egg whites. There are many variations, from the classic version to those flavoured with Savona chinotto or chocolate, or a sugar-free type.

Grinzane Cavour (CN)

Antica Torroneria Piemontese

via Piana Gallo, 48
☎ (+39) 0173239832
✆ www.torrone.it
✉ info@torrone.it
shop: yes
e-commerce: no

For four generations the Sebaste family has specialized in the confectionery industry, above all producing exquisite nougat, but other goodies too. Crucial is the choice of products, firstly PGI Langa Tonda Gentile hazelnuts. Sebaste offer a wide range of confectionery, some gluten-free, with nougat in the front line, in multiple variations and sizes, including a soft version. Then there are sweet truffles in different flavours, chocolate and dried fruit Quadrotte, rum albesi, pralines, baci di dama, chocolate-coated grissini and hazelnuts, and more besides.

Pomezia (RM)

Attilio Servi

via Campobello, 1c
☎ (+39) 069124150
✆ www.attilioservipasticceria.com
✉ info@attilioservi.eu
shop: yes
e-commerce: no

Attilio Servi's sweet creations travel from the workshop in Pomezia to gourmets who are unable to resist the delights made by this iconic patisserie. His experience, creativity and knowledge of the raw ingredients and production methods are apparent in the delicious breakfast pastries, fragrant and soft cakes for festivities like the delicious panettone and colomba. But also lovely modern cakes and a range of sweet and savoury bakes in tasty flavours.

Ales (OR)

Fiorenzo Atzori

via Sardegna, 18
☎ (+39) 078391702
❀ www.fiorenzoatzori.com
✉ info@fiorenzoatzori.com
shop: yes
e-commerce: no

The company was founded in 2001 thanks to Gian Luca's eye for business, but the Atzori family's roots in confectionery are centuries old. In this area almond grove thrive alongside vegetation perfect for production of an excellent honey: two fundamental ingredients for making typical Ales nougat. In addition to this speciality, available in various sizes, there is a wide range of traditional sweets Sardinian patisserie: amaretti, pistoccus de cappa, papassini, gueffus, hood, shortbread and pan'e saba.

Asti

Davide Barbero

via A. Brofferio, 84
☎ (+39) 0141594004
❀ www.barberodavide.it
✉ info@barberodavide.it
shop: yes
e-commerce: no

Well over a century of history upheld by five generations of family members. Quite a calling card for this company specializing in production of superb nougat, above all Friabile Piemontese made according to the traditional Asti recipe. There are various types and weights, including slices, a chocolate-covered pistachio, bite-size nougat, and so on. The company also works with gianduia and chocolate, so try the bars, dragées, gianduiotti, chocolate-covered grissini and chocolates. Great Easter eggs!

Cologna Veneta (VR)

Mandorlato Bauce

v.le Finlandia, 18
☎ (+39) 0442411511 I 3351214884
❀ www.mandorlatobauce.it
✉ info@mandorlatobauce.it
shop: no
e-commerce: no

Just four skilfully dosed ingredients (almonds, acacia honey, sugar, and egg white) are the secret of exquisite mandorlato almond nougat, created in this Verona town in the early 1800s. All the rest is down to the expert manual skills of master confectioners. In addition to the classic version, there is another in chocolate and also a soft type. But also mandorlato with aloe; almonds, honey and rosehip; almonds, honey and blackcurrants; pandorlato, with chocolate; mandorlato nuggets dusted with cocoa; truffles.

Selvazzano Dentro (PD)

Biasetto

via Penghe, 1f
☎ (+39) 049630171
❀ www.pasticceriabiasetto.it
✉ info@pasticceriabiasetto.it
shop: no
e-commerce: no

The fame of master patisseur Luigi Biasetto has long crossed national borders, thanks above all to his many awards and accolades. His skill and creativity, and his passion, have made him the inventor of impeccable delights, verging on perfection, in a triumph of fragrance and flavour. The extensive product range includes dramatic cakes, petit fours, macaroons, chocolates, pralines and tea biscuits. No shortage of panettone, pandoro, colomba and other seasonal treats.

Montevarchi (AR)

Bonci

via A. Vespucci, 101
☎ (+39) 055981225
❀ pasticceriabonci.it
✉ info@pasticceriabonci.it
shop: yes
e-commerce: yes

For more than half a century and for three generations, the Bonci family has been upholding the art of patisserie. Crafting in the traditional way, using select ingredients, and bold enough to experiment are the solid foundation and secret of the company's deserved success. Many specialties, from panbriacone and bria, in various flavours, to panpepato, panforte, pan del cassero, cantucci (chocolate versions too) and ricciarelli. Also shortbreads, jellies, candied fruit, chocolates and pralines with the Mezzasoma brand.

Chivasso (TO)

Bonfante

via Torino, 29
☎ (+39) 0119102157
❀ www.nocciolini-bonfante.it
✉ info@nocciolini-bonfante.it
shop: yes
e-commerce: no

This bakery, one of the Locali Storici d'Italia circuit of Italy's heritage premises, was founded by Luigi Bonfanti in 1922 when he decided to spread the word of his nocciolini further afield. This tiny, mouth-watering biscuit is made with PGI Piedmont hazelnuts, sugar and egg white. Over time, other delicacies were invented and produced, from noccioloni (a kind of handmade brutti e buoni) to nocciolona cake, biscuits (including some with wine), sponge fingers, anicini, torcetti, spreads and a nocciolino liqueur.

Villafranca Piemonte (TO)
Bonifanti

via Vigone, 51
☎ (+39) 0119800718
🕸 www.bonifanti.it
✉ info@bonifanti.com
shop: yes
e-commerce: yes

Founded in 1932 by Vincenzo Bonifanti, the business now belongs to the Grondona family, which has kept faith with the original philosophy of attention to raw materials and to artisanal crafting. The range of sweet treats on offer is extensive: petit fours, baci di dama, amaretti, marron glacé, tortelle (a kind of plum cake), moretti, and chocolate truffles, large and bite-size nougats. Then there are panettone, pandoro and colomba, available in several versions and with elegant gift boxes.

San Marco dei Cavoti (BN)
Cav. Innocenzo Borrillo

via Roma, 64
☎ (+39) 0824 984060
🕸 www.borrillo.it
✉ innocenzoborrillo@libero.it
shop: yes
e-commerce: no

Quality, passion, love, and respect for tradition. This is the explanation for the success of this family company, which has lasted for well over a century. Almonds, hazelnuts, chocolate, honey, and natural aromas are the main ingredients of the tasty nougats made here, where everything happens in full view, as is the tradition, with maximum transparency for the customer. The house special is the bite-size bacio nougat, crunchy and covered with dark chocolate, along with full-size nougats, but fancy biscuits and fresh pastries are not to be underestimated.

Bagnara Calabra (RC)
Careri

via Nazionale, 195
☎ (+39) 0966371349
🕸 www.careritorroni.it
✉ info@careritorroni.it
shop: yes
e-commerce: no

In a Calabrian village renowned for the production of nougat, this family business was opened in 1967 and expanded in the early 2000s. Selected ingredients (mostly almonds, honey and sugar) and careful crafting are the basis for the quality of its production. There are the soft classics in many sizes, chocolate-covered versions, those scented with cinnamon or cloves, orange-flavoured or with white chocolate, in the ice cream option. Then there are fancy biscuits and fresh pastries, and chocolate Easter eggs.

Patisserie, baked goods

Cologna Veneta (VR)
Casa del Dolce

v.le del Lavoro, 11
☎ (+39) 044285961
❀ www.finissimomandorlato.it
✉ finissimomandorlato@gmail.com
shop: yes
e-commerce: no

For years now, the Bertolini family patisserie has been producing the special soft nougat for which the small town of Cologna Veneta is renowned. To make it as "refined" as possible, they only use hand-picked almonds, fresh egg whites, acacia honey and white sugar. The product is available as round cakes, sticks and violins, in various weights. It also produces a selection of baked goods: fragrant colomba and coated panettone, as well as aromatic pandoro.

San Giuseppe Jato (PA)
Pasticceria Cerniglia

via Porta Palermo, 173
☎ (+39) 0918572352
❀ www.pasticceriacerniglia.com
✉ turi.cerniglia@libero.it
shop: yes
e-commerce: no

Founded on the outskirts of Palermo by Salvatore Cerniglia back in 1972, over the years this patisserie has become a real hotbed of the most authentic Sicilian confectionery culture. Tradition is key at this famous bakery where, as well as eating in, visitors can witness the creation of traditional ricotta cannoli originating from Piana degli Albanesi; almond pastries, buccellati biscuits, marzipan fruit and cassata, consumed at gourmet tables Italy and worldwide.

Parona (PV)
Forno F.lli Collivasone

v.lo F. Turati, 1
☎ (+39) 0384253018
❀ www.collivasone.it
✎ info@collivasone.it
shop: yes
e-commerce: no

Tradition has been handed down from father to son here since 1890, producing the tasty offella, a fragrant biscuit typical of the area, whose recipe has never changed: wheat flour, eggs, butter, sugar and olive oil. A chocolate version has now been added. Production also includes corn and rice crackers, and biscuits: whole, rice, Kamut, krumiri, lemon-scented sticks, soy and raisin pizzichi, paronini (good for breakfast). For the festive seasons there are plenty of options. A sugar-free line is also available.

Palazzolo Acreide (SR)
Corsino

via Nazionale, 2
☎ (+39) 0931875035 I 0931875563
✆ www.corsino.it
✉ corsino@corsino.it
shop: yes
e-commerce: yes

Dal 1889

Dolci Tradizioni

Since 1889, the Antica Pasticceria Corsino has embodied a passion for the island's confectionery tradition, with the utmost attention to hygiene and development of the best products. The range is huge: fancy biscuits made with almond paste, arabini, carrubini, malfatti, walnut biscuits, pistachio hearts. Not to mention crunchy quince morsels, citrus peel dipped in chocolate, bars of spicy chocolate, jams and preserves, chocolates, Martorana fruit, large and bite-size nougats. There is also a small selection of savouries.

Verzuolo (CN)
Cradel

via Maestri del Lavoro, 18
☎ (+39) 017586385
✆ www.cradel.it
✉ info@cradel.it
shop: no
e-commerce: no

Since its inception in 1989, this artisan producer has specialized in manufacturing sweets and quality baked goods. Featured products include fried dough strips (bugie di Carnevale) with many different fillings (apricot, chocolate/hazelnut gianduja, cream, cherry etc.), pies, tarts (which are still made by hand and are available with alternative flours such as spelt, rice, corn and whole wheat), biscotti (shortbread, crackers and sugar-free varieties, which are perfect for the health-conscious) and melba toast (also available in spelt and sugar-free varieties).

Bagnara Calabra (RC)
Cundari

via Nazionale, 274
☎ (+39) 0966372505
✆ www.cundarivincenzo.it
✉ info@cundarivincenzo.it
shop: yes
e-commerce: yes

Un Mare di Delizie

Vincenzo Cundari is to be thanked for taking over his father's business and giving it a new lease of life, driven by sheer passion. His flagship is a PGI nougat, made by hand with excellent ingredients and available in many shapes and sizes: soft, coated, with cinnamon, bergamot, rum, orange etc.. Then there are almond and chocolate crisps, coated figs, almond paste, chocolate-coated citrus peel, and typical Christmas recipes like susamelle, mustaccioli, piparelli and panettone.

Patisserie, baked goods

San Pietro al Natisone (UD)

Dall'Ava Bakery

loc. Ponte San Quirino, 1
☎ (+39) 0432727585
✆ www.dallavabakery.it
✉ info@dallavabakery.it
shop: yes
e-commerce: no

In 2012, Carlo Dall'Ava, former head of the San Daniele del Friuli facility that produces excellent cured ham, decided to invest in the art of patisserie. Success followed swiftly, thanks to his hard work sourcing top-quality raw materials and his desire to promote the goodness of the products of the Valli del Natisone. As well as pastries and tarallos, he also makes pastries for festivities using a yeast starter, and special gastronomic delicacies from all over Italy, such as Noto almonds and candied fruit from Calabria and Sicily.

Chiesina Uzzanese (PT)

Desideri

via Livornese di Sotto, 26
☎ (+39) 0572411023
✆ cialdedesideri.it
✉ info@cialdedesideri.it
shop: yes
e-commerce: yes

Since 1911 the Desideri family has devoted itself to the artisanal production of local sweets, safeguarding tradition and paying the maximum attention to production techniques and the quality of ingredients. The cialde di Montacatini are most definitely on center stage. These delicious, fragrant, almond wafer biscuits are also available in a chocolate variety and in an elegant, gift package. They also make brigidini (aromatic, thin, aniseed crisps), cantuccini di Prato and cantumatti (thin almond crisps).

Gaeta (LT)

Di Ciaccio

via Appia, km 136,500
☎ (+39) 0771311010
✆ www.diciaccio.com
✉ info@diciaccio.com
shop: yes
e-commerce: yes

Di Ciaccio
Pasticcieri Artigiani dal 1928

Active from the 1920s, this family firm is an admirable example of how to continue tradition while forging ahead to the future. Confectionery production is of top quality, from yummy sponge fingers to brutti ma buoni, langues de chat, delicious shortbread, girandola or corallo in various flavours. Leavened products include panettone (classic, almond and chocolate), but also typical regional pastries for the festivities: pastiera, susamelli, sciuscelle, rococo and mostaccioli.

Scanno (AQ)
Di Masso

v.le del Lago, 20
☎ (+39) 086474475
🌐 www.dimassoscanno.net
✉ info@dimassoscanno.it
shop: yes
e-commerce: yes

Pan dell'Orso, a traditional local sweet, takes center stage at this bakers' confectionery owned by the Di Masso family. Pan dell'Orso, which is available in different shapes and varieties, gets its name from the bread carried by shepherds in times when bears were still a common sight in the area. The Di Masso family, whose experience goes back generations, also make biscotti, sweets that are common to the area of Abruzzo (amaretti, ferratelle, mostacciuoli), pandolciotto, focaccia 'di nonna Angela' and traditional Easter cakes (colomba pasquale).

Monteroduni (IS)
Dolceamaro

s.s. 85 Venafrana, km 32,896
☎ (+39) 0865493005
🌐 www.dolceamaro.com
✉ clienti@dolceamaro.com
shop: yes
e-commerce: no

An interesting company that has just turned 50 and is managed with passion by the Papa family, specializing in the ancient art of sugared almonds. The range goes from a classic almond dipped in sugar or chocolate to those with fruit and sugar-coated dragées. Over time Papa has expanded production and also makes chocolate, in bars that include spicy ginger, saffron and paprika; dragées, also in various spice and fruit versions; and chocolate-coated coffee beans.

Padova
I Dolci di Giotto

via E. Forcellini, 172
☎ (+39) 0498033100 l 049 8033720
🌐 www.idolcidigiotto.it
✉ info@idolcidigiotto.it
shop: yes
e-commerce: yes

Since 2005, as well as being known for its outstanding products, the Giotto patisserie has proved real social commitment by teaching the art of pastry making to inmates from Due Palazzi prison. The work in the prison is strictly supervised by master pastry chefs who teach their pupils how to follow recipes to the letter. Giotto production is vast and ranges from traditional patisserie for festivities to nougat, biscuits, tarts and the Sant'Antonio line developed in partnership with the monks from the basilica dedicated to Saint Anthony.

Turi (BA)

Dolci Promesse... La Faldacchea

via Filippo Ludovico, 5a
☎ (+39) 0802373574
�',' www.dolcipromesse.it
✉ info@dolcipromesse.it
shop: yes
e-commerce: yes

This is the home of faldacchea, a traditional delicacy of Turi. The chocolate-covered cake contains soft almond paste and sponge enclosing a delicious filling. Cherry, limoncello, coffee, pistachio are just a few of the 19 flavours available (including gluten-free!). The pastries are made by artisanal methods, starting with strict selection of ingredients, finely decorated by hand and presented in individual paper cases.

Modica (RG)

Donna Elvira

via Risorgimento, 32
☎ (+39) 0932764359
🌍 www.donnaelvira.it
✉ info@donnaelvira.it
shop: yes
e-commerce: yes

Traditional Modica specialities produced by Elvira Roccasalva who applies ancient recipes inherited from an elderly lady along with her biscuit store. Elvira offers some offbeat exotic and spicy confectionery like mpanatiggie, sweet dumplings filled with meat and chocolate; Savoia cake of browned marzipan with a heart of almond and orange preserve; and a generous selection of carob pastries and Modica natural, flavoured and single-origin chocolate. In addition, dolci da riposto pantry pastries and Martorana fruit.

Alfonsine (RA)

Forno Fabbri

via Reale, 123
☎ (+39) 054481688 I 349 7213603
🌍 www.fabbrideliziedaforno.it
✉ info@fabbrideliziedaforno.itinfo
shop: yes
e-commerce: yes

The Fabbri family company was established in 1971 and immediately specialized in food. The business developed in two different workshops, one for fine foods and the other for bread and cakes, creating products designed to meet high quality standards. The range includes melba toasts and large cakes for the festivities like colomba, panettone and pandoro. The most recent addition is a line of typical Romagna products, like zucarén made from butter and fresh cream, and scrocladènt, made from almonds.

Zanè (VI)
Filippi

via M. Pasubio, 96a
☎ (+39) 0445314085
❀ www.pasticceriafilippi.it
✉ info@pasticceriafilippi.it
shop: yes
e-commerce: no

The shingle dated 1972 fronts the story of a family that dedicates itself to making patisserie using genuine ingredients and long proving times. Even though the company has had to keep abreast of the times it has never set aside its craft approach. As we mentioned, most of the production is leavened, especially pandoro, colomba and panettone (classic, almond topped without candied fruit, with chocolate, orange and chocolate, sour cherry, fruit, white chocolate and lemon, coffee, chestnut, apricot).

San Vito al Tagliamento (PN)
Dal Forner

via Rosa, 66
☎ (+39) 0434874016
❀ www.dalforner.it
✉ info@dalforner.it
shop: yes
e-commerce: no

dal **Forner**
PANIFICIO E PASTICCERIA
TRADIZIONALE

Oskar Bortoletti creates Forner products with passion and devotion. An artisan whose priority is quality, he runs his bakery-patisserie with his wife Orietta. The ingredients are carefully selected: organic flour and eggs, Belgian butter, top cream, and a love of baked goods made using a sourdough starter. As well as bread and breadsticks they offer baked cakes, pastries and handmade biscots, and products for festivities including colomba and panettone.

Bovolone (VR)
Le Furezze

via San Giovanni, 3
☎ (+39) 3409829822
❀ www.lefurezze.com
✉ info@lefurezze.com
shop: yes
e-commerce: yes

"Furezze" comes from the Venetian dialect word "sfurèso", meaning "delicacies", like those produced using artisanal methods in this workshop, and presented in delightful recyclable packaging. The creations are the fruit of careful ingredient selections, with sophisticated combinations designed to promote and enhance the excellent ingredients. There are lavender buttons, aniseed and liquorice sticks, dark chocolate and chilli slices, and much more.

Cologna Veneta (VR)
Garzotto Rocco & Figlio

via Mabil, 1
☎ (+39) 044285162
🌐 www.garzottorocco.com
✉ garzottorocco@garzottorocco.com
shop: yes
e-commerce: no

In 1840 Rocco Garzotto invented a great Veneto nougat by mixing honey, egg white, peeled and toasted almonds, and a little sugar. Today it is Dino, the fifth generation, who continues to use the family recipe, with the same top quality Italian ingredients, without preservatives, colourings or aromas, in a process lasting almost a year. The nougat comes in various shapes and sizes, and in elegant packaging, even individual servings. Alternatives include bite-size torroncino and a soft nougat using Sicilian pistachios and ground almonds.

Caltanissetta
M. Geraci 1870

via Canonico F. Pulci, 14
☎ (+39) 0934581570
🌐 www.geraci1870.it
✉ geraci@geraci1870.it
shop: yes
e-commerce: yes

A triumph of pure Sicilian sweetness is offered by this iconic family-run company, dating back centuries. Tradition, crafting and quality products come together in small masterpieces of the art of confectionery. There is a large range of products, from excellent nougat (even a bio version), in various sizes and flavours, to marzipan (including Easter lambs); rollò; cassata; cannoli; Martorana fruit; and cakes, like a delicious torta saracena house speciality made with chocolate, almonds and pistachios.

L'Aquila
Kucino

fraz. Preturo I via dell'Aringo, 58a
☎ (+39) 08621956277
🌐 www.kucino.com
✉ info@kucino.com
shop: no
e-commerce: no

This young and dynamic bakery produces top-quality biscotti (both sweet and savory) by bringing together first-rate ingredients, passion and a keen eye for packaging (because first impressions matter)! They've also got fun kits (they call them 'happy kits') that let rookies try their hand at making various types of sweets by simply adding fresh ingredients like eggs, butter or milk. Decadent food lovers won't want to miss out on their line of 'cioccolatosi' biscotti.

Agnone (IS)
Labbate Mazziotta

via Valle di San Lorenzo
☎ (+39) 086578006
🕸 www.labbatemazziotta.it
✉ info@labbatemazziotta.it
shop: yes
e-commerce: no

LABBATEMAZZIOTTA
TRADIZIONE DOLCIARIA DAL 1976

For 30 years this family business has focused on classic Molise patisserie. The secret of its quality is a respect for craft processing, the use of prime products and an ongoing exploration of new scenarios. The company's flagship is its campana, a bell-shaped cake made of nuts and almond flour, and coated with chocolate, in homage to the world's oldest bell foundry located right here. Then there are mostaccioli, wafers filled with walnuts and almonds, dragées, amaretti and aromatized sugars.

Olbia
Loi Dolci Sardi

via Vespignani, 2
☎ (+39) 078950239
🕸 www.pasticcerialoiolbia.com
✉ pasticcerialoididui@gmail.com
shop: yes
e-commerce: no

Founded in 1963 by Maddalena Loi, this traditional patisserie is loyal to Sardinian classics, made with passion and care, using quality ingredients and artisanal processes, without preservatives or additives: honey and saba coppolette; aranzada; bianchini, also with chocolate; jam buns; breakfast biscuits; grape formaggelle with their cheesy filling; iced and plain papassini; tilicas; guelfos; almond pastries; soft amaretti. And lots more too.

Quarrata (PT)
Fratelli Lunardi

via di Lucciano, 33
☎ (+39) 057373077
🕸 www.fratellilunardi.it
✉ info@fratellilunardi.it
shop: no
e-commerce: yes

Massimiliano and Riccardo Lunardi have taken the reins of this family-run business, started in 1966, bringing an innovative, modern perspective to 'home-style' traditional recipes. Ingredients are strictly organic and top-quality, of course. Cantuccini, a local classic, are a mainstay, with a number of enticing and unusual variations available (lemon and lime, chocolate and orange). But we should also mention their mini-biscotti, melba toast, baked goods, cakes, panettoni and various other seasonal treats.

Montesilvano (PE)
Mammamassaia

via Verrotti, 46
☎ (+39) 3351428640 I 0854492521
❀ www.mammamassaiapescara.it
✉ mammamassaia@gmail.com
shop: no
e-commerce: no

Founded in 1992, this small, family-run company has carved out a respectable niche in the national craft pastry segment, in particular for leavened products, and that means about 40 hours of natural proving. Pride of place goes to an admirable range of panettone and colomba in various versions. Then there is an ample selection of all kinds of cakes, tea and fancy biscuits, amaretti, macaroons, traditional Abruzzo patisserie like panaccio, made with almonds, eggs, sugar and dark chocolate.

Prato
Biscottificio Antonio Mattei

via B. Ricasoli, 20
☎ (+39) 057425756
❀ www.antoniomattei.it
✉ info@antoniomattei.it
shop: no
e-commerce: yes

Since 1858 Mattei has been synonymous with Prato biscotti, the traditional almond sweet that's packaged in the unmistakable blue, hand-tied bag. There are also chocolate cantuccini, candied oranges, biscotti della salute, brutti e buoni, biscotti di frolla, mantovana cake, filone (a type of plum cake) and fresh baked sweets. Their Deseo line of products are naturally appealing, with cantuccini available in a number of delicious varieties, sweet and savory biscotti (perfect as a snack before dinner) and cookies.

Roma
Il Mondo di Laura

via Tiburtina, 263
☎ (+39) 065880966 I 3287413765
❀ www.mondodilaura.com
✉ info@mondodilaura.com
shop: no
e-commerce: no

Laura Raccah's world is made up of biscotti. She prepares them with love, using Kosher and certified Slow Food methods, and organic ingredients, in her kitchen workspace. Her creations include the Giuly Cookie (with vanilla and chocolate chips), the Candy Spice (with cinnamon, cloves, ginger and nutmeg) and the Ghilty (with cocoa, orange peel, pieces of dark chocolate and candied orange). The products' packaging looks as good as they taste.

Saint Vincent (AO)
Mauro Morandin

via E. Chanoux, 105
☎ (+39) 0166512690
❀ www.mauromorandin.it
✉ info@mauromorandin.it
shop: yes
e-commerce: no

MAURO
Morandin
MAESTRO PASTICCERE

Mauro Morandin grew up breathing in the fragrance of his father Rolando's bakery, and has become an international maestro of patisserie, preserving the artisan spirit while developing a modern, innovative flavour. He uses the best ingredients to make fresh and dry pastries, chocolate, sugared almonds, and typical Valle d'Aosta sweets like torcetti, tegole and panciucco, popular in Europe and Asia alike. Worth trying are the fragrant colomba and delicious panettone, also in savoury versions like olive, made for the festivities.

Trani (BT)
Premiata Fabbrica di Confetti Giovanni Mucci

via Andria, km 1,290
☎ (+39) 0883586935
❀ www.muccigiovanni.it
✉ mucci@muccigiovanni.it
shop: yes
e-commerce: no

1894
Confetti e dragées
MUCCI
GIOVANNI

Semplicemente Unici

The story of this craft comfit-maker goes back to 1894, when founder Nicola Mucci completed an apprenticeship in Naples and went to set up his own workshop in the heart of Andria. The company has come a long way since then and the family business is now one of Italy's top producers of sugared almonds, chocolate and sweets, using local ingredients where possible. The range goes from classic comfits with almonds and other fillings, to dragées, limoncello or grappa candies.

L'Aquila
Torrone F.lli Nurzia

p.zza Duomo, 74
☎ (+39) 086221002
❀ www.torronenurzia.it
✉ torronenurzia@gmail.com
shop: yes
e-commerce: no

Torrone Fratelli Nurzia

Fratelli Nurzia is a name that conjures up the image of L'Aquila nougat, a delicacy made for Christmas using nuts and cocoa. The company was founded in 1835 and this confectionery tradition has been handed down from father to son until today, stamping the product with its distinctive, inimitable style. The nougats are still prepared with a soft cocoa-based paste or in the classic white version with almonds, and come in different sizes and packaging.

Palermo

I Peccatucci di Mamma Andrea

via Principe di Scordia, 67
☎ (+39) 091334835 I 0916111654
⊛ mammaandrea.it
✉ info@mammaandrea.it
shop: no
e-commerce: no

I PECCATUCCI DI MAMMA ANDREA

Behind this brand, now known worldwide, lie the entrepreneurial spirit and enthusiasm of Andrea De Cesare, who set up the business in 1989 by putting his skills and creative passion for patisserie to good use. The production is massive, with hundreds of items: morsels of plain and flavoured almond paste; tiny marzipan fruits; sospiri; fruit and wine jellies; extra fruit jams and preserves; sweet spreads, nuts in honey; liqueurs and ratafià. Festive pastries for seasonal celebrations and chic gift packaging.

Sant'Egidio del Monte Albino (SA)

Pepe

via Nazionale, 2
☎ (+39) 0815154151
⊛ www.pepemastrodolciere.it
✉ info@pasticceria-pepe.it
shop: yes
e-commerce: yes

The story of Alfonso Pepe and his passion for the art of patisserie goes back to the 1980s. An A.M.P.I. master pastry chef, his career vaunts many awards and covers all branches of patisserie from fresh to dry, and chocolate. Alfonso's very finest achievements have been in the field of larger baked goods, such as panettone and colomba, signature pieces from his Salerno-based workshop. His citrus, apricot and white fig creations are truly lip smacking and must be ordered well in advance.

Bovolone (VR)

Perbellini

via Vittorio Veneto, 46
☎ (+39) 0457100599
⊛ www.perbellini.com
✉ info@perbellini.com
shop: yes
e-commerce: yes

In addition to being identified with fine dining, Perbellini is also known for its white art. The patisserie was opened in 1862 by Giovanni Battista Perbellini, and produces refined pastries of excellent standards: the I' Offella d'Oro, for example, is recipe dated 1891 and is still the house speciality, a tasty version of nadalin, an ancient Verona pandoro. To die for are the strachin millefeuille with soufflé cream filling; the dolce dorato, a small plum cake; buttery sfoiade; sbrisolade; panettone, pandoro, Easter colomba and focaccia.

San Dorligo della Valle (TS)
Pintaudi

via J. Ressel, 2 int. 6, zona industriale
☎ (+39) 040632974
�',' www.pintaudi.eu
✉ info@pintaudi.eu
shop: yes
e-commerce: yes

The passion of Giuseppe Pintaudi, an artisan of taste who has made quality his objective is the inspiration of the fragrant, aromatic biscuit bakery, packaged sweets and the large leavened cakes covered with delicious icing for the festivities. The workshop transforms authentic, naturally good ingredients with no preservatives. There are Trieste's typical presniz, putizze and pinze cakes, classic buttery-vanilla breakfast treats, but also a selection of pastries in different flavours.

Grottaglie (TA)
Pregiata Forneria Lenti

via Raffaello, 11
☎ (+39) 0995665376
�',' www.pregiatafornerialenti.com
✉ info@pregiatafornerialenti.com
shop: yes
e-commerce: no

Emanuele Lenti and his wife Antonella share a passion for baked goods and pastries. Every day they can be found hard at work in their bakery, making cakes true to established local traditions. Their products are baked in an olive wood-fuelled oven and together with the quality ingredients, products are guaranteed an authentic flavour. The range includes bread, tarallo, doughnuts, pandoro, panettone, colomba, and traditional Puglia confectionery like marzipan and other patisserie.

Battifollo (CN)
Primo Pan

via Chiossa, 18
☎ (+39) 0174783322 | 3355712766
�',' www.primopan.com
✉ info@primopan.com
shop: yes
e-commerce: no

PRIMO PAN
Biscotti di Battifollo

In the heart of a small village in the Ligurian Alps, during the years immediately after WW1, Giacomo Biga founded a company specializing in the production of biscuits for which he used entirely artisanal processes. The wholesome ingredients and attention to the production method guarantee tasty goodness with the flavour and fragrance of authenticity. So we find paste di meliga corn biscuits; cereal biscuits (also sugar-free), but also recipes using chestnuts, buckwheat, spelt and hazelnut.

Tonara (NU)
Pruneddu

via Ing. Porru, 7
☎ (+39) 0784638051 3939355216
❀ www.pruneddu.it/com
✉ info@pruneddu.it
shop: yes
e-commerce: no

TORRONIFICIO ARTIGIANO

One of the most famous names in Sardinian nougat production, located in the heart of Barbagia, and founded in 1963 by Salvatore Pruneddu to keep alive old local traditions. The flagship is the torrone classico, a nougat using only selected ingredients, from honey to dried fruit, without sugar, glucose syrup and preservatives. There are three brands: Pruneddu, Barbagia and Arasule. There are various sizes and shapes, from blocks to sticks; from classic nougats wrapped one by one, to fingers with various types of local honey.

Castellinaldo (CN)
Relanghe

via San Damiano, 20
☎ (+39) 01732904201 0173282582
❀ www.relanghe.it
✉ relanghe@relanghe.it
shop: no
e-commerce: no

TORRONI TARTUFI / DRAGÉES
——— A L B A ———

Founded in 1993 with the aim of reviving the artisanal nougat made with the PGI Langa Tonda Gentile hazelnut, the company has undergone changes and converted at corporate level but retains its artisanal approach and abides by its quality philosophy. Nougat is certainly the flagship product but in various shapes and sizes. The range, with some manufacturing support from master chocolatier Guido Gobino, includes pistachio and hazelnut paste, ice cream mixes, dragées, brutti e buoni, and sweet truffles.

Sale (AL)
Rippa

via D. Alighieri, 21
☎ (+39) 013184114
❀ www.bacididamarippa.com
✉ info@bacididamarippa.com
shop: yes
e-commerce: no

RIPPA
DAL 1958

After learning the secret recipe for bacio di dama cookies in Tortona, Sergio Rippa, along with his brother, founded the bakery that bears their name. Since 1958 they have specialized in this traditional sweet (available in different flavors like coffee, almond, hazelnut etc.) and soft amaretti cookies (available in cherry, lemon, orange and apricot). The secret to their success has never changed. It lies in the choice of select ingredients and the artisanal methods used to prepare them.

Genova
Pietro Romanengo fu Stefano

v.le Mojon, 1r
☎ (+39) 010819051
❂ romanengo.it
✉ info@romanengo.com
shop: no
e-commerce: yes

One of the Romanengo family's heritage confectioners, which have delighted generations of consumers not only in Genoa but also further afield. The underpinning for the entire production range is the standard of ingredients sought out and careful crafting at each step. The flagship is certainly the range of sugared almonds in many flavours. Then there are delicious candied fruits and sugar violets, preserves and jams in original combinations, fondants and bonbons, chocolate, chocolates and pralines. A tempting range of seasonal patisserie is also available.

Santa Venerina (CT)
Russo

via Vittorio Emanuele, 105
☎ (+39) 095953202
❂ www.dolcirusso.it
✉ informazioni@dolcirusso.it
shop: yes
e-commerce: no

The vintage patisserie, founded in 1880, has specialized from the start in traditional Sicilian pastries. Recipes of a bygone era skilfully reworked, meticulous research into ingredients and care at each step, ensuring quality is consistently high. The range offered is ample: biscuits with sesame and almond; almond paste pastries, including with citrus aromas; mezzelune; Martorana fruit; ricotta and pistachio cannoli; cassata, including single portions; boiled must; quince jelly, and lots more.

Tramonti (SA)
Sal De Riso Costa d'Amalfi

via Santa Maria La Neve
☎ (+39) 089856446 I 089876932
❂ www.salderiso.it
✉ info@deriso.it
shop: yes
e-commerce: yes

Amalfi Coast lemons, Giffoni walnuts and Battipaglia strawberries are just some of the prime ingredients used in by Sal De Riso in his patisserie. This artist and artisan of sweet pastries imbues his creations with the beauty and fragrance of a magnificent area. The ricotta and pear caprese cake and the lemon Delizia cake are some of the mouth-watering products but the range also includes preserves and liqueurs. All the products are a celebration of the area, the typical style of a patisserie respected in Italy and abroad.

Patisserie, baked goods

Dolo (VE)

Torronificio Scaldaferro

via Cà Tron, 31
☎ (+39) 041410467
✆ www.scaldaferro.it
✉ info@scaldaferro.it
shop: yes
e-commerce: yes

In 1919 the Scaldaferro family linked its name to manufacture and production of almond crisp and nougat. Prime ingredients include local dried fruit, whole virgin Italian honeys, whole cane sugar, egg whites from farmyard hens, vanilla pods. Then, of course, the manual arrangement of individual flakes to make the almond, hazelnut or pistachio, or chocolate-coated nougat in large and small bars, soft nougats, dragées, and almond biscuits. There is a line for celiacs.

Montelupo Fiorentino (FI)

Sfizio

via Virgilio Rovai, 42
☎ (+39) 0571913539 l 349 1731633
✆ www.sfizioitalia.it
✉ info@sfizioitalia.it
shop: no
e-commerce: no

The Sicilian-Japanese union of Antonio Martorana and Aya Yamada, partners in both life and work, and a shared passion for good food and Italian products resulted in this amazing business. They specialize in Tuscan biscuits and cantucci, made by hand as tradition demands, using classic recipes, with unique flavour and sold in practical, stylish packaging. The range of combinations is varied and imaginative: moscato and hazelnut, chocolate and raspberry, fig and walnut.

Velo d'Astico (VI)

Biscottificio Stella

via Riello, 29
☎ (+39) 0445741266
✆ www.stellabiscotti.it
✉ info@stellabiscotti.com
shop: no
e-commerce: no

Since the early 1960s, the Stella family have lovingly managed their bakery. Leavening is done slowly, using a natural yeast starter, organic sugar, select flours, fresh eggs and quality ingredients. Combined with tried and true methods of preparation, the resulting sweets and savory snacks are exquisite. Featured products include shortbread biscotti, canestrelli, krumiri, 'zaeti', baci di dama, almond cantucci, brutti e buoni. But there's more waiting in the wings: grissini breadsticks (available in a 'classic' variety, as well as Kamut and whole wheat) and 'cioppini' biscuits (perfect with a drink). There are also tarts, sbrisolona and 'fugassa' cakes.

Salsomaggiore Terme (PR)
Tabiano

fraz. Tabiano Terme **I** v.le alle Fonti, 7
☎ (+39) 0524565233
🌐 www.pasticceriatabiano.it
✉ info@pasticceriatabiano.it
shop: yes
e-commerce: no

Claudio Gatti is a master baker who uses organic stoneground flour and sourdough starter, while keeping an eye on sugar content and calories. He makes amazingly tasty and light focaccia flavoured with citrus, chocolate, tea, beer and mouthwatering heirloom grains. He also makes pandolce with extra virgin olive oil, Pellegrino and spongata cakes. Claudio is known for his work in promoting focaccia and panettone, attending leading annual events on these products.

Taurianova (RC)
Francesco Taverna

...dal 1945

p.zza Italia, 8
☎ (+39) 0966611106
🌐 www.pasticceriataverna.it
✉ amministrazione@torronetaverna.it
shop: yes
e-commerce: yes

The confectionery pride and joy of this family company, in its 70th year of business, is the nougat, prepared by hand with Avola almonds, Calabrian orange blossom honey, fresh whites from eggs cracked one by one, natural extract of Tahitian vanilla and just a hint of pistachio. But we should mention all Le Chicche variations, in different sizes, from bite-size to large bars, and including ice cream! Among the other goodies are stuffed, coated figs and dates; typical pastries like pitte, biscuits, petits fours; panettone and pandoro.

Patisserie, baked goods

Alghero (SS)
Botarfish

via R. Sanzio, 28
☎ (+39) 079951390
✉ botarfish@tiscali.it
shop: yes
e-commerce: no

Botargo means Sardinia, but also this business, offering tuna and scented mullet botargo packaged in various sizes, or grated. There are also delicacies such as tuna in olive oil of the best quality, or tuna bresaola, both produced in house. Botargo is the undisputed star of regional gastronomy and is still produced using traditional procedures that will guarantee its authenticity and flavour. In the store customers will find Costantino, ready to guide them around his delicious products.

Quartu Sant'Elena (CA)
Bottarsarda

via Dante, 170
☎ (+39) 070883121 I 3935141675
✉ bottarsarda@libero.it
shop: yes
e-commerce: no

Founded at the end of the 1980s, this Sardinian company is a leading artisan producer of mullet botargo. With continuous monitoring and identification of critical points at all stages of processing, top quality is guaranteed while keeping faith with the ancient traditions of the fishermen. Brilliant results and each year an average 100 tons of mullet botargo reach the market. The best Sardinian mullet are selected from the catch to make whole botargo, in jars or sachets.

Cetara (SA)
Cetarii

via Largo Marina, 48/50
☎ (+39) 089261863 I 3355246125
✆ www.cetarii.it
✉ info@cetarii.it
shop: yes
e-commerce: no

Cetarii
Prodotti Tipici Locali

Marinated anchovies, or in olive oil or salted; Mediterranean bluefin and yellowfin tuna with anchovies or peppers, tuna belly and botargo. This company opened in 1995 with the purpose of quality fish preserving and its lengthy list of products are traditional to the Amalfi coast. Today as yesterday, the techniques are the same and the proof is in the anchovies fished by purse-seine, layered with salt in a barrel bottom, and covered with the traditional wooden lid, which is then weighted down. The result of this ancient artisanal process is anchovy colatura sauce.

Avetrana (TA)
Tonno Colimena

via Piave zona Pip, lotto 2
☎ (+39) 0999707955
❀ www.tonnocolimena.it
✉ info@tonnocolimena.it
shop: yes
e-commerce: yes

Known simply as "la fabbrica del tonno" this tuna facility lies between Torre Colimena and Porto Cesario. Colimena applies craft production methods: the tuna is not steamed but cooked in a broth with Mediterranean herbs and natural sea salt. The tuna include albacore, bonito, Ionian little tunny, Strait of Sicily skipjack and mackerel. Agostino Lomartire and Franco Scarciglia have a list of products ranging from the tuna filets to tuna belly, tuna pasta condiments and stuffed chillies.

Vietri sul Mare (SA)
Battista Delfino

via Travertino, 10
☎ (+39) 089761553
❀ www.delfinobattistasrl.it
✉ delfinsrl@tiscali.it
shop: yes
e-commerce: no

Pasquale Battista's children inherited his passion and continue his production of three preservative- and additive-free lines. One is devoted to anchovies (marinated, spicy, salted in traditional clay pots); the top of the range line is tonnara-fished tuna and tuna belly, Cetara anchovy colatura sauce (also in a version with almonds, walnuts, pine nuts, olives, capers and herbs in EVOO); and lastly, creams and sauces in various flavours, including Cetara pesto and turnip green cream with anchovy colatura.

Polesine Zibello (PR)
FoodLab

s.da prov.le per Cremona, 97
☎ (+39) 052496423 I 052496493
❀ www.foodlab.net
✉ info@foodlab.net
shop: yes
e-commerce: no

The Italian Salmon Philosophy

FoodLab, founded by former cook Gianpaolo Ghilardotti, is a company specializing in smoked fish products. Salmon from the best Norwegian and Scottish fish farms, wild salmon caught in Alaska, Atlantic tuna, Pacific swordfish. Manual filleting and salting processes are followed by drying and short, not excessive smoking using beech, oak and walnut smoke. Alongside the smoked products are low-temperature steamed fish products and carpaccio.

San Daniele del Friuli (UD)

Friultrota di Pighin

via Aonedis, 10
☎ (+39) 0432956560
❀ www.friultrota.com
✉ info@friultrota.it
shop: yes
e-commerce: no

Friul Trota
Affumicatori in San Daniele

A pool, Giuseppe Pighin's passion for fishing and for the good things in life. These are the three ingredients of Friultrota, which has been breeding trout in lots of fresh water since the 1970s, with low density of fish bred on a natural diet. An approach that led to the creation of Regina di San Daniele, smoked rainbow trout but also hot-smoked mackerel and swordfish; tuna; sea bass filets; cold-smoked spiced, low-salt herring; and full range of salmon and salt cod.

Vinci (FI)

Ghezzi

s.da prov.le di Mercatale, 155
☎ (+39) 0571501038
❀ www.ghezziitalia.com
✉ info@ghezziitalia.com
shop: no
e-commerce: no

As early as turn of the 20th century this family company was specializing in preserved and semi-preserved fish items, first as an importer and distributor, then as a producer. Ghezzi Alimentari is now in its third generation flanked by the fourth, and has built up partnerships in Italy and abroad to work as one corporation that always has the top catch. The product line includes anchovies, herring, salt cod, botargo, sardines and tuna (filets, in brine or in olive oil).

Bolsena (VT)

Lago Vivo

via Cassia Sud, km 111,700
☎ (+39) 0761780517
❀ www.lagovivo.com
✉ info@lagovivo.com
shop: yes
e-commerce: yes

Lago Vivo was created from the idea and passion of a family of fishermen and artisans in fish processing. Over the last couple of years the company has returned to processing fresh fish from Lake Bolsena. The fish is cold-processed then marinated or smoked, and packaged in a protected environment. The top product is lake whitefish, also available smoked and pre-filleted, for use instead of bacon or pork jowl for flavoursome fish-based dishes.

Carloforte (CI)
Ligure Sarda - Tonno Carloforte

loc. La Punta
☎ (+39) 0781850126 I 010561805
❀ www.liguresarda.it
✉ mail@liguresarda.it
shop: no
e-commerce: no

Founded in 1654, this is the only company producing canned Mediterranean blue-fin tuna in olive oil, fished according to the traditional "mattanza" system. The cans contain only bluefin caught in the Sardinian traps at Carloforte, Portoscuso and Porto Paglia. Ligure Sarda thus vaunts not only experience but also tradition, at the top of its league not only for tuna in olive oil (fleshy parts) and the typical filet cut (leaner part), but also for proposes the classic belly and lower belly in oil.

Anzio (RM)
Manaide

via Ienne, 113
☎ (+39) 3200213191
✉ manaide.anzio@gmail.com
shop: no
e-commerce: no

Luigi Crescenzo and Angela Capobianco founded Manaide in 2013. Since then they have drawn on a core three-pronged philosophy to produce their fish products: seasonal fishing, sustainability and traceability. Every can and jar displays the name of the boat and the precise location where the fish was caught. Their fish is conserved using only extra virgin olive oil and unprocessed salt collected by hand. The result is excellent: anchovies preserved in salt or extra virgin olive oil, sea snails in brine, two different types of octopus, tellins and razor clams in brine.

Osimo (AN)
La Nef - Coda Nera

via Edison, 1
☎ (+39) 0717276042
❀ www.codanera.it
✉ info@lanef.it
shop: no
e-commerce: no

Coda Nera is synonymous with excellent Atlantic salmon smoked for the Label Rouge brand, from qualified, sustainable farms. The processing of this fabled smoked salmon is an ancient method, with the master smoker controlling in person the fileting, light salting, slow maturation of the filets, drying and delicate smoking over a wood fire. Respecting timing and temperatures guarantees wholesome filets, also in the Coda Nera Riserva and Millesimato versions of unparalled quality.

Erice (TP)
Nino Castiglione
San Cusumano

loc. Casa Santa I Tonnara San Cusumano
☎ (+39) 0923562778 I 0923562888
❂ www.ninocastiglione.it
✉ info@ninocastiglione.it
shop: yes
e-commerce: no

NINO CASTIGLIONE
il tonno buono

A long-established business that has been processing tuna for decades. It offers three product lines: Auriga for tuna, including filets, and anchovies; San Cusumano (named after the district where the ancient Castiglione tuna-processing plant stands) for tuna in brine and in oil, belly tuna, tuna botarga powder, mackerel and salmon (also smoked) filets; Specialità including Mediterranean bluefin tuna and yellowfin tuna botarga; milt; air-dried yellowfin tuna filet called mosciame; tuna salami and heart. A new line is dedicated to tinned walleye pollack.

Trappeto (PA)
Nutri Mare

via Valle Fondi, 1
☎ (+39) 0918978174 I 0918989223
❂ www.nutrimare.it
✉ info@nutrimare.it
shop: yes
e-commerce: no

The brand was established 50 years ago and acquired by Nutri Mare, a name englobing centuries of human seafaring experience. One product line is AD 1340 Tonnara dell'Orsa, dedicated to a Sicilian tradition based around tuna and tuna and mackerel belly production. The Mattina range includes skipjack tuna in brine and in olive oil. Lastly, Corona, dedicated solely to bluefish, is a homage to the fishermen of Trappeto (Palermo). The production facility employs only women.

Montemarciano (AN)
Officina di Moreno Cedroni

loc. Marina I via Marina, 46b
☎ (+39) 071698267 I 0719194215
❂ www.morenocedroni.it
✉ info@morenocedroni.com
shop: no
e-commerce: yes

OFFICINA
LABORATORIO ITTICO
Marina di Montemarciano

Officina is a canning facility and brainchild of research undertaken by chef Moreno Cedroni. After his La Madonnina del Pescatore restaurant, the Clandestino sushi bar and the Anikò fish deli, in 2002 the chef began to experiment with craft production of original recipes to can. The experiments were a success. The first to be vacuum-packed were monkfish tripe, cuttlefish with peas, tuna belly, and octopus with potatoes. The line has now grown to include sauces, preserves, condiments and soft drinks.

Susegana (TV)

Orizzonti del Pescatore

fraz. Ponte della Priula I via 4 Novembre, 47e
☎ (+39) 04381798465
❀ www.odpgroup.it
✉ info@odpgroup.it
shop: yes
e-commerce: no

Orizzonti del Pescatore
Qualità, mare e passione

Andrea Rossi's products originate from his deep-rooted passion for fish, a meticulous respect for ingredients and outstanding entrepreneurial skill. These led him to open his own business after years working as a stall assistant in the quaint Rialto market in Venice. The company prepares fish by traditional marinating and specialities include Saccaleva anchovies in EVOO, tartars and carpaccios of tuna and sea bass, marinated salmon flakes, as well as moeche, the green crabs that are the lagoon's greatest delicacy.

Cagliari

La Peonia Cose Buone di Sardegna

via del Lavoro, 8
☎ (+39) 066798552 I 3333175293
❀ www.lapeonia.it
✉ info@lapeonia.it
shop: no
e-commerce: yes

La Peonia

PRODUZIONE DISTRIBUZIONE
BOTTARGA E AFFUMICATI

A new adventure began in 1995 for these botargo producers, already known in Sardinia, who decided to distribute their products throughout Italy, starting with Rome and Milan, where they have two stores. Their strength is a raw material fished in splendid seawaters and the island's timeless processing methods, handed down from one generation to the next. Other key products include Sardinian saffron (in stigmas or in powder), charcuterie, cheeses, local wines and liqueurs. Shop in the center of Rome.

Quartucciu (CA)

Stefano Rocca

loc. Pill'e Mata I lotto, 2
☎ (+39) 0708600012 I 0708476087
❀ www.stefanorocca.com
✉ clienti@stefanorocca.com
shop: yes
e-commerce: yes

ROCCA
STEFANO
dal 1986
La Bottarga

Stefano Rocca began the tradition by producing botargo with the IV Regia fishermen's cooperative of Cagliari's Stagno di Santa Gilla. In the 1980s his grandson, another Stefano, opened a plant inspired by traditional craft production. The striped mullet and tuna (like the marlin that is smoked) no longer come just from Sardinia, given the level of success, but selection is still rigorous. Other products include cream of sea urchin and botargo, but also ready sauces prepared with spiny lobster, European lobster and shrimp.

Ladispoli (RM)
Sapor Maris

via A. Gramsci, 3 Zona Artigianale
☎ (+39) 069911334
✆ www.sapormaris.it
✉ info@sapormaris.it
shop: yes
e-commerce: yes

This artisanal fish-smoking facility on the outskirts of Rome opened in 2009 thanks to the resourcefulness of two true foodies. A passion for angling and a cult approach to cuisine applied for 25 years in the artisanal smoking of fish and roe have made the company a benchmark for the gourmet. Salmon, swordfish, greater amberjack, bluefish, bonito, tuna, grey mullet, smoked marlin and dolphinfish make up the Sapor Maris catalogue.

Bra (CN)
Sapori d'a Mare - Le Baricie

c.so IV Novembre, 25/I
☎ (+39) 0172422057
✆ www.saporidamare.com
✉ info@saporidamare.com
shop: yes
e-commerce: no

The anchovies are from Sicilian waters, processed on the island when freshly caught. The EVOO is Tuscan. The selection, filleting and final cleaning, seasoning and packaging in glass jars are carried out in Piedmont. This is the creation process of Sapori d'a Mare anchovy fillets in EVOO. The company was founded over a year ago by Edoardo Sibona and Enrico Giombini. The fillets are processed with traditional Piedmontese anchovy methods, and are available plain, with chili pepper, with salsa verde and the most recent version is with chives.

Buggerru (CI)
Sarda Affumicati

loc. Portixeddu
☎ (+39) 078154914 I 078154930
✆ www.sardaffumicati.com
✉ produzione@sardaffumicati.com
shop: no
e-commerce: no

Established 22 years ago as Acquacoltura Pizzu Rocca, the purpose of the company was to integrate the eel farming side of business. Smoked whole and in filets, eels gave excellent results and production grew from 1990 onwards. Subsequent expansion of the basic line with the introduction of swordfish, salmon, trout, grouper, angler fish, mackerel and sturgeon, but also of striped mullet and tuna botargo. Another line, Le Delizie di Sardegna, offers octopus, seafood salad, swordfish and grouper carpaccio.

Maierato (VV)
Sardanelli

zona industriale, lotti 20/21
☎ (+39) 0963253713
❀ www.sardanelli.it
✉ tonnosardanelli@sardanelli.it
shop: yes
e-commerce: yes

The iconic Sardanelli can be found in an area of Calabria famous for fishing and blue fish processing. It is a tuna cannery and makes other fish specialities. Tradition and modern technology are the basis of an absolutely crafted process from selection to cutting, cooking in brine and part of the package stage. A lengthy list of canned tuna includes one for fine dining and catering.

Empoli (FI)
Schooner

v.le B. Buozzi, 22
☎ (+39) 0571526331
❀ www.schooner-srl.it
✉ info@schooner-srl.it
shop: no
e-commerce: no

For Schooner certified sustainable fishing is an indispensable condition and the underpinning to its extensive product range. Starting from the shrimp, offered in various types from carpaccio to pre-cooked and peeled, natural, with parsley or Spanish style; pre-sliced natural or smoked tuna and swordfish; octopus soppressa. The salt range includes cod in a starring role, flanked by a line of salmon, octopus and botargo. Last but not least, the company offers ready-to-cook and pre-soaked products.

Cabras (OR)
Spanu

via G. Carducci, 20
☎ (+39) 0783391161 I 0783390151
❀ www.spanubottarga.com
✉ info@spanubottarga.com
shop: yes
e-commerce: no

Giovanni Spanu still offers a product that hands down ancient processing traditions. So his striped mullet and tuna botargo, in filets and minced, are well established on the market thanks to his careful selection of raw materials, workmanship and slow maturing. The Qualità Oro striped mullet botargo is simply mouth-watering, as is the cream of mullet botargo, an enticing pâté whose recipe was inspired by that of the fishermen's wives of Cabras, who prepared it on special occasions.

Preore (TN)

Trota Oro

fraz. Zuclo I loc. Isolo, 1
☎ (+39) 0465322773
✆ www.trotaoro.it
✉ info@trotaoro.it
shop: yes
e-commerce: no

The story of this fish farm begins in 1988 with the production of smoked trout. Then came fresh trout filets, trout marinated in aromatic vinegar, smoked and marinated fresh filet of char, trout eggs, roe and tartare, fresh or smoked common whitefish, grayling. Products crafted with an artisan's skill, without additives or colourings, smoked over mountain softwood shavings. A natural process, which also uses Cervia salt and organic cane sugar.

Collecchio (PR)

Upstream

via 2 Agosto, 7
☎ (+39) 05211566509
✆ www.upstreamsalmons.com
✉ info@upstreamsalmons.com
shop: no
e-commerce: yes

The salmon from the Faroe Islands is particularly impressive because it is farmed in the cool, clean waters of the North Atlantic. The fish is processed and packaged in Ireland, a few hours after the catch. The rest is up to Claudio Cerati, owner of Upstream, who is in charge of marinating and smoking with a blend of woods, primarily beech, from the Parma Apennines. The leading products are Upstream Royal, full side and fillet.

Paesana (CN)
Achillea

via Barge, 84
☎ (+39) 0175987079
❀ www.achillea.com
✉ info@achillea.com
shop: no
e-commerce: no

In 1980 this company, in the heart of the Cuneo Alps, started processing excellent organic produce for healthy food products. Fruit and vegetables, harvested at the right moment of ripeness, are processed, vacuum packed, and packaged using state-of-the-art equipment. Succomio is the line of pure fruit; SuccoBene is a blend of flowers, fruits and herbs. There are also green tea; healthy juices like pomegranate, elderberry and blueberry; the Naturello line of fruit and vegetable mousses for children; jams, cider vinegar, sauces, spreads, honey, canned fruit.

Cori (LT)
Agnoni

c.da Copellaro, 1
☎ (+39) 069678668
❀ www.agnoni.it
✉ info@agnoni.it
shop: yes
e-commerce: no

Now in its fourth generation, this family-run farm produces everything needed to make quality preserves. First there is a good olive oil, a blend of different cultivars, which covers freshly processed vegetables picked in the surrounding countryside: exquisite artichokes on the stem, grilled, sliced, whole etc.; mushrooms; onions in balsamic vinegar; grilled peppers, aubergine and courgette bundles stuffed with tomatoes; pitted olives dressed with capers, sweet cicely and chilli.

Sigillo (PG)
Agribosco

loc. Sant'Anna, 1
☎ (+39) 0759177223
❀ www.agribosco.com
✉ info@agribosco.com
shop: yes
e-commerce: yes

Founded in 1989, this consortium has more than 200 partners and processes organic produce, keeping a close eye on supply chain traceability. They offer a wide range of products: pasta made with bronze dies, spelt pasta, grains (oats, spelt, millet, barley, rye), pulses (chickpeas, adzuki, grass peas, beans, lentils, peas, field pea), soup mixes, muesli, flakes, whole (spelt, chickpeas, buckwheat, millet, rye, lentils) and refined flours, pâtés, jams, hazelnut spreads, canned fruit.

Preserves, jams

Acerra (NA)

Agrigenus

via G. Soriano, 112
☎ (+39) 0815202064
❀ www.agrigenus.com
✉ info@agrigenus.com
shop: yes
e-commerce: no

The company has been on the go for a decade, its mission always to promote typical regional produce, particularly San Marzano PDO and Antico Pomodoro di Napoli tomatoes, a Slow Food Presidium (from the native smek 20 variety), both of which are hand-picked and processed using state-of-the-art machinery. There are also peeled tomatoes (in 400- and 800-gram and 3-kilogram sizes); smooth and chunky tomato purée; baby yellow tomatoes in brine (750-gram glass jar); cannellini beans in 500-gram cans.

Leonforte (EN)

Agrirape

c.so Umberto, 556
☎ (+39) 0935904862 I 3391697299
❀ www.agrirape.it
✉ info@agrirape.it
shop: yes
e-commerce: yes

The brand has a great story behind it, that of the Manna family, which has taken plenty of ups and downs in its stride but never has compromised on quality, and since the early 1950s it has devoted itself to farming, with particular focus on the recovery of heritage crops. Today's production includes jams and preserves, with the star ingredient the famous native peach as well as citrus fruits, peaches in syrup, nut spreads, pulses like black lentils and broad beans, rice, an excellent peach liqueur.

Cavour (TO)

Agroalimenta

via Pinerolo, 208a
☎ (+39) 012169775
❀ www.agroalimenta.com
✉ laboratorio@agroalimenta.com
shop: yes
e-commerce: yes

The Genovesio family had been running its Locanda della Posta restaurant and hotel for years, when it was decided to offer guests a souvenir of the flavours sampled there. The result was a range of delicacies made with tried-and-tested recipes and genuine ingredients. Vegetables in oil, vinegar, or sweet and sour condiment, sauces including with game, dressings and creams, terrines, anchovies, pâtés, olives, jellies, fruit relish, jams and preserves, fruit in syrup and in alcohol, many types of honey and, for those with sweet tooth, biscuits, biscuit cakes, plum cakes and logs.

Braies/Prags (BZ)
Alpe Pragas

Braies di Fuori, 38
☎ (+39) 0474749400
🌐 www.alpepragas.com
✉ info@alpepragas.com
shop: yes
e-commerce: yes

Stefan Gruber, an iconic figure in the industry, makes it look like child's play to make great fruit compotes and achieve a production chain of such excellence. Everything here is handled with intense, Teutonic expertise, from selection of raw materials, all local, from blueberries to currants, gooseberries, and rosehips, to processing and eye-catching packaging. Not to mention the genius of the equally tasty fruit relish, and the fruit smoothies, syrups, jellies, fruit in syrup, fruit spreads and chocolate spreads.

Napoli
Fratelli Andolfo - La Primavera

via L. Volpicella, 62a
☎ (+39) 0817527481
🌐 www.conservelaprimavera.it
✉ info@conservelaprimavera.it
shop: yes
e-commerce: no

The family-run canning and bottling plant opened just after WW2 and still goes about its business with respect for the land, in a constant quest to better its products. Under the Primavera brand name it produces tasty peeled, diced, fileted, pulp, purée, and double concentrate of tomatoes, hillside cherry tomatoes, pepper sauce, Pomorustiche, mushrooms, and roast peppers in brine. There are also various fruits in syrup (fruit salad, pineapple, peaches), and tinned corn, peas, chickpeas, lentils, cannellini, borlotti and Tavo tondino beans.

Albenga (SV)
Anfossi

fraz. Bastia I via Paccini, 39
☎ (+39) 018220024
🌐 www.aziendaagrariaanfossi.it
✉ anfossi@aziendaagrariaanfossi.it
shop: yes
e-commerce: yes

AZIENDA AGRARIA ANFOSSI

Founded nearly a century ago by sugar producer Antonio Anfossi, here 17 hectares of land are given over mainly to basil. The I Freschi brand produces pesto using PDO Genoa basil, including a garlic-free version; walnut, Parmigiano Reggiano and pistachio sauce; cherry tomato and ricotta pesto. Under the company's Olio di Liguria label it produces pesto; basil, artichoke and arugula creams; pitted olives; olive pâté and vegetable pâté. EVOO is also available, as is a good Pigato DOC wine.

Borghetto d'Arroscia (IM)
La Baita&Galleano

fraz. Gazzo
☎ (+39) 018331083 | 018331324
✆ www.labaitagazzo.com
✉ info@labaitagazzo.com
shop: yes
e-commerce: no

About a year ago the renowned La Baita company, famous for its excellent EVOO, merged with Galleano and expanded its product range. The two hectares of terraced vegetable gardens and orchards produce herbs like thyme, borage, savory, dandelion, and wild fennel for drying, but also jams, including a lovely myrtle-leaved orange, candied fruits and fruit in wine, not to mention preserved tomatoes, vegetables in oil with some excellent Albenga artichokes and trombetta courgettes, olives, pâté and pesto.

Loreto Aprutino (PE)
Belfiore

c.da Fontemaggio, 1
☎ (+39) 3391844632 | 0859040426
✆ www.aziendaagricolabelfiore.it
✉ info@aziendaagricolabelfiore.it
shop: yes
e-commerce: no

The Belfiore farm has been established on the Pescara hills since 1851, a byword for monitored crops and processing of quality produce. In addition to its good EVOO and DOC wines like Montepulciano d'Abruzzo and Pecorino, it has an excellent range of vegetables in oil including garlic, turnip greens, mushrooms, jardinière, olives, chilli peppers, dried tomatoes, artichokes and fava beans; tomato sauce; dressings; pesto; fruit jams; honeys; various types of bronze-drawn durum wheat artisanal pasta.

Savona
Besio

via Sant'Ambrogio, 2 a r. - P.A.I.P. Legino
☎ (+39) 019860507
✆ www.besio.it
✉ info@besio.it
shop: no
e-commerce: yes

The company was created in the late 1800s by Vincezo Besio, grocer and confectioner, who also learned the art of candying fruit. Over the years this lovely company has always been family-run and specialized in candied crystallized and glacé fruit, marrons glacés, jams and preserves. The star of the production process is Savona chinotto: candied, preserved in maraschino or used for marmalades, liqueurs and syrups.

Carlentini (SR)
Biosolnatura

via A. Vespucci, 3
☎ (+39) 0957837160
❀ www.biosolnatura.it
✉ info@biosolnatura.it
shop: no
e-commerce: yes

The company was founded in 2001, but since 2013 the passion and drive of its three young partners have pushed the brand into the spotlight. This is really an artisanal workshop whose mission is to promote, preserve and make the most of the inimitable fragrance and flavour of Sicilian products, especially organic options. The lion's share goes to citrus fruits, especially oranges, and particularly marmalade, but there are also extra jams, honey and aromatized Modica chocolate.

San Nicola Manfredi (BN)
Borgo La Rocca

fraz. Monterocchetta I via Elena, 12
☎ (+39) 082440770 I 3288477949
❀ www.borgolarocca.it
✉ info@borgolarocca.it
shop: no
e-commerce: no

Nicola Mercurio has organic certification for his farm and used artisanal processes to preserve vegetables of great quality, starting with peeled tomatoes and tomato purée from crops picked by hand at the right ripeness, processed without acidity regulators and preservatives. Also on offer, a tempting range of vegetables in oil like courgettes, green beans, turnip greens, cauliflower, fava beans, aubergines, mixed vegetables and peppers, but also chillies stuffed with tuna and wild asparagus cream.

Sarconi (PZ)
Per Boschi e Contrade

c.da Cava, 6
☎ (+39) 097566448
❀ www.boschiecontrade.it
✉ info@boschiecontrade.it
shop: yes
e-commerce: no

The de la Ville sur Illon estate includes organic farmlands and generous spaces for hosting various events. The land, however, is the source of the raw materials used to make excellent natural preserves, first of all extra jams, including chestnut and chocolate, carrot and orange, fig and walnut, almond and pumpkin and autumn fruits with vincotto. The fruit, vegetable and spice chutneys are also interesting, as are the different PGI Sarconi beans, pulse and cereal soup mixes, honeys.

Muravera (CA)

Bresca Dorada

loc. Cann'e Frau
☎ (+39) 0709949163
⊗ www.brescadorada.it
✉ mirto@brescadorada.it
shop: yes
e-commerce: no

With 30 years of history behind it, this farm is still committed to developing and offering customers new, top-quality products. The flagships are myrtle liqueurs, including an organic version, made with a syrup of honey and sugar, alcohol and myrtle berries. Then there is a wild fennel matafalua; a prickly pear figu morisca; an orange and lemon liqueur; also, a typical fil'e ferru. Be sure to try the preserves and jams, aromatic compotes, honey, aromatized compotes, creams and even kitchen salt.

Carovigno (BR)

Calemone

fraz. Serranova I c.da Baccatani, 36
☎ (+39) 0831555807
⊗ www.calemone.it
✉ info@calemone.it
shop: yes
e-commerce: yes

The company opened in 2010 and is located in the Torre Guaceto nature reserve, a paradise of pristine Mediterranean vegetation made up of olive groves, vegetable and grain farmlands, and low vegetation on the coastal strip. In addition to olive oil from ogliarola salentina and cellina di Nardò cultivars, the pride of place is taken by the processed tomatoes, all organic, starting with the peeled tomatoes in olive oil and basil. Worthy of note there is also the Torre Guaceto fiaschetto tomato purée, fiaschetto tomato sauce, and dried seeds in olive oil.

Pantelleria (TP)

Cooperativa Produttori
dei Capperi di Pantelleria

c.da Scauri Basso, 11
☎ (+39) 0923916079 I 0923918311
⊗ www.capperipantelleria.com
✉ info@capperipantelleria.com
shop: yes
e-commerce: yes

The consortium was set up in 1971 and has 400 members, who work together to safeguard the quality of PGI Pantelleria Caper production. The best preservative is sea salt, which protects the caper's traits and quality. The buds range from the smallest and most prized to the large size, packed in sachets of different weight. There are also other specialities produced by members, including EVOO, caper berries, oregano, chillies, raisins, and Moscato and Passito wines.

Massa di Somma (NA)
Casa Barone

via A. Gramsci, 109
☎ (+39) 0810606007
❀ www.casabarone.it
✉ casabarone@gmail.com
shop: no
e-commerce: no

Giancarlo Marino has the biggest, most widespread organic farm in Parco Nazionale del Vesuvio. In addition to crops there are olive groves, vineyards and orchards. His main product is the PDO Vesuvio piennolo grape tomato, a Slow Food
Presidium sold fresh in clusters and used for preserves. There are also tinned San
Marzano and yellow tomatoes, extra jams (organic too), preserves, liqueurs and
distillates, and a wide rage of Pagano-branded craft pasta.

San Venanzo (TR)
Casa Corneli

loc. San Vito in Monte I via Ascianghi
☎ (+39) 3293536467 I 3297035253
❀ www.casacorneli.it
✉ info@casacorneli.it
shop: yes
e-commerce: yes

For over two centuries the Corneli family has enjoyed a close bond with San Vito
in Monte, in the hills between Perugia and Orvieto. Here it grows cereals, pulses,
olives and vegetables with sheer passion, applying only organic methods, and processes crops without preservatives, additives or synthetic aromas. Worthy of note,
in addition to the PDO organic EVOO, try Le Pinotte", a refined artisanal range
for pulse soups made with traditional recipes, and organic sauces using tomatoes
grown on the farm.

Ciriè (TO)
Cereal Terra

via Ricardesco, 15
☎ (+39) 0119222629
❀ www.cerealterra.it
✉ cerealterra@cerealterra.it
shop: no
e-commerce: no

The company's talent for organic products and preservation methods was evident
from day one, about 25 years ago. Significant skills that allow this Alto Canavese
outfit to offer some high-level products. The Italian seasonal raw materials are processed fresh; plant and equipment guarantee food hygiene combined with manual
preparation. Some good condiments for cheese include one made with figs and
walnuts, and another with red onions. There are good chickpeas and cannellini
beans in their own juices, as well as mayonnaise and ketchup, creams, dressings
and hors d'oeuvres.

Acquapendente (VT)
Cerqueto

s.da prov.le Torre Alfina
☎ (+39) 0763733355 | 0763732106
❀ www.cerquetosrl.it
✉ info@cerquetosrl.it
shop: no
e-commerce: no

Here in Alta Tuscia, a true powerhouse of products, this company works with its own estate crops, processing and distributing an extensive line of delicacies like pulses and cereals, jams, condiments, vegetables in oil, sauces, pâtés, pesto, dry and egg pasta, tinned and dried soups, polenta flour, chocolate (bars, coated citrus peels, shapes), honey (also with nuts), soup mixes and seasoning for roasts, risotto mixes, cake mixes, tisanes, spices, EVOOs, aromatized oils, and last but not least DOC and IGT wines. A healthy range of organic products is also available.

Ugento (LE)
I Contadini

loc. Torre San Giovanni | s.da prov.le 290 Felline, km 1
☎ (+39) 0833555227
❀ www.icontadini.it
✉ info@icontadini.it
shop: yes
e-commerce: no

The farm covers 200,000 square metres where it grows all the vegetables used for processing and other local items like EVOO to Santa Margherita di Savoia salt. The only "foreigners" are Emilia Romagna vinegar and Sicilian anchovies. Tomatoes, aubergines, peppers, courgettes and dried greens bottled in olive oil, which can then be reused; vegetables in oil, including turnip greens and olives; tomatoes, courgettes, peppers and aubergines stuffed with dried tuna or anchovies; tomato pâtés and sauces.

Massa Lubrense (NA)
Il Convento

via Bagnulo, 10
☎ (+39) 0818789380
❀ www.ilconvento.biz
✉ info@ilconvento.biz
shop: no
e-commerce: yes

LIMONCELLO
IL CONVENTO
AZIENDA AGRICOLA

The Pollio family farm, founded by Antonino and now run by Giuseppe, cultivates lands on the Sorrento peninsula that were once tended by monks. Pollio's respect for the local territory translates into maintaining and improving the heritage crops typical of this strip of land: olives for organic and non-organic EVOO, oranges and mandarins for making liqueurs, and organic Sorrento lemons for producing classic limoncello.

Viadana (MN)

Corte Donda

loc. Salina I via Palazzo, 35
☎ (+39) 0375785697 I 3496694337
🕸 www.cortedonda.com
✉ rizzi@cortedonda.com
shop: no
e-commerce: no

Corte Donda, an 18th-century farmhouse, is set in four hectares of land. Apart from accommodation and a restaurant serving typical cuisine, the farm also has poultry and horses, a vegetable garden and an orchard, the latter producing the crops used for making fruit relishes. Claudio Rizzi makes them in the traditional way, applying rules to the letter, and uses ingredients like cherry tomatoes, pears, figs, campanina apples, quince, plums, melon, celery. He also produces jellies, preserves, jams, sweet spreads, honey and sauces.

Tiglieto (GE)

Dalpian Il Sottobosco

loc. Acquabuona I via Bolla, 7
☎ (+39) 010929298
🕸 www.dalpian.it
✉ info@dalpian.it
shop: yes
e-commerce: no

Dalpian® Il Sottobosco
TIGLIETO - GENOVA

An organic agritourism on the hills behind Genoa, towards Piedmont, with a restaurant serving traditional dishes and home-made ice cream in the summer. It produces syrup, including an unusual rose syrup made with petals from heirloom varieties; honey; sauces; vegetables in oil; seasonings; juices; nectars and preserves made from fresh fruit from its own orchards; fruit in syrup; and dozens of mouth-watering delights, including jams and preserves flavoured with herbs and spices, jellies, creams and mostardas.

Bitritto (BA)

De Carlo

via XXIV Maggio, 54
☎ (+39) 080630767
🕸 www.oliodecarlo.com
✉ info@oliodecarlo.com
shop: yes
e-commerce: no

DECARLO
MASTRI OLEARI DAL 1600

EVOO has no secrets for the De Carlos, who have produced some excellent versions over the last century, including their Elisir, with lemon and tangerine aromas. The oils are also used for preserving vegetables and making creams from processing only seasonal crops. Their Brindisi purple artichokes, picked in March and April are amazing, as are the aromatized semi-dried tomatoes, gathered from late May to July, and olive cream. Also worth sampling, edible muscari in oil and Red Passion cherry tomato cream.

Santa Giustina in Colle (PD)
Del Santo

loc. Fratte I via Pio X, 18
☎ (+39) 049 5790598
⊛ www.delsanto.it
✉ delsanto@delsanto.it
shop: yes
e-commerce: no

The company was founded in 1971 by Gianni De Cecchi, who is now head of Research and Creativity. Applying the short, controlled-chain principle, the outfit vaunts more than a hundred products, typically using only prime raw, seasonal materials and no preservatives, starches, glutamates or chemical additives. You will be spoiled for choice with ready-to-use vegetables; fruit in syrup; vegetables in oil; cereals and pulses boiled or puréed; cream of vegetable soups; sauces and ragouts; tomato purée.

Valsamoggia (BO)
La Dispensa di Amerigo

loc. Savigno I via del Lavoro, 14b
☎ (+39) 0516722262
⊛ www.amerigo1934.it
✉ dispensa@amerigo1934.it
shop: no
e-commerce: no

Trattoria Amerigo has more than 80 years of experience and it was precisely its family expertise that conceived selling its traditional craft preserves to the public. Since 1996 its La Dispensa brand has sold outstanding products, including several Slow Food Presidia. The shopping basket is tempting with PGI Aceto Balsamico di Modena balsamic vinegar; saba; Rosolio, vegetables in oil, pickles; ready sauces and ragouts; cream of vegetable; jams, cream of Parmigiano and of Fossa cheeses. There is also an organic label.

Giarratana (RG)
Fagone

s.da comunale di Buccheri, 5
☎ (+39) 3332694009 I 3881713299
⊛ www.cipolladigiarratana.it
✉ fagone.cipolladigiarratana@gmail.com
shop: yes
e-commerce: no

Giarratana onions are on offer in all possible forms at Fagone, a leader in the production of this Slow Food Presidium vegetable. From July to September, during the harvest, they can be bought fresh on the farm, or shipped throughout Europe, and during the year they are made into delicious preserves by Salvo and Giusy Noto, owners of Fagone. The onions are used alone or with tuna to make patés, and are excellent bottled in extra virgin olive oil.

Imperia
Frantoio di Sant'Agata di Oneglia

fraz. Sant'Agata I s.da dei Francesi, 48
☎ (+39) 0183293472
🌐 www.frantoiosantagata.com
✉ frantoio@frantoiosantagata.com
shop: yes
e-commerce: no

A passionate family whose respect for tradition in almost two centuries is one of the secrets of its quality. In addition to various oils, including a superb PDO Riviera dei Fiori Cru Primo Fiore, a Biologico and a PDO Riviera dei Fiori, there are some great vegetables in oil like artichokes, sundried tomatoes, radicchio, jardinière and chilli. We also recommend the balsamic creams and vinegars, olives with different dressings, pesto and sauces, vegetable pâtés and creams, sauces and pasta. Last but not least tuna, salt cod, mackerel, sea bream and anchovies, all in oil.

Cerignola (FG)
Gaudiano

s.s. 65
☎ (+39) 0885418432
🌐 www.biorganicanuova.it
✉ carlogaudiano@bio-gaudiano.it
shop: yes
e-commerce: yes

The Gaudiano siblings have 200 hectares of land with organic certification and over 35,000 trees, mainly for table olives, including the famous bella di Cerignola cultivar. For 25 years they have produced and processed vegetables to make their delicious, wholesome Biogustiamo range. Why not try marinated garlic; capers in vinegar or in salt; artichokes, mushrooms, onions, aubergines, peppers, sundried tomatoes and dried seeds, courgettes, mixed vegetables, various olive combinations, all in olive oil, and vegetable creams and pesto.

Malo (VI)
La Giardiniera di Morgan

via Montello, 37
☎ (+39) 0445607976
🌐 www.lagiardinieradimorgan.com
✉ lagiardinieradimorgan@gmail.com
shop: yes
e-commerce: no

La Giardiniera di Morgan

Once upon a time the 5 Sensi restaurant served its diners a mouth-watering home-made jardinière that was a huge success. In 2012 owners Morgan and Luciana decided to start bottling a version, making it by hand with prime ingredients. Today that jardinière has developed into five versions, each dedicated to a member of the family, and with small variations depending on the season's crops and a dash of personality. Versatile and delicious, they can stand alone as a starter or accompany meats or cheeses.

Condofuri (RC)
Il Giardino del Bergamotto

c.da Rodì
☎ (+39) 3473732964 I 065002982
✆ www.ilgiardinodelbergamotto.it
✉ info@ilgiardinodelbergamotto.it
shop: no
e-commerce: yes

Elio Attinà owns the organic farm set up by his father in 1942. He decided to take a gamble on bergamot, an aromatic, little-known citrus fruit typical of the Ionian coast in the province of Reggio Calabria. In January 2015 he began using it for excellent juices and sweet preserves, made from the fresh fruit within two hours of harvesting. The bergamot nectar, pure juice, syrup, jams and compotes, some blended with other citrus fruits, candied and dried peel are delicious.

Capua (CE)
Masseria GiòSole

via Giardini, 31
☎ (+39) 0823961108
✆ www.masseriagiosole.com
✉ info@masseriagiosole.com
shop: yes
e-commerce: yes

This 60-hectare estate has been owned by the Pasca di Magliano family for over 300 years, and has always sought innovative production systems, so as to support the economic and social development of the Provincia di Terra di Lavoro district. For more than 20 years part of the fruit and vegetables produced has been used to make excellent fruit juices, jams and preserves, fruit in syrup, tomato purée and sauces, and ready-to-use tomato and vegetable sauces, as well as vegetables in oil and vegetable pâtés.

Bistagno (AL)
Guido Giuso

regione Cartesio
☎ (+39) 0144359411
✆ www.giuso.it
✉ servizioclienti@giuso.it
shop: no
e-commerce: no

Even if Giuso is known for its fillings, toppings and creams (including vegan products), their D'Amore e D'Accordo line of canned fruits can't be overlooked. The fruit is picked just when ripe and then conserved in syrup without additives or conservatives. We suggest their kumquat and cinnamon as well as their lemon and ginger, in addition to the classic chestnuts and vanilla. Their preserves are are also delicious and unusual, 'apricot and wild rose' gives you a pretty good idea!

Montelparo (FM)
La Golosa

c.da Coste, 24
☎ (+39) 0734780030 I 3383591512
❂ www.lagolosacm.it
✉ info@lagolosacm.it
shop: yes
e-commerce: no

In the Aso Valley, in a magnificent unspoiled natural setting, the Curi family's farm has grown, harvested and processed prime fruit at its best ripeness, using artisanal (mainly manual) techniques to preserve all its nutritional properties. There is a large choice of preserves, some classic, some more adventurous like the white watermelon, green apple, Sibillini pink apple and Saturno peach version. Then there is fruit in syrup and juices made with ground fruits.

Angri (SA)
Inserbo

via Generale Gennaro Niglio, 6
☎ (+39) 0818735397
❂ www.inserbo.it
✉ info@inserbo.it
shop: no
e-commerce: no

Piennolo grape, corbara cherry, and organic tomatoes are key products, along with some other, equally important types, processed for tasty canned versions. The company, on the outskirts of Naples, produces classic peeled, diced, pulp and purée; organic purée, filets, pulp, and sauce; San Marzano PDO; baby plum, including the Monti Lattari cultivar. Corbara cherry tomatoes are also used for juices, crushed and in brine; Piennolos are used for sauce, a spicy version, and crushed. Also available ready sauces, boiled organic pulses and vegetables in olive oil.

Nocera Inferiore (SA)
Italianavera

via G. Pepe, 36
☎ (+39) 0810604029
❂ www.italianaverafood.it
✉ info@italianaverafood.it
shop: yes
e-commerce: yes

ITALIANAVERA®
sughi & affini

The story of a woman narrating tradition through the flavour of good, homemade things and eye-catching packaging. This is how Diana Attianese describes her company, set up in 2014 and already respected for the quality of its products. The secret of the success enjoyed by the sauces and creams lies in the authentic ingredients and flavours. Ingredients used include ripe, freshly-picked tomatoes, basil and fresh garlic, extra virgin olive oil and Pantelleria IGP capers.

Pantelleria (TP)
Kazzen

c.da Kazzen
☎ (+39) 0923911770
❀ www.kazzen.it
✉ info@kazzen.it
shop: no
e-commerce: no

For more than 10 years, Fabrizio, Alessandro and Massimo D'Ancona have worked at Kazzen (with the invaluable support of their family members), using artisanal techniques to make and sell the best products on the island. Every stage of production is executed with painstaking care, from harvest to conserving and packaging. It's true that the versatile PGI caper is a star, but there are also plenty of patés, sauces, selections of vegetables in extra virgin olive oil, jams and preserves. There's even oregano, sweets and wine.

Pantelleria (TP)
Konza Kiffi

via Beato L. Palazzolo, 6
☎ (+39) 0923912050 l 3288375507
❀ www.prodottidipantelleria.com
✉ info@prodottidipantelleria.com
shop: yes
e-commerce: yes

The Lo Pinto family estate has been producing and processing prime products for many years. All the island's fragrances and flavours can be enjoyed to the full, a delight for all the senses. First there are PGI capers, caper berries and caper pâtés, but also combined with anchovies, olives, sundried tomatoes, almonds, chilli pepper, and wild fennel. Try the marmalades and extra jams, the latter also made with zibibbo grapes, ideal with cheese. The excellent oregano is worth sampling.

Cutrofiano (LE)
Le Lame

c.da Lame
☎ (+39) 3332951641
❀ www.lelame.it
✉ info@lelame.it
shop: yes
e-commerce: no

In 1981 Antonello Russo started applying biodynamic methods on 16 hectares of land around his historic farmhouse. Today, thanks to his expertise and passion he is an Italian leader for cereals, heritage fruits, vegetables, olives and tomatoes, grown without the use of additives and chemicals, processed for canning in olive oil. Products include Galatina chicory, turnip greens and edible muscari, then tomato purées and ready sauces, excellent peeled tomatoes, sweet and sour dressings, pâtés, pesto, purées and more.

San Giuseppe Jato (PA)
Libera Terra

via Porta Palermo, 132
☎ (+39) 0918577655
✪ www.liberaterra.it
✉ info@liberaterramediterraneo.it
shop: no
e-commerce: yes

A group of cooperatives and farmers manage the land and equipment confiscated from organized crime, working hard to convert to organic farming. The product range is extensive and includes pasta in various shapes, and made from whole and organic flour; flours; tarallini; soups; vegetable pâtés, also organic; hummus and caponata; tomato sauce; marmalades, wine jellies; honey; biscuits; almond paste; EVOO; barley; limoncello and wines.

Scafati (SA)
Fratelli Longobardi

via delle Industrie, 15
☎ (+39) 0818503011
✪ www.longobardi.it
✉ fratelli@longobardi.it
shop: no
e-commerce: no

The key strength of this family company, founded in 1988, is its use of prime raw materials, combined with care for the environment and careful control of each stage of processing. The flagship product is its peeled tomatoes, whole and chopped, followed by tomato pulp, also flavoured with garlic and oregano, basil, peppers and chilli; tomato purées. Also worth trying are the various canned pulses: chickpeas, lentils, several varieties of beans that include cannellini, borlotti, red, butter, tondino).

Cicognolo (CR)
Luccini

via Oglio, 9
☎ (+39) 0372830624
✪ www.mostardaluccini.com
✉ mostardaluccini@libero.it
shop: no
e-commerce: no

Mostarda di Cremona

From an old family recipe, the company produces an excellent Mostarda di Cremona relish, in which the strong, spicy mustard is perfectly balanced by the fruit. Intriguingly versatile tomato, onion, pumpkin, chestnut, fig, blackberry, peach, cherry, apple and pear, watermelon, melon, pineapple, citrus fruits and mixed fruit chutneys lend themselves to some tasty combinations. There are also sauces to serve with meat, courgettes, peppers in sweet and sour brine, peperonata and jardinière.

Preserves, jams

Riccione (RN)
Luvirie

via E. Ferrari, 17
☎ (+39) 0541607774
❀ www.luvirie.com
✉ info@luvirie.com
shop: yes
e-commerce: no

The shingle, in Romagna dialect, means delicacies, which is precisely what the company aims to produce. It selects delicious typical regional titbits that must comply with a single rule: quality. Caramelized figs with ginger; spicy mostarda relish; luviriata cheese sauce; savor and saba; quince jelly; preserves and fruit shakes; wine jellies; honeys; balsamic vinegar pickles; PGI shallots in oil and creamed; stridoli wild plant sauce; Bologna and Cremona mostarda. Not to mention biscuits, Fossa cheese, piadina, PDO extra virgin olive oil.

Senise (PZ)
MAB Masseria Agricola Buongiorno

c.da Rotalupo snc
☎ (+39) 3343104612
✉ masseriagricolabuongiorno@gmail.com
shop: no
e-commerce: no

It was here, in a small hamlet in Pollino National Park, that Enrico Fanelli and Maddalena Guerrieri started MAB, a small food producer that features peppers, a local speciality. Care is taken that the peppers are harvested at the right moment. Then they are sun-dried and finally fried in hot oil. The final step is to vacuum seal them in jars or bags. From there they can be enjoyed as a snack, with a glass of wine, as a garnish or on pasta. They're also available in powder form.

Capaccio (SA)
Maida - Vastola

via Tempa di Lepre, 33
☎ (+39) 0828722975 I 3409811553
❀ www.vastolaitaly.com
✉ info@vastolaitaly.com
shop: yes
e-commerce: yes

Here, in Parco Nazionale del Cilento, the Vastola family upholds age-old preserving traditions, using local produce, tried-and-tested processing methods, and carefully selected raw ingredients. Its vegetables in oil, spreads, sauces and natural jams are all free of preservatives and additives. The vegetables in EVOO and include baby artichokes, wild asparagus and sundried Corbara cherry tomatoes. Its olive cream with cocoa is surprisingly tasty, and it is also worth trying its orange, citron, onion and ginger jam, and its organic papaccelle pepper jam.

Melilli (SR)
Marchesi San Giuliano

loc. Villasmundo I c.da San Giuliano
☎ (+39) 0931959022 I 3928143357
🌐 www.marchesidisangiuliano.it
✉ info@marchesidisangiuliano.it
shop: yes
e-commerce: yes

The Paternò Castello San Giuliano marquises own a splendid farmhouse in an estate that is mainly given over to citrus groves. They produce fruity, cold-pressed EVOO, intense butter biscuits scented with orange, lemon, almond, pistachio, hazelnut and ginger, as well as bottled delights like bio marmalade using oranges, bitter oranges, tangerines, grapefruit, clementines and lemon. Also very tasty are the citrus fruit peel and organic oranges in syrup; and orange blossom, eucalyptus and thyme honey.

Lucera (FG)
Masseria Dauna

s.da per San Giusto c.da Ripatetta
☎ (+39) 3475345907
🌐 www.masseriadauna.com
✉ masseriadauna@gmail.com
shop: yes
e-commerce: yes

MASSERIA
DAUNA

In 2001 the Pozzuto sisters started up this farm in the Daunia hills, intending to continue a rural tradition, following the seasons and the cycles of nature. Apart from their very good EVOO from the peranzana variety, their flagship production is handpicked tomatoes, processed into excellent purée, or peeled tomatoes, cherry tomatoes from the hillside preserved in brine and the sliced tomatoes known as spaccatelle. Lots of ready tomato sauces and vegetables in oil too.

Scorrano (LE)
Le Masserie del Duca Guarini

l.go Frisari, 1
☎ (+39) 0836460257 I 0836460288
🌐 www.ducacarloguarini.it
✉ info@ducacarloguarini.it
shop: yes
e-commerce: yes

DUCA CARLO GUARINI
DAL
1065
IN TERRA D'OTRANTO

Duca Carlo Guarini is an age-old business with 700 hectares of estate that includes vineyards, olive groves and farmland. It produces wines like Negroamaro, Primitivo and Sauvignon, and PGI Malvasianera PGI, as well as olive oil, also aromatized with citruses. Le Masserie del Duca is the brand for the high-end bottled delicacies ranging from classic cream of peppers and of onion and green apple, to artichoke hearts and sundried tomatoes, pitted olives in oil, tomato purée, peeled tomatoes, pesto and pulses.

Matera
Masseria Mirogallo

c.da Mirogallo
☎ (+39) 0835311532
❀ www.masseriamirogallo.it
✉ info@masseriamirogallo.it
shop: yes
e-commerce: no

MASSERIA
MIROGALLO
———— MATERA ————
IL GUSTO DI COLTIVARE E CONSERVARE

Massimo Belfiore grows fruit and vegetables on his farm, with a particular focus on native species, such as sponzali spring onions, red aubergines, king oyster mushrooms, and the edible muscari, a kind of wild onion. In 1998 he opened a workshop for artisanal processing and uses only vinegar, salt and EVOO as preservatives for bottling prime delicacies like vegetable pâtés and creams, sauces and pesto, peppers and sundried tomatoes, vegetables in oil, tomato sauces and purées, jams and vegetable preserves.

Cantiano (PU)
Morello Austera

loc. San Rocco Meleta
☎ (+39) 0721789235 I 3396365417
❀ www.morelloaustera.com
✉ info@morelloaustera.it
shop: yes
e-commerce: no

morell⟨⟩austera

The Lupatelli family's flagship product is the local cantiano sour cherry. Picked, cleaned and pitted, the sour cherries are left to drain of their juice and then cooked quickly with sugar before being bottled in their own syrup. The range of preserves also includes heritage fruit varieties and wild fruit, raspberries in syrup, angelica pear, blackberry and mulberry, white cherry, sour cherry, wild plum and wild strawberry jams.

Lucera (FG)
La Motticella di Paolo Petrilli

c.da Motta della Regina
☎ (+39) 0881523980
❀ www.lamotticella.com
✉ lamotticella@libero.it
shop: no
e-commerce: no

PAOLO PETRILLI

Paolo Petrilli is an enlightened businessman and as early as the end of the 1980s he realized that the organic quality route was the way to go to achieve the level of production needed for making a profit and promoting the area. Today his farm is famous for growing and processing tomatoes and cherry tomatoes, used to make classic peeled, diced, filets, purée (also in a spicy version) and ready-to-use sauces. There is also a durum wheat pasta in various shapes and even an organic wine.

Pantelleria (TP)
La Nicchia

loc. c.da Scauri I via Sotto Kuddia, 7
☎ (+39) 0923916021 I 3803719235
❀ www.lanicchia.com
✉ info@bonomoegiglio.it
shop: no
e-commerce: no

The farm was established in 1949 and is also a caper processing plant with an artisanal workshop. The aim is to grow and select raw materials to be processed using heritage recipes. The flagship is the caper, of course, beginning with the PGI in salt or in olive oil, but also desalted crispy capers, caper berries in olive oil and in salt, caper pâtés, pesto and sauce, sundried tomato and caper pâté, zibibbo jelly and jam, orange and orange, carrot and lemon juices.

Cremosano (CR)
Il Nutrimento

via degli Artigiani, 12a
☎ (+39) 0373290032
❀ www.ilnutrimento.it
✉ info@ilnutrimento.it
shop: no
e-commerce: no

The company, founded in 1990, has a stated mission to offer consumers quality products suitable for vegetarians and those who suffer from gluten intolerance. The products are made according to Italian heritage recipes and use carefully selected products. The range is overwhelming, with vinegars, delicious bruschetta toppings, pickles and vegetables in oil, sauces for pasta and couscous, various pulse recipes, vegetable creams, tomato concentrate and diced tomatoes, pesto, sauces, EVOO and olive oil, preserved olives.

Strevi (AL)
Oliveri

regione Fontane, 56
☎ (+39) 0144322558 I 0144324987
❀ www.oliveri-piemonte.it
✉ info@oliveri-piemonte.it
shop: no
e-commerce: no

A solid family business for three generations that produces speciality foods from prime raw materials picked in the surrounding woods and hills, then carefully processes them with a dash of creativity. Difficult to know which is the best among the ceps, chanterelles, sheathed woodtuft or saffron milk cap mushrooms in olive oil; dried mushrooms; olives; chilli peppers stuffed with tuna, anchovies and capers, goat cheese; vegetables in oil; sauces, creams and ready sauces; jams and relishes; nuts in honey.

San Sebastiano al Vesuvio (NA)
L' Orto del Vesuvio

via Panoramica Fellapane, 43
☎ (+39) 0817714392
❀ www.ortodelvesuvio.com
✉ info@ortodelvesuvio.com
shop: yes
e-commerce: no

The Guidone family opened for business in the 1970s and has been certified organic since 2007. Found in Parco Nazionale del Vesuvio, it has four hectares of land planted with olive groves, vineyards, tomatoes, fruit, and seasonal vegetables. In addition to a good olive oil, the company produces apricot, plum and green tomato jams; piennolo grape tomato sauce; vegetables in oil like aubergines and artichokes; olives; pâtés and more. There is no shortage of excellent distillates, above all limoncello.

Prato
Osteria de' Ciotti - Alla Gusteria

fraz. Tavola I via P. Ciotti, 3a/1
☎ (+39) 0574623992
❀ www.allagusteria.it
✉ info@allagusteria.it
shop: no
e-commerce: no

Cristina Pagliai and husband Fabio Goti own the Nunquam artisanal workshop and monitor every phase of processing to ensure top quality standards. They have two production lines: Alla Gusteria and Osteria de' Ciotti. The former making delicious preserves like friggitelli pepper and apple; relishes; jellies and liqueurs. The latter offers tasty ready meals (reed tripe and Swiss chard with chickpeas; Chianina stew; sauces of venison, salt cod, or sea urchin; mackerel, caper and olive condiment), soups, pickled fruits and vegetables.

Buonvicino (CS)
Paradiso dei Golosi

c.da Palazza, 193
☎ (+39) 098581591 I 3491508238
❀ www.paradisodeigolosi.it
✉ info@paradisodeigolosi.it
shop: no
e-commerce: no

Founded in 1996 by Santo Cauteruccio, who is still the sole administrator, the company is located in a town that is part of Pollino National Park, a basket of excellent products. The premium native and imported raw materials, careful processing, use of the most suitable machinery, and scrupulous monitoring of each phase ensure that standards are very high. Production includes vegetables in oil, with special focus on Sila peppers and mushrooms, ready sauces, preserves and jams (including pepper or onion), spices.

Givoletto (TO)
Pariani

via Avogadro, 7
☎ (+39) 0119947505
✪ www.pariani.org
✉ info@pariani.org
shop: yes
e-commerce: yes

PaRianI

Ricerca ed Eccellenza

Mattia Pariani has a "multisite farm" and has built up cooperations with farmers from other regions of Italy to provide excellent dried fruits that include Bronte PDO green pistachios, Piemonte IGP hazelnuts, Romana della Val di Noto almonds, Parco San Rossore organic pine nuts. They are used to make oils, flours, pastes and grains. As well as semi-finished products, Mattia makes sweet specialities like cocoa and hazelnut or pistachio spreads, candied green walnuts and sbrisolona cake.

Lecce
Perché Ci Credo

via della Ferrandina, 16
☎ (+39) 0832359287
✪ www.perchecicredo.com
✉ info@perchecicredo.com
shop: no
e-commerce: no

PERCHÉ CI CREDO®

Enrico De Lorenzo is enamoured of his Salento home and set up this company to promote the authentic, wholesome flavours and fragrances. It has to be said that his mission has been successful if we are to judge by the quality of these bottled products. A lavish range includes tomato purée; ready sauces (above all the wine version); ricotta sauces; home-style sauces; sides like aubergine caponata, peperonata, turnip greens and others; vincotto and vincotto vinegar; preserves and extra jam.

Rapolano Terme (SI)
Podere Pereto

loc. Podere Pereto I fraz. Serre
☎ (+39) 0577704371
✪ www.poderepereto.it
✉ info@poderepereto.it
shop: yes
e-commerce: no

PODERE PERETO
www.poderepereto.it

The organic farm with farmhouse hospitality was set up in 1993, and includes a petting zoo as well as about 70 hectares of land for cereals, pulses and vegetables, and a small olive grove. Production focuses on native varieties so we find zolfini, coco and toscanelli beans, and piccino and fiorentino chickpeas. There are also ready-to-use lentils, peas, grass peas, pulses and cereals in jars, soups, purées and broths; barley and farro mixes; bronze-extruded pasta; stone-milled flour; tomatoes (peeled, puréed, pulp, in salt, and ragout); oil and vegetables in oil; vegetable preserves and even spelt beer.

San Giovanni al Natisone (UD)
Livio Pesle

loc. Dolegnano I via Abbazia, 11
☎ (+39) 0432757470
❀ www.liviopesle.com
✉ info@liviopesle.com
shop: no
e-commerce: no

These preserves and sauces, all made using local ingredients, can be paired with cheeses, meats, salads and foie gras. There are Picolit and Verduzzo varieties, as well as Hippocras (refosco and spices), the 'Chimichurri' (cabernet, oregano, thyme and garlic), the 'Bishoff' (citrusy with a hint of horseradish), 'Balsamica Universale LP 17 (Modena balsamic vinegar with an anchovy and walnut sauce, excellent on salads), a horseradish sauce (for meats) and pepper sauce (creamed yellow peppers, onion and oil). The latest addition are the delicious 'tubissime'.

Ittiri (SS)
Pinna

c.so Vittorio Emanuele, 259
☎ (+39) 079441100 I 335235571
❀ www.oliopinna.it
✉ info@oliopinna.it
shop: yes
e-commerce: yes

AZIENDA AGRICOLA FRATELLI PINNA

The Pinna family has been in farming since 1940 and has always focused on quality production, following the principle of traceability and respect for the territory. Today the company is run by siblings Antonella, Gavino and Leonardo, each with their own role. In addition to three types of premium EVOO, including an excellent pitted type, they produce artichokes in oil from the Sardinian prickly artichoke, processed in house straight after picking and cut by hand.

Nocera Superiore (SA)
Pomilia

via Croce, 41
☎ (+39) 081931231
❀ www.pomilia.it
✉ info@pomilia.it
shop: yes
e-commerce: yes

Founded by the Salzano family in 1943, the company is a stalwart in quality canned products at competitive prices. Located in the heart of the Agro Nocerino Sarnese district, which is one of the best for farming tomatoes, which are processed to a great standard here. The flagship is the San Marzano PDO, but there are also peeled, diced pulp, finely-chopped pulp, purée, sauces, concentrate and baby plum tomatoes. Not to be overlooked a decent range of pulses, in tins and jars.

Spiazzo (TN)
Primitivizia

p.zza Grande, 93
☎ (+39) 3381034192
❧ www.primitivizia.it
✉ info@primitivizia.it
shop: no
e-commerce: yes

PRIMITIVIZIA

Here in Val Rendena, a magnificent natural setting in the Dolomites, near Adamello, the mountains are this company's inspiration but also the source of the ingredients for producing bottled delicacies. Worthy of note is the unique aromatic and balsamic mountain pine oil to serve with cheeses and desserts, but also an aromatic garlic cream; mountain radicchio; preserved broccoli; condiments for meats (including rose ketchup, horseradish sauce, Fen sauce with flowers and aromatic plants); fruit relish; fruit, pear and chocolate compotes.

Africo (RC)
I Prodotti del Casale

loc. Africo Nuovo I s.s. 106, km 74
☎ (+39) 0964991550 I 3296138376
❧ www.iprodottidelcasale.it
✉ iprodottidelcasale@yahoo.it
shop: no
e-commerce: no

All of the products sold by I Prodotti del Casale are grown on the Pratticò family's own land in Capo Bruzzano, a region known for its clean soil, air and favorable climate. Fruits and vegetables are all harvested at just the right time, using proven natural methods, and then transformed in sauces and preserves. Tomatoes take a leading role, especially the puree, which is bottled with no added salt. We should mention their sweet peppers as well as their selection of organic juices, which include bergamot, tomato (sugar-free) and strawberry.

Alba (CN)
Mariangela Prunotto

fraz. Mussotto I via Osteria, 14
☎ (+39) 0173441590
❧ mprunotto.com
✉ info@mprunotto.com
shop: yes
e-commerce: no

The company grows and processes fruit and vegetables on certified organic soils. The crops are picked by hand and some are even gathered in stages, on different days, so as to ensure the right ripeness. The range is tempting both for the packaging and the contents: tomato purée and pulp, peeled tomatoes and tomato-based sauces; barbecued vegetables in oil; pesto; fruit compotes, mainly of madernasse pears; extra jams; cornmeal; tinned pulses; fruit in syrup, in grappa and in Nebbiolo; honey and nuts in honey, and the new fruit and vegetable juices.

Firenze
Pure Stagioni

via di Castello, 50
☎ (+39) 3494651871
❀ www.purestagioni.it
✉ info@purestagioni.it
shop: no
e-commerce: yes

The quality of the jams and respect for the ingredients are the distinguishing features of this Florentine production company. The ingredients are processed immediately after harvesting to preserve their authentic flavour and are handled as little as possible. They are cooked at high pressure and low temperatures to preserve the colour, consistency, sensory features and nutritional properties. Products include lemon marmalade; blueberry, fig, and strawberry jams; and a Certaldo red onion preserve which is a Slow Food Presidium.

Loro Ciuffenna (AR)
Radici

p.zza S. Pertini, 3
☎ (+39) 0559171171
❀ www.radici.info
✉ radici.radici@tin.it
shop: yes
e-commerce: no

The farm is on the slopes of Pratomagno and comprises several plots of land at different altitudes, which means a wide variety of products are possible. The key here is quality, to the point that it was decided set up an in-house processing line with the same philosophy. A wide range of good things are offered: extra organic jam; fruit in syrup, in spreads and in 100% natural juices; chestnuts in coffee, in wine and in honey; chestnut creams; vegetable pâtés and creams; fruit relishes; sauces, condiments, pesto, vegetables in oil, ready soups and tomato purées.

Capaccio (SA)
Raimo

loc. Cerro I via Feudo
☎ (+39) 0828724424
❀ www.raimocarmine.com
✉ carmine@raimocarmine.com
shop: yes
e-commerce: no

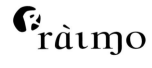

The Raimo farm has always selected the best ingredients and processed them by hand into authentic delicacies for gourmand palates. The range includes tomatoes, peeled and in sauces; ready sauces; various patés made from artichoke, black olive, eggplant, dried tomato; and a wide range of products bottled in oil like cauliflower, peppers, grilled fennel, stuffed chili peppers, bruschetta cilentana, using the farm's own EVOO.

La Loggia (TO)
Cascina Revignano

via Revignano, 40
☎ (+39) 0119627984
✿ www.cascinarevignano.it
✉ info@cascinarevignano.it
shop: no
e-commerce: no

Luca Ferrero selects the very finest materials, processes them with meticulous care and presents them as "madeleines" in his personal quest for the lost flavours of Piedmont's gastronomic tradition. One speciality is vegetables in oil: chillies stuffed with tuna, anchovies and capers; baby onions; artichoke hearts; aubergines; Jerusalem artichokes. All also with bagna cauda. More delicacies include Piedmontese vegetable antipasto, salsa rossa, bagnet vert and tomato sauces. Not to mention preserves and jams, peaches with chocolate and amaretti.

Sclafani Bagni (PA)
Rinascita

c.da Rovittello
☎ (+39) 0921850049 I 3467940864
✿ www.rinascitavalledolmo.it
✉ info@rinascitavalledolmo.it
shop: yes
e-commerce: no

The cooperative, founded in 2004 and currently managed by Tommaso Alessi, specializes in the siccagno di Valledolmo tomato, a native variety with special sensorial traits. The yield per hectare is 8,000 kg, which is very low compared to other varieties, and here it is processed to make an organic purée; astrattu (a fantastic and very fragrant concentrate that is very useful in cooking); sundried tomatoes and ready sauces (alone or with wild fennel).

Genova
Rossi 1947

Passo Ponte Carrega
☎ (+39) 0108601096
✿ www.rossi1947.it
✉ info@rossi1947.it
shop: no
e-commerce: yes

Roberto Panizza's business has achieved well-deserved international repute for producing an excellent pesto, the typical Liguria sauce made from basil, pine nuts, garlic, Pecorino cheese and EVOO. Over the years the range of products on offer has expanded and now includes a very special line of fine salt (pesto, basil and Vessalico garlic flavours too), spices (pepper, curry, vanilla, paprika, nutmeg, cinnamon), and herbs. Roberto will also sell you all you need to make your own pesto, including the traditional marble mortar.

Gragnano (NA)
San Nicola dei Miri

via Pasquale Nastro, 67
☎ (+39) 0818013417
✆ www.pastagentile.it/san-nicola-dei-miri
✉ info@pastagentile.com
shop: yes
e-commerce: no

SAN NICOLA DEI MIRI
GRAGNANO

Here we have the line of craft preserves produced by Pastificio Gentile. Fruit and vegetables hand-picked at the best ripeness, then processed using old family recipes and achieving really good results. The lion's share goes to the tomato, including San Marzano and PDO Piennolo: purée, also in an organic version; filets; sauces, and more. Then there are pâtés and vegetables in oil; extra preserves and jams; fruit in syrup; Cetara anchovy sauce; lip-smacking mini limoncello babas.

Pula (CA)
Santa Margherita Terra e Sole

s.s. 195, km 31,800
☎ (+39) 0709208011
✆ www.smargherita.it
✉ info@saporedisole.it
shop: yes
e-commerce: yes

COOPERATIVA
SANTA MARGHERITA

A model agricultural cooperative, open since 1989 and now with 180 members and 80 hectares of modern greenhouse facilities. It produces, processes and/or packs vegetables from the south of the island, including about ten types of tomatoes, some of which have taken European markets by storm. Then there are peppers, two types of melons and artichokes, including PDO Sardinian prickly artichoke. Also worth trying are the tasty sundried tomatoes and fragrant sauces prepared with each of the varieties of tomatoes.

Pagani (SA)
I Sapori di Corbara

via Corallo, 173
☎ (+39) 3208843878 I 3355852386
✆ www.isaporidicorbara.it
✉ info@isaporidicorbara.it
shop: yes
e-commerce: yes

www.isaporidicorbara.it
info@isaporidicorbara.it
I Sapori di Corbara
Corbarì
IL POMODORINO DI CORBARA

The star of company production is the Corbara cherry tomato, called the Corbarino, a niche variety with distinctive taste and fragrance. The tomatoes are used to make bottled and canned purée; jam; bottled and canned preserves; filets; whole tomatoes in brine. Each of these products can be adapted to different recipes, from pasta to pizza, bruschetta, meat and fish. Last but not least, delicious nectarines in syrup.

Portici (NA)
Sapori Vesuviani

s.da prov.le Pugliano, 16
☎ (+39) 0817753949 I 335310786
⊕ www.saporivesuviani.it
✉ info@saporivesuviani.it
shop: yes
e-commerce: yes

Here in Parco Regionale del Vesuvio, a precious gourmet powerhouse of considerable interest, Pasquale Imperato has devoted himself to his business for many years. His well-deserved success is owed to quality and a short production chain for his flagship PDO Pomodorino del Piennolo del Vesuvio tomato and Vesuvius apricots, of which there are about 100 varieties, used to make juices and jams. Other delicacies include vegetables in oil (purple aubergine, fava bean, cornetto pepper, marrow, San Pasquale courgette); peaches in syrup; jams.

Manzano (UD)
Schianchi

via IV Novembre, 47
☎ (+39) 0432751351 I 3383923996
⊕ www.schianchitalia.com
✉ info@schianchitalia.com
shop: yes
e-commerce: no

schianch*i*

In addition to salt, pepper, sugar and spices, the ten-year-old company vaunts quality products like tea jams (green tea, smoked tea, Earl Grey, excellent with foie gras); fruit and tea jams (rhubarb with vanilla tea, raspberry with smoked tea, Earl Grey with pears, and more); extra jams (including pear and ginger, orange and lavender, mint and strawberry, apple with pepper and cornflower, apple and pepper, apple and blueberry); jams; honeys; fruit and vegetable relish; beer, Champagne, and Sauternes jellies; and much more besides.

Ribera (AG)
Scyavuru

via Chiarenza, 8
☎ (+39) 092563297
⊕ www.scyavuru.com
✉ info@scyavuru.com
shop: yes
e-commerce: yes

SCYAVURU®
STORIE DI GUSTI E SAPORI DI SICILIA

"Sciavuro" is Sicilian dialect for fragrance and inspires the name of the farm, and the fragrance is also evident in the jars of sweet and savoury preserves made by Rosario Tortorici, who started out as a fruit grower and now cans it too. Above all marmalades and jams, including a Slow Food Presidium classic strawberry of Ribera version, alongside that of the late-crop mandarin. There are also vegetable jams, for instance using the Slow Food Presidium Giarratana onion, and vegetable pâtés and pesto, wine jellies, honey, olive oil and wine.

Macerata
SI.GI.

c.da Acquevive, 25
☎ (+39) 0733281462 I 3351253830
✆ www.agricolasigi.it
✉ info@agricolasigi.it
shop: yes
e-commerce: yes

The name is an acronym from the initials of the two owners, Silvano Buccolini, agricultural adviser and oil taster, and his wife Giuliana Papa. In 1996 they began processing prime ingredients, including forgotten fruit varieties, using time-honoured methods and recipes, with remarkable results. The range of products includes fruit (some quite special like quince and sapa) and vegetable jams; vegetables in oil; jellies; fruit in syrup; wine and sour cherries; wine and jujubes; delicious bottled sour cherries; sapa.

San Valentino Torio (SA)
Solania

s.da prov.le 36
☎ (+39) 0819371027
✆ www.solaniasrl.it
✉ info@solaniasrl.it
shop: no
e-commerce: no

Since 1993 the Napoletano family, with vast experience in agriculture and tons of passion, has been at the forefront in defending production quality for San Marzano PDO tomatoes from the Agro Nocerino Sarnese area, whose climate and soils are the most suitable for this vegetable.The Napoletanos do this by gathering the best farmers in the district to help them produce bottled and canned peeled San Marzano PDO tomatoes in a variety of sizes; peeled tomatoes; tomato pulp; cherry tomatoes in brine.

Paternò (CT)
Solo Sole

p.zza del Ficus, 1
☎ (+39) 095853750 I 3485421412
✆ www.conservesolosole.com
✉ info@conservesolosole.com
shop: yes
e-commerce: no

The sun and nature are the two ingredients that make the products used by this company what they are. Filippo Finocchiaro and family produce premium, very versatile preserves that can be used in countless ways. The range includes: caper pâté; artichokes in several versions; aubergines; vegetables in oil; caponata; sweet and sour onions; salted capers; purées, condiments and pesto for pasta and other first courses; olives in delicious recipes; herbs and spices like oregano, wild fennel and chilli; sauces, typical cheeses in oil; salt; jams.

Bagnolo San Vito (MN)
Le Tamerici

loc. San Biagio I via Romana Zuccona, 208
☎ (+39) 0376253371 I 3484224699
❁ www.letamericisrl.com
✉ info@letamericisrl.com
shop: yes
e-commerce: yes

Paola Calciolari, a former pharmacist, is the soul of this company, founded in 1991. Known in Italy and abroad mainly for production of mostarda, Paola's passion led her to rediscover typical but forgotten fruit from her area, and thanks to her boundless imagination the product range is quiet extensive. The relishes are now a classic and we should mention the campanina apple and white watermelon recipe. Then there are extra jams and vegetable and contemplation preserves; wine and vinegar jellies; fruit compotes with Balsamico PGI vinegar; vegetables in oil. There is also a bio line.

Sant'Antonio Abate (NA)
Terra Amore e Fantasia

via de Luca, 23
☎ (+39) 0818735300
❁ www.terramorefantasia.it
✉ info@terraslow.it
shop: no
e-commerce: yes

A family company set up to promote the farming economy of the area. In 1999, after the creation of a Slow Food Presidium to protect Sant'Antonio Abate and Campania tomatoes, retrieving native cultivar seeds and using the cultivation and processing methods of the past, production got under way of tomatoes, Gragnano cherry tomatoes and San Marzano tomatoes but also of Castellammare baby artichokes, mustaccielli bean and Gragnano cornetti peas. There are two lines, Il Miracolo di San Gennaro and the more affordable Terra Amore e Fantasia.

Policoro (MT)
Terravecchia

via Liborio Romeo, 7
☎ (+39) 3389879372 I 3939256835
❁ www.terravecchiaproduce.com
✉ info@terravecchiaproduce.com
shop: yes
e-commerce: no

Everything revolves around the pink Pisticci fig, a variety typical of the town near Metaponto, which turns a beautiful antique pink colour as it ripens. Giovanni Ancona, the owner of the farm, has helped to promote the fig and expand its cultivation. Terravecchia makes them into jams, sometimes with dried fruit; concentrates called ficotto; caramelized figs; honeyed; with chili pepper; candied figs, to pair with Basilicata's mouthfilling cheeses. The company also makes biscuits and strawberry and apricot jams.

Sant'Antonio Abate (NA)
La Torrente

via Paludicella, 3
☎ (+39) 0818796236
🕸 www.latorrente.com
✉ info@latorrente.it
shop: yes
e-commerce: no

This canning and bottling business, with 50 years of experience, has been run by the same family for generations. The star is certainly the tomato, prince of Italian traditional cuisine, harvested only when ripe, processed in various ways and canned or bottled. In addition to the great classics like peeled tomatoes (also with basil), there are filets, pulp (also diced), different types of purées, and cherry tomatoes. Each suited to different type of recipes. Then there are handy ready sauces, pulses and fruit in syrup.

Rivoli (TO)
Tuttovo

via Stura, 24
☎ (+39) 0119575805
🕸 www.tuttovo.com
✉ info@naturaepiacere.it
shop: no
e-commerce: no

"natura è piacere" by TUTTOVO

This brand produces four quality labels: Biogelateria ice creams, creams, sorbets, frappes and lollies sweetened with a hint of cane sugar where necessary; Natura è Piacere, a fine range of vinaigrettes, sauces, condiments including vegan versions, sweet creams, egg-free mayonnaise and Salina capers; Biobontà ketchup and mayonnaise; Mastri Salsieri ketchup and mayonnaise, including vegan versions. All the products are gluten free and are made only with certified organic eggs and milk.

Fossacesia (CH)
Ursini

loc. Villa Scorciosa I s.da prov.le Santa Maria La Nova, 12
☎ (+39) 0872579060
🕸 www.ursini.com
✉ info@ursini.com
shop: yes
e-commerce: yes

ursini
GRANDI OLI, GRANDI SPECIALITÀ

Ursini is renowned for its excellent EVOO, also available in numerous flavours, but it also makes Pestati and Manicaretti vegetable-based products, and Pestati di Bacco, five vegetable, fruit and spice creams conceived to suit a specific type of wine. Then there are sauces, Altri Pasti ready mixes, olives in brine and EVOO. Ursini's fruit preserved in oil is truly unique and includes persimmon and quince slices, ideal for an aperitif to serve with a piece of Pecorino and a glass of fizz.

Verde Abruzzo
Tenuta Fragassi

s.da Gaglierano, 38
☎ (+39) 085960515
✆ www.verdeabruzzo.it
✉ info@verdeabruzzo.it
shop: yes
e-commerce: no

The Conte di Bellomonte label offers not only a variety of EVOOs, including fla-voured versions, but also condiments; PGI Balsamico di Modena vinegar; veg-etables in oil, pâtés and sauces. The Tenuta Fragassi brand includes EVOO, condi-ments, pesto and sauces, while Terra Nostra is used for oils and sauces. Lastly, Pera d'Abruzzo is used for a mouth-watering tomato purée from a production cycle monitored from sowing to bottling, with processing of the native pera d'Abruzzo tomato cultivar on the same day, handpicking only those at just the right degree of ripeness.

Preserves, jams

Livorno Ferraris (VC)

Acquerello - La Colombara

Tenuta Colombara
☎ (+39) 0161477832 I 3346392349
🌐 acquerello.it
✉ info@acquerello.it
shop: no
e-commerce: no

The Rondolino family has owned the Tenuta Colombara since the 1500s. From the very beginning, it has always believed that quality rice, cultivated with respect for nature and aged for a year before being sold, was a successful concept. Since 2000 it has only sown and cultivated the Carnaroli variety. To preserve its qualities, acquired through a long processing procedure that leaves every grain intact, it is sold in practical vacuum-packed tins in various sizes.

Lignana (VC)

Gli Aironi

s.da delle Grange, 8
☎ (+39) 0161344025
🌐 www.gliaironi.it
✉ info@gliaironi.it
shop: yes
e-commerce: no

The Perinotti family has run the business for five generations and is known for its stone milling of rice to preserve the nutritional substances that give the rice its flavour and keep it firm to the bite after cooking. The excellent product range includes: Carnaroli (a wholegrain version also), Vialone Nano, Arborio, Baldo, Rosso Selvatico and Venere Nero. It also sells rice and corn flours, polenta and ready-to-cook risottos, with select ingredients: ceps, cuttlefish ink, radicchio, truffles and so on; delicious sweet and savoury biscuits; interesting crunchy praline rice, drinks and grappa.

Scaldasole (PV)

La Cascina di Ilaria

Cascina Cardinala
☎ (+39) 0382901508
🌐 www.risoedintorni.it
✉ info@risoedintorni.it
shop: yes
e-commerce: yes

Its estate in Lomellina produces a variety of fine rice, all of which are processed mechanically, leaving the crop in its natural state to produce a genuine, natural product with no extra preservatives or additives. It produces a dozen different types, from Carnaroli (including a semi-wholegrain version) to wild Zizania, and classics such as Arborio, Baldo and Vialone Nano. It also sells ready-to-cook risottos, flours, cereals and pulses, biscuits, and other selected products.

Crova (VC)
Cascina Oschiena

s.da Oschiena-Tabalino
☎ (+39) 3922262845
✿ www.cascinaoschiena.it
✉ alicecerutti@cascinaoschiena.it
shop: yes
e-commerce: no

Cascina Oschiena is one of the few farms to grow the traditional Carnaroli variety of rice using integrated pest control. One of the oldest estates in Vercelli, it was the property of the abbey of Santo Stefano di Vercelli from the 16th to the 18th centuries. Now owned by Alice Cerutti, the estate undertakes all production aspects except processing of grains, which is outsourced. As well as Carnaroli, recommended products are Apollo, a fragrant Basmati and Italy's first of this variety, black Venere and Selenio rice.

Bereguardo (PV)
Cascine Orsine

via Cascine Orsine, 5
☎ (+39) 0382920283
✿ www.cascineorsine.it
✉ info@cascineorsine.it
shop: yes
e-commerce: no

BIODINAMICA

A biodynamic farm founded by Giulia Maria Crespi, with the assistance of her son Aldo Paravicini Crespi: 600 hectares of land in the Parco del Ticino. Apart from cattle breeding the farm produces wholegrain, brown and white rice, Marano corn, soft wheat, barley, rye, farro, flours, wholegrain pastas from less common cereals, honey, fresh and mature cheeses, butter, yoghurt, fresh beef and EVOO from the Arezzo farm.

Desana (VC)
Tenuta Castello

p.zza Castello, 8
☎ (+39) 0161318132 I 0161318297
✿ www.tenutacastello.com
✉ info@tenutacastello.com
shop: yes
e-commerce: yes

TENUTA CASTELLO

Riso..Passione Verde di Famiglia

This business has 250 hectares of rice fields and 70 of spelt, corn and poplars. Since 1833 it has produced premium rice, carrying out every phase of processing internally, from preparing the land to harvesting, stone milling and packaging. Its range includes wholegrain and organic Carnaroli, Vialone Nano; and Arborio, hulled by hand and also available in an organic version. There are also wholegrain black and red rice, not to mention various types of pasta, rice and corn flours, saluggini beans, ready-to-cook spelt and risotto.

Occimiano (AL)

Cascina Daneto

Cascina Daneto, 2
☎ (+39) 0142809117
⊛ www.cascinadaneto.it
✉ info@cascinadaneto.it
shop: yes
e-commerce: yes

CascinaDaneto
1948

This family-run company has grown and produced rice since 1948, processing it with a skilful blend of traditional and modern techniques to ensure high quality standards. There are nine varieties available: Carnaroli, Arborio, Baldo, Nuovo Maratelli, Vialone Nano, wholegrain, Fragrance (an aromatic long-grained rice), Venere Nero and Corallo Rosso. It also produces ready-to-cook Carnaroli risottos, flours, pasta, biscuits and sweet mousses made from rice.

Vercelli

Ecorì

via Trino, 200
☎ (+39) 0161271920
⊛ www.ecori.it
✉ info@ecori.it
shop: yes
e-commerce: yes

This 11-partner cooperative was formed in 1999 to package and sell the best rice. Its members, who farm around 1,300 hectares of land overall, are quality conscious and believe in eco-friendly farming methods with low environmental impact. Its products include Carnaroli, Arborio, Vialone Nano, Baldo, Roma, Sant'Andrea, wholegrain, Ermes Rosso, Venere Nero and Apollo rice. It also sells ready-to-cook risottos (including "panissa", a traditional Vercelli dish), biscuits and gift hampers containing a range of delicacies.

Isola della Scala (VR)

Riseria Ferron

loc. Pila Vecia I via Saccovener, 6
☎ (+39) 0456630642 I 0457301022
⊛ www.risoferron.com
✉ latorre@risoferron.com
shop: no
e-commerce: no

Antica e Rinomata Riseria
FERRON ®
Fondata nel 1650

This historic artisanal rice mill was founded in the mid-17th century. It produces two different lines: Ferron, processed with modern machinery for the mass market and local shops; and Pila Vecia, the superior range, for restaurants and delicatessens. The Pila Vecia range includes PGI and pounded Vialone Nano, normal and wholegrain Carnaroli, wholegrain Ermes and Venere rice. The Ferron range includes PGI Riso Nano Vialone Veronese (also in an organic version), Carnaroli, Venere and Ermes rice. The company also produces flours, pastries, baked and gluten-free goods.

Basiglio (MI)

Mario Gennari

via privata Gennari, 16
☎ (+39) 0290753585 I 3355448458
✆ www.risogennari.com
✉ riso@risogennari.com
shop: yes
e-commerce: no

A wonderful 14th-century country residence, set in 35,000 square metres of land, is home to this company run by the Gennari family for over a century. From cultivation to harvesting, drying, husking, whitening and separating the wholegrains, all the production stages are carried out internally using traditional methods. The range includes Carnaroli, Carnaroli Ostigliato Rosso, Vialone Nano, Venere Nero, Basmati and wild red rice.

Ronsecco (VC)

Lodigiana

s.da delle Grange, 20
☎ (+39) 0161816001 I 0161816014
✆ www.lodigiana.com
✉ info@lodigiana.com
shop: yes
e-commerce: yes

The company has been in business for over 100 years, producing, processing and selling rice. Its main aim is to protect the environment, safeguard product quality and traceability from the field to the consumer. It sells the finest varieties grown in the Vercelli area (Carnaroli, Baldo, Arborio, Roma, Sant'Andrea), as well as a line of organic rice. It also produces a wide range of ready-to-cook Carnaroli risottos, delicious rice biscuits, grissini, rice and corn flours, honey and pastas.

Isola della Scala (VR)

Melotti

via Tondello, 59
☎ (+39) 0457300444
✆ www.melotti.it
✉ melotti@melotti.it
shop: yes
e-commerce: yes

Since 1986 this family-run business has been known for its production, processing and sale of Vialone Nano Veronese (PGI, classic, semi-processed, whole and new-harvest) and Carnaroli. It supervises all the production stages: cultivation, growth, harvesting, drying, storage and so on, right up to packaging. It also produces a number of prized heritage varieties like Riso Comune Originario Vialone Nero, Riso Essicato sull'Aia and Riso Nero Beppino, as well as a line of cosmetic products and rice by-products (many of which are gluten free): flour, polenta, biscuits and crackers.

Vercelli
Naturalia

fraz. Larizzate I via N. Bixio, 6
☎ (+39) 0161393222
⊛ www.risonaturalia.com
✉ info@risonaturalia.com
shop: yes
e-commerce: yes

RISO, RISAIE E RISOTTI

Federica Rosso and sisters Simona and Anna Maria, supervised by their mother Giancarla, head this all-female business devoted entirely to rice. The quality-focused farm extends over around 40 hectares and works towards protecting the environment and producing healthy, traceable products. As well as Carnaroli, semi-wholegrain and black rice, it also produces a tasty range of ready-to-cook risottos, its Eclettici range of black and red rice, and its Fioriti range that contains rice, edible flowers, and special herbs and plants grown on the farm.

Trino (VC)
Principato di Lucedio

fraz. Lucedio, 8
☎ (+39) 016181519
⊛ www.principatodilucedio.it
✉ info@principatodilucedio.it
shop: yes
e-commerce: no

PRINCIPATO DI LUCEDIO

This 500-hectare farm lies in a regional park, not far from a historic abbey, and vaunts a story of almost 900 years. Its production processes aim for low environmental impact and its preservative-free products are packaged in a modified environment, guaranteeing freshness and nutritional qualities. Its wide range includes Arborio, Baldo, Carnaroli and Vialone Nano rice; organic Selenio, Ermes Rosso, Venere Nero, wholegrain, Apollo and Basmati rice. It also produces ready-to-cook risottos, flours, cereals and pulses, crackers, grissini and other treats.

Grumolo delle Abbadesse (VI)
Riseria delle Abbadesse

via Roma, 143
☎ (+39) 0444583792
⊛ www.riseriadelleabbadesse.it
✉ info@riseriadelleabbadesse.it
shop: yes
e-commerce: no

This company, founded in 1992, stands out for experience and expertise, meticulous processing methods, cutting-edge technology and prime raw ingredients. Its certified rice is cultivated according to strict rules and milled using traditional methods. It produces two main varieties: the Slow Food Presidium Vialone Nano, and the Carnaroli. It also produces wholegrain red rice, Venere Nero, Canada wild rice, Basmati and other products for the ethnic market, as well as ready-to-cook risottos with carefully chosen ingredients.

Oristano
Riso della Sardegna

via Laconi, 54
☎ (+39) 078371063
❀ www.risodellasardegna.it
✉ info@risodellasardegna.it
shop: no
e-commerce: yes

Riso della Sardegna, founded in 1951, is the first rice producer of its kind in Sardinia. Over three generations the Putzu family has guaranteed a high-quality product thanks in part to the care taken when choosing rice grains. Rice is harvested in October and only made available to consumers after careful cleaning and processing. Their selection is wide-ranging, from organic rice to Basmati, Carnaroli, Venere, rice snacks, risotto mixes and even an array of minestras and legumes (both Sardinian and non-native varieties).

Gropello Cairoli (PV)
Riserva San Massimo

loc. San Massimo
☎ (+39) 0382817239
❀ riservasanmassimo.net
✉ info@riservasanmassimo.net
shop: yes
e-commerce: yes

RISERVA SAN MASSIMO®

This model family-run farm occupies over 500 hectares in the heart of the Lomellina district, in Parco Regionale Lombardo della Valle del Ticino. Here, in an unspoilt environment, they grow superfine Carnaroli rice, with every stage performed using traditional methods, from threshing to packaging. The rice thus retains its flavour, aroma and sensorial traits. Its two flagship products are superfine and wholegrain Carnaroli, both used by some of Italy's top chefs.

Salussola (BI)
Zaccaria

Cascina Margaria, 8
☎ (+39) 0161998235 | 3479256179
❀ www.risozaccaria.com
✉ info@risozaccaria.com
shop: yes
e-commerce: yes

With over 200 hectares of estate, at least 10,000 metric quintals of paddy rice are grown each year, but only a small part is refined and marketed under the company name. The flagship Carnaroli has PDO Riso di Baraggia Biellese e Vercellese certification, as do the Arborio, Sant'Andrea, Balilla and Baldo rice, but not its red and black rice, produced in small quantities. As well as being packed with vitamin B, mineral salts, amino acids and antioxidants, its wholegrain Nero di Baraggia Otello cultivar contains amylopectin, which speeds up cooking and stops the grains breaking up.

San Prospero (MO)
Acetaia del Cristo

via Badia, 41a
☎ (+39) 059907425
❀ www.acetaiadelcristo.it
✉ info@acetaiadelcristo.it
shop: yes
e-commerce: yes

ACETAIA DEL CRISTO
l'Aceto Balsamico Tradizionale di Modena

For over a century the Barbieri family has been a producer of PDO Aceto Balsamico Tradizionale, guaranteed by 2,000 kegs and its own organic vineyards. Careful control of each stage of production, from harvest to boiling of musts, means the best quality balsamic vinegar is obtained and a brand established worldwide. Barbieri has a varied product range, including its I Favolosi flagship line, especially the Diamante Nero, aged for over 25 years, as well as the Collezione della Nonna and the Tradizionali, refined in kegs of various kinds of wood.

Modena
Acetomodena

s.da Borelle, 120
☎ (+39) 059283157
❀ www.acetomodena.it
✉ info@acetomodena.it
shop: no
e-commerce: no

SOCIETÀ AGRICOLA
ACETOMODENA

Today Paolo Vecchi, whose passion for food goes back to early childhood, is at the helm of this historic family-run producer that makes high-quality balsamic vinegar with their own grapes. Aceto Balsamico di Modena PDO Extravecchio is their crown jewel, but their PGI Balsamic (available in both 'gold' and 'black' varieties) is just as good. Their aromatized balsamic dressings and creams also deserve a mention, especially for their versatility in the kitchen. Tours of the facility and tastings are available upon request.

Formigine (MO)
La Bonissima

fraz. Casinalbo I via U. Tonini, 2
☎ (+39) 059512112
❀ www.acetaialabonissima.it
✉ info@acetaialabonissima.it
shop: no
e-commerce: yes

La Bonissima goes back generations, thanks to its being managed with love and care by the De Pietri family. Vinegar is stored in wooden kegs in an old cellar. From there it will go on to adorn tables and enrich foods, lending something precious and, above all, unique in terms of both its flavor and aroma. There is a special focus on packaging, which is elegant and well-suited to every situation. There are a range of products, from PGI to PDO and aged vinegars. Accessories for proper tasting are also on hand.

Albinea (RE)
Il Borgo del Balsamico

fraz. Botteghe I via della Chiesa, 27
☎ (+39) 0522598175
❀ www.ilborgodelbalsamico.it
✉ info@ilborgodelbalsamico.it
shop: yes
e-commerce: yes

IL BORGO DEL BALSAMICO

Cristina and Silvia Crotti have inherited their father's passion and grown it into an internationally renowned business, while keeping faith with the ancient art of making balsamic vinegar. In addition to the PDO Aceto Balsamico Tradizionale di Reggio Emilia, with the 12-year silver and 25-year gold stamp of ageing, both of excellent standard, the company offers a fine range of condiments, with well-designed labels and packaging that make them ideal gifts: balsamic creams, saba, apple and wine vinegar and pralines.

Radda in Chianti (SI)
Castello di Volpaia

loc. Volpaia I p.zza della Torre, 2
☎ (+39) 0577738066
❀ www.volpaia.com
✉ info@volpaia.com
shop: no
e-commerce: no

CASTELLO DI
VOLPAIA

The Mascheroni Stianti family has owned an ancient rural hamlet since 1172, and today includes organic vineyards and olive groves, a restaurant, welcoming accommodation, and some satellite activities like fun cooking classes, organization of receptions and guided tastings. In addition to wine, grappa and olive oil, the family produces an interesting selection of red and white wine vinegars, and five flavoured types: vegetable, spice, floral, herb and fresh, using the herbs grown on the farm.

Scandiano (RE)
Cavalli

CAVALLI cav. FERDINANDO

loc. Fellegara I via del Cristo, 6a-b
☎ (+39) 0522983430
❀ www.balsamicocavalli.it
✉ info@balsamicocavalli.it
shop: yes
e-commerce: no

Fernando Cavalli, farmer and vigneron, is to be thanked for the expansion of the family's balsamic vinegar cellar in the 1950s, to meet the increasing demands of customers. His son Giovanni took up the baton of the family business, which he pursues today with great passion.

Vinegar

Sassuolo (MO)

Compagnia del Montale

via W. Tobagi, 6a
☎ (+39) 0536806434
❀ www.compagniadelmontale.com
✉ info@compagniadelmontale.com
shop: yes
e-commerce: yes

ACETAIA
COMPAGNIA DEL MONTALE

With more than 30 years of history behind it, but with a tradition reaching back to the mists of time, this family company produces PDO Aceto Balsamico Tradizionale di Modena, balsamic vinegars in the 12-year and Extravecchio 25-year versions that have won awards worldwide, and a PGI Aceto Balsamico di Modena. All made according to the classic must boiling process, and ageing in kegs of decreasing size. Also on offer are white and red wine vinegar; Balsamico PGI jelly, great with cheese; balsamic pearls and condiments.

Quarto d'Altino (VE)

Acetaia Ducale Estense Czarnocki Lucheschi

via G. Pascoli, 14
☎ (+39) 0422825750 I 3473581079
❀ www.acetaiaducale.it
✉ info@acetosopraffino.it
shop: yes
e-commerce: no

Some years ago, Andrea Czarnocki Lucheschi, his wife Archduchess Isabella of Austria and the Duke d'Este revived an age-old vinegar cellar and applied a recipe dating back to Cristoforo di Messisburgo, toastmaster of the Dukes d'Este in the 16th century. The vinegar is made by acetification of raw red-grape must, then aged in kegs of decreasing size. There are two versions: the six-year Sopraffino degli Estensi and the Sopraffino degli Estensi Riserva, aged at least 12 years. There are also monovarietal vinegars and the delicate, spicy Vinagro condiments.

Soliera (MO)

Agricola Due Vittorie

via Canale, 35
☎ (+39) 059563876
❀ www.duevittorie.it
✉ info@duevittorie.com
shop: yes
e-commerce: yes

DUE VITTORIE

Davide Maletti is a Modena native and gifted entrepreneur whose enthusiasm and love for his land gave life to Due Vittorie. Their main ingredient is, of course, grapes, which are cultivated in their own vineyards and then transformed into outstanding, natural vinegar through tried and true methods, modern technology, and time (no coloring or preservatives are used). Their wide range of balsamic vinegars are all high-quality, with their organic vinegar standing out, as well as their Extravecchio, which is aged for at least 25 years in casks of decreasing size and different types of wood.

Modena
Acetaia Fabbi

fraz. Collegara I stradello Bonaghino, 56a
☎ (+39) 059469105
✆ www.acetaiafabbi.com
✉ info@acetofabbi.com
shop: yes
e-commerce: no

In a beautiful old house surrounded by trebbiano vineyards, the Fabbi vinegar cellar was set up in 1910. Today there are more than 1,300 kegs of different kinds of wood for maturing and ageing vinegar. Starting in large barrels, where the must ferments, it gradually thickens and is moved to containers decreasing in size until it reaches the smallest, usually oak. There are two PDO vinegars, the Balsamico Tradizionale, aged for 12 years and the Extravecchio 25. There are also two balsamic condiments: the Riserva 4 and the Grand Reserve 8.

Modena
Giuseppe Giusti

loc. Lesignana I s.da Quattro Ville, 155
☎ (+39) 059840135
✆ www.giusti.it
✉ info@giusti.it
shop: yes
e-commerce: no

One of the world's oldest vinegar cellars, dating back to 1605 and now in its 17th generation of vinegar makers. The exceptional quality is well-known and has received many awards, and includes sensational collection vinegars like Aceto Balsamico di Modena PGI Profumato; Aceto Balsamico di Modena PGI Classico: Riccardo Giusti PGI; Quarto Centenario PGI; Banda Rossa PGI; and Biologico PGI. Then the Aceto Balsamico Tradizionale di Modena PDO (minimum ageing 12 years), and Extravecchio (minimum ageing 25 years); the precious Giusti Riserva: Piccole Donne; Eredi, and condiments, creams, salt, chocolates, even panettone.

Concordia sulla Secchia (MO)
Guerzoni

via Taglio, 26
☎ (+39) 053556561
✆ www.guerzoni.com
✉ info@guerzoni.com
shop: yes
e-commerce: yes

Run by Felice, Iride and Lorenzo, the third generation of the Guerzoni family, and the only company of its kind in the world to be certified organic and biodynamic. The range, using strictly controlled processes, includes Aceto Balsamico Tradizionale di Modena PDO, aged up to 24 years, and an Extravecchio, aged over 25 years. Also Aceto Balsamico Tradizionale di Modena PGI gold, silver and bronze versions; Aceto Balsamico di Modena green, white (organic) and red versions; and condiments, creams, saba and grape must.

Vinegar

Formigine (MO)

Leonardi

fraz. Magreta I via Mazzacavallo, 62
☎ (+39) 059554375
⊛ www.acetaialeonardi.it
✉ info@acetaialeonardi.it
shop: yes
e-commerce: no

Since 1871 the name Leonardi has been a byword for balsamic vinegar of the best quality. The company, part of a magnificent estate also open to visitors, offers five product lines: Classica, with various types of balsamic dressings; Good Luxury condiments and Aceto Balsamico di Modena PGI, decanted 2 to 15 times; Gold, condiments including saffron and vanilla; and the Grands Chefs PGI Aceti Balsamici collection; Le Caprice balsamic creams and vinegars. Lastly, Balsamic Diamond, created to commemorate the company's 140th anniversary.

Curtatone (MN)

Mengazzoli

loc. Levata I via della Costituzione, 41
☎ (+39) 037647444 I 0376290228
⊛ www.mengazzoli.it
✉ info@mengazzoli.it
shop: yes
e-commerce: no

Giorgio Mengazzoli turned his dream into a real company and now works with his offspring to ensure ingredients and careful control of the various stages make their product range one of the highest order. The lead role is played by the Balsamico di Modena in both PGI and PDO versions. Then there are wine vinegars, aromatized and monovarietal, and cider vinegar. There are also condiments, cream of balsamic vinegar in special flavours, including macha tea; balsamic pearls; a line of organic vinegars; and the new-born line of liquid gourmet salt.

Castelnuovo Don Bosco (AT)

Acetaia Merlino

via Case Sparse, 23
☎ (+39) 0119976092 I 3319056098
⊛ www.ramodoroaceteriamerlino.com
✉ acetaiamerlino@hotmail.it
shop: yes
e-commerce: yes

Founded by farmers and a group of professionals in the food research field, the Ramo d'Oro cooperative produces vinegar with honey and monovarietal wines contributed by its members. The vinegars are acidified applying ancient methods and age in oak barrels for a minimum of 8–12 months to a maximum of 12 years. The extensive range includes condiments made from boiled grape must and vinegar, called Mostaceti, and flavoured with ginger, juniper, lavender flowers and truffles. There are also mustards, mead and velvety preserves made with fruit or herbs.

Manzano (UD)

Midolini

via delle Fornaci, 1
☎ (+39) 0432754555
❀ www.midolini.com
✉ midolini@midolini.com
shop: yes
e-commerce: no

A record-breaking balsamic vinegar cellar, with over 2,300 kegs and part of the eponymous winery, produces Asperum, an excellent balsamic condiment from native grapes. There are three types: the orange pack, aged for 30 years during which the precious nectar spends time in seven kegs of different woods; Asperum IV, aged "only" 15 years; Asperum V, aged five years and the only one of the range to contain not just boiled must but also 30% wine vinegar. The, there are Asperum chocolates, the brainchild of a partnership with the Mosaic patisserie of Aquileia.

Bomporto (MO)

Paltrinieri

fraz. Sorbara I via Verdeta, 11
☎ (+39) 059902117 I 3388525400
❀ www.acetaiapaltrinieri.it
✉ info@acetaiapaltrinieri.it
shop: yes
e-commerce: yes

A country house is home to this historic Modena company, in business for over two centuries. The vinegar is made from the cellar's own lambrusco and trebbiano musts, applying the classic ageing process in different wood kegs. The flagship product is the PDO Aceto Balsamico Tradizionale di Modena, in Affinato, Extravecchio and Riserva di Famiglia versions, also in gift packs. There is also a PGI Aceto Balsamico di Modena, with different labels indicating the various ageing periods, and balsamic dressing, saba, jelly and vinegars.

Nonantola (MO)

Acetaia Pedroni

loc. Rubbiara I via Risaia, 4
☎ (+39) 059549019
❀ www.acetaiapedroni.it
✉ info@acetaiapedroni.it
shop: yes
e-commerce: yes

Founded in 1862, the vinegar cellar is now managed by Italo Pedroni, a singular fellow and great raconteur, enamoured of his business. He makes five types of PDO Balsamico Tradizionale, named after family members, each with its own character, different ageing time and sensorial profile: Cesare, Claudio, Giuseppe, Umberto, and Italo. Production also includes five types of PGI Balsamico, jelly and cream also made with balsamic vinegar, and some wines from native vines. Next door to the cellars, the Osteria di Rubbiara, a cosy restaurant serving typical dishes.

Faedo (TN)

Pojer & Sandri

loc. Molini, 4
☎ (+39) 0461650342
❀ www.pojeresandri.it
✉ info@pojeresandri.it
shop: yes
e-commerce: no

Founded in 1975 and popular above all with wine buffs for its fine wines and spirits, the company has been making wine and fruit vinegars for 30 years. It uses an age-old method, starting from wine or fruit juice fermented in barrels in contact with mother of vinegar, and without added preservatives. The ingredients used are mainly the cellar's own. In addition to classic white and red wine vinegar, there is a quince version, as well as others from Williams pears, blackcurrant, cherry, raspberry, elderberry and rowanberry.

Castiglione Falletto (CN)

Gigi Rosso

s.da Alba-Barolo, 34
☎ (+39) 0173262369
❀ www.gigirosso.com
✉ info@gigirosso.com
shop: yes
e-commerce: yes

The brand has four farms, all managed by the Rosso family, a father and two sons, Maurizio e Claudio. And it was precisely the latter, a winemaker, who was bitten by the vinegar bug in the early 1980s, following in the wake of an ancient local tradition. The products are mainly red wine vinegars derived from native vines, including Asì Aceto di Barolo, Asì Aceto di Nebbiolo, and Asì Aceto di Moscato. The vinegar flavoured with a blend of Langhe herbs and the balsamic condiment from the moscato grape are both interesting.

Novellara (RE)

Acetaia San Giacomo

s.da Pennella, 1
☎ (+39) 0522651197 I 3487841122
❀ www.acetaiasangiacomo.com
✉ info@acetaiasangiacomo.com
shop: yes
e-commerce: yes

ACETAIA SAN GIACOMO
NOVELLARA (RE) ITALIA

A family tradition handed down from generation to generation for this company, for years the best in the region. The secret of its top quality is production in small batches, minimum boiling of must, and respecting the timing for each step. In addition to the PDO Aceto Balsamico Tradizionale di Reggio Emilia, aged 12–25 years, there are also Essenza, the San Giacomo condiment, Agro sour must, saba, a balsamic jelly delicious with cheese, and even chocolates. The cellars also organize interesting learning visits.

Quattro Castella (RE)

Venturini Baldini

fraz. Roncolo I via F. Turati, 42
☎ (+39) 0522249011
❀ www.venturinibaldini.it
✉ info@venturinibaldini.it
shop: yes
e-commerce: no

A family-run cellar for four generations, founded in 1976, and a producer of Lambrusco and other internationally recognized wines, the company also has an ancient vinegar cellar dating back to the 1700s. Here the range of quality products includes a PDO Aceto Balsamico Tradizionale di Reggio Emilia, aged eight years; a PDO Aceto Balsamico Tradizionale di Reggio Emilia Aragosta, Argento e Oro, aged at least 12 years; and, lastly, Condimento Beatrice, aged for four years.

Vinegar

Termeno/Tramin (BZ)
Alfons Bologna

s.da del Vino, 15
☎ (+39) 0471860916 I 3480462771
❀ www.a-bologna.com
✉ info@a-bologna.com
shop: no
e-commerce: no

This family company vaunts the Sudtirol trademark, a prestigious acknowledgement guaranteeing quality of production that includes only hand-picked apples from integrated organic farming. Juice from fruit washed, chopped and squeezed in a special press, then routinely filtered and pasteurized. Totally free of preservatives, these light, tasty juices are bottled with a screw cap, providing a thirst-quenching and energy-rich drink.

Daverio (VA)
Campo dei Fiori

via C. Battisti, 80
☎ (+39) 0332947481
❀ www.campodeifiori.it
✉ info@campodeifiori.it
shop: no
e-commerce: no

For nearly 70 years the same family has run this company, combining tradition with innovation, and recently extending production from just butter and cheese to include pure fruit juices. The meticulous packaging process was developed to keep intact the properties that Mother Nature bestows on oranges, grapefruits, pineapples and tangerines, cornerstones of the Fior di Succo range of entirely natural juices, with no concentrate content. The Italian organic orange juice is the all-natural newcomer to the range.

Mariano Comense (CO)
Fava Bibite

via per Novedrate, 111
☎ (+39) 031 745282
❀ www.favabibite.it
✉ info@favabibite.it
shop: no
e-commerce: no

A family business now in its third generations that is still riding the crest of the wave thanks to its wide range of soft drinks also produced under licence: iconic Spuma Alpina and Frisco, but also fizzy orange, colas, lemonade, and chinotto. A new line of aperitifs targets the younger age group, as do the sparkling and still organic products. Packaging has been developed to flank glass bottles with safe and 100% recyclable aluminium flasks.

Montepulciano (SI)
Podere Fontecornino

loc. Sant'Albino I via Fontecornino, 2
☎ (+39) 0578798279
❀ www.fontecornino.it
✉ podere@fontecornino.it
shop: yes
e-commerce: no

Alto Adige tradition and experience took a trip to Tuscany in 1992, when Martin Gschleier moved his company down there. Son Michael now continues organic production of apples, which he processes in various ways including tasty juices, vinegar, cider and delicious dried slices. The farm, in an area dear to the Etruscans, cultivates 12 varieties on 11 hectares of land, and the entire chain is managed in house, vaunting prime raw material, pure air and unpolluted water.

Varedo (MB)
Gal's

v.lo Corte Seveso, 7
☎ (+39) 0362580535
❀ www.gals.it
✉ info@gals.it
shop: no
e-commerce: no

Gal's, with a century of experience behind it and using prime raw materials processed with modern technologies, is holding its own. The variety of products is ensured by constant research and study of innovative recipes, targeting top quality. Beverages are all free of artificial colouring and use, instead, natural extracts, derived from flowers and plants, or from natural dyes. There are three flagship products, all sold in glass bottles, all the same size: ginger ale, spuma, and fizzy orange.

Renon/Ritten (BZ)
Kohl

fraz. Auna di Sotto I via Principale/Hauptstraße, 35
☎ (+39) 0471359442
❀ www.kohl.bz.it
✉ kohl@kohl.bz.it
shop: yes
e-commerce: yes

Thomas Kohl has proved that apples will grow at over 900 metres in altitude. Just two decades ago no one took him seriously but his project worked out so well that he has converted his farm entirely to fruit, producing six monovarietal natural mountain apple juices, as well as several versions combining apple with other fruits. His delicious Gran Cru are super vintages that express all the goodness of Ananasrenette and Wintercalville cultivars, whose juice goes into glass, including a magnum size. Award-winning goodness for young and old.

Water, beverages, fruit juices

Nave San Rocco (TN)

Maso del Gusto

loc. Maso del Gusto, 2
☎ (+39) 0461870534
✪ www.masodelgusto.it
✉ masodelgusto@tin.it
shop: yes
e-commerce: no

Maso del Gusto was founded in the 1950s and is the first organic farm in Trentino. After overcoming the difficulties of converting to a new type of cultivation and the consequent downsizing of production, Roberto Loner devoted years to virtuous farming. He uses the fruits of his 18 hectares of orchards (ten apple and three pear cultivars) to produce his famous persecche dried apple slices, a range of bio fruit snacks, and great organic apple juice, including a concentrate version.

Predaia (TN)

Prantil

loc. Vervò di Priò I via della Bonifica, 8
☎ (+39) 0463469262 I 3280178467
✪ www.acetoprantil.it
✉ info@acetoprantil.it
shop: yes
e-commerce: yes

An apple producer for many years, this company's production chain includes cider vinegar and balsamic apple condiment, but also apple juice and dried apples. The essential parameters for harvesting fruit are the sugar content, crispness and hardness: important aspects of quality. The apples are hand pressed and processed directly controlled by experienced farmers. This member of CoCeA, part of Consorzio Melinda, has a traditional and an organic line.

Pergine Valsugana (TN)

Sant'Orsola

loc. Zivignago I via Lagorai, 131
☎ (+39) 0461518111
✪ www.santorsola.com
✉ info@santorsola.com
shop: yes
e-commerce: no

This farmers' association was set up in the early 1970s by ten resourceful young people, who specialized in growing berry fruits, initially only strawberries and late-harvest cherries. Today there are 1,000 associated companies and the fruit types have increased, used to make the Succosi line of healthy, natural products in small and large glass bottles. Without preservatives or colourings, you can savour them natural or diluted with water, and as ingredients for aperitifs and cocktails, alcoholic and non-alcoholic drinks.

Trento
T.V.B.

via G. Manci, 54
☎ (+39) 0630889027
❀ www.tvbitalia.it
✉ info@tvbitalia.it
shop: no
e-commerce: yes

T.V.B.®
pura frutta & basta

Only natural sugars, no preservatives or stabilizers, acidifiers and aromas. Just lots of GMO-free fruits. This sums up TVB's products: only pure blended fruit that retains all the goodness of the raw material and its precious nutrients. Flavours available include great classics and new mixes, each worth two of your recommended five-a-day. The offers eight different wholesome, tasty options, perfect ingredients to mix into fresh, intriguing cocktails.

Carbonera (TV)
Zolla 14

loc. Pezzan I via Cartiere, 14
☎ (+39) 0422445545 I 3384199557
❀ www.zolla14.it
✉ bio@zolla14.it
shop: yes
e-commerce: no

ZOLLA14
Organic Farm Project

This Treviso operation recently celebrated its tenth birthday and continues to farm its 11 hectares of land with biodynamic methods. Its flagship product is its apple juice, both monovarietal and in blends. The precious, limpid liquid is one of seven different "reserve" labels, flanked by peaches in ambra apple juice syrup, a new, one-portion bottled product of 200ml. Respect for diversity and quality are Zolla14's guiding principles, underpinning its ambitious production project.

Leading brands

Agriform

SOMMACAMPAGNA (VR) I via Rezzola, 21
☎ (+39) 0458971800 ✿ www.agriform.it
✉ agriform@agriform.it **shop:** yes **e-commerce:** yes

CHEESE. The cooperative Agriform was established in 1980. They produce, age and sell high-quality local cheeses from the Padana Plain, using local milk, farmed by thousands of ranchers, who are also partners of the producers. Their commitment to quality standards in all respects and throughout all phases of production is commendable; and their range of products is impressive. This includes Grana Padano PDO (including a version aged for 28 months, Oro del Tempo Stravecchio), Parmigiano Reggiano PDO (aged 12-30 months), Oro del Maso (from Alto Adige), fresh and aged Asiago (for up to over 10 months), Piave PDO (also available as an aged cheese), Montasio and Monte Veronese PDO. There's also Gorgonzola, Provolone, Pecorino Romano and mozzarella, not to mention a convenient grated cheese mix that can be used in the kitchen for any number of purposes.

Agroittica Lombarda - Calvisius

CALVISANO (BS) I fraz. Viadana I via Kennedy, 101
☎ (+39) 0309686991 ✿ www.agroittica.it
✉ info@agroittica.it **shop:** yes **e-commerce:** yes

PRESERVED FISH. Today if you think of Italy and caviar, you think of Calvisius (www.calvisius.it). Well, in case you were wondering, they've been making it here since the 1990s! And still today Agroittica are the only group in Europe who've been able to create the conditions necessary to raise the legendary white sturgeon, a prized fish that can live up to 100 years. Their efforts and commitment to traditional, artisanal methods have paid off, thrusting them into pole position with a product that stands out for its high-quality. Their partnership with Italian Caviar has resulted in two new lines of products: Calvisius and Ars Italica Calvisius. The former offers fresh and smoked white sturgeon, Malossol, which is low-salt caviar, and the prized Beluga. The latter features caviar from sturgeons raised in the Ticino Park. There are five varieties to choose from: Oscietra Classic, Royal and Imperial, Da Vinci (made from Adriatic sturgeon) and Sevruga. Salmon, tuna, trout and swordfish stand out among their smoked fish product line.

Agugiaro & Figna

COLLECCHIO (PR) l s.da dei Notari, 25/27
☎ (+39) 0521301701 ✪ www.agugiarofigna.com
✉ collecchio@agugiarofigna.com **shop:** yes **e-commerce:** no

FLOURS, PULSES, CEREALS. The story of the Agugiaro and Figna families has been intertwined with that of the miller's art since the 17th century. Currently they are a single business, with production units in Collecchio (Parma), Curtarolo (Padua), and Magione (Perugia). The entire production range covers the bakery, pastry, pizza, and fresh pasta segments. There are three plants. Molino Agugiaro was first, dating to the early 1400s, established by a noble Venetian family; the last milling plant was inaugurated in 1998 to produce semi-finished baked and pastry products. Molino Vigna, from the eponymous line of millers moved in 1874 from Lugo di Romagna to Parma, thanks to the success achieved by the first plant, and set up a second facility in Collecchio, allowing production of durum wheat and soft wheat to be separated. Lastly, Molino Fagioli, owned by the Figna group since 1997, became part of the Agugiaro & Figna group in 2003, beginning an important production investment plan. The company is certified for organic products.

Alce Nero

MONTERENZIO (BO) l via Idice, 299
☎ (+39) 0516540211 ✪ www.alceneroshop.com
✉ info@alcenero.it **shop:** yes **e-commerce:** yes

NATURAL FOOD. The brand is an umbrella for over a thousand farmers and beekeepers, in Italy and around the world, who have been engaged since the 1970s in producing healthy food. No pesticides and herbicides, eco-friendly production processes that respect raw materials and processing times are the components of the Alce Nero organic range. The catalogue includes pasta, tomato purée and pulp, sauces, EVOO, rice, compotes, fruit juices, flours, cereals and pulses, produced with Italian raw materials, grown by associated farmers and processed by member companies. To these we can added the fair-trade product line. The Alce Nero group has ten members: Conapi, which brings together over 600 beekeepers in Italy; La Cesenate canned food; Finoliva, controlling and processing the product contributed by the national consortium of olive growers; Brio bio fruits and vegetables; the venerable Felicetti pasta factory; Cooperativa Sin Fronteras; Chocolat Stella, quality Swiss chocolate; Pompadour infusions and tisanes; Libera Terra.

Almaverde Bio

CESENA (FC) I fraz. Pievesestina I v.le della Cooperazione, 400
☎ (+39) 0547414111 ⊕ www.almaverdebio.it
✉ info@apofruit.it **shop:** yes **e-commerce:** no

NATURAL FOOD. Almaverde Bio is the Almaverde Bio Italia brand. The consortium brings together several Italian agrifood enterprises and was set up in 2000. It was the first sector brand in Italy and vaunts a unique product range. Respect for the environment, production techniques and quality standards are the fundamental points that unite consortium companies. Starting from Canova, licensee for the fresh and ready-to-consume fruit and vegetables to Fileni, producing organic poultry and eggs since 1978, and Novissime contributing eggs and egg products. Moreover, there are Circeo Pesca's fresh and frozen seafood products; fruit pulp and baby food, deli and vegetable milks, but also Frutta Gel fruit pulp, purées, juices and nectars. In spring 2015 Canova initiated a program to expand the range of products, which includes more than 50 new items across the all lines. The first new product is the Confetto baby tomato grown by Sicilian organic farms.

Liquirizia Amarelli dal 1731

ROSSANO (CS) I loc. Rossano Scalo I s.s. 106 c.da Amarelli
☎ (+39) 0983511219 ⊕ www.amarelli.it
✉ amarelli@amarelli.it **shop:** yes **e-commerce:** yes

PATISSERIE. A venerable Rossano company founded in 1731, which flourished in the 1800s thanks to the improvement of maritime transport and tax advantages granted by the Bourbons. In 1907 Nicola Amarelli introduced a series of technological innovations, which safeguarded craftsmanship and increased production. Today a master liquorice-maker still controls the process, which is totally chemical-free. In addition to raw sticks and pure liquorice, flavoured with aniseed or mint, there are also liquorice comfits, liquorice liqueur, chocolate and biscuits. Firmly convinced that the synergy between companies is a way of enhancing individual skills, Amarelli has created partnerships with other businesses. Among these, Strega Alberti Benevento Spa, Officina Profumo Santa Maria Novella and Tenute Strozzi, but also associations like Les Henokiens, Museimpresa, Comitato Leonardo, Uisi, Gemellati Uist, Aidaf, Aidepi and Soci Onorari Centenari.

Amaro Lucano

PISTICCI (MT) l v.le Cav. Pasquale Vena
☎ (+39) 08354691 ✪ www.amarolucano.it
✉ info@amarolucano.it **shop:** no **e-commerce:** yes

LIQUEURS, SYRUPS, DISTILLATES. Pisticci, Basilicata, 1894. The time and place of the first chapter in the story of Amaro Lucano. In his small biscuit factory, Pasquale Vena experimented and created Amaro Lucano. Still a secret recipe, made with herbs (wormwood, Roman wormwood, clary sage, musk yarrow, sweet orange, gentian, and others), and which brought the rise of a leading business in the Italian spirits market. In the 1950s, after the interruption of activities due to World War 2, the founder's sons Leonardo and Giuseppe upgraded the workshop into a modern facility. In the 1960s production increased significantly and Amaro Lucano became known and appreciated worldwide. With time Sambuca, Limoncello and Caffè were added, products promoted with commitment by the founder's grandson Pasquale Vena, his wife and two children. At the end of 2014 Campari sold Limoncetta of Sorrento (which had joined the Campari group when it acquired the Averna brand) to Amaro Lucano although the liqueur is still bottled by Campari.

Amaro Montenegro

ZOLA PREDOSA (BO) l via E. Fermi, 4
☎ (+39) 051 6170411 ✪ www.montenegro.it
✉ info@montenegro.it **shop:** no **e-commerce:** no

LIQUEURS, SYRUPS, DISTILLATES. Amaro Montenegro's roots go back to 1885, when Stanislao Cobianchi founded the small liquor producer. Initially, they focused on spirits, like ratafià, alchermes, arquebuse, persico, latte di vecchia and rosolio, many of which have since been forgotten. Soon, he created a new, exclusive liquor made with aromatic herbs. It was a subtle, amber, after-dinner drink, perfect for sipping or as a cocktail (Gabriele D'Annunzio called it, 'the liquor of virtues'). Stanislao named it, Amaro Montenegro, in honor of Elena Petrovich Niegos, Princess of Montenegro and the future Queen of Italy. Today, the producer is a full-blown group encompassing various brands, all of them leaders in their respective markets. In addition to Amaro Montenegro, still the house speciality, their portfolio includes Olio Cuore (corn oil and vegetable mayonnaise), Polenta Valsugana (polenta mixes, available in yellow, white, whole grain and multi-grain versions, as well as ready-made), Cannamela (Italy's top producer for spices), Vecchia Romagna (the historic Italian brandy invented in 1939 and easily recognized by its unmistakable, triangular bottle) and Bonomelli (chamomile, herbal teas and infusions).

Ambrosi

CASTENEDOLO (BS) I via dei Ponticelli, 1
☎ (+39) 0302134811 ❀ www.ambrosi.it
✉ info.commerciale@ambrosi.it **shop:** no **e-commerce:** no

CHEESE. Founded in 1942 by Ottorino Ambrosi as a simple, family-run business, today Ambrosi is an international powerhouse. Over the years they have bought up other producers for the purposes of increasing and expanding their presence, including Migali and Bertozzi, both of which are located outside the region. Thanks to the quality of its products, its certifiability, and its distribution network, Ambrosi has become a leader when it comes to high-end, traditional Italian cheeses, focusing on Parmigiano Reggiano and Grana Padano. Part of its success lies in having established close ties with its suppliers, and guaranteeing that the environments, techniques and sources used all correspond to their high standards of authenticity and health. Their main product line includes Pecorino Romano, Provolone, Gorgonzola, Asiago, Taleggio, Fontina and Montasio. There are plenty of organic and fresh dairy products available as well.

Ambrosoli

RONAGO (CO) I via Ambrosoli, 12
☎ (+39) 0313507211 ❀ www.ambrosoli.it
✉ info.ambrosoli@ambrosoli.it **shop:** yes **e-commerce:** no

HONEY. The first honey sweet dates back to 1930, thanks to the ingenious idea of Giovanni Battista Ambrosoli who wanted a practical way to have a small portion of honey constantly available. Ambrosoli was a young industrial chemist working on the family farm, with a mania for honey. He began his business transporting hives from plain areas to the mountains, to benefit from different flowers. After experimenting with other sweet producers in Italy and abroad, the famous honey sweet finally appeared. As well as the natural flavour there are countless variations: milk and honey, coffee, balsamic flavours, aromatic herbs, rhubarb, mint and aniseed (some are also jelly sweets). The original honey from various wildflowers, recommended, is joined today by other versions: acacia, orange flower, eucalyptus, chestnut and Hungarian acacia.

Arrigoni

PAGAZZANO (BG) I via Treviglio, 940
☎ (+39) 0363031203 ❂ www.arrigoniformaggi.it
✉ info@arrigoniformaggi.it **shop:** yes **e-commerce:** no

Semplicemente per passione

CHEESE. Arrigoni bring together cheese-making and farming, making sure they have a hand in every stage of production. Milk is brought in daily, from more than 20 select stables, including their own, and worked into the final product largely by hand. Taleggio PDO is their flagship cheese, followed by Gorgonzola, Salva Cremasco, strachitunt, Arrì Arrì (gorgonzola and mascarpone), Maggengo (conserved in hay), Fior di capra (goat's milk) and Rugiada. Arrigoni offer a fresh cheese line for lighter, summer meals. This includes Quartirolo Lombardo PDO fresco and Stracchino (an organic variety is also available) as well as Primosale and Capriccio. These delicious, high-quality cheeses can be enjoyed by themselves, as a side dish, with salads, to add flavor to a favorite recipe or for more intricate meals. Thanks to innovative production techniques, flavor endures over time and so cheeses can be kept and enjoyed for longer than expected.

Asdomar

GENOVA I p.zza Borgo Pila, 39/26 Corte Lambruschini Torre B
☎ (+39) 0105308711 ❂ www.asdomar.it
✉ info@generaleconserve.it **shop:** no **e-commerce:** no

PRESERVED FISH. Asdomar is part of the Generale Conserve group which works in the packaged fish market. The company is the second largest producer of tuna in oil and this accounts for 60% of its products. The products are sold under the brands Asdomar, the largest, then Janus and Smeralda, as well as private brand names for leading retail companies. In February 2008 the whole production business transferred to Italy, in the newly opened, avant-garde plant at Olbia where the meticulous production process takes place for yellow fin and skipjack tuna from the Atlantic, Pacific and Indian oceans. The company does not use endangered tuna species and has always been aware of environmental sustainability. All Asdomar products are preserved in oil or brine: premium (tuna and tuna belly), medium (tuna with beans or in pâté), and the mackerel and salmon range. In 2013 Generale Conserve expanded its activities with the purchase of Manzotin and the De Rica brand.

Asiago Food

VEGGIANO (PD) I via Santa Maria, 7
☎ (+39) 0495082260 ✆ www.asiagofood.it
✉ info@asiagofood.it **shop:** no **e-commerce:** no

FROZEN FOOD. Established more than 30 years ago by Massimo Azzolini and Monica Ciarfuglia (who are still managing the company), Asiago Food got its start on the Asiago plateau, but later moved down to the plains below it. Today the group are a force to be reckoned with in the Italian food sector. All their fruits and vegetables are frozen and dried within a few hours of harvest. Not only does this protect the quality and freshness of their products, it guarantees that the nutritional properties, flavor, color and texture remain completely intact. An organic line of frozen foods are also available. This includes pitted cherries, berry smoothies, ready-made dishes, as well as vegetarian and vegan dishes (vegetable hamburgers, vegetable and bean purées). They also offer a range of dried mushrooms (porcini mushrooms make up the lion share), in various cuts and shapes. Also here, an organic line is available.

Auricchio

CREMONA I via Dante, 27
☎ (+39) 0372403311 ✆ www.auricchio.it
✉ info@auricchio.it **shop:** no **e-commerce:** no

CHEESE. Auricchio provolone was launched in 1877 in San Giuseppe Vesuviano, by Gennaro Auricchio, who left his secret recipe of a special rennet to his heirs. At the beginning the Auricchio family selected milk and monitored its processing in local dairies. With the increase in production to meet market demand, it was necessary to seek large amounts of good milk in the Po Valley. Since 1976 most of the production has been concentrated in the modern Pieve San Giacomo plant, near Cremona. Provolone Auricchio was already famous in the early 1900s, even overseas, where it was considered an Italian icon. Today it is still produced in the traditional manner, in mild, piquant, young, mature, and reserve version. In recent years the company wished to offer a wide range of cheeses so acquired other brands, flanking the historic label with a number of names from Italy's best dairy tradition: Ceccardi for ricotta and caciotta; Gloria and Locatelli for pecorino cheese; Giovanni Colombo for gorgonzola.

Averna

CALTANISSETTA I via F. Sacchetti, 20
☎ (+39) 0262251 ◉ www.amaroaverna.it
✉ info@campari.com **shop:** yes **e-commerce:** yes

LIQUEURS, SYRUPS, DISTILLATES. Fratelli Averna, former owners of Amaro Braulio, the Frattina grappa company and Limoncetta di Sorrento, was acquired by the Campari group in 2014. Fratelli Averna was founded in 1859, when Salvatore Averna sold fabrics in Caltanissetta and did good works in the Abbazia di Santo Spirito convent. Here one of the monks offered him a gift: an elixir of herbs, roots and citrus fruits from a secret recipe. The bitter was good, with therapeutic and invigorating qualities. So shortly after, Averna started his own small production, then his domestic distillery grew quickly into a factory, and in 1912 Francesco Averna was awarded a royal patent. The business upgraded to a limited company in 1958, with large-scale technical modernization and a nationwide sales network. From 1978 the company focused on diversification of its products and entering foreign markets. Its product range, besides the bitter, includes liqueurs, grappa, sambuca, but also brands of rum, gin and whisky.

Babbi

BERTINORO (FC) I fraz. Capocolle I via Caduti di via M. Fani, 80
☎ (+39) 0543448598 ◉ www.babbi.it
✉ info@babbi.it **shop:** yes **e-commerce:** no

BABBI

◀

PATISSERIE. Babbi, founded in 1952, shows that the line between industrial and artisanal methods is truly thin. The producer, based in Emilia Romagna, has earned itself international recognition thanks to its enticing sweets, but it's also established itself as an important supplier of semi-processed foods and mixes for baked goods. In fact, many similar producers have begun to look at them, and their quality standards, as a model. Given the current trend towards a more globalized marketplace, this is a no small achievement. And examples of excellence abound. Their 'Viennese' wafers with cream filling and chocolate topping are an absolute must, along with their 'babbini' (cream-filled wafers in various flavors), chocolate-filled cialdine, cremini, pralines, wafer cakes, various cream spreads (check out their fig and caramel varieties) and hot chocolate mix. They also offer gluten-free wafer products and ice cream cones.

Baladin

FARIGLIANO (CN) I loc. Prella, 60
☎ (+39) 0173778013 I 0173742130 ✿ www.baladin.it
✉ info@birreria.com **shop:** yes **e-commerce:** yes

BEER. If national and international beer drinkers have gotten to know a 'different' kind of Italian beer, it's thanks to the explosive Teo Musso, the brain behind Baladin (and its founder). His beers are gracing tables in notable restaurants, getting major distribution and, more recently, evening gaining traction abroad. There are more than 30 varieties, from the classics (Nora, Isaac, Super, Wayan, and beers aged for 10 years), to special varieties (like the 'Mielika' with Erica Heather honey and the Open Baladin) and draft beers. There are also drinks, ciders and spirits. There's even a kit for home brewing. Don't forget about their selection of delicious snacks, from fruit preserves to accompany cheese, to panettone, cheese, chocolates and even essential oils (all made with beer)! Baladin have opened pubs all over Italy (Rome, Milan, Turin, Bologna etc.) and abroad (New York and Marocco). Visits are available on request.

Balconi Dolciaria

NERVIANO (MI) I via XX Settembre, 51
☎ (+39) 0331406411 ✿ www.balconidolciaria.it
✉ info@balconidolciaria.com **shop:** no **e-commerce:** no

PATISSERIE. We have Francesco Balconi to thank for having transformed a simple, traditional bakery into a business that today is recognized both nationally and abroad. And over 60 years, their mission hasn't changed: offer baked snacks using only select, Italian ingredients without the addition of OMG, hydrogenated fats, artificial colors or conservatives. And what's more, do it in a way that keeps prices down by reducing production costs, cutting down on waste and improving efficiency by operating non-stop. In addition to the spongy baked snacks that made them famous (trancetti, mini-tiramisù, mini-rolls, snacks with milk or chocolate), Balconi make various types of wafers, rolls, cakes (the 'Viennese', classic and chocolate tiramisù) and, last but not least, breakfast cookies (classic, whole wheat and multi-grain frullini), which are also available in a family-size packaging.

Balocco

FOSSANO (CN) I via Santa Lucia, 51
☎ (+39) 0172653411 ✺ www.balocco.it
✉ info@balocco.it **shop:** no **e-commerce:** no

PATISSERIE. Considering its current scale, it's difficult to imagine that this family-run business got its start in the early sixties as a simple, local bakery. Despite their success, Balocco have managed to stay true to their original philosophy: passion, professionalism and, above all, a strong commitment to the quality of all their products. Their sweets and seasonal cakes (colombe and panettoni, both traditional and reworked) are famous worldwide thanks to the use of only select ingredients and natural yeast starters. And when it comes to production, they're unafraid to take advantage of the best of what modern technology has to offer. All of this has contributed to their reputation for quality and excellence. There are plenty of other treats to enjoy, from chocolate eggs to a host of appetizing biscotti, ideal for breakfast, tea or a snack for the kids. They also produce wafers and frollini, as well as a line for the health-conscious (sugar-free, with multi-grains and fruit...).

Barilla

PARMA I via Mantova, 166
☎ (+39) 0521 2621 ✺ www.barillagroup.it
✉ mediarelations@barilla.com **shop:** no **e-commerce:** no

PASTA. In 1877 Pietro Barilla opened a bakery in Parma, and in 1910 his children increased production, creating the first factory with a continual oven. Later the founder's grandson Pietro joined the business . The post-War revival was an opportunity for restyling the company image and it became a limited company in 1970. It was bought by American multinational W.R. Grace and Company who also then bought Voiello. In 1979 Pietro Barilla repurchased the majority shares. Today the group owns 30 production sites (14 in Italy and 16 abroad), including nine mills which it runs directly, controls Italian and foreign brands Academia Barilla, Filiz, Harry's, Misko, Vesta e Jemina, Mulino Bianco, Pavesi, Wasa. The company has grown over time in the main categories (pasta, sauces and baked goods) and every year launches successful new products: gluten-free pasta, wholemeal brioches and new sauces are just a few examples. In 2015 it invested heavily in the Ames plants in the USA to increase availability of gluten-free pasta.

Bauli

CASTEL D'AZZANO (VR) I via Verdi, 31
☎ (+39) 0458288311 ❀ www.bauligroup.it
✉ bauli@bauli.it **shop:** no **e-commerce:** no

PATISSERIE. The origins of Bauli are the stuff of legends. In 1927 Verona pâtisseur Ruggero Bauli, decided to go to Argentina in search of fortune. He sailed on the Principessa Mafalda, which was shipwrecked and Bauli was saved by miracle. He began his new life in Argentina, where he opened a successful bakery, but just a few years later his homesickness drew him back to his native Verona. In 1937 his bakery was making 5,000 pastries a day, and in 1950s he started producing pandoro, a traditional Verona naturally leavened cake. From working alone he ended up hiring about 20 workers. With the boom, the company expanded, expanding nationwide and becoming more dynamic and modern. In addition to cakes, Bauli began baking a line of snacks and leavened products for various times of day. The group's portfolio of brands vaunts greats of Italian confectionery tradition like Doria, Bistefani, Fbf (a leader in Italian snack product), Motta and Casalini.

F.lli Beretta

TREZZO SULL'ADDA (MI) I via Fratelli Bandiera, 12
☎ (+39) 02909851 ❀ www.fratelliberetta.com
✉ info@fratelliberetta.com **shop:** no **e-commerce:** no

CHARCUTERIE. The head office is at Trezzo sull'Adda while about 20 plants specializing in various charcuterie products are scattered across northern Italy. The story of Beretta pressed meats began at Barzanò Brianza, Lecco, in 1812, and the reins of the company are still held by the same family although the charcuterie business became a joint stock company in 1975. The meat derives from the Prosciutto di Parma circuit and is matured in temperature-controlled chambers and natural cellars. In the 1970s the range expanded to include Wüber frankfurters. In the late 1980s Beretta purchased the Salumificio Brianteo and Cim, both specializing in PDO Parma products, also taking a share in San Carlo (Piacenza charcuterie) and Del Zoppo (bresaola), as well as launching a new venture with French giant Fleury Michon, to form Piatti Freschi Italia. In 2012 they bought Framon, Creuses and Carpegna Prosciutti. Other plants were opened in China, California and New Jersey.

Besana

SAN GENNARO VESUVIANO (NA) **l** via Ferrovia, 210
☎ (+39) 0818659111 ✪ www.besanaworld.com
✉ info@besanagroup.com **shop:** yes **e-commerce:** no

DRIED FRUIT. It all began in 1921, when Emilio Besana and his brother Vincenzo founded the company that 80 years later became the Besana group. In the 1930s the brothers expanded to the USA and to the East, allowing the company to grow on a global scale. A new plant was built in San Gennaro Vesuviano and is still Besana's base. Throughout its history the company has invested in the most advanced technologies, extending its production range: first with almonds from Puglia and Sicily, then with Brazil nuts, dried and dehydrated fruit, seeds, and chocolate. In 1989, Besana UK Ltd opened to introduce the products processed to the United Kingdom and Northern Europe. In 2000 an important alliance was forged with Almaverde Bio, of which Besana was co-founder and exclusive licensee of dried fruits and seeds. Then the partnership with the Mediterranean Fruit Company and Made in Blu Trading (fruit and vegetables). Besana has various establishments around Italy and abroad, and has formed partnerships with other brands over time.

Bevande Futuriste

TREVISO **l** s.da Callalta, 33
☎ (+39) 0422419879 ✪ www.bevandefuturiste.it
✉ info@bevandefuturiste.it **shop:** no **e-commerce:** no

WATER, BEVERAGES, FRUIT JUICES. Bevande Futuriste sets itself apart for, among other things, its sensitivity to the health concerns of today's consumers. The firm manages three brands: DiFrutta (www.difrutta.it), Cortese (www.cortesesoftdrink.it) and ama_tè (www.amatebio.it). The first offers high-quality organic juices, all made with top ingredients and labeled so as highlight nutritional value. Orange and Apple, Wild Blueberry and Tomato are all featured products, along with an Orange, Carrot and Lemon blend. Each juice is as delicious as the next. Cortese is their line of refreshing soft drinks, from chinotto to citron to ginger ale, all made with ingredients of the highest quality. Finally, ama_tè is made up of various flavors of organic green tea. Their infusions include peach and elderflower, mint and lemongrass, lemon and ginger, licorice and fennel, and pomegranate. All varieties offer health benefits, are low-calorie and gluten-free.

Bibanesi - Da Re

GODEGA DI SANT'URBANO (TV) I loc. Bibano I via Borgo Nobili, 9
☎ (+39) 0438782022 I 0438777025 ❂ www.bibanesi.com
✉ info@bibanesi.com **shop:** yes **e-commerce:** yes

BAKED GOODS. In the 1970s Giuseppe Da Re owned one of the leading bakeries in the north-east with considerable production quantities but artisan traditional methods. After some experimentation, he offered a new product in 1989, his bibanesi, a cross between bread and breadsticks, crispy and crumbly, dry and lightly salted, made from extra virgin olive oil with no preservatives or additives. The shape is always different because they are rolled individually by hand after lengthy rising with mother yeast. As well as the classic version other varieties include: milk and honey , wholemeal, Biballegri, flavoured and Kamut bio. The special, limited edition inspired by art is unusual because these unusual breadsticks are little masterpieces. The packaging is designed by Dario Fo. The producer is Da Re di Bibano, of Godega di Sant'Urbano, and a second plant is at Zoppè di San Vendemiano.

Bioland

GRAVINA IN PUGLIA (BA) I c.da San Secondino
☎ (+39) 0803252596 ❂ www.biolandweb.it
✉ info@bioland.it **shop:** no **e-commerce:** yes

FLOURS, PULSES, CEREALS. For the record, Bioland (run by Maria Teresa Leone and Michele Loiudice) is composed of two organic farms. The first is situated right in the hills of Gravina in Puglia and comprises 20 hectares of land. The second is a larger 80 hectares of land and is in San Mauro Forte (MT), in the districts of Piano Miele and Don Filippo. Since 1993, Bioland has been a leader in the area of organic agriculture, at the top of its class in terms of guaranteeing food safety and product traceability. Only ancient varieties of grain are cultivated here. The durum wheats grown include Senatore Cappelli, Khorasan, Dioccum and Monococcum Spelt. The soft wheat varieties comprise Gentil Rosso, Spelt, Triminia, Bianchetta, Risciola and Autonomia. Since 2006 Bioland has had its own certified organic stone grinding mill for transforming grain into flour. Grains are also used to make various types of pasta (including whole wheat), bran, wheat meal and flaxseed. They also grow legumes, including lentils, black chickpeas and cicerchie, a variety of Italian pea. Their shop can be found at 39 Via A. de Gasperi.

Birra del Borgo

BORGOROSE (RI) I loc. Piana di Spedino
☎ (+39) 074631287 ❀ www.birradelborgo.it
✉ info@birradelborgo.it **shop:** yes **e-commerce:** no

BEER. Until recently virtually no one was interested in making beer in Lazio. However, in 2005, Leonardo Di Vincenzo arrived and started shaking things up with his 'Birra del Borgo', shooting to the head of this nascent market. The brew was the result of years of experiments in his small town on the border between Lazio and Abruzzo (indeed, some of his beers are named after the National Park of Monti della Duchessa near where he lived). Passion, talent, quality and brilliant marketing are the keys to the success of beers like the already 'classic' Reale, the Duchessa, the Enkir and the Keto Reporter (made with Tuscan tobacco leaves). Then there are the seasonal varieties (four of them, including gentian and buckwheat), and the 'rarities' (there are about a dozen, including one with chestnuts), produced only once a year and during a specific month. In addition to being able to buy them directly at the brewery, La Birra del Borgo has a shop in Rome and manages an often-packed modern eatery here as well.

Distilleria Bocchino

CANELLI (AT) I via Comm. L. Bocchino, 8
☎ (+39) 01418101 ❀ bocchino.com
✉ info@bocchino.it **shop:** yes **e-commerce:** no

LIQUEURS, SYRUPS, DISTILLATES. It was 1898 when Carlo Bocchino founded a small distillery in Canelli with the aim of making grappa out of pomace from the local Moscato vineyards. Over the years the distillery has reached new heights in terms of quality, thanks in part to the commitment of Giorgio Micco, Carlo's son-in-law, who created their grappa symbol from the name 'Black Seal' ('Sigillo Nero'). Today it is Giorgio's son, Carlo, who manages things, keeping Bocchino a family-run business (with the help of his daughters Miranda and Marta). Their selection of spirits is robust, starting with the Riserva Carlo Bocchino, made from monovarietal grapes and aged at length in specific, designated wood casks. The Cantina Privata collection is for connoisseurs: select vintages, precisely numbered, and aged in wood casks for 8 to 12 years. Decorative gift packaging is also available.

Bonaventura Maschio

GAIARINE (TV) I via Vizza, 6
☎ (+39) 0434756611 ✿ www.primeuve.com
✉ info@primeuve.com **shop:** yes **e-commerce:** yes

BONAVENTURA MASCHIO

LIQUEURS, SYRUPS, DISTILLATES. Cismon del Grappa, late 1800s, the Maschio family cultivates the land and distills grappa on their alembic cart. It is a time of terrible poverty, so the family emigrates. Then, in the early 1900s, grandson Bonaventura develops the distillation into a business and everyone in Gaiarine talks about his stills and his methods. Walking the tightrope of tradition and innovation, in the 1980s the company grew, under the leadership of Italo, inventor of the famous Prime Uve, an aquavit of the finest white prosecco and riesling grapes, distilled under vacuum at low temperature, so as to preserve the original aromas and the sensory experience, reaping remarkable success even beyond national borders. Next up were Prime Uve Nere, from red grapes, above all cabernet and refosco; then Prime Uve Oro, from bianche di collina grapes, aged in oak kegs. The company also produces orange aquavit, Amaro Pratum (from herbs grown by a protected Friuli oasis), other types of grappa and a small line of Charmat-method prosecco.

Bonollo

FORMIGINE (MO) I via Mosca, 5
☎ (+39) 059578700 ✿ www.bonollo.com
✉ info@bonollo.com **shop:** yes **e-commerce:** no

LIQUEURS, SYRUPS, DISTILLATES. Since 1908 the Distillerie Bonollo group has been managed by the family after whom it was named. They now run four distilleries around Italy (in chronological order): in Formigine (Modena), Anagni (Paduni), Osteria della Fontana (Frusinate) and in Torrita di Siena. The oldest, in Fomigine, was opened by Luigi Bonollo, the son of Giuseppe, the man who founded the business in 1908 when he officially registered the first distillate with the state. The whole family has had a part in making the producer one of the most important in Europe. With unflinching determination they have seen to it that the ingredients and processes used to make their grappas, brandies and other spirits are completely traceable and of the highest quality. Today Bonollo also produce tartaric acid (used in various industries), organic and natural mineral fertilizers, and even energy, thanks to their use of biomass materials, 60% of which comes from pomace.

Bonomelli

ZOLA PREDOSA (BO) I via E. Mattei, 6
☎ (+39) 051 6170411 ❂ www.bonomelli.it
✉ info@bonomelli.it **shop:** no **e-commerce:** no

COFFEE, TEA, INFUSIONS. This historic leader in chamomile production got its start in 1908, when the herbalist Luigi Amedeo Bonomelli founded a plant for making liquors and non-alcoholic drinks. The brand, Temperantia, was awarded a gold medal by Real Casa in 1911, and 1920 saw the birth of the Bitter Bonomelli. But we'd only be introduced to the products for which the Bologna producer would become famous, Camomilla Bonomelli and Espresso Bonomelli (a pod of chamomile mixed with other herbs), in 1926. In 1962, they began selling their Thè Infrè, the first ever decaffeinated tea. The producer, always attentive to consumer tastes, diet trends and health/wellness needs, launched a new line of herbal teas in 2009: 'rilassanti' (in addition to chamomile, there are products made with valerian, hawthorn and passion flower), 'digestive' (to promote healthy digestion), 'depurative e drenanti' (to bolster the immune system, to improve circulation and for menopause). Today, the Bonomelli brand is part of the Amaro Montenegro group.

Caffè Borbone

CAIVANO (NA) I loc. Pascarola I zona ASI
☎ (+39) 0817528822 ❂ www.caffeborbone.it
✉ info@caffeborbone.it **shop:** no **e-commerce:** yes

COFFEE, TEA, INFUSIONS. The Borbone brand is owned by Aromatika Ltd., founded in 1997 with the aim of keeping alive Naples's great tradition of coffee, a tradition that every Neapolitan should be proud of. Day in and day out, it's made possible thanks to the use of select ingredients and processing methods that take advantage of the best of what modern technology has to offer. Every step of production is subjected to strict and regular quality controls, so as to guarantee the highest possible standards. And this is why, despite dizzyingly high production volumes, quality is never lacking. Their product line includes blends for cafés and other food/drink establishments, home brew varieties, tisanas and powders, and accessories made on purpose for their products (cups, saucers, trays etc... even sugar). They also have a plant in the United States (New Jersey).

Botalla Formaggi

BIELLA I via E. Ramella Germanin, 5
☎ (+39) 01528163 I 01526353 ✪ www.botallaformaggi.com
✉ info@botallaformaggi.com **shop:** no **e-commerce:** no

CHEESE. Founded in 1947, from the outset Botalla managed to establish itself as a leader among local cheese-makers. Today the producer is managed by siblings Andrea, Simona and Stefano Bonino, along with their father Sandro and mother Maria Teresa. The milk used comes from the nearby mountains and is worked in any of four facilities. It is then aged in natural cellars (that can hold up to 100,000 units) for a period of 60 to 120 days. The constant microclimate in which the cheeses are brushed, turned and worked, one on top of the other along wooden boards, brings out their peculiarities. There are latteria cheeses, toma cheeses, maccagno cheeses, the 'sbirro' (made with Menabrea beer), the ImBufalita (the first aged cheese made entirely of Buffalo milk). There are both aged cheeses and fresh ones, cheeses made with goat's milk and sheep's milk, as well as the vegetarian 'Veggy'. Finally, don't forget about the delightful 'Botallini', bite-sized cheese balls in oil (no conservatives!), available in a variety of natural flavors (truffle, peperoncino chili, aromatic herbs...)

Fratelli Branca Distillerie

MILANO I via Resegone, 2
☎ (+39) 02 85131 ✪ www.branca.it
✉ info@branca.it **shop:** yes **e-commerce:** yes

LIQUEURS, SYRUPS, DISTILLATES. In 1845 Bernardino Branca invented the bitter that took the world by storm in just a few years. Its 27 herbs and spices, gathered from 4 continents, were in the original recipe and are unchanged today. The family has carefully kept its secrets for 5 generations. In 1893 the logo made its debut with the Branca world, designed by Leopoldo Metlicovitz. In 1907 Dino Branca conquered the markets of Europe and America, opening new plants in Buenos Aires, Saint Louis and Chiasso. In 1963 the revolutionary Brancamenta was launched, an especially refreshing bitter, its herb and spices formula enriched with an essential oil from Piedmontese peppermint. Over the years, the group has expanded its offerings and today its products, besides Fernet–Branca, Brancamenta and Stravecchio Branca, include Caffè Borghetti, Grappa Candolini, Grappa Sensèa, Punt e Mes, Carpano Classico and Bianco, Antica Formula, Sambuca Borghetti, the premium spirit Magnamater, Sernova vodka, Villa Branca Chianti Classico wines, Bellarco sparkling wine and, most recently, Carpano Dry.

Brendolan

SAN DANIELE DEL FRIULI (UD) I via Aonedis, 13
☎ (+39) 0432956592 ✪ www.brendolanservice.com
✉ info@brendolan.net **shop:** no **e-commerce:** no

CHARCUTERIE. Over three generations this company has nurtured a passion for the art of curing meat. With a foundation of experience, passion, tradition and commitment, the typical, original production methods fully respect the strict criteria established by the consortia for PDO and PGI specialities. The head office at San Daniele del Friuli includes a slicing centre for PDO Prosciutto San Daniele and other traditional Italian charcuterie. All phases of the production process are carefully monitored: from genetic selection of the pig breeds to their diet, butchering and selection of the meat, processing and the art of ageing. These are the features of the high quality range of charcuterie, prosciuttos and various types of sausage, distributed on a well-established international market, particularly the USA. Brendolan Service is part of the group with a range of speciality food products.

Brezzo

MONTEU ROERO (CN) I fraz. Tre Rivi, 87
☎ (+39) 017390109 ✪ www.brezzo.it
✉ miele@brezzo.it **shop:** yes **e-commerce:** no

HONEY. Brezzo was founded just after the end of WWII, in the early 1950s. Since then it has grown exponentially, both in terms of experience and achievement. Today the third generation has brought its skills and ideas to the table in the hopes of expanding the business's future prospects for growth. Their vision is one of adapting to consumer needs and changing tastes, while staying true to Brezzo's deep roots. Their selection of monofloral honeys is impressive (cardoon, strawberry tree, eucalyptus, lavender, sunflower) as are their royal blends (apple, pollens, propolis and royal jelly). Their selection also includes Mielcream (cocoa and Roero honey), Frutta Golosa (fruit conserved in honey), honey candies, organic honey vinegar, acacia honey with truffle, as well as hazelnut and almond honey spreads.

Buitoni

ASSAGO (MI) I via del Mulino, 6
☎ (+39) 0281811 ✿ www.buitoni.it
✉ relazioni.esterne@it.nestle.com **shop:** yes **e-commerce:** no

PASTA. In 1827 enterprising Giulia Boninsegni Buitoni and her husband opened a small production facility in the square of Sansepolcro. The pasta was made with durum wheat from Puglia, which was practically unknown at the time. In 1856 her son opened another pasta business in Città di Castello and the company became suppliers to the Savoy House, but the turning point came in 1861 with Giovanni Buitoni who began the production of gluten-rich pasta, a new dietary speciality. Advertising, praise and commitment to social issues continued the long story of this company whose products include today: bread substitutes (crackers and rusks), liquid and ready bases, pizzas, snacks, pesto and sauces (also gluten-free), traditional filled pastas, ready meals, frozen foods (La Valle degli Orti) and the latest line, Buitoni Idea (ready-to-cook chicken in paper flavoured with herbs. Buitoni is part of the Nestlé group.

C.C.OR.A.V. - Consorzio Cooperativo Ortofrutticolo Alto Viterbese

GROTTE DI CASTRO (VT) I loc. Salcinella
☎ (+39) 0763796117 I 0763796118 ✿ www.ccorav.it
✉ ccorav@ccorav.it **shop:** yes **e-commerce:** no

FLOURS, PULSES, CEREALS. C.C.OR.A.V. is a consortium that brings together five farm cooperatives from six municipalities in central Italy (Lago di Bolsena, Tuscany and Umbria). It's an area famous for its legumes, thanks to its volcanic, potassium-rich soil. The more than 600 farmers involved provide the consortium with pearled spelt, a variety of beans (fagiolo del Purgatorio, borlotto, ciavattone, della stoppia, cannelino and verdolino), Valentano chickpeas, Onano lentils, black chickpeas and, most importantly, potatoes (Alto Viterbese PGI, Alta Tuscia, red and purple varieties). They also sell a variety of bottled legumes, excellent Proceno red garlic (a pungent type of garlic that has myriad health benefits) and Jerusalem artichokes (white and red), recommended for those with celiac disease or diabetes. They also offer a range of interesting, alternative pasta varieties, with Senatore Cappelli wheat or chickpea flour, bronze wire-drawn into different shapes (penne, sedanini, fusilli, gnocchetti sardi...).

Cademartori

MILANO I via F. Gioia, 8
☎ (+39) 0243356111 ✪ www.cademartori.it
✉ ext.comm@it.lactalis.com **shop:** no **e-commerce:** no

CHEESE. Eugenio Cademartori opened his first dairy in Introbio, in Valsassina, in 1882. Since then production traditions have remained intact, as proved by the fact that cheese is still ripened in natural caves at Introbio. Taleggio cheese, from a native lactic ferment and salted by hand, was launched in 1923 thanks to Guido Cademartori, who took over the family business. In 1957 production was transferred to Società Lattiera di Certosa di Pavia, in the heart of the Po Valley, to optimize the milk collection cycle. In the early 2000s, the company joined the French group Lactalis and, eight years later, the Lactalis Italia holding was set up to include Cademartori, Galbani, Invernizzi, Locatelli and Président. The Cademartori label products include PDO Quartirolo, PDO Taleggio goat and sheep cheeses, caciotta, Provolone and other specialities.

Caffarel

LUSERNA SAN GIOVANNI (TO) I via Gianavello, 41
☎ (+39) 0121958111 ✪ www.caffarel.com
✉ caffarel@caffarel.com **shop:** yes **e-commerce:** no

CHOCOLATE. This was Italy's first chocolate factory. In 1826 Paolo Caffarel and his son had the brilliant idea of buying an old factory near Porta Susa, in Turin, and starting to manufacture chocolate there. In 1865, another intuition led to the creation of the gianduiotto. The Caffarels experimented with a new recipe that cut down the percentage of cocoa and increased the amount of hazelnuts, which abound in Piedmont. After 150 years the Caffarel gianduiotto still requires a high percentage of PGI Piedmont hazelnuts, mixed with the world's top cocoa and then extruded. It is no longer made by hand but with a machine designed specifically for the company and with the same rigorous attention to raw materials. Besides the classic and dark chocolate gianduiotto, there is the nocciolotto cube of gianduia and hazelnut; the Gentile hazelnut crisp; and the artisanal pralines. In 1997 Caffarel was acquired by Lindt & Sprüngli AG, but the confectionery company based in Luserna San Giovanni, retains its autonomy and its brand and product identity.

F.lli Caffo
Vecchio Amaro del Capo

LIMBADI (VV) I G. via Matteotti, 11
☎ (+39) 096385025 I 096385922 🖰 www.caffo.com
✉ info@caffo.com **shop:** yes **e-commerce:** no

UN SECOLO DI PASSIONE

Vecchio Amaro del Capo
l'Unico piacere ghiacciato!

LIQUEURS, SYRUPS, DISTILLATES. At the end of the 1800s, in the Etna foothills, Giuseppe Caffo started to distil marc in a business now about to celebrate its centenary. In 1915, Caffo acquired an old Sicilian distillery and began making liqueurs from aniseed and aromatic and medicinal herbs. The skills were handed down to future generations and then extended to include brandy and soft drinks. In 1966 Sebastiano Caffo took over the company Vecchio Amaro del Capo with his son Giuseppe Giovanni, today president of the group, which also has branches abroad. Next came a new plant next to the Limbadi distillery and in 2006 the acquisition of a distillery in the Udine area, Friulia, specializing in grappa processing. In 1999, the Caffo Beverages Inc. became importer of spirits, wines and other company products for America. Wild Orange Srl was opened in 2001, managing group business, and in the same year that Liquirizia Caffo Vibo Valentia plant, making Calabria liquorice and herb extracts under the Caffo and Taitù brands. Lastly we find Typical Srl, based in Leipzig and aiming to conquer the German market. Since 2013 the Caffo group also manages Borsci San Marzano.

Tonno Callipo

MAIERATO (VV) I s.s. 110, km 1,6
☎ (+39) 0963996211 🖰 www.callipo.com
✉ marketing@callipogroup.com **shop:** yes **e-commerce:** no

Storie di mare

PRESERVED FISH. When we say tuna, we immediately think of Callipo, the classic brand created in 1913 and renowned for the quality of its preserves, especially tuna in oil. The company uses the widespread yellowfin tuna, fished in the Atlantic and Indian oceans, frozen on board and processed in the Maierato plant, but also the increasingly rare Mediterranean bluefin. Products are bottled by hand. The company also offers botargo, anchovies, tuna belly, salmon, and mackerel, all of an excellent standard despite the large production quantities. The Callipo group includes Gelateria Callipo, which continues the Pizzo ice-cream tradition with products based on heritage recipes. Recently, this Maierato producer introduced a new line of preserves dedicated to the flavors and traditions of Calabria: marmalades made with citrus fruit, figs or pomegranate; compote of red onion, peperoncini or green tomatoes; and bottled 'nduja di Spilinga (a spicy condiment).

Distillerie Camel - Bepi Tosolini

POVOLETTO (UD) I via della Roggia, 20
☎ (+39) 0432664144 ✪ www.bepitosolini.it
✉ info@bepitosolini.it **shop:** yes **e-commerce:** yes

LIQUEURS, SYRUPS, DISTILLATES. This company has established itself in the upper ranks of national production of spirits, with the Bepi Tosolini line named after the founder, who built manual steam alembic stills that are still used today, the secret behind an excellent product. In 1973 the large distillery opened in Povoletto, with its traditional stills, again steam-fired and artisan, like the new bain-maries which were added. Bepi Tosolini products are divided into lines: single variety grappas, the Most series (obtained from distillation of selected grapes with the best array of aromas, and available in finely crafted bottles, glass and ampoules) and grappas from mixed grapes (prestigious black grapes, single variety moscato rosa, ramandolo, fragolino, ribolla gialla and the legendary picolit). The I Legni series consists of selected spirits aged in barriques in the Tosolini family cellars. Over time these have been joined by digestifs, spiced liqueurs and brandies.

Gruppo Campari Cinzano

SESTO SAN GIOVANNI (MI) I via F. Sacchetti, 20
☎ (+39) 0262251 ✪ www.cinzano.it
✉ campari@campari.com **shop:** yes **e-commerce:** yes

LIQUEURS, SYRUPS, DISTILLATES. In their small Turin shop, Giovanni and Carlo Cinzano, master spirit distillers, launched a new trend in aromatic wines, made with local herbs and spices in 1757. About 30 years later they were appointed official suppliers to the Royal Household and the Savoy family asked the Cinzanos to create a sparkling wine to compete with champagne. Thus, in 1840, the first Italian spumante was created, and is still a must in Italy with various types (dry, rosé, sweet). Since the late 19th century, vermouth (the quintessential base for Italian mixed drinks) and spumante conquered the rest of the world, reaching South Africa and South America. In 1887 a widespread advertising campaign was launched and in the early 20th century Cinzano opened its first production centre abroad, in Chamberry, France. From designer illustrations to television ads, from the post-War to the Sixties, Seventies and Eighties, advertising has played a fundamental role for Cinzano. Since 1999, Cinzano has been part of the Campari Group, which also includes the Aperol brand.

Campisi

PACHINO (SR) I fraz. Marzamemi I c.da Lettiera
☎ (+39) 0931841166 ✆ www.campisiconserve.it
✉ info@campisiconserve.it **shop:** yes **e-commerce:** yes

PRESERVES, JAMS. This family-run business (est. 1854), still upholds a centuries-old tradition of processing and transforming seafood. But there's a lot more to Campisi than that. Their product line can be divided into six categories: blue, azure, yellow, green, bordeaux and orange. The bulk of their products are made with tuna, available in different cuts and sizes: ventresca or tarantello (bottled chunks of tuna), buzzonaglia, lattume (longer, thick strips), smoked tuna, bottarga (dried and cured roe), garum (a kind of offal paté). Then there's their selection of anchovies, mackerel, grouper, swordfish, octopus and squid (also available in creams and patés). They have an assortment of salts, sauces and mixes (for example with certified cherry and datterini tomatoes), pestos and ready-made sauces. There are also wines, extra virgin olive oils, various types of pasta, Modica chocolate, honey, candies and preserves, various dried fruits and much more. You can even customize your own elegant gift packages.

CAO Formaggi

ORISTANO I loc. Fenosu I Perda Lada
☎ (+39) 0783301831 ✆ www.caoformaggi.it
✉ info@caoformaggi.it **shop:** yes **e-commerce:** no

CHEESE. CAO is a cooperative of sheep farmers founded in 1966 (the initials stand for Cooperativa Allevatori Ovini) that today boasts about 700 members (including president Renato Ilotto). Thanks to their efforts, CAO is a model of sustainability and quality. More than 26 million litres of milk, all produced on trusted local farms, undergo rigorous controls. The milk is then processed with care and respect for environmental impact, with the help of modern facilities. Pecorino PDO, both Roman and Sardo, is their pride and joy. The cheese is available in different ages and sizes (their bocconcini make convenient, bite-sized snacks). They also offer enticing, naturally flavored varieties: truffle, spicy peperoncino chili, myrtle and black pepper. In addition to soft and aged pecorino, they offer light and salted ricotta and pecorino cream (extremely versatile in the kitchen). Their high-end line, Pastore Sardo, features the bold and tangy Gran Riserva, which is aged for at least three months.

Antico Molino Caputo

NAPOLI I c.so San Giovanni a Teduccio, 63
☎ (+39) 0817520566 ✪ www.molinocaputo.it
✉ info@molinocaputo.it **shop:** no **e-commerce:** no

La Farina di Napoli

FLOURS, PULSES, CEREALS. Since 1924, the name Caputo has been synonymous with flour, both in Naples and beyond. Over several generations the producer has represented, and still represents, in the best possible way, the culture and tradition of 'the white art'. It all starts with having the right wheat, both Italian and foreign-grown varieties, making sure they all meet the highest standards of quality. Environmental impact is reduced by guaranteeing the minimum possible waste throughout all phases of processing, which is also carried out slowly so as to protect the nutritional integrity of the flour. Neither conservatives, nor enzymes nor chemicals are used in the so-called 'Caputo method' (a well-kept secret), which also ensures that the flavor is natural and authentic. There are several varieties, including 00 pastry flour, 'strong flour', whole wheat, multi-grain, organic and gluten-free flours. Indeed, there is a flour for every need, from making bread to pizza to pasta or pastries.

Carozzi

PASTURO (LC) I via Provinciale, 14a
☎ (+39) 0341955173 ✪ www.carozzi.com
✉ info@carozzi.com **shop:** yes **e-commerce:** yes

CHEESE. In the heart of Valsassina, for more than half a century, Carozzi has been producing high-end cheeses with both an eye towards tradition and a sensitivity to today's consumer tastes. Quality milk, favorable climate, experience, passion and care are all at the foundation of their products, which include a selection of rare, internationally recognized, award-winning cheeses. They also make various flavors of yogurt (with cow's milk or goat's milk), ricotta, stracchino (also available with goat's milk), mozzarella, mascarpone, robiola and primo sale (cheese made with sheep's milk). They have cheeses with 'natural rinds' (like ricciolo, montanara and fontal) as well as 'washed rinds' (Vaalassina 'valunt', crottino and salva cremasco), all the way up to their certified PDO line (Gorgonzola, Quartirolo and Taleggio, all available in different ages). To purchase or simply taste a sample of this veritable treasure trove, or for a meal or snack, check out la Formaggeria, a simple, cozy shop and eatery that's open all day.

Carpenè Malvolti

CONEGLIANO (TV) I via A. Carpenè, 1
☎ (+39) 0438364611 ✤ www.carpenemalvolti.com
✉ info@carpene-malvolti.com **shop:** yes **e-commerce:** no

LIQUEURS, SYRUPS, DISTILLATES. Passion and tradition for 147 years. Antonio Carpenè's brainchild was founded in 1868 to produce a sparkling wine from the grapes of the Conegliano and Valdobbiadene hills. It was the first to make fine prosecco using good quality, scientifically monitored production systems instead of the more empirical versions of the time. It is no coincidence that Antonio Carpenè perfected the Charmat method in Italy, applying it to prosecco with decisive and significant modifications. His love for the land, culture and wine led him to set up the Scuola Enologica in Conegliano Veneto. The longstanding commitment of this family, now in its fourth generation, is responsible for the first official Prosecco di Conegliano, written on the label back in 1924. Today Carpenè's leading products are still Prosecco DOC and DOCG (from Brut to Extra Dry) as well as fine quality spirits (grappa and brandy). The historical headquarters is at Conegliano Veneto and the cellar is at Follina. Since 2010 the business has worked with Gruppo Italiano Vini for distribution on the national market.

Selezione Casillo

CORATO (BA) I via Sant'Elia Zona Industriale
☎ (+39) 0808726673 ✤ www.selezionecasillo.com
✉ info@selezionecasillo.com **shop:** no **e-commerce:** no

FLOURS, PULSES, CEREALS. Boosted by sixty years of experience in the industry, the Casillo Group has become a leader in wheat processing and sales. With the help of their president, Francesco Casillo, the firm has set itself apart for innovating and experimenting with new processing techniques, for its tightly regulated operations, the transparency and traceability of the ingredients used and the care it takes in securing its facilities. All this guarantees consistent (and consistently high) standards of quality, despite the high volumes of flour produced and sold. And there are many types (including stone ground varieties, multi-grain and a 'signature' series promoted by famous chefs), varieties for home use and for professionals, all adapted to specific needs, from bread to pasta, pizza, focaccia, sweets and even for batters. Tomato sauces are also sold, as well as pre-cooked, semolina couscous. During the year they organize courses for food lovers and professionals.

Casoni Fabbricazione Liquori

FINALE EMILIA (MO) I via Venezia, 5a
☎ (+39) 0535760811 ❖ www.casoni.com
✉ info@casoni.com **shop:** no **e-commerce:** no

LIQUEURS, SYRUPS, DISTILLATES. Opened in 1814, today Casoni is a solid business and one of the leading brands in Europe in the production of liqueurs and spirits. Over the years the Modena company has expanded its range of products, specializing mainly in typical Italian regional liqueurs, with an eye to new consumer trends and increasingly mindful of exports. Its strengths are a bond with tradition, specialist know-how, flexibility, in-house production of infusions and distillates, and large-scale production capacity, guaranteed by the production plants: two in Finale Emilia (Via Venezia and Via San Lorenzo) and one in Slovakia (near Kosice). Casoni produces hundreds of liqueurs and spirits, including Sambuca, Amaro, Amaretto, Anicione, Limoncello di Sorrento, Nocino di Modena, Bitter, Fernet, Crema Caffè and Aperitivo 1814, a refreshing bitter-sweet, low-alcohol beverage made with the Casoni family's venerable recipe of herbs, fruits and seeds.

Roberto Castagner

VAZZOLA (TV) I fraz. Visnà I via Bosco, 43
☎ (+39) 0438793811 ❖ www.robertocastagner.it
✉ info@robertocastagner.it **shop:** no **e-commerce:** no

LIQUEURS, SYRUPS, DISTILLATES. One of the leading distilleries in Italy, still protecting tradition today, in an ideal blend with innovation in the plants at Visnà di Vazzola, in the province of Treviso at the foot of the Conegliano hills. Roberto Castagner has no ancestors, and represents his own first generation, producing grappa (also for large-scale distribution) with passion, respect for nature and intelligent entrepreneurship alongside his daughters and grandchildren, the latest addition to the business. An avant-garde spirit, excellent ingredients (fresh smoked single variety marc), copper stills alongside glass and gold, and experience as master distillers: these are the ingredients of the traditional line which includes various jewels like Fuoriclasse Leon (an extraordinary product in content and bottle shape) and the Collezione Capolavoro, Le Torbate, Le Millesimate, a line of spirits, drinks, vodkas, brandies and some wines.

Citterio

RHO (MI) I c.so Europa, 2016
☎ (+39) 02935161 ✆ www.citterio.com
✉ info@citterio.com **shop:** no **e-commerce:** no

CHARCUTERIE. Giuseppe Citterio Ltd. was founded in 1878 and is among Italy's first and oldest producers of deli meats. Their approach, which is about staying current while passionate and committed to tradition, has allowed them to solidify their reputation as a top-quality producer and a leader in the field. With more than 100 years of experience, and a knowledge of ancient, proven recipes, they know what it takes to guarantee quality and flavor. But they also aren't afraid to adapt to today's consumer, with a host of products that includes organic meats, speck, cooked ham, prosciutto, bresaola, baked turkey breast... They offer seasonal meats like cotechino and zampone, as well as classics like mortadella and salami (including Cacciatore PDO), Vienna sausage, coppa and pancetta. Some of their meats are also available in convenient snack-size packaging.

Coam

MORBEGNO (SO) I v.le Stelvio, 286
☎ (+39) 0342604411 ✆ www.coamspa.it
✉ info@coamspa.it **shop:** yes **e-commerce:** yes

PRESERVED FISH. Coam got its start in 1964, selling bottled porcini mushrooms and vegetables like artichokes, peppers, eggplant etc., which are still available today under the brand name Le Conserve di Morbegno. Ten years later they began dealing in prized salmon, using the brand Scandia. Caught by hand and only delivered through the cold chain from well-equipped vessels, the fish is completely wild, as is their Mediterranean and Indian Ocean swordfish and tuna (yellow and longfin). The same is true of their Norwegian and Scottish salmon, sturgeon, lobster, crab, prawns, octopus, Trentino lake trout and Lombard lavarello lake fish. They also offer farm-raised salmon, both Scottish and Norwegian varieties, all carefully controlled. They have smoked fish, as well as raw and steamed fish, fish in oil or marinated in herbs. They also distribute fish roe (salmon, lumpfish, tuna bottarga and mullet) and offer elegant gift packaging for an unusual but always well-received gourmet present.

Giulio Cocchi

COCCONATO (AT) I via Liprandi, 21
☎ (+39) 0141600071 ✆ www.cocchi.it
✉ cocchi@cocchi.com **shop:** yes **e-commerce:** no

LIQUEURS, SYRUPS, DISTILLATES. In 1891 Giulio Cocchi moved to Asti to open a home distillery/winery, producing his own speciality aromatic wines. Today the selection includes fragrant vermouths, like 'The Americano' (now world famous and a common ingredient in cocktails), Barolo Chinato, the amaro vermouth Dopo Teatro, the aged 'reserve', La Venaria Reale, and the Cocchi Rosa (a mix of Piedmont red wine, herbs and spices like gentian, quinine, citrus peels and rose petals). Then there's their grappas, 100% Dorée di Moscato d'Asti, white grappa (made with the fragrant pomace of Barbera grapes from the Monferrato hills), and for die-hard fans, their Aquaforte brandy. Standouts from their Alta Langa sparkling wine selection include Bianc 'd Bianc, vintage and 'Primosecolo', made with 100% chardonnay. For those who are interested in tasting their products, they have bars in Turin, Savona and Levanto (in Cinque Terre).

Colussi

MILANO I via G. Spadolini, 5
☎ (+39) 02847841 ✆ www.colussigroup.it
✉ colussi@colussigroup.it **shop:** no **e-commerce:** no

PATISSERIE. Venice, 1911. Angelo Colussi opened his first artisan workshop, a bakery making only bread at first, but soon specializing in baicoli, the city's traditional biscuit. In the 1930s his children took over the business and started a transition to an industrial scale, opening their first factory with cutting-edge facilities. The memorable Gran Turchese butter biscuit was launched in 1953, consumed at breakfast by generations of Italians. In the 1980s, product diversification arrived, flanking biscuits with new lines dedicated to melba toasts and crackers. The 1990s continued without setback and growth thanks to market launches of pasta, rice and condiments, baked goods and pastries. The development of the Colussi Group followed, to address overseas markets. The group owns factories in Piedmont, Lombardy, Liguria, Tuscany and Umbria, comprising five top Italian brands like Colussi, Misura, Agnesi, Flora and Sapori Siena 1832.

Concast - Gruppo Formaggi del Trentino - Trentingrana

PREDAIA (TN) I loc. Segno I via della Cooperazione, 4
☎ (+39) 0463469256 ✿ www.formaggideltrentino.it
✉ info@formaggideltrentino.it **shop:** yes **e-commerce:** no

GRUPPO FORMAGGI del TRENTINO
Gustatevi il nostro mondi

CHEESE. The Gruppo Formaggi del Trentino, born in 2010 from the synergy of different local cheese-makers (Trentingrana and Concast, Consorzio dei Caseifici Sociali Trentini), processes, ages and markets its own milk from partners, public and private companies. There are two lines: Trentingrana (a type of Grana Padano) and Tradizionale (dedicated to other typical regional soft-paste cheeses). The genuineness of the products comes primarily from the healthy nutrition of cattle fed with the scented hay of mountain pastures and non-GMO feed, which guarantees the sensorial qualities of the milk. The company's flagship is Trentino grana, a hard cooked-paste cheese with delicate but decisive fragrances if made with summer milk; when ripened it develops a strong, slightly savoury flavour. Alongside there are other cheeses including Moena puzzone, Trentino vezzena, Val di Sole casolet, Cavalese fontal, Sabbionara affogato, Primiero tosela. There are other mountain pasture products in the range as well as Trentino butter.

Condorelli

BELPASSO (CT) I c.da Timpa Magna
☎ (+39) 095913630 ✿ www.condorelli.it
✉ condorelli@condorelli.it **shop:** yes **e-commerce:** yes

PATISSERIE. Francesco Condorelli was just 21when he became the owner of the Borrello patisserie, but he was then involved in the war and his business ground to a halt. Back in Sicily, he returned to work at Belpasso, at the foot of Mount Etna, and it became a magnet. From 1933 the story continued until the company grew to the point that it became today's Dolciaria Belpasso. The real breakthrough, however, came in the 1960s with the invention of a bite-size soft iced nougat, called Condorelli, and which conquered the world market. The facilities make 160 specialities for the festivities and for daily consumption, products made with the best raw materials (Sicilian almonds, Bronte pistachio, local honey) and, of course, the nougats (white chocolate, vanilla, orange, lemon, coffee or classic milk chocolate). But Condorelli also produces almond milk, confectionery, chocolate and specialities like marzipan and jams.

Le Conserve della Nonna

RAVARINO (MO) I via Confine, 1583
☎ (+39) 059900432 ✆ nonsolobuono.it
✉ info@nonsolobuono.it **shop:** no **e-commerce:** no

La natura diventa bontà

PRESERVES, JAMS. Founded in 1973, in the lush Modena countryside, Conserve della Nonna is a well-known brand of the Fini Group. The principles underlying their production approach are simple: only select products are used, all of which are '0 kilometer' (from local orchards and farms); fruits and vegetables are only harvested when ripe, and then processed within 24 hours so as to guarantee their freshness and flavor. No additives or conservatives are used and cutting-edge technology sees to it that nutritional properties remain intact, along with color, flavor and texture. There are more than a hundred items to choose from: canned fruits, preserves, sauces, ragus, pestos, pickles and bottled vegetables, vegetable patés and creams. They also have certified organic products and have taken pains to respect the environment: the company installed enough solar cells to provide almost all their own energy needs.

Conserve Italia

SAN LAZZARO DI SAVENA (BO) I via P. Poggi, 11
☎ (+39) 0516228311 ✆ www.cirio.it
✉ conserveitalia@ccci.it **shop:** no **e-commerce:** no

PRESERVES, JAMS. Not many people know that Francesco Cirio began his business in Turin, at the Porta Palazzo vegetable market. Here he started trading fruit and vegetables to France and England. In 1856 he was only 20 years old when he opened his first Cirio plant, using the preservation method devised by the Frenchman Appert. In 1867 he presented his products at the Paris Expo and later opened other canning plants in the south of Italy. When he died, in the early 1900s, his partner Pietro Signorini laid solid foundations in the Naples area. By the 1920s, thanks to advertising and promotion, Cirio became a household name for Italians and consumption of its products spread throughout the country. In 2004 it was acquired by Gruppo Cooperativo Conserve Italia, the European leader in the canning industry. Today the company produces tomato preserves, concentrate, peeled and puréed, sauces and condiments. Also available are pulses, vegetables, oil and vinegar. Cirio has always paid great attention to research and innovation, to ensure excellent quality products with high service content.

Corsini

CASTEL DEL PIANO (GR) I via delle Cellane, 9
☎ (+39) 0564956787 I 0564957308 ✿ www.corsinibiscotti.com
✉ info@corsinibiscotti.com **shop:** no **e-commerce:** no

PATISSERIE. Among the woods and pastures of Monte Amiata you'll find Corsini, the historic bakery that has dominated Maremma Toscana since 1921. The history of the Corsini family is one of bread and biscotti. It has its beginnings in the oven of Corrado and Solidea, who set in motion a long tradition that has passed down from one generation to the next right through to today. Indeed, even if the company has allowed itself to evolve over time, growing into a modern facility with a number of employees, it has managed to maintain its artisanal roots and, most importantly, emphasis on care when it comes to ingredients and quality. Among its many specialities, its cantuccini deserve a special place (available in many varieties, including 'classic'). Their truly alluring selection of ancient Tuscan recipes includes Polendina made with chestnut flour, Amiata focaccia and Pandesanti. And, of course, biscotti and sweets abound: soft amaretti cookies, cavallucci, ricciarelli, panforte, melba toast, sweets, tarts and tart slices and cakes. They also produce seasonal specialities like nougat, panettone and colombe Easter cakes.

Mario Costa

CASALINO (NO) I loc. Orfengo I via dell'Industria, 26
☎ (+39) 0321877566 ✿ www.mariocosta.it
✉ info@mariocosta.it **shop:** no **e-commerce:** no

CHEESE. In 1919 Mario Costa founded his industrial cheese-making facility, but today most of the cheese made there is still worked by hand, according to tradition (with only select milk, rennet, and cultures) using tried and true practices. Gorgonzola PDO is their speciality, with care taken throughout all phases of production, starting with processing the milk. International audiences have shown favor to this sharp, tangy cheese in particular, and demand keeps growing. The extended aging process used guarantees its high-quality and means that it is suitable for those who have difficulty digesting lactose (as bacteria consume the lactose during fermentation). There are four types of this versatile cheese: Gran Riserva, Dolcificato (sweet), Piccante (with more bite than usual) and with mascarpone. Don't underestimate their Taleggio PDO, another excellent product that's worth trying.

Curtiriso

VALLE LOMELLINA (PV) I via Stazione, 113
☎ (+39) 0384700011 ❀ www.curtiriso.it
✉ info@curtiriso.it **shop:** no **e-commerce:** no

RICE. The company's history began around 1875 when Virginio Curti set up the first refinery in Gemonio on the foothills of the Varese Pre-Alps. Not long after, the old rice processing systems began to be replaced with modern machinery, and this phase was completed in 1911. The War stopped production, but new plants appeared with the economic upturn. Curti was probably the leading Italian rice manufacturer with the most carefully selected growers, and in the 1970s already had five production plants. In 1987 the company was sold to Buitoni, which merged with Nestlé Italiana in 1992. Since 1996 they have invested in clean energy and also produce organic rice. Today the company controls Antica Riseria Campiverdi, Riso Ornati, Pigino, Riso Rolo and is part of the Euricom group. A wide range of different types of rice is accompanied by rice-based products (cereal crackers, also organic) and a line of ready-to-serve risottos.

Fratelli D'Acunzi

NOCERA SUPERIORE (SA) I s.da prov.le 81 via Porta Romana, 85
☎ (+39) 0815144949 ❀ www.dacunzi.it
✉ dacunzisrl@tiscali.it **shop:** yes **e-commerce:** no

PRESERVES, JAMS. Thanks to its modern facility and its reputation for safety and environmentally-friendly practices, this family-run business has become one of the most important producers in the region. The D'Acunzi family (brothers Filippo, Giovanni and Pasquale and sister Raffaella) make sure that every stage of production is subject to careful controls, from harvest, which is timed to guarantee ripeness, to packaging and labeling. D'Acunzi manage two brands: La Carmela and Orto d'Oro. The former includes peeled San Marzano tomatoes, canned/bottled fruits and vegetables (peppers and mushrooms) and legumes (various types of beans, lentils, chickpeas and peas). They also have cooked grain for 'la pastiera', a traditional sweet in Campania. Orto d'Oro comprises tomatoes in various forms (peeled, finely chopped, concentrate, double concentrate, purée) and peach purée.

Andrea Da Ponte

TARZO (TV) I fraz. Corbanese I via I Maggio, 1
☎ (+39) 0438933011 ❂ www.daponte.it
✉ info@daponte.it **shop:** yes **e-commerce:** no

LIQUEURS, SYRUPS, DISTILLATES. The art of distillation is at home here. In 1896 Matteo Da Ponte published a manual of distillation, illustrating for the first time his patented alembic stills and the first concentration columns for alcohol steam, made to refine and soften an authentic spirit but with a rough and ready flavour. This is the Da Ponte method, invented by a worthy heir of the head of the dynasty, Andrea Da Ponte, predecessor of Liberale Fabris, the founder's grandson, who created a monovarietal grappa in the 1960s from prosecco marc, and gave rise to the Vecchia Grappa di Prosecco aged in barriques. With the aim of improving this spirit and raising its quality, in 1979 he transferred the distillery to the Corbanese di Tarzo basin. The story and tradition is carried forward by his son who shows vision and skill, also revealed in the production of many different ranges of liqueurs and some excellent spumante wines alongside the leading product, prosecco grappa 120° (limited edition with only 1,000 numbered champagne bottles).

Olio Dante

MONTESARCHIO (BN) I via Badia zona Industriale
☎ (+39) 0824894141 ❂ www.oleificimataluni.com
✉ info@mataluni.com **shop:** no **e-commerce:** no

EXTRA VIRGIN OLIVE OIL. After being sold to foreign companies the brand returned to Italy in 2009, purchased by Oleifici Mataluni (which includes Dante, Oio, Olita, Topazio and Vero). The Sommo Poeta label came home, and not long after, production was moved to Montesarchio (Benevento) in a modern plant equipped with a highly specialized laboratory for quality control and a research centre for developing oil materials and innovative packaging (Criol).This is the most recent history but the older part dates back to 1849 when Andrea Costa started trading in oil in Genoa with cargo ships and were the forerunners of the famous Costa Crociere liners. The name was coined to association oil with Italy. The leading products are 100% extra virgin olive oil and Terre Antiche, alongside the seed oils with added vitamins.

Leading brands

De Cecco dal 1886

FARA SAN MARTINO (CH) I zona Industriale
☎ (+39) 08729861 ✪ www.dececco.it
✉ dececco@dececco.it **shop:** yes **e-commerce:** yes

PASTA. Before producing pasta at Fara San Martino, don Nicola De Cecco made the best flour in the district in his stone mill. His son Filippo began making pasta, and in 1886 the Molino e Pastificio dei Fratelli De Cecco was created. Combining artisan experience and engineering ideas, they made a low-temperature drying machine. The boom after World War 2 grew the company to its present size, and in 1950 the Pescara pasta factory was opened. Much has changed over the years, except the basic principles of the founder, to use premium wheat, fresh flour, bronze machinery, slow, low temperature drying and quality control. Today F.lli De Cecco di Filippo Spa is an Italian food company specializing in the production of pasta, flour, olive oil and sauces, with a central plant and two more in Fara San Martino and Caldari di Ortona.

De Rica

GENOVA I p.zza Borgo Pila, 39 Corte dei Lambruschini Torre B
☎ (+39) 0105308711 ✪ www.derica.it
✉ info@generaleconserve.it **shop:** no **e-commerce:** no

PRESERVES, JAMS. In 1912, a factory with 20 workers in the Piacenza countryside was using cooking and pureeing equipment to can tomatoes and vegetables. In 1932, Giuseppe Bianchi bought the company and developed production without setbacks, even during the war. The factory was enlarged and in 1953 the first trials for mechanical peeling of tomatoes were set up. The preserves crossed national borders, travelling to England, Germany, North America, and Japan. In 1957 the company was acquired by Luigi Tononi, owner of Industria Conserve Alimentari, which focused entirely on tomato production. The De Rica brand was not developed until 1963, for a name easy to identify and remember. Production diversified with sauces, pulses, fruit in syrup and jams. For a time it was part of Cirio Bertolli De Rica Spa, but in 2013 switched to Generale Conserve of Genoa.

Defendi

CARAVAGGIO (BG) I fraz. Vidalengo I via Francesca, 4
☎ (+39) 0363305076 ❀ www.caseificiodefendi.it
✉ info@caseificiodefendi.it **shop:** yes **e-commerce:** no

CHEESE. Defendi specializes in the production, aging and selling of cheeses common to northern Italy, though Gorgonzola, the most famous of Italy's blue cheeses, and Taleggio, a local speciality, are on center stage here. Bolstered by more than 150 years of experience, production focuses on these two crown jewels and includes Sweet and Sharp Gorgonzola PDO (Bacco and Bacco Verde, respectively), Capriccio (Gorgonzola and Mascarpone), Taleggio PDO (Il Caravaggio), Quartirolo Lombardo PDO, Primavera di Caravaggio (a washed-rind cheese made with cow's milk, whose flavor is both sweet and mild). There are also cheeses made with buffalo milk. Their Baffalo Blu is a blue cheese, and they offer a buffalo Camembert. Bufaletto is a buffalo-cow milk mix (a washed-rind cheese that's similar to Taleggio). Their cheeses are made through a combination of modern technology and manual methods using only Italian milk from select producers.

Delicius Rizzoli

TORRILE (PR) I fraz. San Polo I via Micheli, 2
☎ (+39) 0521813525 ❀ www.delicius.org
✉ info@delicius.it **shop:** no **e-commerce:** no

PRESERVED FISH. Delicius Rizzoli, which got its start in Parma in 1974, is a leader in the field of canned fish. Over the course of its more than 40 years of operations, Delicius has managed to achieve an important position in the market, as well as expand the selection of products offered. Thanks to their multi-plant strategy, the producer has facilities in five Mediterranean countries, and the scale of operations is global, assuring them a presence in those locations where fish are first caught, then selected and controlled. Their selection of products includes anchovies, tuna, mackerel and sardines, all preserved in pull-tab aluminium cans. There's also a top-of-the-range line in glass jars and organic products, as well. Here, tradition goes hand-in-hand with innovation. Indeed, over the years, they've also introduced more creative products, like the Alici Double (a rich anchovy paste), grilled mackerel and sardines, a line of products known as Fantasie, and a spicy selection. They also produce shrimp and clams in glass jars.

Delverde

FARA SAN MARTINO (CH) I zona Industriale
☎ (+39) 08729951 ⚘ www.delverde.eu
✉ info@delverde.it **shop:** yes **e-commerce:** yes

DELVERDE

SORGENTE DEL FIUME VERDE
SOURCE OF THE VERDE RIVER

ITALY

PASTA. Quality, respect for the environment and tradition are the commandments that Delverde has always observed since it opened for business. Of course, the pure water of Mount Majella, the best durum wheat flour, bronze dies and low drying temperatures make a big difference compared to other pasta brands. This production philosophy, which today embraces oil, preserves and ready sauces, dates back to 1967 when the company began to exploit centuries-old Abruzzo traditions. Today Delverde Spa produces 130 different types of fresh and dry pasta, egg pasta, organic white and wholemeal, and cutting-edge products introduced in 2016, from special flours blended with chickpeas and linseed. The parent company Molinos Rio de la Plata s.a. company, a leader in the farm food sector in Latin America, bought the majority share in Delverde in 2009.

Vincenzo Di Iorio

PIETRADEFUSI (AV) I fraz. Dentecane I via Roma, 145
☎ (+39) 0825962097 ⚘ www.torronediiorio.com
✉ info@torronediiorio.com **shop:** yes **e-commerce:** no

PATISSERIE. Just off highway A16, tucked away in a hamlet of Irpinia, lies an exemplary family-run business that has for generations, over three centuries, upheld the national art of the turrón. Artisanal craftsmanship ('manual' might be a better word for it) and select ingredients (honey, Giffoni hazelnuts, Azola almonds, cocoa etc.) are at the foundation of this brand's success. They offer a diverse, and delicious, product line, starting with classic almond or hazelnut nougat, either coated or filled with chocolate. Then there are the 'bi-flavor' nougats, sweet blocks filled with chocolate and vaniglia, double decker cubes called 'cremini di torrone', a sponge cake 'pantorrone' (also available in a limoncello variety) as well as soft, crumbly and crunchy varieties of turròn nuggets (almond or hazelnut). There are also plenty of confetti candies (almond, hazelnut, with or without chocolate), chocolate covered hazelnuts, soft amaretti cookies, maron glacé and mostaccioli (including the decadent 'imbottita' variety).

Di Martino

GRAGNANO (NA) I via Castellammare, 82
☎ (+39) 0818012984 I 0818018251 ✆ www.pastadimartino.com
✉ info@dimartinonline.it **shop:** yes **e-commerce:** no

PASTA. True passion and dedication, an indivisible pairing for Giuseppe Di Martino since he began his business, whose cornerstone was a production process closely linked to Gragnano tradition. He worked in the cells of the factory and once he became an expert mixer the owner allowed him some shares in the pasta factory. It was 1912 and that was how Di Martino began, with its own secret source of mineral water: it was the age of pasta sold loose or in tin boxes, which often crossed the Ocean. A family history made of old skills and quality, inscribed today in the long and short forms of pasta, also the wholemeal and bio versions. Through the Dicado company, owned by the Di Martino family, the company bought the Amato pasta factory and thus saved it from extinction.

Divella

RUTIGLIANO (BA) I l.go D. Divella, 1
☎ (+39) 0804779111 ✆ www.divella.it
✉ divella@divella.it **shop:** no **e-commerce:** yes

PASTA. While the company founded by Francesco Divella way back in 1890 has evolved and developed over time, it's also managed to stay true to a few important principles: constant quality controls, careful selection of ingredients, the use of the best modern technology, attention to consumer health and safety and, last but not least, respect for the environment and social responsibility. They offer a vast selection of products, starting with a host of classic dried pasta varieties. Then there is their line of bronze wire-drawn pasta, their speciality pasta brand (including traditional regional pastas like orecchiette), egg noodles and rice. And they've got plenty of toppings to go with all that pasta: peeled and sliced tomato sauce, ready-made sauces, canned beans, balsamic vinegar and extra virgin olive oil. There's also a product line for making breads and pastries, a variety of flour, biscotti, snacks and breakfast snacks and hazelnut cream spread.

Domori

NONE (TO) I via Pinerolo, 72
☎ (+39) 0119863465 ✿ www.domori.com
✉ domori@domori.com **shop:** yes **e-commerce:** yes

CHOCOLATE. Gianluca Franzoni (also known as Mack Domori), founder and president of Domori, is a true champion of chocolate culture. He is the first producer in Italy to oversee every stage of chocolate production from start to finish, starting with his own plantation, the Hacienda San José, in Venezuela. From there, dozens of varieties of aromatic cocoa are shipped to his facility near Turin, where they are processed using systems designed to respect each cocoa's specific sensorial qualities, in the fewest possible cycles and low temperatures. And from there, it's all about what doesn't happen: no vanilla, cocoa butter or soy lecithin. Just cocoa and cane sugar. The producer, now part of the Illy group, targets purists, especially their Single Origins and Criollo lines. We recommend their Porcelana, Canoabo and Chuao. Their cream spreads are deliciously enticing, as are their chocolate bars with hazelnuts (obviously certified Tonda Gentile Piemonte PGI).

La Doria

ANGRI (SA) I via Nazionale, 320
☎ (+39) 0815166111 ✿ www.gruppoladoria.com
✉ commerciale.italia@gruppoladoria.it **shop:** no **e-commerce:** no

PRESERVES, JAMS. Doria opened in 1954 at Angri, the Agro Nocerino Sarnese, the heart of the "red gold" district. At the time the area was known for its intensive cultivation of San Marzano tomato, whose massive presence contributed to the development of agri-industrial production. It is still the main national hub for processing tomato preserves. Today the La Doria group is a leader in the production and marketing of products derived from tomatoes, fruit juices, ready sauces, canned pulses and pasta. In Italy it has seven manufacturing facilities and a trading company in the UK. The brands that make up the group, in addition to Doria, are La Romanella, Vivi G, Vivi G bio and Cook Italian.

EcorNaturaSì

SAN VENDEMIANO (TV) I via Palù, 23 Z.A.
☎ (+39) 0438720410 ❀ www.ecornaturasi.it
✉ info@ecornaturasi.it **shop:** no **e-commerce:** no

NATURAL FOOD. In 2009 Ecor, the largest national distributor of organic and biodynamic products merged with NaturaSì, the main national supermarket specializing in organic and biodynamic products. The results was EcorNaturaSì. The group's philosophy focuses on promoting healthy diet and their initiatives include supporting biodynamic farms that work towards sustainability and environmentally sound practices. Constant, rigorous controls on behalf of consumer health are central to their mission. Only seasonal fruits and vegetables are sold. Harvests are timed so as to guarantee maximum freshness, flavor and nutritional value. Their large selection includes products for those with gluten, lactose and yeast intolerances.

Elah Dufour

NOVI LIGURE (AL) I s.da Serravalle, 73
☎ (+39) 0143313311 ❀ elah-dufour.it
✉ info@elah-dufour.it **shop:** no **e-commerce:** no

CHOCOLATE. A glorious century and a half of history stretches behind Elah Dufour, the group that today embraces 4 important brands in the confectionery sector: Elah, Dufour, Novi, and Baratti & Milano. The oldest of these is Baratti & Milano, a company founded in Torino in 1858, specialized in the classics of Piedmontese sweet traditions: gianduiotti, cremini, cuneesi, braidesi, and pralines with Piedmontese hazelnuts as well as "Baratti" candies. Over time, the production site moved to Bra (near Cuneo), while the historic shop is in the centrally located Piazza Castello of Torino, the city of the royal Savoia family. The store still has its original 19th century décor. Next came Novi, established in Novi Ligure in 1903 and devoted to chocolate production: Fondentenero, Gran Cru Nero Nero, Gianduja Piemonte, gianduiotti, Otello pralines, Novi spreadable cream. Elah, dedicated to the preparation of sweet spreads, puddings and desserts, was founded in 1909 in Genoa by Francesco Ferdinando Moliè. The Dufour family, also in Genoa, in 1926 created the firm that carries its name, specialized in fruit gelatin candy, chocolate bonbons and a wide variety of filled candies.

Fabbri 1905

BOLOGNA I via Emilia Ponente, 276
☎ (+39) 0516173111 ✆ www.fabbri1905.com
✉ info@fabbri1905.com **shop:** no **e-commerce:** yes

PATISSERIE. Black cherries in syrup are the symbol of this century-old producer from Emilia Romagna. For four generations (the fifth is on its way), they have packaged and sold their 'amarene' in the classic blue and white ceramic vase, an idea that goes back to their founder, Gennaro Fabbri. Perfect for sweets, as a topping on ice cream or in fruit cups, their flavor is unmistakable. Their product line includes their famous syrups, which are used in refreshing, cold drinks (they also have an organic mint variety). Then there are their sweet sauces, various types of toppings (a recent addition is there organic agave), gelatin topping (powdered or spray on etc.), fruit juice concentrates (excellent for cocktails), fruit in liquor, marron glacé, almond milk, hot chocolate mix and mixes for jellies, sorbets etc. There's also a line of products for food professionals: ice cream makers, cafés, bakers, restaurant owners... Their mission is and always has been simple: quality.

Farchioni

GUALDO CATTANEO (PG) I via Centrale Madonna del Puglia
☎ (+39) 074292951 I 0742929595 ✆ www.farchioni.eu
✉ farchioni@farchioni.com **shop:** no **e-commerce:** no

EXTRA VIRGIN OLIVE OIL. Since 1780 this Spoleto company has produced oil, wine and flour, moving to Giano dell'Umbria in 1920. Since then it began selling its own oil, from the best olives. Today Farchioni's green gold is the fruit of decades of work, research and experience. From its foundation to the present day the company has reached significant competitive levels. The product lines include PDO oils, single cultivars, 100% Italian, products for restaurant use and flavoured oil. Today Gruppo Alimentare Farchioni consists of many farms, farm industries and services. Since 2000, with the creation of Terre della Custodia, it has also produced wine.

Felsineo

ZOLA PREDOSA (BO) I via C. Masetti, 8
☎ (+39) 0513517011 ۞ www.felsineo.com
✉ info@felsineo.com **shop:** no **e-commerce:** no

CHARCUTERIE. Since 1947, generations of Raimondi family have made sure that the name Raimondi means mortadella, the traditional Italian lunch meat from Emilia Romagna. At their plant in Zola Predosa Felsineo they produce only that, though in a number of varieties, including the excellent Bologna PGI (about a third of the entire PGI on the market, making it the leading brand in Italy by far). There's the Sciccosa, which comes wrapped in a dark skin, the Sincera, suitable for those with gluten or lactose intolerances, the Nera, seasoned with pieces of black truffle, the Rossa, flavored with peperoncino chili, the Rustica, with pieces of prosciutto, and much more. The list of ingredients is short: lean pork shoulder, pork fat, tripe, garlic, salt, pepper and conservatives. With its warm pink color, its compact texture, the pleasingly occasional chunk of meat and odd piece of fat, their mortadella is the result of tried and true recipes and techniques. Digestibility is a main priority, and they're determined to seek out new ways to please consumer expectations without compromising flavor and quality.

Ferrarelle

RIARDO (CE) I c.da Ferrarelle
☎ (+39) 0823649111 I 02574608 ۞ www.ferrarelle.it
✉ commerciale@ferrarelle.it **shop:** no **e-commerce:** no

WATER, BEVERAGES, FRUIT JUICES. Ferrarelle is one the most popular mineral waters with Italians. It springs from the Riardo countryside in the province of Caserta, from an ancient volcanic source between the extinct volcano of Roccamonfina and Campania's Apennine foothills. Work to channel Ferrarelle water began in 1893, while the commercial launch as a table water was in 1900, during the national hygiene exhibition in Naples. Today, this water, rich in mineral salts and carbon dioxide (which gives it its natural effervescence), is exported to 40 countries worldwide. In 2005, LGR Holding Spa acquired Ferrarelle, Santagata, Natìa and Boario, followed by Vitasnella, in 2012. The name Ferrarelle Spa currently identifies the group with its iconic trademark.

Ferrarini - Vismara

REGGIO EMILIA I loc. Rivalta I via Rivaltella, 3
☎ (+39) 05229321 ✆ www.ferrarini.com
✉ marketing@ferrarini.com **shop:** yes **e-commerce:** yes

CHARCUTERIE. The story begins in an old villa in the fields among the green hills of Reggio, at Rivaltella, where the Gruppo Ferrarini still has its head office. When it began producing cooked ham in 1956 it was the first company in Italy to offer this product without added polyphosphates, which was revolutionary in the sector. The company adheres to a strict quality policy for its products, and promotes research and study into new flavours and manufacturing techniques. Traditional items are flanked by new products like lonzotto, practically fat-free, and coriandoli di cotto, gluten-free with no milk protein, and further adds to health benefits by being low in salt and higher in potassium. In 2000 Ferrarini purchased Vismara and has various plants in Italy and abroad.

Ferrero

ALBA (CN) I p.le Pietro Ferrero, 1
☎ (+39) 0173 295111 ✆ www.ferrero.it
✉ info@ferrero.it **shop:** no **e-commerce:** no

FERRERO

CHOCOLATE. Pietro Ferrero opened a workshop in Alba, where he began some mouth-watering experiments. In 1946 ingredients were hard to find, but using one of the area's most abundant gems, the hazelnut, he invented Giandujot, the ancestor of Nutella, a gianduia paste that could be sliced and spread on bread. It was such a success that a single-serving version was made, called a Cremino. Expansion abroad began in the 1950s, and in 1957 Michele Ferrero gave his company a multinational dimension. The 1960s saw the creation of Pocket Coffee, TicTac and, above all, Nutella, which was an immediate worldwide success. The Kinder revolution dates back to 1968, first with Kinder milk chocolate fingers, then with Kinder eggs. Ferrero Spa today is an Italian multinational company, specializing in confectionery products and 100% owned by P. Ferrero & C.

La Fiammante

SAN SEBASTIANO AL VESUVIO (NA) I p.zza della Concordia, 7
☎ (+39) 0815615316 I 0815616290 ✿ www.lafiammante.it
✉ info@lafiammante.it **shop:** no **e-commerce:** no

PRESERVES, JAMS. La Fiammante is the flagship brand of ICAB (Industria Conserve Alimentari Buccino), the food giant that also distributes La Paesana dei fratelli Paudice and La Reale. The producer is founded on the principles of careful selection of ingredients, constant monitoring of terrain and plants, and the continual updating of technology, all of which guarantee that the consumer is getting the best possible product. Tomatoes reign supreme, with an array of sauces (there's also organic and with basil), peeled varieties (including the prized San Marzano PDO), finely chopped (pure organic). Their sweet, fragrant cherry tomatoes are perfect for gourmet meals and deserve a special mention, as do their Piennolo PDO tomato products, datterini (red and yellow), Corbarini tomatoes, cherry tomatoes 'a pacchetelle' (red and yellow). And don't forget about their canned and bottled vegetables (mushrooms, peppers, artichokes and friarielli), corn and legumes (beans, peas, chickpeas and lentils).

Fiasconaro

CASTELBUONO (PA) I p.zza Margherita, 10
☎ (+39) 0921677132 ✿ www.fiasconaro.com
✉ info@fiasconaro.com **shop:** yes **e-commerce:** no

FIASCONARO

PATISSERIE. From generation to generation the Fiasconaro family has handed down the secrets of the art of traditional Sicilian confectionery, but with some creative touches. The flagships are the extensive range of leavened products, colomba and panettone, some classic, others enriched with the family's own spreads made with manna, pistachio, chocolate and coffee. A line for lactose intolerance is also available. Then there are cubaiat, full-size and bize-size nougats, and Martorana fruit. An excellent line of natural jams and preserves is made with island fruit. A similar line exists for honey. The raw materials are all sourced in Sicily and processed painstaking craftsmanship. The various product lines now also include passito and sparkling wines.

Fieschi 1867

CREMONA I via dei Lanaioli, 24
☎ (+39) 037232495 ✆ www.fieschi1867.com
✉ info@fieschi1867.com **shop:** no **e-commerce:** no

PATISSERIE. An unwavering attention to quality and respect for tradition have been at the heart of this producer's philosophy since Augusto Fieschi founded it in 1867. Mostarda is their core product. The perfect accompaniment for stewed meats, it's made according to an old recipe that requires fruit to be harvested at the right moment, then candied and immersed in an sweet syrup infused with mustard seed oil. Their product line also includes spicy fruit sauces, produce bottled in oil and fruit preserves. Their nougat, made with select almond and honey, deserves a special mention (there's also a chocolate and coffee variety, as well as a nougat cake). Then there's the 'cotognata' made with 70% quince (excellect with cheeses), their sweet cream spreads, fruit preserves, pralines, drageés, the sbrisolona (a local treat), hazelnut cakes and, during the seasons, panettone and pandoro.

Acqua Filette

GUARCINO (FR) I via delle Cartiere, 6
☎ (+39) 0775469012 ✆ www.acquafilette.it
✉ marketing@acquafilette.it **shop:** no **e-commerce:** no

WATER, BEVERAGES, FRUIT JUICES. Acqua Filette (Est. 1894) bottles water from the spring from which it has taken its name. At 900 meters above sea level in the lush, green heart of Ciociaria, they bottle more than 50 million litres a day, taking pains to guarantee the highest standards of health and safety. With a quantity of total dissolved solids at less than 500 mg per litre, the water is certified low mineral content and so particularly healthy, inasmuch as it promotes diuresis and can be consumed in large quantities. Moreover, it is completely free of nitrates. Three varieties are available: 'naturally natural' (still water), slightly sparkling and sparkling. Acqua Filette was chosen by the Umberto Veronesi Foundation to receive support in its research activities and, in particular, the campaign 'Pink is Good'. Since 2013 this initiative has focused on fighting breast cancer through promoting awareness and scientific research.

Filotei

ARQUATA DEL TRONTO (AP) **I** fraz. Pescara del Tronto **I** via Salaria zona industriale
☎ (+39) 0736808117 ✆ www.filoteigroup.it
✉ filotei@funghi.it **shop:** yes **e-commerce:** no

MUSHROOMS, TRUFFLES. Filotei Group srl can be found at the foot of the Sibillini Mountains, on the border between Umbria and Marche. This is one of the most famous and long-lived food companies in the province of Ascoli Piceno, involved in the marketing and processing of typical foodstuffs, in particular mushrooms and truffles. The company is over 50 years old, selling a series of products like sauces and creams (white, black, summer, Norcia truffles; ceps), also with vegetables; whole mushroom specialties (red and black ceps, button, also frozen); sundried mushrooms and tomatoes; vegetables in oil or vinegar (often mixed). The company also has a catering lines.

Finagricola

BATTIPAGLIA (SA) **I** v.le Spagna zona industriale
☎ (+39) 0828614511 ✆ www.finagricola.it
✉ info@finagricola.it **shop:** yes **e-commerce:** yes

Così Com'è

PRESERVES, JAMS. In 1986 a group of expert farmers joined forces and founded Finagricola, a farming cooperative located in Piana del Sele (Campania). Their 300 hectares of terrain is located in an area particularly well-suited to growing fruits and vegetables, thanks to its favorable weather conditions. Here, every stage of production is carefully executed and documented, so as to guarantee product authenticity and traceability. There are several varieties of tomato and lettuce, endives, arugula, peppers, eggplant, spinach and melons, all chosen so as to offer a variety of healthy produce. There are two product lines: GranGusto and Così Com'è. The former includes bottled yellow and red datterini (dried and semi-dried) in oil, semi-dried yellow and red peppers in oil, scarola with raisins and pine nuts, as well as broccoli rabe. The latter comprises red and yellow datterini and pizzutelli tomatoes (fresh or bottled). They also produce quality extra virgin olive oil.

Findus

ROMA I via Caterina Troiani, 75
☎ (+39) 0694331 ❀ www.findus.it
✉ **shop:** no **e-commerce:** no

FROZEN FOOD. The company opened for business in 1964 at the Cisterna Latina plant, and so began the story of fine quality Italian frozen products. The market has developed and extended its range, as ever guaranteed by meticulous observation of health and hygiene regulations, and a high standard of professionalism from all associates. In 1967 Findus invented its famous cod fish fingers, followed later by Croccole, plaice filets, salmon fingers and, more recently, fish burgers. In 1975, Sofficini crispy pancakes arrived, followed in 1996 by 4 Salti and subsequently a range of pasta, risotto, vegetable and meat dishes. The new Dolce Buongiorno includes ideal breakfast products ready in just a few minutes. In 2010 the company was purchased by Birds Eye Iglo (now the Iglo Group).

Fini

MODENA I via Rizzotto, 46
☎ (+39) 053559190 ❀ www.acetaiafini.it
✉ info@acetaiafini.it **shop:** yes **e-commerce:** no

VINEGAR. In the beginning there was the speciality store and restaurant, opened by Telesforo Fini in 1912. Even then, Aceto Balsamico Tradizionale di Modena and Aceto Balsamico di Modena vinegars were being produced in the back of the store, so it comes as no surprise that Fini is one of the founders of today's Consorzio Aceto Balsamico di Modena. In the company attic, one of the oldest vinegar cellars in the industry, some wooden barrels date back to the 18th century. The product is appreciated the world over and today, as in 1912, the tradition is unchanged, using the best must, patiently aged in cherry, chestnut, oak and mulberry casks. In addition to the original, traditional vinegars, also in a spray version and as a limited edition, there are glazes, oils and special seasonings. The Fini group owns the Fini Modena brand specializing in the production of fresh filled pasta, and Le Conserve della Nonna, producing in the Ravarino plant. The group recently acquired Greci Industria Alimentare, a leader in the catering sector.

Fior di Loto

ORBASSANO (TO) I Interporto S.I.TO Prima Strada, 1a
☎ (+39) 0114018511 ✪ www.fiordiloto.it
✉ info@fiordiloto.it **shop:** no **e-commerce:** no

NATURAL FOOD. Founded by Riccardo Maschio in 1972 as a small, family-run business, Leone is the oldest distributor of organic products in Italy and the first to produce puffed rice cakes (now everywhere) according to Japanese tradition. Moreover, since 1993 they have made it a priority to offer food products for individuals with food allergies, starting with a gluten-free line and following with lactose and yeast-free varieties. Today their selection is amazing for both its quality and variety: flours, grains, seeds, pastas, rice, soups, cereals for breakfast or as a healthy snack, sweet and savory snacks, drinks, preserves, enticing baked goods, dried fruit... And don't forget about their fresh produce: eggs, milk, yogurt, cheese, ready-made meals, smoked snacks, fish burgers, condiments, stuffed pasta and a whole lot more. Dietary supplements are also available, as are speciality raw-food items, household cleaning and personal hygiene products.

Fiorentini Alimentare

TORINO I s.da del Francese, 156
☎ (+39) 0114704568 ✪ www.fiorentinialimentari.it
✉ info@fiorentinialimentari.it **shop:** yes **e-commerce:** no

NATURAL FOOD. The story begins in the 1940s when Vittorio Fiorentini's shop in the centre of Turin, opened in 1918 by Leonildo Fiorentini, began selling special food products from all over the world, from couscous and unleavened bread to sauces, spices and tropical fruit. Roberto and Adriana Fiorentini continued and developed this direction, and grasped the full potential of the new trend towards healthy food. So in 2002 Fiorentini production started to specialize in bread substitutes and gluten-free, vegan and organic products including breakfast cereals, biscuits, melba toasts, pasta, rice, supplements, condiments, drinks and fruit juices, desserts and more. With almost 15 years of experience in the sector, today Fiorentini offers a wide range of products, both own brand and private label, and is one of the European leaders in the production of corn and rice cakes and snacks under distributor's brands.

Cesare Fiorucci

POMEZIA (RM) I loc. Santa Palomba I v.le Cesare Fiorucci, 11
☎ (+39) 06911931 I 0691193670 ✪ www.fioruccifood.it
✉ informazioni@fioruccifood.it **shop:** yes **e-commerce:** no

CHARCUTERIE. Innocenzo Fiorucci was from a Norcia family of butchers and cured meat producers. In 1915 the family moved to Rome and gradually set up a chain of pork butchers, renowned throughout the city. In 1950 Cesare Fiorucci created Industria Romana Carni e Affini, IRCA, to bring together artisan tradition and industrial production to protect product quality. In 1975 the Fiorucci brand was officially created, with the small Norcinetto salami, the first product to be sold throughout Italy. In the 1980s investments were made to update technology and expand business abroad. In 2011 Fiorucci became part of leading meat processor, the Campofrio Food group. Today there are five different product lines: Cinque Stelle, Suprema, Amarsi d+ (gluten-free charcuterie with reduced fat and salt), Rostello and Naturissimo (without chemical additives). In 2013 Fiorucci was bought by Chinese company Shuanghui International Holdings, the largest Asian pork production business.

Flamigni

FORLÌ I via M.L. King, 17
☎ (+39) 054383200 ✪ www.flamigni.it
✉ flamigni@flamigni.it **shop:** yes **e-commerce:** no

PATISSERIE. Brothers Armando, Lieto and Aurelio Flamigni opened their pastry store in Forlì, in 1930. Soon the stores began to multiply and became a magnet for all travellers arriving from northern Italy to the Adriatic coast. High professional standards, top ingredients, craftsmanship: these were the secrets of such rapid success. In the 1970s a turning point driven by Marco Buli, son-in-law of one of the founders, with which he increased numbers and made the nougat and all its versions crucial to production. Gradually panettone, pandoro and colomba, patisserie, marrons glacés and various other specialities came to the fore. The Flamigni Srl factory is in Forlì and Flamigni&Langhe produces in Rodello, province of Cuneo.

Riso Flora

MILANO I via G. Spadolini, 5
☎ (+39) ✆ risoflora.it
✉ colussi@colussigroup.it **shop:** no **e-commerce:** no

RICE. The Flora brand, part of the Colussi group, began as a specialist producer of parboiled rice in the late 1960s. Thanks to its significant innovations in the sector, the brand became a leader for rice that does not overcook and developed its capacity for perfect cooking through a range of simple, tasty products ideally suited to the pace of modern life, especially for quick preparation times without loss of flavour. Today Flora is a pledge for best results in the kitchen, thanks to a selection of excellent strictly Italian rice varieties, monitored throughout the production process. The extensive range of rices includes parboiled, white (Carnaroli, Arborio, Ribe and Originario) and whole.

Formec Biffi

SAN ROCCO AL PORTO (LO) I via Piacenza, 20
☎ (+39) 037745401 ✆ www.formec.it
✉ info@formec.it **shop:** no **e-commerce:** yes

PRESERVES, JAMS. Formec Biffi markets 95 products under 1,600 labels. A multitude of goodness for a company that is the result of Pietro Casella's entrepreneurial skills. Formec Biffi opened in the late 1960s, at San Rocco al Porto, near Milan, with two brands: Biffi and La Gaia. It grew its success over the years thanks to continuous investment in research. Everything began with mayonnaise, a product the founder was targeting before it was popular and when ready foods were an exception in Italy. La Gaia, Italy's leading producer of sauces, makes ketchup, mustard, pesto, sauces and creams, while Biffi (opened in 1852, in Milan, and acquired in the 1990s) produces pastries and coffee, fruit relish, mayonnaise, fresh sauces and condiments. The latest addition is the line of vegetable sauces. Top raw materials and attention to manufacturing processes are the company's strengths.

Birra Forst

LAGUNDO/ALGUND (BZ) I loc. Foresta I via Venosta, 8
☎ (+39) 0473260111 � www.forst.it
✉ info@forst.it **shop:** yes **e-commerce:** no

BEER. It all started in 1857, when two Merano businessmen founded the brewery in Maso Unterkofl, in Foresta, known as Forst in German. The area has excellent water from mountain springs and natural ice to use in summer. In 1863, Josef Fuchs, founder of Fuchs, now in its fourth generation, bought the property and started important technical improvements, introducing cooling compressors, and thus allowing production to continue whatever the season. Always at the forefront in the use of modern technology, the new heating room inaugurated recently ensures safety, quality and environmental respect, thanks to a modern recovery system of energy that is used for subsequent heating. Still owned by the same family, Forst today produces a line of excellent beers, a true expression of tradition and the experience of its brewmasters.

Fraccaro

CASTELFRANCO VENETO (TV) I via Circonvallazione Ovest, 25
☎ (+39) 0423491421 � www.fraccarospumadoro.it
✉ spumadoro@fraccarodolciaria.it **shop:** yes **e-commerce:** yes

Fraccaro Spumadoro S.p.A.

PATISSERIE. Born as a Castelfranco bakery in 1932, the tradition it initiated endures today. Bread, but also many sweet specialities. A second bakery opened soon after, in Borgo Pieve, for focaccia and panettone. Despite the years that have passed, quality and craftsmanship have remained intact. In the 1970s the current Fraccaro Spumadoro Spa opened and the company gradually became green, then greener, thanks to the use of renewable and recyclable packaging. The cornerstones of the entire product line, including an organic selection, are the sourdough and the slow proving: from festive cakes (panettone is still made with spelt flour) to various others, some traditional, others less so. The recipe of Aroma Spumadoro, a mixture of citrus oils and water-based essences, dates back to 1940 and is used to prepare focaccia, fluffy cakes, snacks and much more.

Francia

SONNINO (LT) I via Argine Amaseno
☎ (+39) 077394961 ❂ www.francialatticini.it
✉ info@francialatticini.it **shop:** no **e-commerce:** no

CHEESE. Francia is a family-run company, founded about half a century ago. Despite having developed an industrial strength, (they've gone from producing 5,000 kilos of mozzarella a day to 50,000) they still maintain their original philosophy and artisanal approach. They have two facilities in Italy, one in Sonnino (LT) and another in Pontinia (LT), but the latter focuses on products made from buffalo milk. They also have a plant in Germany. Their product line is impressive, starting with their selection of cow milk mozzarella, which is available in various shapes and sizes (bite-size bocconcini, 'confetti', ovoli (little ovals), twists, filone strips, 'julienne-style'), and then there's their buffalo mozzarella PDO (also available in a variety of sizes and shapes), their organic line (including ricotta), their fresh cheeses (scamorza, provoloncino, ciambella, cacio, classic or smoked), ricotta (from cow, sheep or goat's milk), yogurt, mozzarella for pizza, the 'Zarina' (their high-end fiordilatte cheese) and, finally, ready-made pizzas, topped with either buffalo or cow mozzarella.

Distillerie F.lli Francoli

GHEMME (NO) I c.so Romagnano, 20
☎ (+39) 0163844711 ❂ www.francoli.it
✉ info@francoli.it **shop:** yes **e-commerce:** yes

LIQUEURS, SYRUPS, DISTILLATES. Head of the family Luigi Guglielmo Francoli performed his first experiment with a rudimentary alembic still in 1875 at Campodolcino in the province of Sondrio. It was 20 years later that his children created Distilleria F.lli Francoli and the passion for distilling remained in the family until 1951 when Distilleria Luigi Francoli was created by one of Luigi Guglielmo's descendants. Here the best grappas in the area were bottled and sold. In 1999 Grappa Luigi Francoli was released and is the original line (including the commemorative stravecchia in a limited edition) alongside Sorsi di Luce, the Premium range and black grape marc grappa (up to 50°). In 2006, the business joined the Impatto Zero environmental project.

Pastificio Gaetarelli

SALÒ (BS) I loc. Cunettone I via E. Fermi
☎ (+39) 036541567 ✪ www.gaetarelli.it
✉ info@gaetarelli.it **shop:** yes **e-commerce:** no

PASTA. This family-run producer has been making high-quality pastas since 1964. The key to their success lies in the choice of select ingredients (preferably local), and a combination of artisanal methods and cutting-edge technology (used with the utmost respect for health and safety standards). Their facilities are even equipped with a kitchen designed to organize proper tasting tests. All their efforts have resulted in delicious products free of additives, colors and conservatives. There are three product lines: fresh, egg noodles (tagliatelle, pappardelle, taglioni, lasagna, bigoli, garganelli and so on), stuffed pastas (ricotta and spinach tortelloni, meat quadrucci, tortellini etc.) and their 'specialties' (tortelli with Bagòs cheese, medaglioni with radicchio and Asiago PDO, tortelli with venison salmì and more). Their '25 grammi' line is designed to cut back on waste by offering smaller portions... a nice idea indeed (frozen varieties are also available).

Galbani

MILANO I via Flavio Gioia, 8
☎ (+39) 0243356111 ✪ www.galbani.it
✉ ext.comm@it.lactalis.com **shop:** no **e-commerce:** no

CHEESE. Galbani is an larger-than-life company, which opened in 1880, when Egidio Galbani started to produce cheese with the intention of competing with the French. Robiola Galbani was then launched and was a great success, its fame crossing national boundaries. Bel Paese, a raw-paste cheese was next, in 1906, and also destined for international acclaim. In the 1920s the company grew, adding several factories and modern technologies. In 1928 the production of processed cheese began, using an innovative procedure for Italian industry. During the 1930s it was the turn of Certosa and Certosino. Galbani expanded abroad in the 1950s, with branches and stores in 52 countries. In the 1980s a pressed meat facility opened in Melzo, for production of Galbani gluten-free items without added polyphosphates and milk derivatives, with the two flagships salame Galbanetto and Galbacotto cooked ham. In 2006 the Galbani brand is part of the Lactalis group.

Galbusera

COSIO VALTELLINO (SO) I v.le Orobie, 9
☎ (+39) 0342609111 I 03963741 ✿ www.galbusera.it
✉ info@galbusera.it **shop:** yes **e-commerce:** no

PATISSERIE. In 1938, in a small bakery in a village in the province of Sondrio, brothers Mario and Enea began to bake biscuits using wholesome, genuine ingredients. The products soon became popular throughout Valtellina and since then the Galbusera family has always invested in prime raw materials, food safety, and making sure its range is delicious. As the years passed, these factors made the company a market leader for nutritious baked goods. No GMOs are used by the company, which aims to combine good flavour with good health, and never uses additives or hydrogenated fats. Galbusera also produces gluten-free biscuits and a tasty diet range. The products are ideal for breakfast and snacks, and the Cosio facility ships these very Italian goodies worldwide.

Riso Gallo

ROBBIO (PV) I v.le Riccardo Preve, 4
☎ (+39) 03846761 ✿ www.risogallo.it
✉ info@risogallo.it **shop:** no **e-commerce:** yes

RICE. With 150 years of business celebrated in 2006, Riso Gallo is one of the biggest rice processors is Europe. It started business in Genoa in 1856, opening a factory that used to export products to South America but success soon led the Preve family to focus on growing in Italy, and it transferred headquarters to Novara, then to Robbio Lomellina in the heart of the Pavia area. In the early 1940s Riccardo Preve had an extraordinary intuition: not to sell rice loose, but to package it under a brand name. At this time, there was a high level of illiteracy in Argentina, and animals were used to identify varieties of rice: lion, giraffe, tiger, eagle and rooster, the most prestigious quality and which gave the brand its name. Today Riso Gallo is sold in 73 countries and the range of products has expanded and diversified.

Garofalo

GRAGNANO (NA) I via dei Pastai, 42
☎ (+39) 0818011002 ✆ www.pastagarofalo.it
✉ info@pastagarofalo.it **shop:** no **e-commerce:** yes

PASTA. Pastificio Garofalo dates back to 1789 when the Gragnano Municipal council gave Michele Garofalo and Salvatore Montella exclusive rights to produce and sell "good quality macaroni". Today Garofalo blends the artisan spirit of the past with the selection of the best flours prepared with advanced technology, and industrial, export production quantities. The company offers all the traditional Neapolitan formats (and wholemeal and gluten-free versions), giving the pasts substance and weight like the macaroni-makers did back in the day. The company also produces flour, potato gnocchi and 100% Italian extra virgin olive oil. In 2014 the Spanish rice, pasta and sauce multinational Ebro took over 52% of the company shares.

Gentilini

ROMA I via Tiburtina, 1302
☎ (+39) 064123571 ✆ www.biscottigentilini.it
✉ info@biscottigentilini.it **shop:** yes **e-commerce:** no

PATISSERIE. Pietro Gentilini opened his first bread and biscuit bakery in 1890. At that time, a dry biscuit of English origin, called Oswego, was becoming popular in Italy and Pietro sensed its potential. He dedicated himself to the study of a recipe that would enhance the original and that is how Osvego was born. The Gentilini flagship biscuit is now also available with five grains. In the years that followed, new products were developed: novellini, frollini, brasil, vittorio, tripolini, margherite, wafers, amaretti, melba toast, jams, and honey, a milk and honey spread. Not to mention panettone, pandoro and the traditional Roman Easter speciality, pizza di Pasqua.

Gragnano in Corsa

GRAGNANO (NA) I via Nuova San Leone, 53
☎ (+39) 0818733341 ✪ www.gragnanoincorsa.it
✉ e.petrone@gragnanoincorsa.it **shop:** yes **e-commerce:** yes

PASTA. Since 2006 Vincenzo Petrone and Filomena Sorrentina have been at the helm of this Gragnano pasta maker. Thanks to their skills and commitment to quality, they've already gained a steady slice of the market, especially abroad. They start by selecting the right ingredients (their semolina is 100% Italian, mostly from Luca and Puglia), which are then carefully checked and ground in such a way as to protect the integrity of the grain starches and keep their nutritional properties intact. Pure Monti Lattari water is then added until the dough is 33% water, after which it is pressed and then bronze wire-drawn into any of a variety of pasta shapes (both classic and 'special' varieties are available). Finally, the pasta is dried at a low temperature, with impressive results.

Granarolo

BOLOGNA I via Cadriano, 27/2
☎ (+39) 051 4162311 ✪ www.granarolo.it
✉ **shop:** no **e-commerce:** no

CHEESE. The Granarolo group includes two different but synergic businesses: Granlatte, a consortium of milk producers, and a public limited company, Granarolo Spa. It is Italy's leading milk chain, based on an integrated production system. It was founded in 1957, near Bologna, by a small cooperative. Now it has 12 production facilities located throughout Italy. In the 1970s and 1980 it grew and strengthened over time, also abroad, acquiring production branches of other dairy companies. There followed internationalization and export, with subsidiaries in various parts of the world. The latest acquisition was Gennari Spa (Parmigiano Reggiano, Grana Padano, Prosciutto Crudo di Parma), in addition to Yomo, Accadì, Pettinicchio, Ferruccio Podda, Pinzani, Croce di Magara, Amalattea, and the Calabria, Perla, Casa Azzurra, Bioleche, and Granarolo dairies. Its products cover the entire dairy product range. In the last two years it has added about 20 new items, including desserts, butter, eggs, béchamel sauce and ice cream.

Grandi Molini Italiani

ROVIGO I via Aldo Moro, 6
☎ (+39) 045209111 ✆ www.grandimolini.it
✉ info@grandimolini.it **shop:** no **e-commerce:** yes

il primo ingrediente

FLOURS, PULSES, CEREALS. This was the first Italian milling group, one of the leaders in Europe in the production of common and durum wheat flours for domestic, industrial and professional purposes. Its origins date back to the mid-1800s, when Antonio Costato founded the first family mill on the banks of the Po, at Guarda Veneta, followed by another in Rovigo, in 1921, thanks to Marcello Costato, whose son took the company nationwide. A third opened in Rome, then mills in Porto Marghera, Coriano Veronese and Cordovado were acquired. In 1997, GMI became single shareholder of Trieste Terminal Cereali, while in 2000 saw it becoming a leading exporter of flour around the world. The Livorno plant was built and a network of branches developed, completing group restructuring. The year after a 50% stake in Molini Riuniti was acquired.

Grandi Salumifici Italiani

MODENA I s.da Gherbella, 320
☎ (+39) 059586111 ✆ www.grandisalumificiitaliani.it
✉ info@grandisalumificiitaliani.it **shop:** no **e-commerce:** no

Grandi Salumifici Italiani®

CHARCUTERIE. The business began with Peter Ferdinand Senfter who started artisan speck production in a San Candido butcher, for local consumption in Val Pusteria, using his own animals. In the early 20th century the Senfter butcher business became the official supplier of the imperial Hapsburg court. By the 1960s it was a real industry and in 1981 it divided into butcher and charcuterie. The company began exporting to Germany and the plant was renovated before the turning point came in 2001, when the Senfter group and the Emilian cooperative Unibon created Grandi Salumifici Italiani Spa, with head offices in Modena. Senfter products include Alto Adige PGI speck, smoked Prague ham, and frankfurters, but the group (also a leader in ready meals) includes cured meat brands like Casa Modena, Parmigiani, Cavazzuti, Alcisa and Gruppo Alimentare in Toscana (PGI Finocchiona).

Pasta Granoro

CORATO (BA) I s.da prov.le 231, km 35,100
☎ (+39) 0808721821 ❖ www.granoro.it
✉ pasta@granoro.it **shop:** no **e-commerce:** yes

PASTA. Synonymous with fine pasta, this company also produces a range of ready sauces, condiments, rice, boiled legumes and extra virgin olive oil. Their story began in Corato, Puglia, where a generation of industrial pasta makers had worked since 1930. Attilio Mastromauro opened a pasta factory in 1967 with the Granoro brand name. His wife Chiara worked with him. He modified the production machines to his own technical specifications, personally supervised the production process, and monitored quality while keeping the plants in Corato. Today the company is run by his daughters Marina and Daniela, who have consolidated their brand on the Italian market and abroad. A varied range of pastas (with a bio and a bronze-drawn line), in which the grano arso stands out (the grain remains on the ground after harvesting, and is then gathered and stone-ground). The latest addition is biscuits, fat- and preservative-free, made with excellent, non-GMO ingredients.

Grondona

GENOVA I via Campomorone, 48
☎ (+39) 010785901 ❖ www.biscottificiogrondona.com
✉ info@grondona.com **shop:** no **e-commerce:** yes

PATISSERIE. Grondona is a historic, family-run baker with decades of experience in the industry. Here they've made it clear that traditional Genoese food reigns supreme, with ancient recipes that continue to get passed down from one generation to the next. Their dough is made with natural yeast starters, kept 'alive' thanks to a tried and true daily ritual. Ingredients are chosen only after a careful selection process, from flour to butter to dried and candied fruit to natural flavoring (orange flower, lemon juice, Madagascar vanilla). Artificial coloring, conservatives and flavors are prohibited. Their Biscotto Lagaccio Antica Genova is their crown jewel (available in a more decadent variety with chocolate chips), followed by their 'corleggeri' (available with or without sugar), canestrelli, gallette 1803 and ciambellone (Italian donuts). Other sweet specialities include pandolcini, moretti cookies, baci di dama and cantucci. During the holidays, don't miss out on their traditional pandolce with raisins, fruit and dried fruit.

Hausbrandt Trieste 1892

NERVESA DELLA BATTAGLIA (TV) I via Foscarini, 52
☎ (+39) 0422889200 I 04228891 ✆ www.hausbrandt.com
✉ info@hausbrandt.com **shop:** yes **e-commerce:** yes

COFFEE, TEA, INFUSIONS. The Specialità Caffè Hausbrandt brand was created in 1892. Over the years advertising became its strong point with classic ads and the famous design of branded cups. These were its origins. More recently, in 1968, came young entrepreneur Martino Zanetti who rented a small coffee roasting factory in Marca Trevigiana, and by the late Eighties had a strongly established business. In 1988, with a series of purchases, the classic Trieste brand Caffè Hausbrandt joined the company, thus combining tradition and innovation in the Nervesa della Battaglia headquarters. This is now the home of Hausbrandt Trieste 1892 Spa which guarantees distribution of its coffee all over the world. Alongside the range of coffees (granulated, ground, pods, capsules, decaffeinated, espresso, single origin) is barley coffee, cocoa, ginseng and festive cakes (panettone and colomba). The classic Birra Theresianer and the Tenuta Col Sandango winery are part of the group.

Iasa

PELLEZZANO (SA) I loc. Cologna I via Nofilo, 25
☎ (+39) 089566347 ✆ www.iasa.it
✉ iasasrl@tin.it **shop:** no **e-commerce:** no

PRESERVED FISH. In the market since the early 1900s, Iasa have existed in their current form since 1969. They got their start salting anchovies in the distinctive wooden barrels. Then, in 1970, they began producing and packaging anchovy fillets (in small glass jars and pull-tab aluminum cans) and anchovy paste (in tubes). Thanks to the quality of their products, in almost no time they were able to seize a sizable piece of the market. In 1980 they decided to deal in tuna and were the first in Italy to use glass jars with a screwable top, the aluminum cans came later. In both cases, the company have prided itself on upholding its artisanal methods and respect for tradition. Their other products all reflect the same dedication to quality, from their Cetara anchovies to their Colatura anchovy sauce, tuna chunks in extra virgin olive oil and tuna bottarga (dried fish roe). They're also targeting a younger audience with their grilled tuna line and tunamburger.

Ica Foods

POMEZIA (RM) I s.s. Pontina, km 27,650
☎ (+39) 069106911 ❀ www.icafoods.it
✉ info@icafoods.it **shop:** no **e-commerce:** yes

SNACKS. The company, an Italian leader in the production and distribution of savoury snacks, was founded in 1949 by Carlo Finestauri. He began with artisanal production of potato crisps using methods he had learned in the US. The secret of the company's success has always been attributable to the quality of raw materials used: selected potatoes and only the best sunflower and extra virgin olive oils, with a little salt. Strict quality controls do the rest to ensure only safe products reach the market. With over 60 years of experience, today Ica Foods is present in over 25 countries worldwide. It owns the trademarks Crik Crok (under which they market traditional and special gluten-free crisps and snacks); Puff (famous for cheese-flavoured corn puffs); Le Contadine (specializing in rustic extra virgin olive oil crisps, sweets, biscuits and baked products like croutons, melba toasts, sliced bread); Bliz (a line of sweets like liquorice and gums; and savoury dried fruit and nachos).

Icam

LECCO I via Pescatori, 53
☎ (+39) 03412901 ❀ www.icamcioccolato.com
✉ reception.orsenigo@icamcioccolato.it **shop:** yes **e-commerce:** no

CHOCOLATE. A sweet tale that began in 1942, with Silvio Agostoni's bakery in Morbegno, producing confectionery. A war was on, so just a little sugar, mixed with chestnut flour, a hint of cocoa, and the Torta Montanina saw the light. An immediate success. In 1946 the founder procured equipment for refining sugar and his own machinery for processing cocoa. Then he began to produce Dolcao cream and moved to Lecco. In 1967, Icam opened another plant. When oldest son Angelo took over management he established direct relationships with cocoa producers in Africa and Latin America. The exquisite hazelnut praline Blue Rose was launched in 1985. In 1997 an organic chocolate product came to the market. The new production hub at Orsenigo was opened in 2008, and in 2014 the Vanini line of certified, gluten-free, kosher organic Italian chocolate was presented. Today total control of the production chain is a guarantee of a complete range of chocolate made in Italy and known worldwide, including chocolate patisserie, sweets and a professional line.

Igor

CAMERI (NO) I s.da N. Leonardi 32
☎ (+39) 03212001 ✪ www.igorgorgonzola.com
✉ info@igornovara.it **shop:** no **e-commerce:** no

CHEESE. Founded in 1935 by Natale Leonardi, today Igor's super modern facility of 22,000 square metres (easily reached from highway A4) is equipped with systems for producing, aging and packaging cheese. The third generation of family haven't let down their guard in terms of guaranteeing quality and investing in innovation while respection tradition and the environment. Gorgonzola is their crown jewel. Made with free-range milk and aged for 70 days, the cheese is gluten and lactose-free. There are different versions, from the aged Gran Riserva to the sweet PDO, extra-sharp gorgonzola, Casa Leonardi (soft and creamy) and organic. There are also tomini cheeses, mozzarella, mozzarella and ricotta, taleggio, grana and gorgonzola cream. Their Blu di Capra, made from goat's milk, sets itself apart for its particularly delicate blue cheese flavor.

Illy

TRIESTE I via Flavia, 110
☎ (+39) 0403890111 ✪ www.illy.com
✉ info@illy.com **shop:** no **e-commerce:** yes

COFFEE, TEA, INFUSIONS. In 1933 Francesco Illy created a coffee production and sales business in Trieste. In 1935 he patented the forerunner of espresso machines and a modern preserving system, making it possible to export coffee to bars all over Italy. In subsequent years he took the culture of espresso coffee over national borders and in 1957 a department was set up for producing tins, with the advent of products for home consumption. In 1974 pre-portioned coffee was perfected so that people could enjoy bar-quality espresso at home. Then Matteo Thun designed the white cup: in 1992 the first artist series came out, followed by designer tins. Thus, in 2000, the University of Coffee was created and three years later, the Illy Bar Concept project, the chain of Italian-style coffee bars worldwide, which would become Espressamente Illy in 2005. Now present in over 140 countries, the Illy group controls Domori, fine quality chocolate; Dammann Frères, tea; Mastrojanni wines; and holds shares in Agrimontana jams and pastries, and Gromart ice cream.

Inaudi

BORGO SAN DALMAZZO (CN) I c.so G. Mazzini, 148
☎ (+39) 0171266189 ✆ www.inaudi.com
✉ inaudi@inaudi.com **shop:** yes **e-commerce:** yes

MUSHROOMS, TRUFFLES. Operational since the early 1950s, this family-run business has always believed in the quality of their local produce and the possibility of making it more widely available. Indeed, Inaudi specializes in using artisanal methods to process and sell both mushrooms and truffles, mostly from right in their own territory. Over time, their selection of products has expanded. Today both dried mushrooms and mushrooms bottled in oil are sold (both porcini and other varieties), along with vegetables, snails, anchovies, truffles (white, black and 'bianchetto'), condiments (truffle and mushroom flavored oils and vinegars), pestos and sauces, truffle anchovies and toma cheese, truffle butter and salt, honeys, canned fruit, preserves, pralines and egg pasta with mushrooms, truffles or wine. In addition to their showroom and shop (both on-site), they have retail points in Alba and Cuneo. Guided visits are available on request.

Invernizzi

MILANO I via Flavio Gioia, 8
☎ (+39) 0243356111 ✆ www.invernizziformaggi.it
✉ ext.comm@it.lactalis.com **shop:** no **e-commerce:** no

CHEESE. In 1908 Giovanni Invernizzi founded his eponymous company. Then, in 1914, moving to Melzo, the company became the hub of dairy production. The purchase of the Caravaggio facility marked the start of production of stracchino, Gorgonzola, taleggio, and processed cheese. In the 1960s, Carolina the Cow was invented and the company gained second place, behind Galbani, in the production of fresh cheese. In 1974, mozzarella Mozzarì was born. In 1985 the company merged with Kraft Foods and in December 2003 it was acquired by French Lactalis group. The range of products includes processed cheese slices, crescenza Invernizzina, Invernizzino string cheese and mascarpone.

Italia Alimentari

GAZOLDO DEGLI IPPOLITI (MN) I via Marconi, 3
☎ (+39) 03766801 ❂ www.italiaalimentari.it
✉ info@italiaalimentari.it **shop:** no **e-commerce:** no

CHARCUTERIE. Italia Alimentari is famous in the Italian food industry as a charcuterie specialist. It was created in 2012 by the merger of Gruppo Cremonini and Montana Alimentari, and also includes classic brands Cortebuona, Ibis and Montana. Ibis, in the group since 2002, covers the whole Italian charcuterie panorama, and the feathers in its cap include PDO culatello di Zibello, cooked culatello, and Grand Ducato mortadella. The meat for the PDO charcuterie and the more prestigious lines derive from heavy pigs from Prosciutto di Parma breeders. Cortebuona, created in the early Nineties, works at four different plants: Bussetto (Parma), Gazoldo degli Ippoliti (Mantua), Paliano (Frosinone) and Postalesio (Sondrio), each concerned with different types of pressed meat. The pork comes from Italian breeders connected to the leading national PDO for prosciutto crudo. The company specializes in culatta and culatello. Montana, founded in 1953, was the first Italian company to produce tinned meat and gradually increased the number of production plants and the range, with tinned, fresh and frozen meats.

Ki Group

TORINO I s.da di Settimo, 399/11
☎ (+39) 0117176700 ❂ www.kigroup.com
✉ kigroup@kigroup.com **shop:** no **e-commerce:** no

NATURAL FOOD. A pioneer in the organic produce industry, Ki Group have used their specialized retail channels to become leaders in the widespread distribution of organic, biodynamic and natural foods. The number of products distributed is staggering, around 2,500 of the best brands, all carefully selected and subjected to strict controls in terms of quality, health and safety, and authenticity. In addition to distribution, the group controls 100% of La Fonte della Vita, a leader in organic food, and vegetable meat and cheese substitutes (tofu, seitan etc.). There truly is a bit of everything to satisfy every possible need, even for those with allergies and intolerances, from gluten to lactose to yeast, and for diabetics, vegetarians, vegans and those on a raw-food diet. Don't forget about their supplements, eco-friendly household cleaning and personal hygiene products, as well as cosmetics.

Caffè Kimbo

MELITO DI NAPOLI (NA) I via Appia, km 22,648
☎ (+39) 0817011200 ❂ www.kimbo.it
✉ info@kimbo.it **shop:** yes **e-commerce:** yes

KIMBO

COFFEE, TEA, INFUSIONS. A Neapolitan tradition for 50 years, the Rubino brothers were born into the coffee business, working alongside their father in the family bar-patisserie. The fame of their espresso coffee spread quickly outside the district and gradually their reputation grew, bringing with it ideas, including that of sharing the pleasure of Neapolitan coffee with cafés and homes worldwide. In the 1960s they grabbed the opportunity offered by new packaging techniques so thanks to the revolutionary new vacuum tin, real, traditional, Neapolitan coffee could travel anywhere. This was the goal behind Cafè do Brasil Spa (now Kimbo Spa) in 1963, which soon became one of the leading coffee businesses in Europe. Kimbo coffee became famous everywhere with a full range for home, bar and office. The company also produces coffee under the Kosè brand.

Latteria Soresina

SORESINA (CR) I via dei Mille, 13
☎ (+39) 0374349111 ❂ www.latteriasoresina.it
✉ info@latteriasoresina.it **shop:** yes **e-commerce:** no

CHEESE. Now vaunting 220 members, Latteria Soresina was founded in 1900. Its mission as a cooperative was to process milk produced by its members, united by a bond seen in its huge attachment to its territory. Latteria Soresina's four facilities work only with milk produced by the 48,000 cows reared in nearby dairy farms, which helps to ensure top quality of the raw materials delivered, as well as precise and constant control of the entire chain. The company produces excellent cheese, butter and milk, including lactose-free, and for Latte Milano and Latte Bergamo brands, but also cream, béchamel sauce, yogurt, Grana Padano, and Parmigiano Reggiano.

Latteria Vipiteno

VIPITENO/STERZING (BZ) I s.da Passo Giovo, 108
☎ (+39) 0472764155 ✿ www.latteria-vipiteno.it
✉ info@latteria-vipiteno.it **shop:** no **e-commerce:** no

MILCHHOF STERZING
LATTERIA VIPITENO

CHEESE. Founded in 1884, this cooperative is among the oldest in the region. Every day, Vipiteno's almost 600 members produce about 150,000 liters of fresh, top quality milk from cows raised in local mountain pastures. The delicious and unique milk is then worked into yogurt, fresh cream, butter and commercially available milk. Naturally, the coop has never let down their guard in terms of guaranteeing quality, obtaining certifications, and meeting consumers' constantly changing needs. To this end, they have introduced a new organic line as well as convenient, snack-sized yogurts, perfect for a quick lunch break. Moreover, almost all their selection is suitable for those with gluten intolerances. For a small fee (and on request), guided visits of the plants are available. Visitors get to see up close the various stages of production, quality controls and packaging.

Latterie Vicentine

BRESSANVIDO (VI) I via San Benedetto, 19
☎ (+39) 04441425000 ✿ www.latterievicentine.it
✉ info@latterievicentine.it **shop:** yes **e-commerce:** no

genuini come noi

CHEESE. Formed in 2001, Vicentine is the result of a merger between two local, decades-old producers. Their mission is, and always has been, to continue local cheese-making traditions with the aid of modern technology and using only high-quality milk. Over the years, Latterie Vicentine has kept growing and today, in terms of members and milk produced, it is the largest in Veneto, not to mention the largest producer of Asiago PDO in Italy (for which it has received international awards and recognition). With this in mind, it's easy to imagine what their standards are like. And they've managed to guarantee them across their whole product range: fresh milk, yogurt, tosella, mascarpone, stracchino, cheese spreads, butter, ricotta, cream, mozzarella, Asiago, Grana PDO, sharp cheeses including Cuor di Vezzena (aged for a minimum of eight months), Castelgrotta (minimum five months) and Morlacco (more than two months).

Lauretana

GRAGLIA (BI) **I** fraz. Campiglie, 56
☎ (+39) 0152442811 ✆ www.lauretana.com
✉ info@lauretana.com **shop:** no **e-commerce:** no

LAURETANA®
L'acqua più leggera d'Europa

WATER, BEVERAGES, FRUIT JUICES. The Italian company that produces Europe's lightest water, in Graglia (Biella). About 50 years ago, Teresio Rossello discovered an artesian spring and took a sample of its water to be analysed. The first plant was built at 850 metres above sea level, near the spring, from which the water was piped directly downhill in stainless steel pipes. The bottling plant opened in 1965 and the water was marketed with the name Lauretana. Since then Biella's blue gold has managed to conquer the world: Europe, United States, Australia, China, Japan, Russia. The water comes in still, slightly sparkling or sparkling versions, is bottled in PET, or glass for the catering industry. A product of excellence with bottle design by Pininfarina.

Lavazza

TORINO **I** c.so Novara, 59
☎ (+39) 01123981 ✆ www.lavazza.it
✉ info@lavazza.it **shop:** no **e-commerce:** yes

LAVAZZA

COFFEE, TEA, INFUSIONS. At age 25 Luigi Lavazza left Monferrato and moved to Turin, never imagining that his name would one day be famous. In 1895 he took over a grocery shop and soon decided to focus on coffee, creating his own blend. In 1927 Lavazza became a limited company and production increased. In the 1950s the large coffee roasting industry began and the first, unforgettable advertising campaigns. The subsequent years were devoted to exports, to conquer foreign markets. Today Lavazza is represented in over 90 countries, covering the sector of coffee at home and outside the home and the Horeca channel, celebrating 120 years of business with commemorative 100% Arabica packs. The company holds about 8% of shares in Green Mountain Coffee Roaster Inc. (which works with the pod coffee machine section) and owns Ercom Spa, leader of the Italian sector for top range hot drinks and preparations for sorbets and ice cream, with products sold under the Eraclea, Dulcimea and Whittington brands.

Lenti Rugger

SANTENA (TO) **I** via Tetti Giro, 7
☎ (+39) 0119456333 ✿ www.lenti.it
✉ info@lenti.it **shop:** no **e-commerce:** no

DAL 1935 PURO COTTO PER PURO PIACERE

CHARCUTERIE. In 1935 Attilio Lenti started up the first cooked ham production plant and today the company still produces over 5,000 tons of quality cooked meats per year. It pays particular attention to consumers and every product is free from gluten (AIC certified), lactose and caseinates (SGS certified), polyphosphates, glutamates, and GM ingredients. Products also have low salt content and are flavoured with an infusion of spices from a recipe perfected by the founder in the early years of business. The meat is purchased from national and EU markets. The company was among the first producers of organic roast turkey, ostrich ham and cooked ham.

Leone

COLLEGNO (TO) **I** via Italia, 46
☎ (+39) 011484759 ✿ www.pastiglieleone.com
✉ info@pastiglieleone.com **shop:** yes **e-commerce:** yes

dal 1857

PATISSERIE. Leone was founded in 1857 in Alba (CN) by Luigi Leone. The sweets producer later transferred to Torino where, in 1934, it was taken over by the Monero family, who still manage it today. The family, who have taken pains to respect the culinary traditions of Piedmont, have succeeded in making the name Leone famous, primarily for the hundreds of varieties of sweet pastilles, easy to recognize in their classic box (we particularly appreciated their citrus 'Tassoni', classic 'Violetta', 'Al Biscotto', and chocolate cake varieties). There's also their candies (which include particular flavors like sage, anise and cinnamon), fruit jelly drops (available in mint, anise, 'gommose' and sugar-free), various other drops, fondant candy, sugar-free and gluten-free varieties. Don't forget about their extensive selection of chocolate (completely gluten-free and, in the case of their dark chocolate, also lactose-free): dark, milk, sugar-free, aromatized, in differents types of bars, balls and hazelnut/chocolate gianduiotti. Their metal cans make great collectable items.

Leporati

LANGHIRANO (PR) I fraz. Pastorello I s.da Langhirano, 29
☎ (+39) 0521854421 ✪ www.leporati.it
✉ info@leporati.it **shop:** no **e-commerce:** no

CHARCUTERIE. Leporati is a top industrial producers of Prosciutto di Parma in several different lines: alongside the standard, with a minimum 16 months ageing, there are Ouverture (minimum 18 months ageing), and Riserva, an uncertified niche ham matured at length. Thigh joints are used from heavy pigs born, raised and butchered in Italy, compliant with the PDO Consortium regulations. Most of the production processes are carried out manually (salting, finishing, piercing, and pork fat application), while machines are used for manipulation and washing. The meat is dried in temperature-controlled chambers and aged in semi-underground cellars with wooden shelves. The company also produces Felino salami, culatello, coppa di Parma and rolled pancetta. Leporati Prosciutti Langhirano Spa exports to various parts of the world.

Levoni

CASTELLUCCHIO (MN) I via Matteotti, 23
☎ (+39) 0376434011 ✪ www.levoni.it
✉ levoni@levoni.it **shop:** yes **e-commerce:** no

CHARCUTERIE. Ezechiello Levoni founded his empire in 1911, after a long apprenticeship with Francesco Peck of Prague, one of the most prestigious pork butchers of all time. Levoni won the gold medal at the London International Exhibition in 1913 for his special smoking of Hungarian ham. His children created many new products including Paisanella, cubes of bacon mixed into salami. In the 1960s, under the third generation, the business expanded and two ham factories opened, one in Lesignano de' Bagni (Parma) and the other at San Daniele del Friuli. Today the Levoni Spa group is in the fourth generation and well-known abroad for its many types of salami, cooked and cured ham, mortadella and a whole series of speciality products.

Liguori

GRAGNANO (NA) l via dei Pastai, 50
☎ (+39) 081 i8726502 ❀ www.pastaliguori.com
✉ info@pastaliguori.com **shop:** yes **e-commerce:** no

PASTA. Back in 1975 Don Gaetano Liguori obtained permission from the municipal council to make and sell good quality macaroni. Since then, Pastificio Liguori
has handed down its old tradition. Don Gaetano's descendants include Vincenzo
Liguori who created the company that exists today, in 1820. The best blends of
Italian durum wheat, Gragnano spring water, bronze drawing equipment and the
skill of master pasta makers, low temperature drying: these are the main ingredients of Liguori pasta, long, short or special, like the famous paccheri, candele
and mafaldine.

Loacker

RENON/RITTEN (BZ) l fraz. Auna di Sotto/Unterinn l via Gasters, 3
☎ (+39) 0471344000 ❀ www.loacker.it
✉ info@loackerconsumer.com **shop:** no **e-commerce:** no

SNACKS. In 1925 Alfons Loacker founded a small, artisanal bakery to serve his
community. Today the company is among the most famous in Italy and has earned
worldwide recognition. Despite the heights it has reached, Loacker refuses to rest
on its laurels. Research and development are constant, as is their emphasis on
regular quality controls and taking advantage of the latest, best technology. Only
quality, select ingredients are used, and artificial coloring, conservatives, and hydrogenated fats are all absolutely prohibited. The wafer, in all its infinite varieties,
reigns supreme here. Thanks to its flavor, the way it crumbles and crunches, its
creaminess (when filled), this is the product for which Loacker is probably most famous. It comes in all shapes and sizes, including 'mini' and 'maxi', and flavors like
the hazelnut 'Napolitaner alla nocciola', lemon, vanilla, coconut, milk and cocoa
as well as different coatings. Their Gran Pasticceria line features irresistible cakes
in several varieties and don't forget about their original pralines, snacks and bars.

Loison Pasticceri dal 1938

COSTABISSARA (VI) I s.da prov.le Pasubio, 6
☎ (+39) 0444557844 ❖ www.loison.com
✉ loison@loison.com **shop:** yes **e-commerce:** yes

PASTICCERI DAL 1938

PATISSERIE. Originally a small bakery, opened in 1938 by Tranquillo Loison, this is now an artisan facility run by his grandson Dario, but the searching out of raw materials and the respect for tradition are still the same. "All stages of product processing are identical to those used by my grandfather", says Dario, "from 72 hours of proving with natural sourdough to cooling". The panettone, pandoro, colomba, and other leavened cakes are worked, cut, frosted and packaged by hand, one by one. A wide range of flavours are available, from late-harvest Ciaculli mandarin to Bronte pistachio, black cherry and cinnamon, chinotto etc.. Smart gift packaging is on offer. Check out the delicious range of biscuits.

Lurisia

ROCCAFORTE MONDOVÌ (CN) I via delle Terme, 62
☎ (+39) 0174 583000 ❖ www.lurisia.it
✉ info@lurisia.it **shop:** no **e-commerce:** no

PREMIUM BEVERAGES

WATER, BEVERAGES, FRUIT JUICES. Lurisia has historical ties to the mineral waters of the Santa Barbara and Pini springs, liquid gold in glass bottles whose striking design is recognized worldwide. The company's mission for the quality of its water and attention to the environment is renowned and now also includes Unico, a soft drink made with Piedmontese barbera grapes, apples and pears, totally free of preservatives and colourings. A tasty treat that flanks the chinotto and orange drinks made with Savona sour oranges and Gargano oranges, both Slow Food Presidia. A joint venture with Teo Musso, father of Baladin beer, created Lurisia ale, a limited edition produced in a number of variants. Lurisia–Acque Minerali Srl co-production policy has brought about other products of excellence.

Luxardo

TORREGLIA (PD) I via Romana, 42
☎ (+39) 0499934811 ❀ www.luxardo.it
✉ luxardo@luxardo.it **shop:** yes **e-commerce:** no

LUXARDO

LIQUEURS, SYRUPS, DISTILLATES. This company's history begins far away in Zara, Dalmatia, and continues in Italy at Torreglia (Padua) where the family still produce their famous maraschino and other liqueurs like Sangue Morlacco, cherry brandy from marasca cherries and Sambuca. In 1821 Girolamo Luxardo opened the maraschino factory in Zara, after his wife Maria Canevari had begun making the product at home with enthusiastic reactions from friends. After years spent perfecting the product it obtained the privilege of exclusive use by the Emperor of Austria. After destruction of the plant in World War 2 and subsequent events, Giorgio Luxardo (fourth generation) courageously reopened the company at Torreglia, and it is now a world leader in the sweet liqueur sector. Luxardo Spa is also a leader in cake liqueurs and produces grappa and other spirits, jams, fruit syrups and wines (Luxardo De Franchi Castel Venda).

Maina

FOSSANO (CN) I fraz. Tagliata I via Bra, 109
☎ (+39) 0172640111 ❀ www.mainapanettoni.com
✉ info@mainapanettoni.com **shop:** yes **e-commerce:** no

MAINA

PATISSERIE. Founded in Turin in 1964, Maiana moved to its current site in Fossano 10 years later. Over half a century, the bakery has enlarged its facilities (now a shining example of architecture and design) and line of production. In addition to panettone and colombe Easter cakes they make pandoro cakes and chocolate Easter eggs. They take pains to see to it that every stage of production is carefully controlled, and their approach, which draws on traditional methods of preparation, is decidedly artisanal. Take, for example, their decision to use only natural yeast starters, which guarantees easier digestibility, and the choice to use only select, natural products that are free of chemicals, conservatives and OGM. But they aren't afraid to take advantage of the latest technology either. These characteristics have all contributed to their success. Their panettoni and pandori come in all different varieties, including Christmas gift packaging. We also recommend their cakes (starting with their tiramisù), colombe Easter cakes (the 'chocobrownie' is a particularly enticing recent addition), and their 'gran nocciolato' Easter eggs, available in milk chocolate, dark chocolate and hazelnut gianduia.

Majani

VALSAMOGGIA (BO) I loc. Crespellano I via G. Brodolini, 16
☎ (+39) 051969157 ☯ www.majani.it
✉ info@majani.com **shop:** yes **e-commerce:** yes

Il cioccolato dal 1796

CHOCOLATE. Since 1796, the name Majani has meant quality chocolate, and not just for the region of Emilia Romagna. Ever since its inception, their guiding principles have been the same: the use of only top-quality cocoa and careful production combined with a healthy dose of creativity. The result is a product that is both unique and impossible to imitate. Their core product, and probably their most famous, is the Fiat, a four-layered, creamy chocolate candy that goes back to 1911 when it was commissioned by the famous, national car manufacturer. Today it is available in various delicious flavors. The 'sfoglia nera', thin sheets of chocolate that are available in both classic and dark chocolate varieties, are another delectable treat. Try them with cognac, rum, sweet wines, Balsamic vinegar or a nice espresso. Don't forget about their sugar-free line, chocolate covered citrus peels, various types of chocolates, chocolate bars, cream spreads, liquors, hot chocolate mixes, chocolate Easter eggs, nougat and, for the summer, soft fruit jelly drops. In addition to their factory outlet they have a shop in downtown Bologna.

Malpighi

MODENA I fraz. San Donnino I via Barca, 20
☎ (+39) 059465063 ☯ www.acetaiamalpighi.it
✉ info@acetaiamalpighi.it **shop:** yes **e-commerce:** yes

VINEGAR. Since 1850, the name Malpighi has stood for traditional Balsamic vinegar, with five generations of family dedicating their life to making and selling this product 'par excellence'. Their selection is impressive: the Ermes Malpighi has been aged more than 30 years, then there's the Affinato, the Extra Vecchio, the Riserva Ciliegio, Riserva Ginepro, and Riserva Secolare (a 'meditation' vinegar). Let's not overlook their Balsamic-based condiments: the Saporos and Prelibato (both of which are available in aged varieties), the Gustoso, sauces and toppings, all available in alluring packaging. For those who are interested in knowing more, it's possible to book free guided visits at Tenuta del Cigno (just outside Modena), where you can visit their vineyards, the old vinegar factory and the area where the vinegar is aged (the barrel warehouses, which store about three thousand barrels, some of which go back to the Napoleonic period). You can then taste and purchase any of a variety of products. There's also a showroom near Palazzo Ducale, in the heart of Modena.

Mangiarsano Germinal

CASTELFRANCO VENETO (TV) I via Staizza, 50
☎ (+39) 04231770 ❀ www.mangiarsanogerminal.com
✉ info@mangiarsanogerminal.it **shop:** no **e-commerce:** yes

Gruppo
MangiarsanoGerminal

NATURAL FOOD. Mangiarsano Germinal got their start in Brescia in 1981 but currently operate out of Veneto. The group, who sell organic and health products, strive to uphold quality standards while respecting the environment. Their 12,000 square meter facility houses two product lines, comprising the group's five brands. The first is Germinal Bio (www.germinalbio.it), various organic and health foods, including products for those who have special allergies and intolerances. The second is Gaia Bio Alimenti, organic products made from select, alternative grains. Then there's Bio Bimbo and Bio Junior (www.bio-bimbo.it), which, as you might have guessed, deal mostly in organic products for babies and children. Next there's Mangiarsano and, last but not least, Zizzola (www.zizzola-srl.com) which deals in sweets made according to ancient Venetian recipes like, for example, the torta fregolotta.

Manicardi

CASTELVETRO DI MODENA (MO) I stradello Massaroni, 1
☎ (+39) 059799000 ❀ www.manicardi.it
✉ info@manicardi.it **shop:** yes **e-commerce:** no

MANICARDI

VINEGAR. Founded in the early eighties by Enzo Manicardi, this vinegar producer has, from the outset, sought to bring together the best of tradition, authenticity and modern technology. They grow their own grapes, mostly Pignoletto and Lambrusco Grasparossa, and from these they are able to produce a truly impressive array of vinegars, starting with Aceto Balsamico Tradizionale di Modena PDO, Extravecchio (aged about 25 years) and the Affinato (aged about 12 years). Then there's Botticella (available in silver and gold varieties), Acetaia degli Scudi (particularly well-suited to cooking), the Neroelisir (also available in gold), their line of green, yellow, blue and fuschia-labeled vinegars (which include suggestions for pairing in such a way as to best bring out the vinegar's flavor), and the Triangolari (aged in various types of barrels, including oak, chestnut and cherry). They offer organic products as well as alternative condiments like the Condibianco (made with wine vinegar and unfermented grapes), wine and apple vinegars, creams and chocolates with Balsamic vinegar.

Martini & Rossi

TORINO I c.so Vittorio Emanuele II, 42/44
☎ (+39) 011 81081 ✪ www.martinierossi.it
✉ eobert@bacardi.com **shop:** yes **e-commerce:** no

LIQUEURS, SYRUPS, DISTILLATES. Four traders set up the Distilleria Nazionale di Spirito di Vino all'uso di Francia in 1847, in Turin. In 1879 the company name became Martini & Rossi, owned by Alessandro Martini (one of the founders) and Luigi Rossi, a liqueur producer from Turin. The company met with sweeping success in the new century: branches were created all over the world and in the 1950s and 1960s multiple projects were linked to the company image (Terrazze Martini appeared in many capitals), while in Pessione, the current headquarters, the Museo Martini of the history of winemaking opened in 1961. Vermouth is the keystone of production but the range includes spumante (especially Asti Martini), fernet, bitters (since the 1870s) and quinine cordial. In 1993 the company joined the Bacardi Group. Today the five Martinis, sparkling wines and liqueurs made under this iconic Made-in-Italy trademark are sold in 120 countries.

Marzadro

NOGAREDO (TN) I via per Brancolino, 10
☎ (+39) 0464 304555 ✪ www.marzadro.it
✉ info@marzadro.it **shop:** yes **e-commerce:** no

LIQUEURS, SYRUPS, DISTILLATES. We have Sabina Marzadro and her brother Attilio to thank for this now internationally renowned distillery, established in a humble country home during the difficult post-war period in Trentino. It was she who got it in her head to make grappa out of the pomace left out in the courtyards of local winegrowers. Her stubbornness paid off, and today the Marzadro family are a quintessential Italian success story. In their large facility, which blends naturally and easily into the countryside, they produce grappa that is firmly rooted in tradition, sophisticated and elegant, from monovarietal grappas (Marzemino, Nosiola, Chardonnay, Prosecco etc.) to blends, to herbal infusions and aged grappas. They also make liquors, which stand out for their dynamic, modern quality and are available in a variety of natural flavors (pear, blueberry, raspberry, apricot, peach, Williams pear...). They also organize interesting and informative guided visits of the facility.

Mauri

PASTURO (LC) I via Provinciale, 11
☎ (+39) 0341955700 ❂ www.mauri.it
✉ mauri@mauri.it **shop:** yes **e-commerce:** no

CHEESE. In 1920 Emilio Mauri had an idea, use the best equipment available to make traditional Lombardy cheese. Today, Mauri is headquartered in Valsassina, in a lush green area at the foot of Mount Grigna. Their facilities includes a cavern for aging cheeses and a plant in Treviglio, in Bergamot. Their product line is robust and delicious, starting with their aged cheeses. Their Remauri blue cheese is aged for a minimum of 90 days. Then there's their taleggio (both classic and aged) and their gorgonzola, which is available in sweet or sharp 'piccante', as well as with mascarpone or with walnuts. Their fresh cheeses are particularly enticing: goat cheese (also available with herbs, lactose-free or in a crescenza variety), quartirolo, mozzarella (from cow or buffalo milk), mascarpone and ricotta. Their decision to offer their specialty cheeses in unique gift packaging has been much appreciated. Guided visits can be organized (on request), along with delightful tastings on site, all in a beautiful, renovated lodge immersed in the natural surrounding landscape.

Menabrea

BIELLA I via R. Germanin, 4
☎ (+39) 0152522320 ❂ www.birramenabrea.com
✉ info@birramenabrea.com **shop:** no **e-commerce:** no

BEER. The Menabrea brewery, founded in 1846, has gotten to where it is by staying true to its original mission: make high-quality beer. This has been possible thanks to their modern facilities and the careful selection of ingredients (from the water used to the hops, the yeast and the malts) but mostly thanks to their skill, passion and experience. The brewer, part of the Forst Group since 1991, has also stayed true to its artisan approach and roots. Their product line includes a special 150-year-anniversary edition (blond, amber, strong and red), beer for restaurants, their special Christmas brew (only seasonally available and sold in attractive gift packaging) and finally their pure malts. It's possible to book visits of their Beer Library and Museum, where you can see old equipment, utensils, tools, steins, drawings and photos, as well as advertising material and pamphlets.

Mila - Milkon

BOLZANO/BOZEN I via Innsbruck, 43
☎ (+39) 0471451111 ✿ www.mila.it
✉ info@mila.it **shop:** yes **e-commerce:** no

CHEESE. Milkon Alto Adige is a dairy cooperative, founded in 1997 by merging Mila, the Latteria Sociale di Brunico (Senni), and the Südtiroler Bergziegenmilch cooperatives. Milkon has two production facilities equipped with cutting-edge technologies, each specializing in different types of dairy products. Brunico makes cheeses, both fresh and ripe, including PDO Stelvio; cream; yogurt and mascarpone. Dairy products are crafted with fresh milk brought daily from the mountain farms of Alto Adige, including a lactose-free line and a goat milk type. The merger of the Mila and Senni cooperatives in 2013 forged the Latte Montagna Alto Adige (ex Milkon) cooperative.

Distilleria Moccia

FERRARA I via G. Marconi, 21
☎ (+39) 053252611 ✿ www.distilleriemoccia.it
✉ moccia@zabovmoccia.it **shop:** yes **e-commerce:** no

LIQUEURS, SYRUPS, DISTILLATES. Artisan production and slow rhythms for an egg-based liqueur that is part of history, registered in 1948 by Distillierie Moccia under the brand Zabov, combing the word zabaglione and "ovo", or egg. This was an idea by young Mauro Moccia and it became famous all over Italy. Towards the end of the 1960s the company was already producing 70 different types of liqueur, like Greek Sambuca and Amaretto Moccia. It began to expand abroad, and advertising and a partnership with Festival Bar did the rest. In the 1980s Moccia became part of the Ori family who still own the company, and remains a leader in the liqueur sector. The leading label is Zabov, available in two versions since the 1980s, coffee and chocolate, joined later by Chupito and Bombardino, based on rum instead of brandy. The range of products includes cordials, maraschino, nocino, genepì, and bitters. In 2013 it was bought by Campari Punch Barbieri, another important traditional Italian brand.

Molinari

CIVITAVECCHIA (RM) I via Aurelia Nord, km 75,300
☎ (+39) 076658301 ✿ www.molinari.it
✉ molinari@molinari.it **shop:** yes **e-commerce:** yes

MOLINARI

LIQUEURS, SYRUPS, DISTILLATES. In 1945 Angelo Molinari launched Sambuca Extra Molinari on the market, beginning with just a few bottles. By 1959 the first semi-industrial plant opened the way for others. The boom of Sambuca Molinari came between the 1950s and 1960s in the Rome of the ?Dolce Vita?. In 1971 it was selling three million bottles, and more than double in 2001. In the collective imagination Molinari is synonymous with sambuca. The classic version is joined by a coffee version with top secret ingredients. The range includes Limoncello di Capri (no flavourings or preservatives) and Elisir Gambrinus, a unique liqueur with over 165 years of history. In 2012 Molinari purchased Distilleria Giacomo Ceschi, the oldest in Friuli, and the Vov brand.

Molino di Ferro

VEDELAGO (TV) I loc. Fanzolo I via Molino di Ferro, 6
☎ (+39) 0423487035 ✿ www.molinodiferro.com
✉ web@molinodiferro.com **shop:** no **e-commerce:** no

FLOURS, PULSES, CEREALS. The company expressed Luigi Marconato's passion for quality cornmeal. A family tradition maintained intact over time, even by his children, who seek out carefully selected and only Italian corn, applying scrupulous attention to work processes, from delicate grinding operations and, before that, expertise of the various phases of cleaning raw materials, which come from a chain under constant and strict control. The product line includes pasta (without special gluten, including organic and with fibre for coeliacs), instant polenta, biscuits, grissini, condiments, sauces, lasagne, gnocchi and snacks, all gluten-free.

Il Mongetto

VIGNALE MONFERRATO (AL) I Cascina Mongetto, 10
☎ (+39) 0142933469 ❀ www.mongetto.eu
✉ mongetto@mongetto.eu **shop:** yes **e-commerce:** yes

PRESERVES, JAMS. In the heart of Basso Monferrato, an area teeming with exceptional food products and towering wines, Mongetto is comprised of tracts of farmland, 16 hectares of vineyards and a charming, late 17th century agritourism facility called Dré Casté. But since the 1980s, Mongetto is most famous for having conquered our tastebuds with its gourmet, bottled produce. They are probably best known for their peperoncini peppers, stuffed with anchovies and capers, but it doesn't stop there. Their bagna cauda dip is outstanding. Then there's their line of produce bottled in oil (anchovies, artichokes, shallots and peppers), their various sauces (for example a 'bagnet' for stewed meat), capers and anchovies in salt, fruit preserves (including pumpkin, figs and quinces, which go perfectly with cheese), their jams, their surprising Moscato peaches with mint leaves, Martin Sec pears in Grignolino and their delicious grape mostarda. Custom gift baskets are available.

Monini

SPOLETO (PG) I s.s. Flaminia, km 129
☎ (+39) 074323261 ❀ www.monini.com
✉ info@monini.com **shop:** no **e-commerce:** yes

EXTRA VIRGIN OLIVE OIL. In 1920 Zefferino Monini began producing extra virgin olive oil in the Spoleto area, with its many olive-covered hillsides yielding oil with an intense but balanced flavour. Back then most Italians used only olive oil, especially in the city, and Monini decided to see extra virgin, revolutionizing the sector and market. His sons Giuseppe and Nello worked alongside him in the artisan laboratory and soon transformed the business into a modern industry which over the years became a benchmark for quality, authenticity and oil culture and it remains so today with the new Monini generation at the helm. In 2003 the Frantoio del Poggiolo opened, not only to produce extra virgin olive oil but also for research, seminars, and public tasting courses. Alongside the classic, organic and PDO versions are flavoured oils, spreads and vinegars.

Montali

LANGHIRANO (PR) I loc. Riano I s.da per Riano, 51
☎ (+39) 0521357121 ✆ www.montali.it
✉ info@montali.it **shop:** no **e-commerce:** no

CHARCUTERIE. Carefully selected ingredients, a tradition-centered approach and top-of-the-line equipment are the secrets behind the success of Montali, the Emilia Romagna meats producer founded in the 1950s. The pork used is only from trusted sources and their meats are expertly handled, from salting and curing to aging. Their deboned Prosciutto San Giorgo is certified Parma and therefore corresponds to all the high quality standards of the consortium - so as to best meet consumers' needs, three different types are available. Then there's their prosciutto crudo San Giorgio (with bone), which weighs about 9 kilos, their prosciutto San Daniele, whose flavor and fragrance are impossible to imitate (with bone and not associated with any specific classification), the tasty prosciutto Riano 'nostrano', the Carniel and the Mec, all available in different cuts, each one with its own specific characteristics.

Latteria Montello

GIAVERA DEL MONTELLO (TV) I via Fante d'Italia, 26
☎ (+39) 04228833 ✆ www.nonnonanni.it
✉ info@latteriamontello.com **shop:** yes **e-commerce:** no

CHEESE. In 1947 Giovanni Lazzarin, aka Nanni, had a small dairy in the Marca Trevigiana district of Treviso. Even then the cheese was distinctive for its natural, artisanal goodness. Today his sons and grandsons maintain that tradition, combining quality and technology. In the 1970s building of a new plant started in Giavera del Montello and the company passed to the direct heirs. In 1985 the Nonno Nanni brand was launched and today, becoming Latteria Montello in the third generation, it took leadership of the premium stracchino market segment in Italy. The traditional quality of the entire product range is unvaried and now includes not only classic stracchino (also with yoghurt and probiotics), but also squaquerello, robiola, mascarpone and a fresh cheese with rocket. Other trademarks are Ca' Serena (crescenza) and Nonna Rina, dedicated 20 years ago to Nonno Nanni's wife, and identifying a line of sweet crêpes, gnocchi (some with fillings and others flavoured), and crespelle pasta.

Birra Moretti

SESTO SAN GIOVANNI (MI) I v.le Edison, 9
☎ (+39) 02270761 ✪ www.birramoretti.com
✉ export@birramoretti.it **shop: no e-commerce: no**

BIRRA MORETTI

BEER. Luigi Moretti opened for business in 1859, when he started his brewery and ice factory in Udine. In 1860 he bottled his first beer and began to make a name for himself in the region. In the 1950s the brand's moustachioed drinker appeared on the label, said to have been a regular customer of a trattoria near Udine, whose photograph was taken by Commendator Lao Menazzi Moretti, since he saw him to be the perfect expression of the beer. The Moretti brand spread thanks to advertising but the trademark also sponsors many sporting events. By the 2000s it was exporting to 40 countries and reaching an annual production of two million hectolitres. The range offers various products, from Ricetta Originale lagers to special beers made with pure malts and fine grains selected directly in the field; regional from Piedmont, Sicily, Friuli and Tuscany; Gran Cru and even Zero, an alcohol-free beer. In 1996, Moretti was acquired by Heineken.

Mutti

MONTECHIARUGOLO (PR) I loc. Piazza I via Traversetolo, 28
☎ (+39) 0521652511 ✪ www.mutti-parma.com
✉ muttispa@muttispa.it **shop: no e-commerce: no**

PRESERVES, JAMS. More than 100 years of presence on Italian tables may suffice to describe the history of the Parma company located in the heart of the Parma food valley. Founder Giovanni Mutti understood the importance of alternating crops, still applied today. In 1899, his grandson Marcellino founded F.lli Mutti in Basilicanova, with a facility dedicated to tomato processing. In 1951, with the launch of tomato paste in aluminium tubes, packaging that had so far only been used for toothpaste, the company soared to the top of the canning industry. Then, in 1971, with a finely-chopped tomato pulp, it consolidated its success. Mutti SpA today is the market leader in the concentrates and pulp segment, an area where quality is a fundamental value. The whole production chain is non-GM certified and today also includes tomato vinegar and ready sauces. In 2014, Mutti took over the Fiordagosto factory, in Salerno and gave the name to a new double paste. A production hub opened in Oliveto Citra.

Muzzi - IDB Group

BADIA POLESINE (RO) I via Cà Mignola Nuova, 1577
☎ (+39) 0425596211 � www.pasticceriamuzzi.com
✉ info@idbgroup.it **shop:** yes **e-commerce:** no

PATISSERIE. Founded in 1795 as a comfit-maker, famous for its aniseed-filled anisini, today this family-run patisseur is one of the best in Italy, whose attention to quality goes hand-in-hand with love of the environment. Products include tea and fancy biscuits, sweet cantucci but also a delicious savoury version; chocolate and pralines; coated hazelnuts and citrus peel. During festivities they produce a range of colomba, Easter eggs, nougats in different sizes, and classic and not-so-classic panettone.

Bortolo Nardini

BASSANO DEL GRAPPA (VI) I Ponte Vecchio, 2
☎ (+39) 0424227741 I 0424220477 � www.nardini.it
✉ nardini@nardini.it **shop:** no **e-commerce:** yes

B.^{LO} NARDINI
DISTILLERIA A VAPORE

BASSANO
—— al PONTE dal 1779 ——

LIQUEURS, SYRUPS, DISTILLATES. At Bortolo Nardini, seven generations of distillers have seen to it that grappa culture has a place in the world. Indeed, it was in 1779, a year proudly displayed on their logo, that the story of this prestigious producer began in Bassano del Grappa, making Bortolo Nardini the first and oldest distillery in Italy. Their selection of spirits features classic, traditional pomace brandies that use white grapes, or grapes aged in wood, and distillates flavored with rue or gentian. Their impressive variety of liquors is modern and versatile. It includes juniper, cedar water, mistrà anise liquor, the 'tagliatella' (made of grappa, marasca cherry, orange and herbs... the recipe is a family secret), amaro, rhubarb, quinine and fernet. Their 'Selezione Bortolo Nardini' is also worth looking into. Dedicated exclusively to the HORECA market (the European food and service industry), they come in elegant bottles designed by the noted architect, Renzo Piano. Many of their products are used to prepare outstanding cocktails. Guided visits are available.

Noberasco

CARCARE (SV) I loc. Paleta, 1
☎ (+39) 01822055001 ❀ www.noberasco.it
✉ info@noberasco.it **shop:** no **e-commerce:** yes

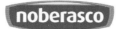

DRIED FRUIT. A story of hard work in the fruit industry that started in 1908, when Benedetto Noberasco began to collect and package fruit and vegetable products from the Albenga plain. Soon he established relationships with foreign countries that allowed him to import dried fruit: his famous oval box is still a classic in date packaging. Success grew and Benedetto's son Pier Luigi took over the company until 2000. During the 1950s and 1960s the number of warehouses in Italy grew to 48. Later an innovative processing system and new plant opened at Mongrassano Scalo, in the province of Cosenza. Packaging was given a facelift, then an organic line was added, and a new production site opened in Vado Ligure (Agri Food Srl). In 2013, the Noberasco product range was expanded to include a pocket version of dried fruit, made a production facility at Carcare.

Nonino

PAVIA DI UDINE (UD) I fraz. Percoto I via Aquileia, 104
☎ (+39) 0432676331 ❀ www.grappanonino.it
✉ info@nonino.it **shop:** yes **e-commerce:** no

LIQUEURS, SYRUPS, DISTILLATES. The Nonino family have made a name for themselves not only for their distillery, which was founded in 1897 and has since accumulated an impressive number of awards and recognitions - they are also responsible for protecting Friuli's native grapes, which otherwise risked being lost. Indeed, today Nonino is one of grappa's great producers, but it's also one of its great sponsors both in Italy and throughout the world. Today the distillery is in the hands of four driven and capable women: Giannola and the younger Cristina, Antonella and Elisabetta. The selection of spirits they produce features limited edition wine acquavit and honey distillates, all marked by the famous logo representing the Medieval symbol for alcohol. Don't forget about their amaros, liquors and fruit brandies (apricot, raspberry, Williams pear, cherry). All these products have proved versatile and can be used to make cocktails. In 1975, Nonino established the prestigious Nonino Award, given to those who have distinguished themselves for their research and/or study of grapes native to Friuli.

Nuova Castelli

PONTE BUGGIANESE (PT) I via del Porrione, 118/122
☎ (+39) 0572932411 ✿ www.alival.it
✉ alisales@alival.it **shop:** no **e-commerce:** no

CHEESE. Alival Spa is the parent company that has operated in the dairy sector since the 1980s, and now has two plants, respectively at Ponte Buggianese (Pistoia), specializing in the production of mozzarella for pizza and various other dairy specialities, including the famous Condipizza; and the plant in Porcari (province of Lucca), where spun and fresh cheese such as mozzarella and ricotta are made. In the early 1990s the company initiated a group policy with which it managed to bring to market STG and PDO products, rare until that time and which marked the start of its success. Alival recently joined in Nuova Castelli of Reggio Emilia.

Beppino Occelli

FARIGLIANO (CN) I reg. Scarrone, 2
☎ (+39) 0173746411 ✿ www.occelli.it
✉ info@occelli.it **shop:** no **e-commerce:** no

CHEESE. Few dairy producers have been able to maintain the passion and perseverance shown by Occelli. Founded in 1976 by Beppino Occelli, they got their start in Langhe, gradually spreading out to Cuneese, the pastures of Castelmagno and Valgrana and finally reaching Valcasotto (a Medieval hamlet that has since been completely renovated). Their product line features works of art like their fresh cream butter, considered one of the best 13 butters in the world by Wine Spectator. But there's a whole lot more, from fresh and aged cheeses to semi-aged and blue cheeses, some of which have even been trademarked. In the dark of their old caverns, time is at work, along with air and water, making sure their cheeses are aged perfectly. Experts in the art turn the cheeses periodically, checking them, working them until the day they are ready to be served and enjoyed. Just to name a few: robiola, truffle crutin, testùn, Valcasotto, Raschera, Castelmagno, Bra.

Orogel

CESENA (FC) **I** via Dismano, 2600
☎ (+39) 05473771 ✪ www.orogel.it
✉ info@orogel.it **shop:** yes **e-commerce:** no

FROZEN FOOD. Over 2,000 producer-members in the large food group, a consortium joint-stock company which works the best Italian farmlands to offer the best fruit and vegetables, fresh, frozen and in preserves. The whole production process is closely monitored from sowing to harvesting, from processing to distribution, through a patented tracing system. The farm work follows the seasons and the production process undergoes strict monitoring to guarantee quality standards. This was the first company in the frozen food sector to obtain product certification and its SGS label guarantees monitoring of the production chain, nutritional value and absence of GMOs. Consorzio Orogel believes in the principles of sustainable development, preserving the local area and the environment. The extensive range of products under this brand name includes herbs, vegetables (also grilled), fish, potatoes, soups, ice cream, single-portion first and second courses.

Ortogel

BELPASSO (CT) **I** loc. Piano Tavola **I** zona industriale
☎ (+39) 0956141300 ✪ www.ortogel.com
✉ info@ortogel.com **shop:** no **e-commerce:** no

FROZEN FOOD. In 1869 Alfio Sapienza Grasso set up a wine business near Catania railway station. In 1890 Giacomo Tamburino planted a blood orange orchard nearby. This is the old story, but the modern adventure began in 1978 when Ortogel was set up by a family group of citrus growers and operators in the farm food sector in the industrial zone of Caltagirone. In 1981 they began production of frozen vegetables and not long after converted the factories for production of natural juice of Sicilian blood oranges and other citrus fruits. The production chain was completed with cold technology and quick freezing. The products were launched in Italy and abroad with the Gelidea brand and it expanded from the Nineties until 2010 with a series of technological innovations. Today the company produces natural and organic NFC juices, concentrate juices, cold-extracted essential oils, cubes of orange and lemon zest in salt solution or frozen, flours, dried citrus zest and fibres.

Fattorie Osella

CARAMAGNA PIEMONTE (CN) I v.lo Sant'Abbondio, 6
☎ (+39) 0172828211 I 0172828241 ✆ www.fattorieosella.it
✉ info@fattorieosella.it **shop:** yes **e-commerce:** no

CHEESE. In 1952, in Caramagna Piemonte, a rural haven close to Mount Monviso, a stone's throw from the Langhe, Dario Osella and his brother Gino Tommaso opened their dairy. Over six decades dairy production has expanded but the strong point continues to be the milk procured from selected farms in the area. In the mid-1980s the agreement with Kraft Foods led to today's Mondelez Italia, to which Osella sold a part of the company, now listed in its portfolio alongside other brands. Modern technologies used in the respect of quality raw materials and age-old cheese recipes place the company in the Italian and international spotlight. The product range is extensive with the Cremosi robiola and goat cheeses; the Freschissimi primo sale and stracchino, as well as ricotta; the Piumati like Alpino Osella, one of the flagships; and Specialità, including Conte di Cavour and Alba Berbera. All tasty and wholesome, without preservatives.

Pallini

ROMA I via Tiburtina, 1314
☎ (+39) 064190344 ✆ www.pallini.com
✉ info@pallini.com **shop:** yes **e-commerce:** no

LIQUEURS, SYRUPS, DISTILLATES. Nicola Pallini, an enterprising young man from Civitella del Tronto, moved to Antrodoco to expand his trade: the products included his own liqueur. In 1875 Antica Casa Pallini was created and the talent of his descendent Virgilio did the rest. In 1922 the business moved to Roma where he met a young Russian with a passion for chemistry. This fortunate meeting brought family experience and tradition to the fifth generation in Rome's only distillery. The company is a leader in liqueur production in Italy, with Mistrà and Sciroppi, and other products include Sambuca 313, created in 2010 to celebrate 135 years of business, and limoncello, Antico Amaro, maraschino and Gran Caffè, from a venerable company recipe.

Caffè Palombini

ROMA I via di Tor Cervara, 273
☎ (+39) 06228951 ۞ www.palombiniespresso.com
✉ info@palombiniespresso.com **shop:** yes **e-commerce:** yes

COFFEE, TEA, INFUSIONS. It all began in the 1940s from an idea by Giovanni Palombini, a creative man with a gift for innovation, as well as a great coffee expert. He set up the company and it soon became a benchmark for Roman consumers, and he was proud that his coffee was always mentioned as Pope Paul VI's favourite. His son Aldo inherited his passion and led the industrial development of the family business, establishing and expanding it over time with patient care over the production process, meeting consequently with success and distribution in Europe, North America and Asia. Today the range covers all taste demands: strong coffee for the morning, Arabica with low caffeine content for breaks at work, and decaffeinated to end the day without foregoing the pleasure of a good espresso.

Paluani

VILLAFRANCA DI VERONA (VR) I fraz. Dossobuono I via dell'Artigianato, 18
☎ (+39) 0458614411 ۞ www.paluani.it
✉ paluani@paluani.it **shop:** no **e-commerce:** no

PATISSERIE. Paluani got its start in 1921 making naturally leavened baked goods (back then they called themselves 'Prodotti Paluani'). In 1968, they got their big break when two families decided to invest in the business, bringing new technology and research and enlarging their product line to include chocolate, using only Italian ingredients. They were the first in the industry to be certified GMO free. More certifications followed, testifying to their commitment to protect consumer interests. Paulani are famous for their seasonal Christmas and Easter sweets, and rightly so. In fact their selection of panettoni, pandori, colombe Easter cakes, agnelli and chocolate eggs is formidable (there are classic varieties, as well as those with certified Piedmont hazelnut, with chocolate, without candies, filled with different types of creams, organic etc.) There are also cakes, sweet snacks and chocolate bars (milk chocolate, dark chocolate and hazelnut).

Paoletti

ASCOLI PICENO I loc. Marino del Tronto I via dei Peschi, 5
☎ (+39) 0736341470 � www.paolettibibite.it
✉ info@gassosa.it **shop:** yes **e-commerce:** yes

WATER, BEVERAGES, FRUIT JUICES. Given its achievements, Paoletti, founded by Enrico Paoletti in the early 1900s, can be considered as one of Italy's most notable historic businesses. For more than four generations the family has persevered in their quest for quality, pouring their energy into identifying the best ingredients and carefully controlling production, while seeing to it that their equipment and facilities are upgraded and modern. And considering a new thirst for traditional, Italian beverages, a host of classics are being reborn: the Bitter, the Gassosa (the absolute first to be produced) and the Spuma, not to mention the drink that has become an icon of the producer (also thanks to its flashy design), the Frizzatina. Of course we shouldn't forget about the Tonica, the Cedrata, the Limonata, Aranciata and the Pompelmo, all drinks that are available in single bottles, both plastic and glass.

Parmalat

COLLECCHIO (PR) I via delle Nazioni Unite, 4
☎ (+39) 05218081 � www.parmalat.it
✉ info@parmalat.it **shop:** no **e-commerce:** no

CHEESE. A world leader in the production of primary foods like milk and its derivatives, but also of fruit-based drinks. It brands milk in all its variants: fresh and long-life, from Premium Blue, the first in Italy made with microfiltration, to Zymil, the easy-to-digest milk with reduced lactose content. With Chef, a brand established in 1970, it created the market for long-life savoury cream and béchamel, later flanked by the salmon, four-cheese, ham, and porcini mushroom versions. Among the most innovative products is there YOChef, a cream and yogurt sauce that tastes just like cream with only 6.5% fat and low in cholesterol. In July 2011 the company was acquired by the French group Lactalis.

Parmareggio

MODENA I via Polonia, 30
☎ (+39) 059414711 ✆ www.parmareggio.it
✉ marketing@parmareggio.it **shop:** no **e-commerce:** no

CHEESE. This cheese producer got its start some 35 years ago in an area best-known for its Parmigiano Reggiano. Over the years, it has evolved, keeping up with the times, updating its systems and modernizing equipment, thus establishing itself as a leader in the cheese sector (as well as butter, since 2009). Parmigiano Reggiano is, of course, at center stage. A variety of forms are available, starting with their so-called 'pezzi' (pieces) of varying ages, from 22 to 30 months. There's also a variety made from the milk of the prized red cow, or mountain cattle, and their Parmigiano made with organic milk. Their line of snacks is interesting and appetizing, and their freshly grated cheeses are convenient and versatile in the kitchen. Don't forget about their selection aimed at younger consumers, and for snack breaks. Last, but not least, they offer a practical line of pre-sliced cheeses (sweet and sharp Provolone, classic and smoked Scamorza, Edamer and sweet Alpina Dolce), as well as butter. At Christmas time, they also offer gift packages.

La Pasta di Camerino

CAMERINO (MC) I loc. Torre del Parco, 1
☎ (+39) 0737640498 ✆ www.lapastadicamerino.it
✉ info@pastaentroterra.com **shop:** no **e-commerce:** no

PASTA. It all started 30 years ago in a small workshop created by Gaetano Maccari. His aim was to offer consumers a product that respected local pasta making traditions. Over time, and with the coming of new generations (Federico and Lorenzo, Gaetano's sons), that small project became a reality. Thanks to a combination of manual skill, mastery and modern technology, today the producer churns out about 20,000 kilos of pasta a day, and they're set to keep expanding (to the point where they regularly have to enlarge their facility). Their high-quality egg pasta, made using only Italian ingredients, is bronze wire-drawn and dried slowly at low temperatures. The result is a pasta that is pleasantly rough and porous (a variety of shapes and sizes are available). Their semolina pasta and organic spelt pasta are also increasingly popular with consumers.

Pavesi

PARMA I via Mantova, 166
☎ (+39) 05212621 ✪ www.pavesi.it
✉ webline@mail.barilla.it **shop:** no **e-commerce:** no

PATISSERIE. In 1937 Mario Pavesi and three staff started producing biscuits in a small Novara bakery. In the post-war period he launched biscuits of an original shape and light texture that would give energy without being too heavy, suitable for children. Called Pavesini, not surprisingly the first advertising campaigns targeted mothers. In 1955, returning from a trip to the United States, Pavesi started producing crackers, perfect for a changing Italy. In the 1960s it was the turn of Ringo, biscuits conceived for teenagers raving over the Beatles. In 1970 along came Togo, chocolate-coated finger biscuits, and in the 1980s were joined by Amici del Mattino, a line of breakfast butter biscuits. In the 1990s, Pavesi joined the Barilla group.

Confetti Pelino

SULMONA (AQ) I via Introdacqua, 55
☎ (+39) 0864210047 ✪ confettimariopelino.com
✉ pelino@pelino.it **shop:** yes **e-commerce:** yes

PATISSERIE. Since 1783, the Pelino family have seen to it that their name means quality. The secret to this confectioner's unrivaled success (international by now) lies in having the best ingredients (Avola almonds, Tonda Gentile hazelnuts, Belgian chocolate etc.), an artisanal approach and the carrying out of careful quality controls throughout all stages of production. The range of products offered is impressive: honey and hazelnut or almond candies, licorice candies, chocolate candies, cherry, orange, marzipan candies, not to mention their pralines, bon bons and fruit jelly drops (also available 'confettata')… a whole world of sweet goodness. If you happen to visit, don't miss their museum (founded in 1988), where you can see, among other things, old equipment and candy making tools, antiques and rare objects having to do with the ancient art of confectionery.

Pellini Caffè

BUSSOLENGO (VR) I via I Maggio, 8
☎ (+39) 0456763311 ✿ www.pellinicaffe.com
✉ pellinicaffe@pellinicaffe.com **shop:** no **e-commerce:** no

COFFEE, TEA, INFUSIONS. This company, founded in 1922 in Verona, has always focused attention on research and development. The large new production centre in Bussolengo, inaugurated in 2005, represents a significant piece of engineering work in industrial architecture, with avant-garde technology in the processing plants. The company is part of Consorzio Sao Caffè, set up in 1971, and currently consisting of four separate companies, each a leader in its area thanks to care over ingredients and production process (Pellini, Caffè Trombetta, Guglielmo, Saicaf). The vast production range includes: top Arabica 100% (moka, decaffeinated, natural, espresso); bio Arabica 100%; Pellini Espresso Superiore (velvet, creamy or traditional flavour); the bar range and Pellini Luxury Coffee pods. The products are enjoyed in over 30 countries around the world and were awarded the title of Coffee Flavour of the Year in 2015.

La Perla di Torino

TORINO I via Catania, 9
☎ (+39) 0112482149 ✿ www.laperladitorino.it
✉ info@laperladitorino.it **shop:** yes **e-commerce:** yes

CHOCOLATE. After discovering that he had a gluten intolerance, Sergio Arzilli dedicated himself to making chocolate. Passion for craftsmanship is at the heart of his work, as evidenced by his decision in 1992 to dedicate an entire production line to Turin, the city where his creations are made using a mix of high-quality cocoa and only select ingredients. Their chocolate truffle, the Perla Nera, is literally their crown jewel, but they offer a wide range of products, like cream spreads (including pistacchio, a recent addition), the dark chocolate truffle (which is suitable for vegans), the pistachio truffle, sugar-free milk chocolate and dark chocolate, hazelnut gianduja chocolate bars, mini-truffles (pistachio, stracciatella, hazelnut white chocolate with dark chocolate flakes), the Regio (a creamy praline) and the Perla Blanca, a white hazelnut chocolate truffle. Care, effort and attention to detail go into their elegant packaging and to their recipes, all of which has contributed to their success at home and abroad.

Pernigotti

NOVI LIGURE (AL) I v.le della Rimembranza, 100
☎ (+39) 01437791 ✿ www.pernigotti.it
✉ info.direzione@pernigotti.it **shop:** yes **e-commerce:** yes

PATISSERIE. In the beginning, in about 1860, Pernigotti of Novi Ligure produced fruit relish and nougat, wines and musts, enjoying immediate success. National sales were such that in 1882 it became an official suppliers to the royal family. In the 1920s Paolo Pernigotti made the quantum leap and from a family business it became an industry, expanding its production lines. In 1927 the famous gianduiotto won the Grand Prix at the Turin national and international exhibition. In subsequent years, many new products arrived: ice cream mixes, the acquisition of Sperlari and Streglio. In the 1970s, alongside classic almond nougat, a superfine hazelnut recipe was launched. In 1995 came the encounter with Averna, which helped keep alive Pernigotti tradition and quality. In 2013 Averna sold Pernigotti to the Turkish Sanset group, owned by the Toksöz family. in addition to the classic pralines, the company makes gianduia creams, bars and slabs of chocolate (including extra-large), and snacks.

Birra Peroni

ROMA I via Renato Birolli, 8
☎ (+39) 06225441 ✿ www.birraperoni.it
✉ info@peroni.it **shop:** no **e-commerce:** no

BEER. In 1846 Francesco Peroni opened a small brewery in Vigevano. He split production almost immediately, opening a facility in Rome. Then his offspring expanded the company with two new production sites, in Bari and in Naples. In 1953 Franco Peroni continued expansion policies, adding three more plants. From the 1970s to the 1980s the company opened abroad and extended its product portfolio and international partnerships. In 1990 it consolidated leadership in the premium sector. In 2003 the Birra Peroni group entered the SABMiller PLC group, one of the largest beer producers in the world. In Italy there are three production sites (Rome, Padua and Bari) as well as the Saplo malthouse. The product range today is very extensive and in addition to classic Peroni and Peroncino, includes double malt, red, pure malt Gran Riserva, and the Lemon Chill. Its other brands include Nastro Azzurro, Miller Genuine Draft, Raffo, Pilsner Urquell and Wührer.

Perugina

ASSAGO (MI) **l** via del Mulino, 6
☎ (+39) 0281811 ❂ www.baciperugina.it
✉ relazioni.esterne@it.nestle.com **shop:** yes **e-commerce:** no

CHOCOLATE. It was 1907 when Francesco Andreani, Leone Ascoli, Francesco Buitoni and Annibale Spagnoli founded Società Perugina for making comfits. By 1915 the small business had become an industry, expanding the range with sweets, chocolate and cocoa powder. In 1917, the company launched the Luisa chocolate bar, named after Annibale's wife. This became the company's flagship along with the Bacio Perugina chocolates and Rossana sweets. In 1923, the Buitoni family took control of the company and the name became simply Perugina. The sweet chain lengthened over time, adding boxed chocolates and other chocolate bars. The brand expanded abroad and in 1973 Buitoni Perugina (Ibp) was born. In 1991 Nestlé arrived and along came Collezione Perugina: Baci in Rosso, dark chocolate and cherry in liqueur; in white and milk chocolate; the Nudi, without wrappers, simply boxed. Dessert and patisserie lines flank a gluten-free range.

Petti

CAMPIGLIA MARITTIMA (LI) **l** loc. Venturina Terme **l** via E. Cerrini, 67
☎ (+39) 0565855150 ❂ www.petticonserve.com
✉ info@petticonserve.com **shop:** no **e-commerce:** no

Solo Pomodoro TOSCANO
- lavorato a bassa temperatura -

PRESERVES, JAMS. In 1925 Antonio Petti, an Agro Nocerino Sarnese landowner, founded his eponymous company. In the 1940s, his son Pasquale began working in the company and the name was changed to Antonio Petti e Figlio. In 1950 his wife joined the company to supervise production personally. At the end of the 1960s, Pasquale imported the Roma tomato to Italy for the first time and decided to grow it with other varieties in Tuscany, in Val di Cornia. In 1973, the company became Antonio Petti fu Pasquale Spa. The 2013, a unique line of products dedicated to the Italian market was launched. Today, in addition to the parent company (with the plants in Nocera Superiore), the group includes Italian Food Spa (Venturina, Livorno), CGA Spa and Conserveria Africana Ltd. Quality is still the key ingredient in puréed, pulp, peeled and paste products. There is also a bio range of baby plum and San Marzano tomatoes.

Leading brands

Peyrano - Jacopey Cioccolato

TORINO I c.so Moncalieri, 47
☎ (+39) 0116602202 ❧ www.cioccolato-peyrano.it
✉ peyrano@peyrano.com **shop:** yes **e-commerce:** yes

CIOCCOLATO

CHOCOLATE. In Turin, where the company was founded in 1915, Peyrano means chocolate. Antonio Peyrano opened his famous chocolate workshop in Corso Moncalieri and by 1920 was supplying the House of Savoy. He invented the recipes still used today, and the 1950s created specialities like the Alpini, a top secret blend and the company's pride and joy. In the 1960s Peyrano partnered Vogue and the world of haute couture. In the 1990s, Ettore Sottsass designed collectable boxes for the company. Peyrano controls the complete production cycle, from the cocoa bean onwards, working with antique machinery and complying with the pace of tradition, including conching for 72 hours. Today Peyrano offers approximately 80 chocolate gourmandises, from the original Alpino to diablottino, gianduiotto, cuore, Conca d'Oro, Giulietta, Romeo, astri, cremini, and the very light quadrett in five flavours: milk and dark chocolate, mint, coffee, bitter chocolate.

F.lli Pinna

THIESI (SS) I s.s. 131 bis via F.lli Chighine, 9
☎ (+39) 079886009 ❧ www.pinnaspa.it
✉ info@pinnaspa.it **shop:** yes **e-commerce:** no

CHEESE. Here in the green countryside of Meilogu, Sassari, during the 1920s, the Pinna family started making and selling cheese, founding what has since become one of the most important producers in the region. Now the third generation are carrying on the tradition, processing about 260,000 liters of milk a day with cutting-edge equipment and skilled craftsmanship. Despite such a high production volume, quality standards are never compromised. Their two product lines feature cheeses like the Pecorino Sardo PDO (both sweet and aged), Fiore Sardo PDO and the Pecorino Romano PDO. Then there's their Brigante, an excellent fresh pecorino that's available in a number of varieties (lactose-free, with peperoncino chilli, black pepper and rosemary). They also make ricotta (their smoked ricotta is outstanding), caprini Goat cheese and pecorinos of varying ages.

Acqua Plose

BRESSANONE/BRIXEN (BZ) I via J. Durst, 12
☎ (+39) 0472836461 ✿ www.acquaplose.com
✉ info@acquaplose.it **shop:** no **e-commerce:** no

NATURAL MINERAL WATER

WATER, BEVERAGES, FRUIT JUICES. The water bottled by Acqua Plose flows from a source set high among the mountain peaks of South Tyrol, at 1870 meters above sea level. Founded by Giuseppe Fellin in the early 1950s, the company pride themselves on their sustainable practices, using renewable energy sources so as to reduce their CO_2 emissions by more than 500 tons a year. Their water boasts total dissolved solids of only 22 mg per liter. Such a low quantity means that it's particularly light and healthy. They sell still, sparkling and very sparkling water in a variety of formats (all in glass), with the utmost respect for the environment. They also produce juices made using organic fruit and teas (also organic and sold in glass bottles) available in a number of varieties (standouts include their green tea and white ginger) and finally their refreshing vintage drinks (citron cedrata, chinotto, spuma, gassosa and cola).

Poli

SCHIAVON (VI) I via G. Marconi, 46
☎ (+39) 0444665007 ✿ www.poligrappa.com
✉ info@poligrappa.com **shop:** yes **e-commerce:** yes

POLI
1898

LIQUEURS, SYRUPS, DISTILLATES. In a small town in Vicenza, just a few kilometers from Bassano del Grappa and in the shadow of Marostica Castle, you'll find Poli Distillery. The Poli family settled here in the 16th century and began distilling a few centuries later, in 1898. Theirs is a long tradition that today extends across three product lines: Jacopo Poli, which includes vintage-dated distillates like their limited edition Poli Barrique, aged 13 years in oak barrels, or the Torchio d'Oro made with Torcolato di Breganze wine; then there's Poli, their fruit spirits made with select pomace (cherry, pear and raspberry), gin, brandy and grape spirits; last but not least is their Poli Museo, their blended grappas (also organic and kosher) and liquors (chocolate, coffee, blueberry, honey, elixirs etc.). They also organize interesting and informative guided visits of the distillery (where a successful TV sitcom was shot) and their Grappa Museum (an experience not to be missed).

Pomì

RIVAROLO DEL RE ED UNITI (CR) I s.da prov.le 32
☎ (+39) 0375536211 ✆ www.pomionline.it
✉ info@pomionline.it **shop:** no **e-commerce:** no

O così. O Pomì.

PRESERVES, JAMS. It all began in 1982, when a Parma company specialized in tomato processing since the early 1900s, was the first in the world to use new production technologies to package Pomì tomato purée. In 2007 the Pomì brand and its production plants were bought by Boschi Food & Beverage, a company processing tomatoes, with stakes held by Consorzio Casalasco del Pomodoro and Consorzio Interregionale Ortofrutticoli CIO. The merger arrived in 2012. The direct relationship with over 300 farms in the provinces of Parma, Piacenza, Cremona, and Mantua, allows Pomì to control the entire chain, certifying that tomatoes are 100% Italian. The product line for Italy, in addition to classic and rustic, pulp and cubes, also includes ketchup, purée and L + tomato juice, rich in lycopene, a pigment that gives the fruit its red colour. The company is present in over 50 countries.

Aceto Ponti

GHEMME (NO) I via E. Ferrari, 7
☎ (+39) 0163844111 ✆ www.ponti.com
✉ info@ponti.com **shop:** no **e-commerce:** no

VINEGAR. In 1867, Giovanni Ponti, farmer and wine and vinegar producer, began business in Sizzano, in the Novara area. In 1911, son Antonio received the diploma of honour for wines and vinegars at the Paris international fair. In 1939 the company added canned vegetables to its production. The fourth generation began a massive expansion action, acquisition of top competing vinegar-makers, and conquest of international markets. In 1986 the new Peperlizia line was launched and in 1991, with the takeover of Modenaceti, production of Aceto Balsamico di Modena began, taking Ponti to world leadership (also for wine vinegar) at this moment in time. In 2008, Ponti acquired Achillea, a Cuneo company specializing in production of organic cider vinegar, fruit juices and jams. There are five facilities: two in Piedmont, and one each in Veneto, Emilia Romagna, and Lazio. The product range includes two types of IGP Aceto Balsamico di Modena; wine, aromatized and cider vinegars; rice and pasta condiments; vegetables in oil and in vinegar; ready sauces and condiment sachets.

Birrificio Angelo Poretti

INDUNO OLONA (VA) I via Olona, 103
☎ (+39) 0293536911 ✆ www.birrificioporetti.it
✉ info@carlsberg.it **shop:** yes **e-commerce:** no

BEER. Angelo Poretti toured Europe and met the best brewmasters, learning the secrets of their craft, before returning to Italy and investing his savings. The idea was to introduce a new type of beer, Bohemian Pilsner, to Italy and in 1877 it was decided to start production in Induno Olona, near the Valganna caves, where there are very pure water springs, essential for a real beer. The Poretti brewery was born. The founder's legacy was carried forward by his grandchildren, in 1901, but in 1939 the brewery began to struggle because of the war. It was rescued by the Bassetti family, which owned the Spluga di Chiavenna brewery. In 1969 Splügen Bock and the first dry beers appeared. In 1982 an agreement was signed with the Carlsberg group for marketing its brand in Italy, and in 2002 the Danish multinational bought the company, which became Carlsberg Italia Spa (Poretti, Tuborg, Splügen, Carlsberg). Poretti beers today included the original recipe Saison Chiara, and 3, 4, 5, 6, 7 (seasonal specials) and 9 types of hops. The precious champagne beer has 10.

Principe di San Daniele

SAN DANIELE DEL FRIULI (UD) I via Venezia, 222
☎ (+39) 0432942083 ✆ www.principefood.com
✉ info@principefood.com **shop:** yes **e-commerce:** yes

CHARCUTERIE. Principe di San Daniele has been a leader in the quality cured meats sector for over 70 years, combining tradition and advanced production technology. The company was founded by and has always been the property of the Dukcevich family, who also own the prosciutto company King's in Sossano, near Vicenza. Besides being the top producer of Prosciutto di San Daniele DOP among the 30 members of the consortium, Principe also offers a wide range of traditional salumi, or cured meats. The acorn logo can be found on DOP prosciutto crudo, aged prosciutto and cured ham, prosciutto Praga, würstel, pancetta, bresaola, speck, mortadella, salami and other specialties. The company's wide-ranging, quality offerings also include a number of pre-sliced products, some of which are in gluten-free versions.

Molino Quaglia

VIGHIZZOLO D'ESTE (PD) I via Roma, 48
☎ (+39) 0429649110 I 3358485497 ✪ www.molinoquaglia.com
✉ marketing@molinoquaglia.com **shop:** yes **e-commerce:** yes

FLOURS, PULSES, CEREALS. For more than four generations, Qualia has been work-ing to produce top-quality flours using 100% Italian grain. Their success has been well deserved. There are two brands, Petra (started in 2007, these are sustainably farmed, soft wheat flours that are ground by stone) and Molino Quaglia, both of which offer a variety of different flours, all suitable for different types of situations and foods, from bread to sweets, from pasta to pizza to batters. There are spelt and whole spelt flours, buckwheat, rye, corn, chickpea and pea flours. They offer more than one type of gluten-free flour, as well as flaxseed, oatmeal, bran etc. Flours are ground in such a way as to protect the nutritional value of the original grain, they are then given a number, so as to identify their unique characteristics and their direct connection to the mill. Qualia organize cooking, baking, bread and pizza making courses at their school, Scuola del Molino (www.lascuoladelmolino.com), though other sites are available as well.

Rana

SAN GIOVANNI LUPATOTO (VR) I via Pacinotti, 25
☎ (+39) 0458587311 I 045547317 ✪ www.rana.it
✉ info@rana.it **shop:** yes **e-commerce:** no

PASTA. Giovanni Rana began working as a child in his family bakery but in 1961 he began his own production of tortellini, in a small production facility in San Giovan-ni Lupatoto, near Verona. At the beginning they were only made to order: the filling was prepared on Thursday, and the tortellini were made on Friday and Saturday, to be delivered on Sunday. In 1968 the first machine entered the production facility and in the 1970s a new phase began with a new factory: production was automated and distribution expanded and in the Eighties Pastificio Rana conquered the Italian market. In 1990 Rana was the testimonial for his advertising campaign, guarantee-ing the quality of his products himself. The message made a good impression and won the trust of Italian and European consumers alike. The range now includes filled pasta (the latest is Duetto, with two different fillings), long pasta, lasagne sheets, durum wheat pasta, gnocchi (also filled), pasta bases and fresh sauces. The brand is famous around the world.

Redoro

GREZZANA (VR) I via G. Marconi, 30
☎ (+39) 045907622 I 3484904510 ✆ www.redoro.it
✉ info@redoro.it **shop:** no **e-commerce:** no

EXTRA VIRGIN OLIVE OIL. Established in 1895, Redoro got its name from its two founders, Regina and Isidoro Salvagno. Defined by its long tradition, the producer is still in the hands of the same family who oversee about 3,800 plants spread across 40 hectares of land. Additional olives, when needed, are only used after a careful selection process. Olives are then pressed using one of the three presses (one at their main facility, one in Mezzana and one near Lake Garda, used only for extra virgin Garda PDO), according to the strictest standards of quality control. Their quality selection of oils are sold both nationally and abroad and comprise an organic line, Veneto Valpolicella PDO and aromatized oils. They also sell organic vegetables bottled in oil, sauces, pestos, patés, cosmetic products and wine, all available on site or online. They also organize guided visits and tastings.

Refresco

CADORAGO (CO) I fraz. Caslino al Piano I via alla Fonte, 13
☎ (+39) 031886111 ✆ www.refresco.it
✉ info@refresco.com **shop:** no **e-commerce:** no

WATER, BEVERAGES, FRUIT JUICES. The history of Refresco goes way back to 1888 when Domenico and Regina Verga started producing a pleasingly fizzy and refreshing drink, the Spumador. The beverage, with its characteristic cap, was followed some years later by the Spuma, a mix of 10 medicinal herbs made according a secret family recipe. In 1996 Refresco purchased the mineral spring Fonte Sant'Antonio, thus expanding their product line to include water. Today the company, whose central office isn't far from their roots, distribute a number of mineral waters: Primula, San Francesco, Mood, San Carlo, Valverde and, obviously, Sant'Antonio. Their carbonated beverage line, Spumador, includes tonic water, ginger ale, chinotto, citrus cedrata, canned beverages, aperitifs (the clear Dorino and the red Aperì), energy drinks, aranciata orange soda, colas, fruit juices in various (and some cases unusual) flavors, various teas, and vitamin drinks for athletes.

Leading brands

Renzini

UMBERTIDE (PG) I loc. Montecastelli I via D. Renzini, 2
☎ (+39) 0759418600 ✤ www.renzini.it
✉ marketing@renzini.it **shop:** yes **e-commerce:** yes

CHARCUTERIE. It all started in the 1920s, in a small, speciality salami shop that would later, in 1952, become a full-blown business. Then, as now, it was run by the Renzini family. An assortment of deli meats are still being made, including wild boar mortadella and speck, game meats, and meats seasoned with truffle. But you'll find the classics as well, albeit suited to the modern diet (less fat, less salt and drastically fewer additives), all produced according to strict sanitary guidelines. Renzini oversee various facilities in the upper Valle del Tevere. The meat used is partly from the Parma and San Daniele pork circuits (certified prosciutto di Norcia PGI) and partly from northern Europe. Their select wild boar are from Umbria and around Europe. Aging is carried out in ventilated rooms.

Rigamonti

MONTAGNA IN VALTELLINA (SO) I via Stelvio, 973
☎ (+39) 0342535111 ✤ www.rigamontisalumificio.it
✉ info@rigamontisalumificio.it **shop:** no **e-commerce:** no

CHARCUTERIE. A leader in bresaola production, a few years ago Rigamonti joined the Brazilian JBS SA group, the world leader in processing animal protein, which bought all the shares in this venerable Valtellina company, founded in 1913. The meat, frozen Brazilian beef, is processed in Valtellina. The bresaola, IGP and uncertified for the more prestigious line, is produced in Montagna in Valtellina, at the historical headquarters, and also in the newer plants in Poggiridenti (1970s) and Mazzo in Valtellina, which opened in 1986. The company also makes horsemeat, turkey and Aberdeen Angus bresaola, as well as ham, speck and pancetta, and exports to 16 countries.

Rigoni di Asiago

ASIAGO (VI) I via Oberdan, 28
☎ (+39) 0424603611 ✆ www.rigonidiasiago.com
✉ info@rigoniasiago.com **shop:** no **e-commerce:** no

Rigoni
di Asiago

HONEY. Rigoni was created after the World War 1 thanks to Elisa Antonini. After 80 years as a small beekeeping business on the Asiago upland, it became the largest bottler of organic Italian honey and one of the biggest names in the sector. In 1979 the business changed from processing the product to production itself, but the real turning point came in 1992 when Elisa's grandchildren, Vittorio and Narcisio Rigoni, decided to produce organic honey in response to the products sold in Europe of Eastern origin. Monofloral honey from Italy's best suited areas comes to the factory in barrels, emptied through a constant temperature-controlled system, and is meticulously analyzed in the laboratory. Rigoni lend their name to about 15 types of honey, from the classic chestnut, to less common fir, strawberry tree and rhododendron, as well as honey in a special squeezable bottle, jams, hazelnut spread and DolceDì, a dense sugar extracted from organic apples.

Riomare

CERMENATE (CO) I via L. Einaudi, 18/2
☎ (+39) 031779111 ✆ www.riomare.it
✉ info@riomare.it **shop:** no **e-commerce:** no

PRESERVED FISH. It was the 1960s, with a boom in the economy and a fashion for modern things, also at the table. Rio Mare hit the bull's-eye by meeting the new Italian demands. Starting with the famous pink tin, which was to become an icon for tuna in oil, tuna so tender it can be cut with a breadstick. In the 1970s the brand was well-established in Italy and began to make its name abroad. Then it was followed by tuna in brine and in EVOO, alongside its famous salads. In the 1990s these were joined by salmon and mackerel (today also grilled) and in the Noughties, by hand-prepared, pressure-cooked tuna filets. The range of products includes pasta sauces and tuna with pulses or vegetables. Rio Mare is part of the Bolton group.

Riunione

GENOVA I via privata Gualco, 50e
☎ (+39) 010803344 ✪ www.lariunione.it
✉ info@lariunione.it **shop:** no **e-commerce:** yes

PRESERVED FISH. Riunione was established in 1988 and, thanks to the ability, professional skill and passion of its founders, the producer has been able to evolve over time into the successful national and international business that it is today. And their success is well-deserved. In addition to their attention to quality, they've managed to stay abreast of consumer needs, studying and researching products that are able to satisfy changing tastes and trends. Salmon is, of course, at the heart of their line of smoked fish, from wild Red King to Irish, Norwegian, Scottish and organic varieties. They also offer interesting and unusual varieties with seasoning, coriander, lemon and dill, sesame and poppies. They also have smoked tuna, swordfish, halibut, cod, trout, herring and mackerel. Their Nature line (not smoked) features thinly sliced fish carpaccio, tartar, cubes, pre-soaked baccalà cod, bottarga fish roe, squid ink, fish broth, sea urchin meat, crab meat and shrimp... There's so much that it's hard to choose.

Rizzoli Emanuelli

PARMA I via E. Segrè, 3 quartiere S.P.I.T.
☎ (+39) 0521211111 ✪ www.rizzoliemanuelli.com
✉ info@rizzoliemanuelli.it **shop:** no **e-commerce:** no

PRESERVED FISH. There is the tang of the ocean in the story of this company, founded in 1898, when Luigi Rizzoli started to filet and package anchovies in Turin, a city on the ancient salt road. Luigi's son Emanuele moved to Parma in 1906 and later generations have carried on the tradition from here. There are several lines of preserved foods: Classica, Le Selezioni, Le Riserve di Famiglia, Gli Artigiani del Mare, Il Faro di Bontà, all based on anchovy filets in various recipes, such as spicy sauce, natural, with lemon, chopped, with capers or with olives. The production chain is monitored and guaranteed, and pays attention to sustainable fishing. The motto of this company, one of the oldest in the sector, is "ante lucrum nomen", included in the trademark to prove that for Rizzoli quality in the products and production process come first.

Roberto

SUSEGANA (TV) I via dei Colli, 145
☎ (+39) 043863564 ◈ robertoalimentare.com
✉ info@robertoalimentare.com **shop:** no **e-commerce:** no

BAKED GOODS. Roberto got its start in 1962 as a modest, local baker specializing in breadsticks. In more than half a century it has grown into a multifaceted producer specializing in a range of foods and with a number of certifications to its name. Their breadsticks are still a featured item, especially the classic 'torinesi' but over time they've added other varieties, including fat free, whole wheat, sesame 'crocchini', rosemary, mignon (mini breadsticks available in a variety of flavors) or simply salted. They also have delicious, crunchy 'bruschettine' (tomato and basil, garlic and basil, rosemary and herbs) or crostini croutons for soups, minestras and salads. Then there's their sliced breads (white, multi-grain, whole wheat), pan-fiocco bread and sandwich bread, bread for bruschetta, hamburgers and hot dogs. Don't forget about their flat bread and tortillas or their 'Linea Essenza', which is aimed at the health-conscious or those who have food intolerances.

Distilleria Romano Levi

NEIVE (CN) I via XX Settembre, 91
☎ (+39) 0173677139 I 3480055656 ◈ www.distilleriaromanolevi.com
✉ info@distilleriaromanolevi.com **shop:** yes **e-commerce:** yes

LIQUEURS, SYRUPS, DISTILLATES. Romano lost his father and five years of age and his mother at 17, after which he began distilling liqueurs with his sister Lidia, drawing on the family's ancient tradition. This was to be his life's work. In the 1970s he became famous thanks to Veronelli, who named him "the angelic grappa producer". Inside his distillery is the same artisan equipment with a discontinuous alembic still working on direct heat, so that only small quantities of product are distilled. The labels of his bottles are very famous for being designed by his own hand: the best known of his subjects is the wild woman. His grappas are still made from the marc of great DOC and DOCG wines of Piedmont, and there is also Grappa Gentile alla Camomilla (by Lidia and Romano Levi), the classic grappas, collection items in limited editions, and riservas. The Levi house-distillery is a living, productive grappa museum, an island in time where Romano's genius hovers above.

Roner

TERMENO/TRAMIN (BZ) I via Zallinger, 44
☎ (+39) 0471864015 I 0471864010 ✪ www.roner.com
✉ info@roner.com **shop:** yes **e-commerce:** no

LIQUEURS, SYRUPS, DISTILLATES. In 1946 Gottfried Roner, spurred on by a gut feeling and a strong entrepreneurial spirit, started a home distillery. Today the business he created is on its third generation and, thanks to its commercial success, in 1999 it purchased Ritterhof, one of the leading producers of gewurztraminer wine in Alto Adige. Roner holds a top spot in terms of fruit distillates and spirits, with a selection that features Williams pear and Gravensteiner apples. They aren't lacking in grappas either, with an offering that includes a pinot nero Riserva and a number of interesting monovarietals. Their selection of liquors is robust. They've got wild strawberry, limoncello, gentian, juniper, blueberry, plum, chocolate, zabaione and an Alpine herb amaro. And there's more: gin, rum, single malt whisky, white and red vermouth, all perfect for sumptuous cocktails and drinks. There are even decadent chocolates made with Williams pear liqueur and glasses to serve it all in.

Rovagnati

BIASSONO (MB) I p.zza Paolo Rovagnati, 1
☎ (+39) 0392752000 ✪ www.rovagnati.it
✉ info@rovagnati.it **shop:** no **e-commerce:** no

CHARCUTERIE. After the war, Angelo Rovagnati decided to become a wholesale trader in butter and cheese. These early steps as a company, with his son Paolo at his side, convinced him to follow the salami route. Cooked ham was still seen as an inferior product at this time, but by researching and experimenting with new production methods Rovagnati achieved high quality, and this meant growth. In 1985 his company was producing 20 types of cooked ham, alongside pancetta (also in a lean version), and then came the Gran Biscotto brand. In 1990 he purchased a typical pig farm to ensure full control of ingredients, and sliced meat in trays appeared. 2002 was the year of the Panatine and the Gusto & Benessere line. Since 2006 the company has been ageing prosciutto crudo (riserva and prime) as well as producing cured meats and cheeses. The original factory in Biassono, in the province of Milan, is now joined by other plants in Arcore, Villasanta and Faenza. Today Rovagnati exports to many European and non-European countries.

Rummo

BENEVENTO I c.da Ponte Valentino
☎ (+39) 0824331111 ❀ www.pastarummo.it
✉ crm@pastarummo.it **shop:** no **e-commerce:** no

PASTA. It all began in 1846 when Antonio Rummo chose the fertile lands of San-nio to develop the ancient art of wheat growing. Today Pastificio Rummo is in its sixth generation, and the excellent quality of the past is also guaranteed by tech-nological research. The secret of the high quality standard is in the selection of prestigious ingredients and a slow processing method with lengthy mixing times. The result is an excellent product with a typical wheaty aroma, lingering and firm, ideal to be cooked twice, and approved by the Federazione Italiana Cuochi. By using a tri-generator Rummo has reduced its carbon emissions by over 30%. In 2011 it produced an organic line, which added to the many types of dried pasta format, including Le Leggendarie (paccherotti, scialatielli, candellotti and more).

Sabelli

ASCOLI PICENO I zona industriale Basso Marino
☎ (+39) 073630671 ❀ www.sabelli.it
✉ info@sabelli.it **shop:** yes **e-commerce:** no

CHEESE. In 1962 Archimede Sabelli registered the first patent for the invention of a machine that manufactured mozzarella. In almost a century of business, the family's dairy tradition has clearly combined dependable raw materials with ad-vanced technologies and manufacturing systems to ensure the artisanal quality is not lost even on large numbers. The Marche plant processes only milk from farms in the Gran Sasso area, which retains all its natural goodness in fresh cheeses such as mozzarella and burrata. Sabelli produces a wide range of dairy specialities, and as well as classics for delicatessen sales, products include items that meet the specific needs of catering professionals. Ranges offer soft-paste and spun-curd cheese, white and smoked provola and scamorza, Pecorinos, caciottelle, either plain or flavoured with chili, olives, truffles, walnuts.

Saclà

ASTI I p.zza Amendola, 2
☎ (+39) 0141 3971 I 0141 352700 ✿ www.sacla.it
✉ info@sacla.it **shop:** yes **e-commerce:** yes

PRESERVES, JAMS. The story began in Asti, in 1939, when Secondo "Pinin" Ercole had a brilliant idea, and decided to use surplus seasonal vegetable crops to make preserves to be consumed during the rest of the year. He and his wife founded the Società Anonima Commercio Lavorazione Alimentari, called simply Saclà. Initially production was local, but by the 1950s the number of consumers of Saclà vegetables in oil, pickles vegetables and olives was growing thanks to revolutionary family-size glass jars. There have been many innovations over the years, from the first twist- off cap to sachets of pitted olives. Then came the Acetelli, followed by long-life pasta condiments targeting for foreign markets. Still owned by the Ercole family, Saclà is a market leader and exports ready sauces to more than 40 countries. The wide range of products includes the brands Saclà, Gustitalia, Saclà Fresco, Almaverde Bio and Dispensa di Lorenzo.

San Benedetto

SCORZÈ (VE) I v.le Kennedy, 65
☎ (+39) 0415859505 I 0415859500 ✿ www.sanbenedetto.it
✉ info@sanbenedetto.it **shop:** no **e-commerce:** no

WATER, BEVERAGES, FRUIT JUICES. San Benedetto was set up in 1956, at Scorzè in the province of Venice, to bottle mineral water in glass. In the late 1970s, it used innovative disposable glass, but in the 1980s was the first Italian company in the industry to launch PET containers. During that decade San Benedetto also signed two agreements, one with Cadbury Schweppes International and another with Pepsi Co. International, to manufacture and market for Italy the Schweppes product range and the Pepsi and Seven Up brands respectively. A new plant opened in Popoli, province of Pescara. From the late 1990s, new companies arrived and various agreements were signed. As time passed, the company leaned increasingly towards sustainability and in 2012 came the new Eco Green line of regenerated plastic bottles. Mineral waters, infused waters, fruit-based beverages, cold tea, soft drinks, sports drinks and aperitifs are all part of the Veneto group's portfolio now, working under the brands Acqua Minerale San Benedetto, Primavera–Acque d'Italia, Acqua di Nepi and Guizza.

San Bernardo

GARESSIO (CN) I via O. Rovere, 41
☎ (+39) 0174805211 ❀ www.sanbernardo.it
✉ info@fontisanbernardo.it **shop:** no **e-commerce:** no

WATER, BEVERAGES, FRUIT JUICES. The Fonti S. Bernardo company was set up in 1926 and immediately bottled in glass at Garessio, province of Cuneo, and in 1991 also at Ormea. Known since antiquity as miraculous water with therapeutic properties, it is particularly light. The glass bottle was the only container until 1982, when the first PET bottle was produced. The range was then renewed with the 75cl returnable glass bottle, taking the first step for restyling the entire range, which now includes a 100cl returnable glass bottle for catering, door-to-door 50cl for restaurants of first and second level, 33cl returnable and disposable glass bottle for restaurants and coffee bars, all in the natural, slightly sparkling or sparkling versions. In 2012, a 50cl PET bottle was launched for San Bernardo Sorgente Rocciaviva. In April 2015, the company was sold by the Montecristo group.

San Carlo

SAN GIULIANO MILANESE (MI) I fraz. Sesto Ulteriano I via Basento, 8
☎ (+39) 02982911 ❀ www.sancarlo.it
✉ mailbox@unichips.com **shop:** no **e-commerce:** no

SNACKS. Founded in 1936 by Francesco Vitaloni, San Carlo snacks just celebrated their 80 year anniversary. Once just a simple deli, they became famous for their crunchy potato chips, a product they now produce 100 tons of every day. And with production volumes that high, they're able to guarantee quality standards that are the envy of the industry. Their 'classic' potato chip is still at the top, but they've been able to adapt to the times, offering a 'light' version as well as a special anniversary variety. They offer a range of snacks: peanuts and peanut-based snacks, pistachios, crackers and rice crackers, potato sticks, dried and toasted seeds. And on the bread front there's sliced bread (available in a variety of flavors), buns, flat bread, melba toast, breadsticks, croutons and bread crumbs.

Cascina San Cassiano

ALBA (CN) I c.so Piave, 182

☎ (+39) 0173282638 ✿ www.cascinasancassiano.com

✉ info@cascinasancassiano.com **shop:** no **e-commerce:** yes

PRESERVES, JAMS. The Rossetto family have built Cascina San Cassiano drawing on an artisanal approach, experience and using high-quality Italian ingredients (except for Caribbean cane sugar), most of them PDO and PGI certified. The company, founded in the early 1990s, has evolved astonishingly fast. Their product line, some of which is currently seeing a packaging makeover, is staggering in terms of the variety of products offered, including an organic food selection. Featured products include fruit mostarda, wine and vinegar preserves, oil and vinegars, all types of pastas and rices, candies (available with stevia), canned fruit, sweets, products bottled in oil (including cheese and salami), sauces, creams, pestos, ragus, mayonnaise, truffle delicacies, aromatized butter, honeys with dried fruit and sweet cream spreads. Basically, there's something for every moment of your day, from breakfast to an early evening snack, from lunch break to dinner.

San Pellegrino

ASSAGO (MI) I via del Mulino, 6

☎ (+39) 0231971 ✿ www.sanpellegrino-corporate.it

✉ sanpellegrino@sanpellegrino.telecompost.it **shop:** yes **e-commerce:** no

WATER, BEVERAGES, FRUIT JUICES. The Sanpellegrino Group is Italy's principal company in the mineral water and non-alcoholic beverage sector. It includes a portfolio of mineral waters such as San Pellegrino, Acqua Panna, Levissima, Nestlé Vera and Recoaro as well as a wide assortment of drinks such as Sanpellegrino, Aranciata, the iconic Chinò, iced-tea Beltè , and aperitifs, including Sanbittèr, Gingerino and a new range called Emozioni. The excellence of Sanpellegrino goes beyond the intrinsic quality of its products. It is rooted in a strong dimension of typically Italian values that are embodied in its name. The most evident example is San Pellegrino mineral water, distributed today in 145 countries. It has become a symbol of Italy around the world, and is tastefully associated with an Italian lifestyle, brilliant, cultivated, original, food-loving and appreciative of the pleasures of spending time together. San Pellegrino has ably become part of the rediscovery of Italy and the Italian way of life.

Frantoio di Sant'Agata d'Oneglia

IMPERIA I loc. Oneglia I s.da dei Francesi, 48
☎ (+39) 0183293472 ❀ www.frantoiosantagata.com
✉ frantoio@frantoiosantagata.com **shop:** no **e-commerce:** no

EXTRA VIRGIN OLIVE OIL. Founded in 1827, Sant'Agata d'Oneglia, undoubtedly one of the most enduring oil producers of the region, has been in the hands of the Mela family for generations. Today Sant'Agata d'Oneglia is managed by Antonio and Paola, together with their daughters Cristiana and Serena. Their some 8,000 Taggiasca olive trees are spread over dozens of hectares of land, and they own a press as well, which allows for the processing of olives soon after harvest. In addition to a variety of extra virgin olive oils, they sell olives and olive paté, various products bottled in oil (vegetables, tuna, anchovies, codfish, mackerel, yellow tail), creams and sauces, vinegars and condiments, different types of semolina pasta, delicious truffle products, cosmetics made with olive oil (soaps, detergents, face, hand and body creams), breadsticks, panettone and even limoncello. It's all available on their easy-to-use online shop.

Sant'Anna

VINADIO (CN) I fraz. Roviera
☎ (+39) 0171959433 ❀ www.santanna.it
✉ info@santanna.it **shop:** no **e-commerce:** no

WATER, BEVERAGES, FRUIT JUICES. Sant'Anna was founded in 1996 by the Bertoni family, who've since seen to it that the brand is a leader in the field. Indeed, the company can now boast having the largest bottling plant in the world, a true jewel of technology and design. Sant'Anna water is exceptionally light, having an extremely low quantity of dissolved solids and sodium content. This makes it a healthy choice at any age. There are sizes available for every need and occasion, from a quarter liter to two liters, and they make sparkling water as well. The company prides itself on having been the first in the world to create a completely biodegradable bottle (except for the cap). Other products include their Santhé, refreshing iced teas available in a variety of flavors (lemon, peach, green tea and decaffeinated) and sizes (including pocket size). Then there's SanFruit, fruit drinks available in peach, pear and apricot (100% gluten-free). Their most recent addition is their Karma line, fruit and vegetable drinks that are gluten-free and free of conservatives.

Sapori di Siena

MILANO I via G. Spadolini, 5
☎ (+39) 02847841 ◈ www.saporidisiena.it
✉ colussi@colussigroup.it **shop:** no **e-commerce:** no

PATISSERIE. Virgilio Sapori opened his Siena business in 1832, producing panforte in a small bakery. Almost two centuries have passed since the opening of that workshop, two hundred years characterized by constant renewal that has kept alive ancient Tuscan confectionery traditions. Alongside the famous festive specialities like panforte, ricciarelli, cavallucci, and cantuccini, also fragrant new haute patisserie to be served every day. Sapori di Siena today is still a confectionery brand expressing its message of quality, refinement and careful selection of raw materials, able to satisfy fully the tastes and demands of the whole family, for every special moment. In 2004 the company became part of the Colussi group.

Sarchio

CARPI (MO) I via dei Barrocciai, 42
☎ (+39) 059658552 ◈ www.sarchio.com
✉ info@sarchio.com **shop:** no **e-commerce:** yes

NATURAL FOOD. Sarchio's mission is and always has been offering consumers a line of organic products with close ties to the earth and farming traditions. Founded in 1982, in 2006 the company was the first to produce an array of gluten-free foods and today it offers an equally varied selection for vegans as well. Their product line offers something for every meal of the day, starting with breakfast, which we all know is so important for overall health. This includes jams, breakfast cookies, cereals, cream spreads and fruit juices. But they have plenty of savory and sweet snacks as well, featuring crackers, bread substitutes, snacks for kids, seeds, pasta, rice, condiments and bouillon cubes, sweeteners, flours, tomatoes sauces, sauces, bottled vegetables and legumes and much more. There's also a line of completely natural vitamin supplements, including products for those with weight problems.

Fattoria Scaldasole

MONGUZZO (CO) **l** via Gaetano Donizetti, 7
☎ (+39) 03161491 ✆ www.fattoriascaldasole.it
✉ info@scaldasole.it **shop:** no **e-commerce:** no

Fattoria
Scaldasole

NATURAL FOOD. Almost 30 years ago, in Anzano del Parco, north of Milan, the Roveda husband-and-wife team founded this company. In the beginning there were bio juices made from oranges and blood oranges. The crucial factor from the start was procuring certified raw materials for healthy, natural products with low environmental impact and recyclable packaging. Soon the Rovedas moved on to production of various types of yogurt using organic and certified biodynamic milk, garnering gluten-free certification in 2012. Lastly, there is a dessert line. In 2005, Fattoria Scaldasole, formerly part of the Heinz Group (Plasmon), was acquired by the French agri-food giant Andros.

Scarpato

VILLA BARTOLOMEA (VR) **l** via Olmetto, 27
☎ (+39) 0442637327 ✆ www.scarpato.it
✉ scarpato@scarpato.it **shop:** no **e-commerce:** no

PATISSERIE. Founded way back in 1888, Scarpato are proud of their panettoni Christmas cakes, colombe Easter cakes, and baked sweets, all leavened naturally over three days so as to guarantee a light, easy to digest treat. In addition to the classics, there are unique varieties like ricotta and citrus fruit, 'cioccococco', cherry and Chantilly cream, strawberries and Champagne, coffee with anise, pineapple, pistachio, pumpkin and amaretto, marron glacé, citrus fruit, whole wheat with honey, and even varieties for vegans, diabetics and those with lactose intolerance. But these shouldn't overshadow the rest of their product line, which includes decadent biscotti like baci di dama (with hazelnut or zabaione), brownies, soft amaretti cookies, their soft schiacciata, megamuffins, sweet truffles (with amaretto, pistachio or chocolate), chocolates, variety of nougat, babà (with rum or lemon) and the sbrisolona. We should also mention their lovely gift packaging, which makes it all that much better.

Dr. Schär

POSTAL/BURGSTALL (BZ) I Winkelau, 9
☎ (+39) 0473293300 ✪ www.schaer.com
✉ info.it@drschaer.com **shop:** no **e-commerce:** no

NATURAL FOOD. Since 1922 the company has been producing and marketing products for healthy eating. At first everything revolved around the nutritional requirements of young children but it soon introduced its first series of dietary products without gluten, developed specially for children who suffer from gastrointestinal disorders. In 1981, the first selection became a full line of gluten-free products and ever since the company has grown, increasing its facilities, not just in Italy, but also in Germany, USA, and Spain, incorporating other brands and becoming an international group. Today's product range includes bread, pasta, flour, snacks, cereals, patisserie, biscuits, frozen food and ready meals.

Riso Scotti

PAVIA I via Angelo Scotti, 2
☎ (+39) 03825081 ✪ www.risoscotti.it
✉ info@risoscotti.it **shop:** yes **e-commerce:** yes

RICE. When Pietro Scotti founded Riso Scotti in 1860 the company processed the cereal and sold it to third parties. In 1890 his son Ercole moved to Villanterio and two of his eight children, Angelo and Gaetano, would follow in his footsteps, working in rice shipping. The company developed to such an extent that it changed from an individual business to a de facto corporation, F.lli Scotti, and the original artisanal rice processing soon became industrialized. In 1953 Ferdinando Scotti, Angelo's son, purchased an old rice-processing mill at Torretta a Pavia, refurbished it and transferred the head office from Villanterio to Pavia. Today, over 150 years later, Scotti SpA is the parent company of a team of high-tech rice businesses, some specializing in growing, research and experimentation, others in processing, transformation and sales. The product range includes various types of rice, rice flour pasta and bread, biscuits, patisserie, condiments and vegetal drinks.

Segafredo Zanetti

PIANORO (BO) I via Puccini, 1
☎ (+39) 0516202111 ✆ www.segafredo.it
✉ info@segafredo.it **shop:** yes **e-commerce:** yes

COFFEE, TEA, INFUSIONS. An icon of Made-in-Italy espresso, Segafredo Zanetti was established in the early 1970s and thanks to expansion became the world's first private coffee sector group. It is the fifth largest producer, with three million sacks of raw coffee sold every year, as well as the only group to be 100% integrated with control of the whole production chain, from plant to cup. The ingredients come from their own plantations in Brazil, Costa Rica and Hawaii, guaranteeing a high and consistent standard in the end product. The company offers a full range of coffees for all requirements as well as infusions, teas, barley coffee and ginseng, sugar and chocolate. The company belongs to the Massimo Zanetti Beverage group, a holding company consisting of a large network of businesses which are constantly and rapidly growing around the world.

Segnana

TRENTO I via Ponte di Ravina, 13
☎ (+39) 0461972311 ✆ www.segnana.it
✉ info@segnana.it **shop:** yes **e-commerce:** no

LIQUEURS, SYRUPS, DISTILLATES. In 1860 Paolo Segnana began distilling pomace in his portable still, installed atop a wagon. And so it was that the Segnana distillery was born. In the 1980s Segnana was bought by the Lunelli family, who'd already been producing Ferrari sparkling wines and owned vineyards in Tuscany and Umbria (as well as Surgiva water). Today, this cutting-edge distillery is situated next to the Ferrari winery, thus reducing the time needed to transport the pomace to the still, and guaranteeing its freshness, fragrance and flavor. Their selection of spirits is varied and compelling. We were struck by their sun-aged grappa, and grappa aged in Sherry barrels. There are plenty of monovarietal grappas as well. For enthusiasts, they offer the Segnana 150°, produced every year in 1,860 elegant, numbered bottles and featuring the year of the distillery's founding on the label. Guided visits of the facility are available on request.

Sibona

PIOBESI D'ALBA (CN) I via Castellero, 5
☎ (+39) 0173614914 I 0173610577 ❀ www.distilleriasibona.it
✉ info@distilleriasibona.it **shop:** yes **e-commerce:** no

LIQUEURS, SYRUPS, DISTILLATES. In a lovely town in the heart of Roero you'll find Sibona, a distillery with over a hundred years of history. Sibona is situated in an area of Piedmont that's famous for its prestigious vineyards, distilling grappa using local nebbiolo, barbera, arneis and moscato grapes. The pomace is worked while it is still fresh, so as to conserve its fragrance. Thanks to their skill, strict quality controls and well-maintained equipment, the standard of quality is consistently very high. In addition to their selection of young grappas, Sibona also produce aged spirits, using barrels in which some of the most prized wines and distillates are also aged, from Port to Sherry, Madeira and Tennessee Whiskey. Their vintage line features a series of complex and elegant grappas. You'll also find more novel products like their chamomile and aloe liquors, their decadent grappa filled chocolates (using Moscato grapes), chocolates made with amaro, and finally their 'drinkable cigars', single-shots of grappa. Their elegant gift wrapping is a nice touch.

Molino Sima

ARGENTA (FE) I via Circonvallazione, 2
☎ (+39) 0532804524 ❀ www.molinosima.it
✉ info@molinosima.it **shop:** no **e-commerce:** no

FLOURS, PULSES, CEREALS. The brand is represented by a farmer association that is currently one of the largest in Italy, the Cooperativa Agricola Giulio Bellini. With a century under its belt as far as production is concerned, it also pays great attention to the environment and to technological innovation. Since 1992 the brand has produced organic flour obtained from cereals grown by members, especially spelt and wheat grown in the Ferrara area. It was one of the first to import Kamut® khorosan, and today is a major producer at world level. The range includes many types of flour (including stone- ground), special, bio and Senatore Cappelli durum wheat. From sowing to harvest, milling, storage of flour, everything is strictly controlled and certified.

Sommariva

ALBENGA (SV) I via G. Mameli, 7
☎ (+39) 0182559222 ✆ www.oliosommariva.it
✉ info@oliosommariva.it **shop:** yes **e-commerce:** no

PRESERVES, JAMS. In the heart of the medieval town of Ponente Ligure, you'll find Sommariva, the producer founded by Domenico Sommariva in 1915. In addition to fine extra virgin olive oil (including aromatized varieties), there are salts, vinegars, various types of pasta, a line of cosmetic products, spices and herbs. Indeed, they offer a wide range of products: Genoese pesto (there's also organic, without garlic, vegan and with PDO basil), red and dill pesto, vegetable cream sauces (arugula, tomatoes and artichokes), walnut sauce, delicious bottled produce (dried tomatoes and seeds, grilled artichokes and peppers, mixed vegetables, tomino cheese, seasoned lard, capers in vinegar or salt, sardines and tuna) and treats, including Italian peppers stuffed with tuna or anchovies and capers. Their 400 square meter museum is worth a visit. Here you can learn about olive oil history and culture, but there's also modern art, from painting to sculpture all the way to photography and works of literature.

Molino Spadoni

RAVENNA I fraz. Coccolia I via Ravegnana, 746
☎ (+39) 0544569056 ✆ www.molinospadoni.it
✉ info@molinospadoni.it **shop:** yes **e-commerce:** no

FLOURS, PULSES, CEREALS. Molino di Vinovo, built between Ravenna and Forlì by the historic Pier Capponi family, has been milling grain since 1445. Owned by the Spadoni family since 1923, it has chosen to invest in cutting-edge milling technology with the objective of ensuring the highest quality for all its customers. For this reason, it is the international leader in marketing flours and special blends for both domestic and professional use. The company is headquartered in Coccolia (Ravenna), where the main plant is active, with the mill and warehouse. It is now attested on the domestic market, Europe and worldwide, also producing yeast, bread substitutes, rice, liqueurs and wine, as well as cold ready foods (puddings and custards).

Acqua Sparea

LUSERNA SAN GIOVANNI (TO) I via Ponte Pietra, 3
☎ (+39) 0121954002 ❀ www.acquasparea.com
✉ crosso@damilanog.com **shop:** no **e-commerce:** no

WATER, BEVERAGES, FRUIT JUICES. The Piedmontese brand of the Pontevecchio Acque Minerali group owned by the Damilano family. On the market for 40 years, it is now a cutting-edge business on mineral water scenario, bottling from five mountain springs in the Alps, at the foot of Mount Frioland. The founder is Giovanni Damilano and headquarters are in Lucerna San Giovanni, in the province of Turin. Production started up in 1971 with a line for bottling industrial mineral water and Sparea spring water in returnable glass. Today it also bottles Valmora, Alpi Cozie, Fonti delle Alpi and Monviso waters. The chic bottles contain pure, light water in natural, slightly sparkling and sparkling versions (blue, red or yellow) label. Also available in PET.

Sperlari

CREMONA I via Milano 16
☎ (+39) 03424821 ❀ www.sperlari.it
✉ info@leaf.it **shop:** no **e-commerce:** no

··Sperlari··

PATISSERIE. In Cremona, Enea Sperlari opened a shop for artisanal production and sale of typical traditional local specialities: nougat and fruit relish. That was in 1836 and the products were a huge success, so by the end of the century the Sperlari brand had even gone overseas, reaching numerous Italian communities. In 1950 its range of products extended to include sweets and turned them into an outright cult object. In the 1960s the Sperlari gift pack was launched, an appealing casket of sweets that was a great alternative to the classic box of chocolates: in just one year 8,000,000 were sold. Today Sperlari is a Cloetta Italia srl brand and is a leader in the markets of nougat bars, bite-size nougats, pralines, fruit relish and, of course, sweets.

Molini Spigadoro

BASTIA UMBRA (PG) **I** via IV Novembre, 2/4
☎ (+39) 0758009216 ☉ www.molinispigadoro.com
✉ info@molinispigadoro.com **shop:** no **e-commerce:** yes

FLOURS, PULSES, CEREALS. Molini Spigadoro operates in Umbria, the green heart of Italy. Its origins and its geographical location make it a company attentive to environmental values. It performs 30,000 checks across the production chain, offering a range of superior quality products. Thanks to dynamic and consistent entrepreneurial development, inspired by experimentation and the pursuit of excellence, the company is present on the flour market with a range of professional and domestic products. Its extensive range is very characteristic: from classic flour to bakery products (including organic and gluten-free) to those specific to patisseries and pizzerias, and a line of products with high nutritional value.

Stainer

PONTREMOLI (MS) **I** Zona Industriale Novoleto
☎ (+39) 0187830091 ☉ www.stainerchocolate.it
✉ info@stainerchocolate.it **shop:** no **e-commerce:** yes

CHOCOLATE. Stainer's founders were inspired by the Austrian dessert tradition. Indeed, here tradition and innovation come together to create unique products that maintain the original characteristics, peculiarities and nuances of the ingredients used, all of which are carefully selected. Thanks to constant research and experimentation, Stainer's line of products is truly impressive, starting with dozens of varieties of chocolate bars, which are also available in sugar-free, lactose-free, gluten-free and organic varieties, as well as with goat's milk, soy milk, milk from the Alps and coconut milk (just to give you an idea). And that's not to mention their spiced chocolates, their gourmet line and a host of chocolate candies and pralines available in different flavors (and with optional gift wrap packaging). Don't forget about their supplements, coffee beans, chocolate covered cocoa beans and ginger, hazelnut gianduia cream spread, as well as mixes for pudding, mousse, sorbet, frappés, ice cream, baked goods and hot chocolate.

Stock

MILANO I via Tucidide, 56 bis
☎ (+39) 0249681201 ✪ www.stockspirits.com
✉ reception@stock-spa.it **shop:** no **e-commerce:** no

LIQUEURS, SYRUPS, DISTILLATES. The story began in Trieste, in 1884, when 18-year-old Lionello Stock from Dalmatia opened a small steam distillery, intending to distil local wines which were popular with the French for cognac production after an outbreak of late blight destroyed their harvest. This was the birth of Cognac Stock Medicinal, joined in 1935 by the 1884 Cognac Fine Champagne, which was to become the famous Brandy Stock 84 in 1955. After the First World War many factories were built in Europe and elsewhere: his success was based on marketing and advertising. Later Stock relaunched itself using its brandy, and between the 1950s and 1960s Stock products were distributed in 125 countries, expanding into whisky, vodka, grappa, bitters, gin and sweet liqueurs. In 1995 Stock was purchased by German company Eckes AG., a company producing alcoholic drinks and fruit juices. In 2007 Stock Spirit Group became the owner of American fund Oaktree, which numbers many brands today including Stock Original, Stock Napoleon and Stock 84.

Strega Alberti

BENEVENTO I p.zza Vittoria Colonna, 8
☎ (+39) 082454292 ✪ www.strega.it
✉ info@strega.it **shop:** yes **e-commerce:** yes

LIQUEURS, SYRUPS, DISTILLATES. Giuseppe Alberti, father of Strega liqueur, opened a café in the main square of Benevento, which would become the meeting place for liberal thinkers of the period. He began producing Strega in 1860, and it was named for the legend claiming that the city of Benevento was the site of witchcraft rituals. His children consolidated the business and expanded production of the liqueur to new markets. In 1947, on the initiative of Maria and Goffredo Bellonci and Guido Albert, the Premio Strega was invented, which is the most important Italian literary award. In the economic boom years Strega became popular abroad with production in Sao Paulo, Brazil, and Buenos Aires. Later the Alberti sweet industry began, with Strega nougat, chocolates with and without Strega, and speciality cakes like caprese, pannocchio, colomba, panettone and pandoro, naturally with Strega. These have recently been joined by a gluten-free range.

Surgital

CONSELICE (RA) I fraz. Lavezzola I via Bastia, 16/1
☎ (+39) 054580328 ❀ www.surgital.it
✉ surgital@surgital.it **shop:** yes **e-commerce:** no

L'italiana preferita dallo chef.

FROZEN FOOD. Laboratorio Artigianale Tortellini was created in 1980 by Edoardo Bacchini and his wife, who have generations of experience in pasta-making. Their two great plans were: selling fresh pasta to local restaurants, and freezing. In 1984 Edoardo patented a machine for garganelli romagnoli, after which production became faster and the cold chain was increasingly employed. By the 1990s there were about 60 types of fresh pasta distributed to various parts of Italy, and two production lines were started: pre-cooked lasagne, under the Prontosfoglia brand name, and potato gnocchi. In 1998 Surgital Spa and the Fiordiprimi lines appeared, for quality ready meals. The market developed throughout the world. Today there are nine brands and the same number of product lines of frozen fresh pasta, single or multi-portion ready dishes, and frozen sauces in pellet form. The company is a benchmark for the catering industry, bars, hotels and fast-food venues.

Acqua Surgiva

CARISOLO (TN) I via Pignole, 10
☎ (+39) 0461972311 ❀
✉ contact@surgiva.it **shop:** no **e-commerce:** no

Surgiva

ACQUA MINERALE
NATURALE

WATER, BEVERAGES, FRUIT JUICES. Part of the Lunelli group, the owner of Ferrari, the famous winery making the sparkling wine most loved by Italians; of the historic Segnana distillery, synonymous with refined, elegant grappas; a line of regional wines; and of Locanda Margon. The name of this water is a homage to the immaculate peaks of the Parco Naturale Adamello Brenta in the heart of Trentino, where its springs forth in all purity at high altitude near Madonna di Campiglio. It is bottled in the Carisolo plant with technologically advanced installations, and is one of the lightest waters found, with very low nitrate content.

 (left margin, vertical text)

Leading brands

Distilleria Toschi

SAVIGNANO SUL PANARO (MO) I via Genova, 244
☎ (+39) 059768711 ✪ www.toschi.it
✉ toschi@toschi.it **shop:** yes **e-commerce:** no

TOSCHI
Gustosa, la vita

LIQUEURS, SYRUPS, DISTILLATES. Toschi was created in 1945 in Vignola (Modena) thanks to an idea from Giancarlo and Lanfranco Toschi, to make the famous Vignola cherries in syrup so they could be enjoyed all year round. In 1953 the packaging inspired by the Ferrari car appeared, containing Toschi liqueurs, while 1957 saw the creation of a cherry brandy made from an infusion o f black cherries (called morette) in alcohol. In its 65 years of business the company, whose headquarters is in Savignano sul Panaro, has vastly expanded its range which now includes fruits in alcool syrup, liqueurs (Fragolì, Mirtillì, Nocino, Nocello, Lemoncello), syrups and mixes for cakes and ice cream (toppings, garnishes and base mixes), drinks, IGP Aceto Balsamico di Modena, and products for coeliacs, vegans and vegetarians.

Tre Cime Mondolatte

DOBBIACO/TOBLACH (BZ) I via Pusteria, 3c
☎ (+39) 0474971300 ✪ www.3zinnen.it
✉ info@mondolattetrecime.com **shop:** yes **e-commerce:** yes

CHEESE. The origins of Latteria Tre Cime date back to the end of the 1800s. Today it is a cooperative that collects the milk of Alta Val Pusteria from 180 member farms, from a total of 2,500 cows fed with untreated forage from the region, and ensuring a unique flavour. The raw material is processed by the Schwarz method of cold milk creaming. The production range is rich and tasty: cream, butter, milk, yogurt, and cheese, including Dobbiaco; caciotta; fontal; Ortus with tomato and garlic; Diavolo with pepper and chilli; Bacchus with red wine; and a very fragrant herb cheese.

Le Tre Marie

EMPOLI (FI) I via Tosco Romagnola, 56
☎ (+39) 0221791 ✆ www.tremarie.it
✉ info@tremarie.it **shop:** yes **e-commerce:** yes

PATISSERIE. Legend has it that in 1150, the Milan bakery of the Quattro Marie Christian confraternity offered the needy bread and flour in exchange for copper coins depicting the Virgin Mary, Mary Magdalene, Mary Salome and Mary of Cleophas. Then the image of the Blessed Virgin was separated from the three minor Marys and they became the current shingle. In 1896 the legendary bakery turned into the elegant Tre Marie patisserie, whose speciality was panettone. Its more recent history began in the 1960s, when the owners sent 150 letters to the best pastry shops in Italy, inviting them to be exclusive agents for their area, driving a relaunch. From the 1970s to the present, production has added ice cream and other desserts. The artisanal skills of bygone times survive in the pastry specialities and leavened products that preserve the flavour and fragrance of pastries of yesteryear. In 2013 Galbusera Spa bought the Tre Marie Ricorrenze company, owner of the Tre Marie brands for celebration products, biscuits, crackers and ready-made cakes.

Tre Valli Cooperlat

JESI (AN) I via Piandelmedico, 74
☎ (+39) 07312381 ✆ www.trevalli.cooperlat.it
✉ info@trevalli.cooperlat.it **shop:** no **e-commerce:** no

CHEESE. Trevalli Cooperlat consists of 15 basic cooperatives and associates about 1,000 agricultural producers who provide the milk. Today it is a major agribusiness, one of the top players in the Italian dairy sector, and increasingly important abroad. With two main lines of products split into Tre Valli's Noi brand, linked to tradition and local trademarks, and Hoplà, a leader in the field of vegetable creams, it ensures ongoing improvement of product quality, diversification of production and research. The range is extensive, from fresh and long-life milk to butter, yoghurt, ice cream, ricotta, mozzarella and the various types of cheeses.

Trentin

CEREA (VR) I via Genova, 19 Zona Industriale
☎ (+39) 0442398111 ✪ www.trentingroup.it
✉ commerciale@trentingroup.it **shop:** no **e-commerce:** no

CHEESE. The well-deserved success of the Trentin Group, founded and still run by the Trentin family, can be traced back to their continued passion and commitment, their deep knowledge of cheesemaking, their long and enduring experience (accumulated over generations), their use of the latest technology (for production but also packaging and storing), and their sensitivity to the changing demands of consumers and markets. It goes without saying that all their cheeses are subject to strict quality controls, which are carried out at every stage of production. Their certified Parmigiano Reggiano meets all the difficult demands required by this cheese. The same is true of their Pecorino Romano, Gorgonzola, Grana Padano, Montasio, Provolone Valpadana, Asiago and Fontina, all available directly from the producer or at major distributors. There's also a practical cheese mix called 'Festival', a versatile resource in the kitchen.

Turri

CAVAION VERONESE (VR) I loc. Cantinegirelli I s.da Villa, 9
☎ (+39) 0457235598 ✪ www.turri.com
✉ info@turri.com **shop:** no **e-commerce:** no

EXTRA VIRGIN OLIVE OIL. Since 1951 the Turri family have cultivated olives. Today Mario, Laura, Luisa and Giovanni, the third generation, grow more than 27 types of olives common to Garda and Veneto, and olives from other parts of Italy as well. They also have an old wooden press and a more modern facility where their crop is transformed into oil shortly after it is harvested. Six types of oils are produced, each one with its own specific characteristics, including the fruity Garda Orientale PDO (which has gained notable national recognition) and an organic line. There are also aromatized oils, olives, delicious bottled produce, vinegars and a line of cosmetics made with olive oil. Visits and tasting events can be organized year-round.

Acqua Uliveto

VICOPISANO (PI) I fraz. Uliveto Terme I s.da prov.le Vicarese
☎ (+39) 050788194 I 050789069 ❂ www.uliveto.it
✉ cogedi@cogedi.it **shop:** no **e-commerce:** no

WATER, BEVERAGES, FRUIT JUICES. In a book he published in 1835, the renowned physician Giuli spoke openly of the beneficial effects of this water, whose springs are at Uliveto, a small town where the olive rules. At the turn of the 1900s his studies were observed carefully by other distinguished Italian clinicians whose work also contributed to the development of the spa facilities. In 1910, given the important health benefits afforded by this water, the Società per Azioni Acqua e Terme di Uliveto company built the first bottling plant. The natural mineral water springs are still the same, located near Vicopisano, in the province of Pisa, and the water is immediately bottled by the Uliveto Terme plant. The company is part of the Co.Ge.Di. Uliveto-Rocchetta group.

Urbani Tartufi

SANT'ANATOLIA DI NARCO (PG) I s.s. Valnerina, km 31,300
☎ (+39) 0743613171 ❂ www.urbanitartufi.it
✉ info@urbanitartufi.it **shop:** yes **e-commerce:** no

MUSHROOMS, TRUFFLES. For the Urbani family truffles have always been and still are a raison d'être. A bloodline that began with Costantino Urbani in 1952 and continued in time thanks to a love for the land, the trust shared with the hunters, the creation of an academy, a confraternity and a museum dedicated to the truffle. Today's Urbanis have opened leading branches overseas. In about a century, the range offered has expanded and diversified, also opening up to the world of mushrooms with a dedicated line. There are fresh and frozen truffles (all varieties), oils, sauces, ready condiments (artichoke and truffle; cream and truffle; tomato and truffle), butter, cream, oil and much more. There are also organic, kosher and vegetarian options.

Vallelata

MILANO I via F. Gioia, 8
☎ (+39) 0243356111 ❖ www.vallelata.it
✉ ext.comm@it.lactalis.com **shop:** no **e-commerce:** no

CHEESE. Vallelata was founded in 1990 as a Galbani brand. It has always been identified with fresh cheeses of good quality and intense milky flavour. From mozzarella to ricotta, robiola and scamorza, the cheeses are made from raw materials processed with all the care needed to preserve quality intact and safeguard the freshness and simplicity that only Nature can create. Vallelata mozzarella is processed with eco-friendly production methods, inspired by Italian dairy traditions: only good milk and no preservatives. The range also includes buffalo mozzarella, burrata and fiordilatte. Vallelata is part of the Lactalis Italia group.

Valsoia

BOLOGNA I via I. Barontini, 16/5
☎ (+39) 0516086800 ❖ www.valsoiaspa.com
✉ info@valsoia.it **shop:** no **e-commerce:** no

PRESERVES, JAMS. Valsoia is a reassuringly constant presence among Italian food manufacturers. For years it has been at the forefront in terms of quality and identifying new products capable of satisfying the increasingly health-conscious tastes of consumers. It has made a name for itself by choosing quality ingredients, using top-notch technology and offering a variety of products. They manage four brands of products, starting with Valsoia (www.valsoia.it), which offers a wide range of plant-based products, including desserts and ice creams. Next there's Naturattiva (www.naturattiva.com), with its line of soy and rice products. Then there's Santa Rosa (www.santarosa.it), which has dealt in high quality preserves and fresh sorbets since 1968. Finally, there's Pomodorissimo (www.pomodorissimo.it), a line of fragrant tomato sauces, available in classic or chunky varieties, and even fat-free. They also work with Weetabix, distributing their healthy cereal and grain breakfast products.

Distilleria Varnelli

MUCCIA (MC) I via G. Varnelli, 10
☎ (+39) 0737647000 ✪ www.varnelli.it
✉ varnelli@varnelli.it **shop:** yes **e-commerce:** no

LIQUEURS, SYRUPS, DISTILLATES. This is Marche's oldest liqueur business, founded in 1868 by Girolamo Varnelli who lived in Cupi di Visso, in the Sibillini mountains. His knowledge of herbs brought about Amaro Sibilla, based on yellow gentian, cinchona, and other medicinal plants. Then his son Antonio moved the business to Pievebogliana and expanded the range with various products including the flagship Varnelli, a special dry anise and sophisticated interpretation of Marche mistrà. Antonio also imposed organizational structure on the company. In later years Varnelli became a leader in the anise sector, establishing the liqueur as the favourite addition to coffee. Throughout the generations the family's experience in herbs has remained intact along with the old artisan processing methods and secret recipes. Today production takes place in Muccia, in the province of Macerata, with a range of products from anise to liqueurs, bitters, punch and a line of pastries.

Venchi

CASTELLETTO STURA (CN) I via Venchi, 1
☎ (+39) 0171791611 ✪ www.venchi.com
✉ info@venchi.com **shop:** yes **e-commerce:** yes

il cioccolato dal 1878

CHOCOLATE. Silvano Venchi opened his confectionery workshop in Via degli Artisti in Turin, in 1878. The company soon conquered the palate of many Torinese, above all with its Nougatina, a sweet made from chopped, caramelized hazelnuts coated with a chocolate glaze. In the 1900s Venchi grew fast and its products become famous far beyond Piedmont. Recently Venchi joined forces with Cuba, a confectionery company owned by Pietro Cussino, a master pâtissier from Cuneo. Today, maintaining quality at the highest levels, without chemicals or preservatives, Venchi exports its products to 55 countries. Its flagships include gianduiotti, chocolate and hazelnut cream, Crema Cubana al rum, and Chocaviar (minute chocolate beads that look like caviar), then ice cream, fruit jellies and a line of organic chocolate. All products are gluten-free.

Vergnano

SANTENA (TO) **l** s.s. Torino-Asti, km 20
☎ (+39) 0119455111 ✿ www.caffevergnano.com
✉ italia@caffevergnano.com **shop:** yes **e-commerce:** yes

COFFEE, TEA, INFUSIONS. The trademark shows 1882 as the year in which the adventure began. Domenico Vergnano opened a small grocery store in Chieri, a small town at the foot of the Turin hills. In just a few years it developed into coffee roasting and sales, with considerable success. The business grew with the first three warehouses in Turin, Alba and Chieri, but the real quantum leap took place in the 1930s, with the purchase of a coffee farm in Kenya. Today, after earning space on the international overview with exports to 60 countries, Vergnano promotes coffee culture through the Coffee Shop 1882 project, a network of Italian-style cafés around the world. Their commitment to the environment shows in the Cialde line of coffee pods of low environmental impact.

Vicenzi

SAN GIOVANNI LUPATOTO (VR) **l** via Forte Garofolo, 1
☎ (+39) 0458262800 ✿ www.vicenzi.it
✉ info@vicenzi.it **shop:** no **e-commerce:** no

PATISSERIE. Vincenzi got its start in 1905 as a small, completely family-run enterprise. Today the group comprises three brands: the international Matilde Vicenzi (www.matildevicenzi.it), Grisbi (www.grisbi.it), and Mr. Day (www.mrday.it). Despite their accomplishments, they still maintain the same values and principles on which the business was founded: respect for tradition, the use of select ingredients (only stone-ground Italian flours, free-range eggs, fresh butter, 'real' fruit preserves etc.) and, especially, attention to quality. Moreover, they are constantly researching methods to make new products and make their old products better. Among the most famous of Matilde Vicenzi's 'sweets' are their fragrant, savoiardi, amaretti cookies, their flaky millefoglie, their cantuccini, biscotti, 'minivoglie' pastries, as well as their bigné (with whatever filling you like) and spongecake for various types of desserts.

Molino Vigevano 1936

TORRE D'ISOLA (PV) I via dell'Artigianato, 5
☎ (+39) 0384298479 I 0384876121 ◈ www.molinovigevano.com
✉ molinovi@molinovigevano.it **shop:** no **e-commerce:** no

FLOURS, PULSES, CEREALS. Easy to reach from the A7 Pavia Nord-Bereguardo highway, this historic flour producer, bought by Gruppo Lo Conte in 2013, has more than 80 years of experience in the sector. They produce two lines of flours: those for ordinary, domestic cooking and those for commercial activities like pastry shops, bread makers, pizza makers, restaurants etc. In fact, it's for exactly these types of kitchens that they realized products like their Oro di Macina flour, stone-ground and produced using cold extraction, both of which protect the original grain and make it easier to work with. Home cooks can choose from semi-whole wheat flour, risciola, moreschina, manitoba strong flour, flours for sweets, flours for pizza and focaccia, for soft desserts, tarts and cookies, for frying and batters. There's also a line of yeasts (natural yeast starters and organic), made using ancient, stone-ground Risciola flour (100% Italian) and vital wheat germ.

Villani

CASTELNUOVO RANGONE (MO) I via E. Zanasi, 24
☎ (+39) 059534411 ◈ www.villanisalumi.it
✉ info@villanisalumi.it **shop:** no **e-commerce:** no

CHARCUTERIE. This company was the brainchild, in 1886, of Ernesta and Costante Villani. Today there are five production plants between Bassa and Friuli, in the PDO and IGP zones. The fifth generation of the family is now in charge of what is Italy?s oldest charcuterie business, nationally renowned in the sector. The artisan spirit behind its origins and a strong connection with the land have always been ingredients of company philosophy. Today Villani produces an excellent range of products: starting with its 'cru', Prosciutto di San Daniele and Prosciutto di Parma 24 Mesi; pancetta and culatello; PDO and IGP charcuterie (some gluten-free); cooked hams, mortadella, sliced meats and other delicatessen specialities. There is also the Poderi Santa Maria del Tiepido line of EVOO, balsamic vinegar and Lambrusco Grasparossa di Castelvetro. Villani recently acquired the Maletti brand, which specializes in charcuterie production and fine food hampers.

Virgilio Latterie Mantovane

MANTOVA I v.le della Favorita, 19
☎ (+39) 03763861 ✪ www.consorzio-virgilio.it
✉ info@consorzio-virgilio.it **shop:** no **e-commerce:** no

CHEESE. The consortium got its start in 1966 and today comprises 70 member dairy producers and more than 2,000 milk suppliers. Their aim is to provide consumers with excellent products that respect traditional methods and quality standards but also take advantage of the best of what technology has to offer. Virgilio Latterie Mantovane is the only Italian consortium that has managed to bring together producers of Grana Padano PDO and Parmigiano Reggiano PDO, a feat made possible by the fact of having a presence that spans the left and right banks of the river Po. Parmigiano Reggiano, aged anywhere from 18 to 30 months, is their crown jewel. Then there's their Grana Padano, available aged 16, 18 or 24 months, and as a sliced cheese or small cheeses. They also offer whipped cream, cream, milk and besciamella. They also make butter, mascarpone, stracchino, certified squacquerone di Romagna and coffee desserts as well.

Zafferano 3 Cuochi - Bonetti

MILANO I via delle Forze Armate, 320
☎ (+39) 024562082 ✪ www.zafferano-3cuochi.it
✉ info@3cuochi.it **shop:** no **e-commerce:** no

CONDIMENTS: SALT, SPICES, HERBS. The venerable 3 Cuochi brand is a leader in the Italian saffron market. The story begins in 1935, when Gianni Mangini founded a production company, now run by the third generation, and created the brand that immediately met with success. Tradition and avant-garde technology combine in the sachets of 3 Cuochi pure saffron powder obtained from the best batches of spice from various countries, which undergoes careful quality control throughout processing, and is packaged with materials that preserve its qualities at length. Delicate, bright red 3 Cuochi saffron has none of the white specks that indicate lower quality of the original ingredients. The saffron is dry and slips easily from the sachet, making it easy to use in dishes because it dissolves and doses more easily than saffron threads, giving uniform flavour and colour.

Zanetti

LALLIO (BG) I via della Madonna, 1
☎ (+39) 035201511 ✿ www.zanetti-spa.it
✉ commerciale@zanetti-spa.it **shop:** no **e-commerce:** no

CHEESE. Zanetti began at the end of the 19th century as a small, artisanal operation for aging hard cheeses. Over time they evolved, enlarging, upgrading and increasing the number of facilities and eventually purchasing other producers. Indeed, today Zanetti, whose presence goes beyond national boundaries, is one of the most valued and important dairy producers in Italy. Grana Padano PDO is their crown jewel, available as an aged Riserva, grated or packaged in small portions. Parmigiano Reggiano PDO, also available in various ages, is just as important to their core business. There's even an organic variety. Then there's Provolone Valpadana PDO, pecorino cheeses, local Bergamo specialities (including Branzi, Taleggio PDO, stracchino, robiola, Blutunt, Formai del Mut), and a wide selection of dairy products (mascarpone, mozzarella, ricotta, burrata etc.), goat cheeses, speciality cheeses for the cheese connoisseur (Ubriaco del Piave, Cuor di tartufo, Gran Riserva al pepe, Caciocavallo in vinaccia) and more.

Zarotti

PARMA I s.da nuova di Coloreto, 15a
☎ (+39) 0521243371 ✿ zarotti.it
✉ info@zarotti.it **shop:** no **e-commerce:** no

PRESERVED FISH. Zarotti, also known as "those anchovy guys", is among Italy's leading brands in the field of canned fish. In 1993, Zarotti was bought by a family from San Marco di Castellabate, the Scerminos, who already owned a plant that operated in the sector. Their logistical center is in Parma (administration, sales, marketing, distribution). Production still occurs along the Cilento coast in a modern plant equipped with the latest technology. All phases of production are subject to strict controls, from fishing to final sale. In keeping with a strategy of delocalizing production, they've opened plants in Albania and Morocco. Their selection mostly centers on anchovies and tuna, both of which are processed in the place where they are caught, and sold in a variety of formats, including a organic line and their Mar Cantabrico (anchovies), packed in glass or in cans. Zarotti is certified IFS (International Food Standard) and "Friend of the Sea".

Zuegg

VERONA I via Francia, 6
☎ (+39) 0458292611 ✆ www.zuegg.it
✉ info@zuegg.it **shop:** no **e-commerce:** no

Passione per la frutta, amore per la vita

PRESERVES, JAMS. Maria Zuegg founded her company over a century ago, making fruit juices and jams. In 1890 she began selling apples, which she exported as far as Saint Petersburg. In 1923 came the first jam production, which was very successful on northern Italy markets. In 1954 the Lana d'Adige facility began producing fruit-based drinks: apricot, peach and pear juices. In the 1960s a new plant was inaugurated in Verona, processing semi-finished fruit-based products, yogurt items, tarts and ice cream for food industries. A facility opened at Luogosano (near Avellino) on 1985, and in subsequent years factories opened in Germany, France, Austria, and Russia. Short production chain and zero waste have become fundamental aspects in Zuegg's production philosophy. Latest additions to the range are fruit velvets and organic Cremose, a smooth product made only with organic fruit.

Fresh fruits &vegetables

Fresh fruits&vegetables

Valle d'Aosta

MELE

PERE MARTIN SEC

APPLES

MARTIN SEC PEARS

Cofruits

SAINT-PIERRE (AO) I loc. Cognein, 6
☎ (+39) 0165 903282 - (+39) 0165 903436
✆ www.cofruits.it ✉ info@cofruits.it

Consorzio Gran Paradiso Natura

VILLENEUVE (AO) I loc. Trepont, 90
☎ (+39) 348 7384543 ✆ www.granparadisonatura.vda.it

Cooperativa Consorzio Produttori Frutta

GRESSAN (AO) I fraz. Chez le Ru, 21
☎ (+39) 0165 250205 - (+39) 340 4148141

Piedmont

CASTAGNA CUNEO IGP

MARRONE DELLA VALLE DI SUSA IGP

NOCCIOLA PIEMONTE IGP

PGI CUNEO CHESTNUT

PGI VALLE DI SUSA CHESTNUT

PGI PIEDMONT HAZELNUT

Consorzio per la valorizzazione e la tutela della Castagna Cuneo Igp - Asprofrut

LAGNASCO (CN) I via Praetta, 8
☎ (+39) 0175 282311 ✆ www.asprofrut.com ✉ info@assortofrutta.eu

Consorzio Tutela Nocciola Piemonte Igp

CASTAGNITO (CN) I via Alba, 15
☎ (+39) 0173 210311 ✉ info@nocciolapiemonte.it

Liguria

BASILICO GENOVESE DOP

CHINOTTO DI SAVONA

PDO GENOA BASIL

SAVONA SOUR ORANGES

Consorzio di tutela del Basilico Genovese

GENOVA I Villa Doria Podestà via Pra, 63
☎ (+39) 010 5601152 ✆ www.basilicogenovese.it ✉ info@basilicogenovese.it

Associazione Produttori Chinotto di Savona

FINALE LIGURE (SV) I fraz. Finalborgo via Aquila II, 15
☎ (+39) 019 692441 - 339 2665855

Lombardy

MELA DI VALTELLINA IGP	*PGI VALTELLINA APPLE*
MELONE MANTOVANO IGP	*PGI MANTUA MELON*
PERA MANTOVANA IGP	*PGI MANTUA PEAR*
ZUCCA MANTOVANA	*MANTUA PUMPKIN*

Agronomia (READY-TO-EAT VEGETABLES)
SAN PAOLO D'ARGON (BG) I via Puccini, 5
☎ (+39) 035 951137 ✪ www.agronomia.biz ✉ agronomia@agronomia.biz

Bonduelle Italia (READY-TO-EAT VEGETABLES)
SAN PAOLO D'ARGON (BG) I via Trento
☎ (+39) 035 4252411 - 800903160 ✪ www.bonduelle.it
✉ servizio.consumatori@bonduelle.com

Consorzio Tutela Mele della Valtellina
TOVO DI SANT'AGATA (SO) I via Roma, 57
☎ (+39) 0342 770122 ✪ www.meladivaltellina.it ✉ infoctm@melavi.it

Consorzio del Melone Mantovano
SERMIDE (MN) I via Ludovico Ariosto, 30a
☎ (+39) 335 6087178 ✪ www.melonemantovano.it ✉ info@melonemantovano.it

Consorzio Perwiwa
MANTOVA I via Giuseppe Mazzini, 16
☎ (+39) 0386 757323 ✪ www.ersaf.lombardia.it ✉ coop.corma@tin.it

Consorzio Agrituristico Mantovano "Verdi Terre d'Acqua"
MANTOVA I s.da Chiesanuova, 8
☎ (+39) 0376 324889 - 329 2127504 ✪ www.agriturismomantova.it
✉ info@agriturismomantova.it

Facchini (READY-TO-EAT VEGETABLES)
PONCARALE (BS) I via Martiri della Libertà, 23
☎ (+39) 030 2640537 ✪ www.facchininatura.it ✉ info@facchininatura.it

La Linea Verde - Dimmidisì (READY-TO-EAT VEGETABLES)
MANERBIO (BS) I via Artigianale, 49
☎ (+39) 030 9373611 ✪ www.lalineaverde.it ✪ www.dimmidisi.it
✉ export@lalineaverde.it ✉ commerciale@lalineaverde.it

Mioorto Società Agricola (READY-TO-EAT VEGETABLES)
CAROBBIO DEGLI ANGELI (BG) I via Don Severino Tiraboschi, 41
☎ (+39) 035 952422 ✪ www.mioorto.it ✉ info@mioorto.it

439

Orto Bellina (READY-TO-EAT VEGETABLES)

GORLAGO (BG) I via Virgilio, 5
☎ (+39) 035 951145 ✪ www.ortobellina.it ✉ info@ortobellina.it

Sab Ortofrutta (READY-TO-EAT VEGETABLES)

TELGATE (BG) I via Cesare Battisti, 80
☎ (+39) 035 4491480 ✪ www.sabortofrutta.it ✉ sab@sabortofrutta.it

Trentino Alto Adige

MELA ALTO ADIGE O SUDTIROLER APFEL IGP	*PGI ALTO ADIGE OR SUDTIROLER APPLE*
MELA VAL DI NON DOP	*PDO VAL DI NON APPLE*

Consorzio Mele Alto Adige – Südtiroler Apfelkonsortium

TERLANO/TERLAN (BZ) I Jakobistrasse/via Jakobi,1a
☎ (+39) 0471 054066 ✪ www.suedtirolerapfel.com ✉ info@suedtirolerapfel.com

Consorzio Melinda

CLES (TN) I via Trento, 200/9
☎ (+39) 0463 671111 ✪ www.melinda.it ✉ melinda@melinda.it

Associazione Produttori Ortofrutticoli Trentini

TRENTO I via del Brennero
☎ (+39) 0461 823730 ✪ www.apot.it ✉ info@apot.it

Veneto

ASPARAGO BIANCO DI BASSANO DOP	*PDO BASSANO WHITE ASPARAGUS*
CILIEGIA DI MAROSTICA IGP	*PGI MAROSTICA CHERRY*
MARRONE DI SAN ZENO DOP	*PDO SAN ZENO CHESTNUT*
PESCA DI VERONA IGP	*PGI VERONA PEACH*
RADICCHIO DI CHIOGGIA IGP	
RADICCHIO DI VERONA IGP	*PGI CHIOGGIA RADICCHIO*
RADICCHIO ROSSO DI TREVISO IGP	*PGI VERONA RADICCHIO*
RADICCHIO VARIEGATO DI CASTELFRANCO IGP	*PGI TREVISO RED RADICCHIO PGI CASTELFRANCO SPECKLED*

Consorzio per la tutela dell'Asparago Bianco di Bassano Dop

BASSANO DEL GRAPPA (VI) I via G. Matteotti, 39
☎ (+39) 0424 521345 ✪ www.asparagobiancobassano.com ✉ info@asparagodop.it

Consorzio per la tutela della Ciliegia di Marostica Igp

c/o Comunità Montana dall'Astico al Brenta I BREGANZE (VI) I p.zza Mazzini, 18
☎ (+39) 0445 873607 ❀ www.ciliegiadimarosticaigp.it ✉ info@ciliegiadimarosticaigp.it

Consorzio di tutela del Marrone di San Zeno Igp

SAN ZENO DI MONTAGNA (VR) I c.da Ca' Montagna, 11
☎ tel. (+39) 045 7285017 ❀ www.marronedisanzeno.it ✉ info@marronedisanzeno.it

Consorzio di tutela della Pesca di Verona Igp

SAN GIOVANNI LUPATOTO (VR) I via Ca' Nova Zampieri, 15
☎ (+39) 045 8750873 ❀ pescadiverona.it ✉ info@pescadiverona.it

Consorzio di tutela Radicchio di Chioggia Igp

c/o Mercato Orticolo di Chioggia I CHIOGGIA (VE) I loc. Brondolo
☎ (+39) 349 5934459 ❀ www.radicchiodichioggiaigp.it
✉ consorzio@radicchiodichioggiaigp.it

Consorzio di tutela Radicchio Rosso di Treviso e Radicchio Variegato di Castelfranco Igp

QUINTO DI TREVISO (TV) I p.le Indipendenza, 2
☎ (+39) 0422 486073 ❀ www.radicchioditreviso.it ✉ consorzio@radicchioditreviso.it

Consorzio per la tutela e la valorizzazione del Radicchio di Verona Igp

VERONA I via Sommacampagna, 63h
☎ (+39) 335 218 677 - 339 709 6780 ❀ www.radicchiodiverona.it
✉ consorzio@radicchiodiverona.it

Cultiva (READY-TO-EAT VEGETABLES)

TAGLIO DI PO (RO) I via San Basilio, 129
☎ (+39) 0426 377025 - 0426 377021 ❀ www.cultiva.global ✉ cultiva@legalmail.it

L'Insalata dell'Orto (READY-TO-EAT VEGETABLES)

MIRA (VE) I via Giare, 144a
☎ (+39) 041 5675206 ❀ www.linsalatadellorto.it ✉ info@linsalatadellorto.it

Ortoromi Società Cooperativa Agricola
(READY-TO-EAT VEGETABLES)

BORGORICCO (PD) I via Piovega, 55
☎ (+39) 049 7480800 ❀ www.ortoromi.it ✉ marketing@ortoromi.it

Fresh fruits&vegetables

Friuli Venezia Giulia

ASPARAGO BIANCO DEL FRIULI VENEZIA GIULIA	*FRIULI VENEZIA GIULIA WHITE ASPARAGUS*
BROVADA DOP	*PDO BROVADA*
FIGO MORO DA CANEVA	*MORO DA CANEVA FIG*
RADICCHIO ROSA DI GORIZIA	*GORIZIA PINK RADICCHIO*

Associazione per la valorizzazione dell'Asparago Bianco del Friuli Venezia Giulia

TRICESIMO (UD) I fraz. Adorgnano via San Pelagio, 141
☎ (+39) 0432 851678

Associazione per la valorizzazione della Brovada Dop

PAVIA DI UDINE (UD) I via Selvuzzis, 19
☎ (+39) 0432 675105 ✪ www.brovadafvg.it ✉ info@brovadamansutti.it

Consorzio per la tutela e valorizzazione del Figo Moro da Caneva

c/o Gelinova I PORDENONE I Interporto Centro Ingrosso settore G/3
☎ (+39) 333 2399111 ✪ www.figomoro.it ✉ info@figomoro.it

Associazione Radicchio Rosa di Gorizia

c/o Biolab I GORIZIA I via dei Vegetariani, 2
☎ (+39) 0481 539877✪ www.rosadigorizia.com ✉ info@rosadigorizia.com

Emilia Romagna

CILIEGIA DI VIGNOLA IGP	*PGI VIGNOLA CHERRY*
FUNGO DI BORGOTARO IGP	*PGI BORGOTARO MUSHROOM*
MARRONE DI CASTEL DEL RIO IGP	*PGI CASTEL DEL RIO CHESTNUT*
PATATA DI BOLOGNA DOP	*PDO BOLOGNA POTATO*
PERA DELL'EMILIA ROMAGNA IGP	*PGI EMILIA ROMAGNA PEAR*
PESCA E NETTARINA DI ROMAGNA IGP	*PGI ROMAGNA PEACH AND NECTARINE*

Consorzio di tutela della Ciliegia di Vignola Igp

VIGNOLA (MO) I via dell'Agricoltura, 110
☎ (+39) 059 773645 ✉ consorziodellaciliegia@tin.it

Consorzio del Fungo di Borgotaro Igp

BORGO VAL DI TARO (PR) I via Nazionale, 54
☎ (+39) 0525 90155 ✪ www.fungodiborgotaro.com ✉ info@fungodiborgotaro.com

Fresh fruits&vegetables

Consorzio Melapiù

FERRARA I via Giorgio Caselli, 13/b
☎ (+39) 0532 229608
❀ www.melapiu.com ✉ info@melapiu.com

Consorzio Castanicoltori del Marrone di Castel del Rio

c/o Comunità Montana della Valle del Santerno I FONTANELICE (BO) I via Mengoni, 7
☎ (+39) 0542 92638 ❀ www.marronedicasteldelrio.it ✉ info@marronedicasteldelrio.it

Consorzio della Patata di Bologna Igp

CASTENASO (BO) I loc. Villanova via Tosarelli, 155
☎ (+39) 051 5872419 ❀ www.patatadibologna.it ✉ info@patatadibologna.it

Consorzio di tutela e valorizzazione Pera dell'Emilia Romagna Igp

c/o Centro Servizi Ortofrutticoli I FERRARA I via Bologna, 534
☎ (+39) 0532 904511 ❀ www.csoservizi.com ✉ info@csoservizi.com

Consorzio di tutela e valorizzazione Pesca e Nettarina di Romagna Igp

c/o Centro Servizi Ortofrutticoli I FERRARA I via Bologna, 534
☎ (+39) 0532 904511 ❀ www.csoservizi.com ✉ info@csoservizi.com

Tuscany

CASTAGNA DEL MONTE AMIATA IGP	PGI MONTE AMIATA CHESTNUT TUSCAN BLACK KALE
CAVOLO NERO RICCIO DI TOSCANA	
	PGI MUGELLO CHESTNUT
MARRONE DEL MUGELLO IGP	
MARRONE DI CAPRESE MICHELANGELO DOP	PDO CAPRESE MICHELANGELO CHESTNUT
PINOLO DEL PARCO DI MIGLIARINO SAN ROSSORE	PARCO DI MIGLIARINO SAN ROSSORE PINE NUT

Associazione per la valorizzazione della castagna del Monte Amiata Igp

ARCIDOSSO (GR) I loc. Colonia
☎ (+39) 0564 96528 ✉ info@castagna-amiata.it

AS.P.O.R.T. - Associazione Produttori Ortofrutticoli
(Cavolo nero riccio di Toscana)

CECINA (LI) I via F. Turati, 4
☎ (+39) 0586 632255 - 0586 632256 ❀ www.asport.it ✉ asport@asport.it

Consorzio del Marrone del Mugello Igp

c/o Unione Montana Comuni del Mugello I BORGO SAN LORENZO (FI)
via P. Togliatti, 45
☎ (+39) 055 845271 ✆ www.ilmarronedelmugello.it
✉ biocastellina@libero.it

Consorzio Produttori di Marrone dell'Alta Valle Senio

CASOLA VALSENIO (RA) I via Valdrio, 16
☎ (+39) 055 8046816 ✆ www.marrone-altavallesenio.it ✉ altavallesenio@yahoo.it

Umbria

PATATA ROSSA DI COLFIORITO IGP   *PGI COLFIORITO RED POTATO*

Associazione Patata Rossa di Colfiorito

FOLIGNO (PG) I fraz. Popola, 14d
☎ (+39) 335 5799489 ✉ commerciale@lenticchie.it

PAC 2000 A Società Cooperativa (READY-TO-EAT VEGETABLES)

PERUGIA I loc. Ponte Felcino via del Rame, zona industriale
☎ (+39) 075 59161 ✆ www.pac2000a.it ✉ info@pac2000a.it

Marche

OLIVA ASCOLANA DEL PICENO DOP   *PDO PICENO ASCOLANA OLIVE*

Consorzio di tutela dell'Oliva Ascolana Dop

ASCOLI PICENO I via Ruffini, 9
☎ (+39) 0736 277927 - 338 8577644 ✉ leonardo.seghetti@tin.it

Lazio

CARCIOFO ROMANESCO DEL LAZIO IGP	*PGI ROMANESCO DEL LAZIO PGI ARTICHOKE*
CASTAGNA DI VALLERANO DOP	*PDO VALLERANO CHESTNUT*
CICORIA DI CATALOGNA (puntarelle)	*CATALOGNA ENDIVE* (puntarelle)
KIWI LATINA IGP	*PGI LATINA KIWI FRUIT*
NOCCIOLA ROMANA DOP	*ROMAN HAZELNUT*
OLIVE DI GAETA	*GAETA OLIVES*
PATATA DELL'ALTO VITERBESE IGP	*PGI ALTO VITERBESE POTATO*

Biolatina (READY-TO-EAT VEGETABLES)
SABAUDIA (LT) l via Litoranea, km 11,400
☎ (+39) 0773 534807 ✿ www.biolatina.it ✉ info@biolatina.it

Consorzio di tutela del Carciofo Romanesco Igp
CERVETERI (RM) l via del Cavaliere, 1
☎ (+39) 06 9941478 ✿ www.carcioforomanesco.it ✉ info@carcioforomanesco.it

Associazione Castanicoltori Vallecimina
VALLERANO (VT) l via Torrione
☎ (+39) 0761 751949 ✉ vallecimina@alice.it

Associazione Gaetavola (Puntarelle)
GAETA (LT) l c.so Cavour, 6
☎ (+39) 335 6989626 ✿ www.gaetavola.org

Consorzio Kiwi Latina
c/o Op Kiwi Sole l BORGO CARSO (LT) l via Podgora Appia, 8c
☎ (+39) 0773 638328 - 0773 638337 ✿ www.kiwilatina.it
✉ amministrazione@opkiwisole.org

Consorzio per la Tutela e la Promozione dell'Oliva di Gaeta Dop
c/o Coop. Unagri l ITRI (LT) l via A. Padovani, 40
☎ (+39) 0771 727928 - 0771321020

Consorzio Pataticolo dell'Alto Viterbese Co.Pa.Vit.
ACQUAPENDENTE (VT) l via Rugarelle, 8
☎ (+39) 0763 733264 ✉ copavit@libero.it

San Lidano Società Cooperativa Agricola
(READY-TO-EAT VEGETABLES)
SEZZE SCALO (LT) l via Migliara, 46
☎ (+39) 0773 89791 ✿ www.sanlidano.it ✉ marketing@sanlidanogroup.it

Abruzzo

AGLIO ROSSO DI SULMONA	*SULMONA RED GARLIC*
CAROTA DELL'ALTOPIANO DEL FUCINO IGP	*PGI FUCINO CARROT*
PATATA DEL FUCINO IGP	*PGI FUCINO POTATO*

Consorzio Produttori Aglio Rosso di Sulmona
SULMONA (AQ) l via Q. Sella, 5
☎ (+39) 370 3309173 - 338 5080981 ✿ www.agliorossodisulmona.org
✉ info@agliorossodisulmona.org

Az. Agr. Orto.Be.Mar. (Patata del Fucino Igp)

SAN BENEDETTO DEI MARSI (AQ) I via Grande, 9
☎ (+39) 0863 867806 - 348 3825993 ✆ www.lacarotadelfucino.it
✉ info@lacarotadelfucino.it

AMPP - Associazione Marsicana Produttori Patate

CELANO (AQ) I via Borgo Strada 14, 87
☎ (+39) 0863 79501

Molise

PATATA LUNGA DI SAN BIASE	*SAN BIASE LONG POTATO*

Campania

ALBICOCCA DEL VESUVIO	*VESUVIUS APRICOT*
CARCIOFO DI PAESTUM IGP	*PGI PAESTUM ARTICHOKE*
CASTAGNA DI MONTELLA IGP	*PGI MONTELLA CHESTNUT*
FICO BIANCO DEL CILENTO DOP	*PDO CILENTO WHITE FIG*
LIMONE COSTA D'AMALFI IGP	*PGI AMALFI COAST LEMON*
LIMONE DI SORRENTO IGP	*PGI SORRENTO LEMON*
MARRONE DI ROCCADASPIDE IGP	*PGI ROCCADASPIDE CHESTNUT*
MELA ANNURCA CAMPANA IGP	*PGI CAMPANIA ANNURCA APPLE*
NOCCIOLA DI GIFFONI IGP	*PGI GIFFONI HAZELNUT*
POMODORINO DEL PIENNOLO DEL VESUVIO DOP	*PDO VESUVIO PIENNOLO GRAPE TOMATO*
POMODORO SAN MARZANO DELL'AGRO SARNESE-NOCERINO DOP	*PDO SAN MARZANO DELL'AGRO SARNESE-NOCERINO TOMATO*

Ente Parco Nazionale del Vesuvio (Albicocca del Vesuvio)

OTTAVIANO (NA)I Palazzo Mediceo via Palazzo del Principe
☎ (+39) 081 8653911 ✆ www.parconazionaledelvesuvio.it
✉ parconazionaledelvesuvio@pec.it

Assessorato Agricoltura - Regione Campania Settore Sirca (Albicocca del Vesuvio)

NAPOLI I via G. Porzio Centro Direzionale Isola A 6
☎ (+39) 081 7967306 - 081 7967302 ✆ www.sito.regione.campania.it

Consorzio di tutela Carciofo di Paestum Igp

EBOLI (SA) I via Bagnolo San Vito
☎ (+39) 0828 601213 ✆ www.carciofodipaestum.it ✉ info@carciofodipaestum.it

Cooperativa Castagne di Montella

MONTELLA (AV) I c.da Sottomonticchio
☎ (+39) 0827 69129 - 0827 61401 ✪ www.castagnedimontella.it
✉ info@castagnedimontella.it

Consorzio di tutela del Fico Bianco del Cilento Dop

PRIGNANO CILENTO (SA) I p.zza Municipio, 1
☎ (+39) 0974 831039

Consorzio di tutela del Limone Costa d'Amalfi Igp

MAIORI (SA) I c.so Reginna, 71
☎ (+39) 334 3647427 - 366 4576491 ✪ www.limonecostadamalfiigp.com
✉ info@limonecostadamalfiigp.com

Consorzio di tutela del Limone di Sorrento Igp

PIANO DI SORRENTO (NA) I via dei Platani, 15
☎ (+39) 081 5636060 – 081 5636049
✪ www.limonedisorrentoigp.it ✉ info@limonedisorrentoigp.it
✉ consorziotutelalimonesorrento@pec.coldiretti.it

Consorzio di tutela del Marrone di Roccadaspide Igp - Cooperativa s.c.a.r.l. "Il Marrone"

ROCCADASPIDE (SA) I loc. Spinosa
☎ (+39) 0828 947496

Consorzio di tutela della Mela Annurca Campana Igp

CASERTA I via G. Verdi, 29
☎ (+39) 0823 325144 ✪ www.melannurca.it ✉ info@melannurca.it

Consorzio di tutela della Nocciola di Giffoni Igp

GIFFONI VALLE PIANA (SA) I via Valentino Fortunato zona PIP
☎ (+39) 089 8424053 ✪ www.igpnoccioladigiffoni.it ✉ info@igpnoccioladigiffoni.it

Consorzio di Tutela del pomodorino del piennolo del Vesuvio dop

c/o Casa Barone I SAN SEBASTIANO AL VESUVIO (NA) I p.zza della Meridiana, 47
☎ (+39) 081 0606007 ✉ piennolodop@gmail.com

Consorzio di tutela del Pomodoro San Marzano dell'AgroSarnese-Nocerino Dop

SARNO (SA) I via Lanzara, 27
☎ (+39) 081 5161819 ✪ www.consorziopomodorosanmarzanodop.it
✉ info@consorziopomodorosanmarzanodop.it

Rago Società Cooperativa Agricola (READY-TO-EAT VEGETABLES)

BATTIPAGLIA (SA) I s.da p.le, 312
☎ (+39) 0828 671404 ✪ www.ragogroup.com ✉ info@ragogroup.com

Fresh fruits&vegetables

447

Puglia

ARANCIA DEL GARGANO IGP	*PGI GARGANO ORANGE*
CARCIOFO BRINDISINO IGP	*PGI BRINDISI ARTICHOKE*
CLEMENTINA DEL GOLFO DI TARANTO IGP	*PGI GOLFO DI TARANTO CLEMENTINA*
OLIVA LA BELLA DELLA DAUNIA (o di Cerignola) DOP	*PDO LA BELLA DELLA DAUNIA (or Cerignola) OLIVE*
UVA DI PUGLIA IGP	*PGI PUGLIA GRAPE*

Consorzio di tutela Agrumi del Gargano
(Arancia del Gargano Igp e Limone Femminello del Gargano Igp)

RODI GARGANICO (FG) I via Varano, 11
☎ (+39) 0884 966168 ❁ www.garganoagrumi.com ✉ info@garganoagrumi.com

Associazione Terra dei Messapi (Carciofo Brindisino)

MESAGNE (BR) I via A. Albricci, 3
tel. (+39) 0831 734929
❁ www.terradeimessapi.it ✉ info@pec.terradeimessapi.it
✉ pubblicherelazioni@terradeimessapi.it

Consorzio di tutela della Igp Clementina del Golfo di Taranto

c/o Az. Agr. Frisino I PALAGIANO (TA) I via L. Da Vinci, 4
☎ (+39) 347 5860593 - 393 9722281 ❁ www.orfruttafrisino.it ✉ f.frisino@gmail.com

Consorzio di tutela Oliva Dop La Bella della Daunia Cultivar Bella di Cerignola

c/o Assessorato Aree Produttive del Comune di Cerignola I CERIGNOLA (FG)
p.zza della Repubblica, 1
☎ (+39) 0885 410219 ❁ www.consorziotutelaolivabella.com

Consorzio Uva di Puglia Igp

APEO - Associazione Pugliese Esportatori Ortofrutticoli I BARI I via C. Rosalba, 47j
☎ (+39) 080 5044127

Basilicata

MELANZANA ROSSA DI ROTONDA DOP	*PDO RED ROTONDA AUBERGINE*
OLIVA DI FERRANDINA	*FERRANDINA OLIVE*
PEPERONE DI SENISE IGP	*PGI SENISE PEPPER*

Consorzio di tutela della Melanzana Rossa di Rotonda Dop

c/o ALSIA ROTONDA (PZ) I c.da Piano Incoronata
☎ (+39) 0835 244575 ❀ www.biancoerossadop.it ✉ info@biancoerossadop.it

Consorzio Terre di Lucania (Oliva di Ferrandina)

FERRANDINA (MT) I via Ridola, 43
☎ (+39) 0835 312097 ✉ leterredilucania@yahoo.it

Consorzio di tutela del peperone Igp di Senise

c/o Confederazione Italiana Agricoltori I SENISE (PZ) I via Sottotenente Panzardi, 53
☎ (+39) 0973 585733 ✉ agazzaneo65@gmail.com

Calabria

CIPOLLA ROSSA DI TROPEA CALABRIA IGP	*PGI RED TROPEA CALABRIA ONION*
CLEMENTINA DI CALABRIA IGP	*PGI CALABRIA CLEMENTINA*
FICO DI COSENZA DOP	*PDO COSENZA FIG*
PATATA DELLA SILA IGP	*PGI SILA POTATO*

Consorzio Cipolla Rossa di Tropea Calabria Igp

VIBO VALENTIA I loc. Vena Superiore via Roma
☎ (+39) 0963 260631 - 0963 42149 ❀ www.consorziocipollatropeaigp.com
✉ info@consorziocipollatropeaigp.com

Consorzio di tutela Clementina di Calabria Igp

c/o Osservatorio Fitopatologico I CORIGLIANO CALABRO (CS)
Porto di Corigliano Calabro
☎ (+39) 329 9117924 - 328 2152255 ❀ www.igpclementinadicalabria.it
✉ info@igpclementinadicalabria.it

Consorzio Fichi di Cosenza Dop

BISIGNANO (CS) zona industriale
☎ (+39) 0984 949106 ✉ consorzio@fichidicosenza.it ✉ info@fichidicosenza.it

Consorzio di tutela della Patata della Sila Igp

SPEZZANO DELLA SILA (CS) I loc. Camigliatello Silano via Forgitelle, 28
☎ (+39) 0984 578693 ❀ www.patatadellasilaigp.com ❀ www.patatadellasila.it
✉ info@patatadellasila.it

Fresh fruits&vegetables

449

Sicily

ARANCIA DI RIBERA DOP	*RIBERA ORANGE*
ARANCIA ROSSA DI SICILIA IGP	*PGI SICILIAN RED ORANGE*
CAPPERO DI PANTELLERIA IGP	*PGI PANTELLERIA CAPER*
FICO D'INDIA DELL'ETNA DOP	*PDO ETNA PRICKLY PEAR*
FICO D'INDIA DI SAN CONO DOP	*PDO SAN CONO PRICKLY PEAR*
LIMONE DI SIRACUSA IGP	*PGI SIRACUSA LEMON*
LIMONE INTERDONATO MESSINA IGP	*PGI INTERDONATO MESSINA LEMON*
MANDORLA DI AVOLA	*AVOLA ALMOND*
MANDORLA DI NOTO	*NOTO ALMOND*
OLIVA NOCELLARA DEL BELICE DOP	*PDO NOCELLARA DEL BELICE OLIVE*
PESCA DI BIVONA IGP	*PGI BIVONA PEACH*
PESCA DI LEONFORTE IGP	*PGI LEONFORTE PEACH*
PISTACCHIO VERDE DI BRONTE DOP	*PDO BRONTE GREEN PISTACHIO*
POMODORO DI PACHINO IGP	*PGI PACHINO TOMATO*
UVA DA TAVOLA DI CANICATTÌ IGP	*PGI CANICATTÌ TABLE GRAPE*
UVA DA TAVOLA DI MAZZARRONE IGP	*PGI MAZZARRONE TABLE GRAPE*

Consorzio di tutela Arancia di Ribera Dop

c/o Centro Direzionale per l'Agricoltura I RIBERA (AG) I via Quasimodo
☎ (+39) 0925 561522 ✿ www.aranciadiriberadop.it

Consorzio di tutela Arancia Rossa di Sicilia Igp

CATANIA I via San Giuseppe La Rena, 30b
☎ (+39) 095 7232990
✿ www.tutelaaranciarossa.it ✉ aranciarossadisicilia@gmail.com
✉ consorzioditutelaaranciarossadisiciliaigp@arubapec.it

Cooperativa Agricola Produttori di Capperi di Pantelleria

PANTELLERIA (TP) I c.da Scauri Basso
☎ (+39) 0923 916079 ✿ www.capperidipantelleria.com ✉ info@capperipantelleria.com

O.P. Consorzio Euroagrumi – Fico d'India dell'Etna

BIANCAVILLA (CT) I via Cristoforo Colombo, 124
☎ (+39) 095 7711510 ✉ euro@euroagrumi.it ✉ dino@euroagrumi.it

Consorzio di tutela del Limone di Siracusa Igp
SIRACUSA I via De Caprio, 57
☎ (+39) 0931 38234 ❀ www.limonedisiracusa.org ✉ info@limonedisiracusa.org

Consorzio Limone Interdonato di Messina Igp
NIZZA DI SICILIA (ME) I via Umberto I, 369
☎ (+39) 0942 717072 ❀ www.limoneinterdonatoigp.it
✉ contatti@limoneinterdonatoigp.it

Consorzio Mandorla di Avola
AVOLA (SR) I p.zza Umberto I, 5
☎ (+39) 347 9257136❀ www.consorziomandorlaavola.it
✉ consorziomandorla@gmail.com

A.Pro.Ma.S - Associazione Produttori Mandorle di Sicilia
c/o Bongiovanni I MAZZARINO (CL) c.da Piano San Salvatore
☎ (+39) 0934 974487 - 368 3191242
❀ www.mandorledisiciliabongiovanni.it ✉ bongiovannisrl@virgilio.it
✉ preventivibongiovanni@gmail.com

Consorzio di Tutela Oliva Nocellara del Belice Dop
CASTELVETRANO (TP) I via IV Novembre, 11
☎ (+39) 0923 89322 ❀ www.consorzionocellaradelbelice.com
✉ info@consorzionocellaradelbelice.com

Consorzio di tutela Pesca di Leonforte Igp
LEONFORTE (EN) I p.zza Branciforti, 2
☎ (+39) 0935 904515 ❀ www.pescadileonforte.it ✉ info@pescadileonforte.it

Consorzio di tutela del Pistacchio Verde di Bronte Dop
BRONTE (CT) I p.zza Nunzio Azzia, 14
☎ (+39) 095 7723659 ❀ consorziopistacchioverde.it
✉ presidente@consorziopistacchioverde.it ✉ vicepresidente@consorziopistacchioverde.it
✉ info@consorziopistacchioverde.it

Consorzio di tutela del Pomodoro di Pachino Igp
MARZAMEMI (SR) I via Nuova
☎ (+39) 0931 595106 ❀ pomodoro.igppachino.it ✉ segreteria@igppachino.it

Consorzio di tutela Uva da Tavola di Mazzarrone Igp
MAZZARRONE (CT) I via Botteghelle, 7
☎ (+39) 0933 28227 ✉ uvaigpmazzarrone@libero.it

Fresh fruits&vegetables

Sardinia

CARCIOFO SPINOSO DI SARDEGNA DOP

PDO SARDINIA SPINY ARTICHOKE

Consorzio Carciofo Spinoso di Sardegna Dop

VALLEDORIA (SS) I c.so Europa, 33

☎ (+39) 079 582248

🌐 www.carciofosardodop.it ✉ carcspindisardegna@tiscali.it

Indexes

Alphabetical Index

Alphabetical Index

Alphabetical Index

Alphabetical Index

Index by category

COFFEE, TEA, INFUSIONS

Index by category

Index by category

Index by category

www.gamberorosso.it